S0-BUG-117

ALLE ZEIT WACH
1842

Louis F. Pau · Claudio Gianotti

Economic and Financial Knowledge-Based Processing

With 67 Figures

Springer-Verlag
Berlin Heidelberg New York
London Paris Tokyo
Hong Kong Barcelona

Research Professor Louis F. Pau
Technical University of Denmark
Bldg. 348/EMI
DK-2800 Lyngby/Denmark

Dr. Claudio Gianotti
Via Renato Birolli no 7
I-20125 Milano/Italy

ISBN 3-540-53043-6 Springer-Verlag Berlin Heidelberg New York Tokyo
ISBN 3-387-53043-6 Springer-Verlag New York Heidelberg Berlin Tokyo

2142/7130-543210

To my daugther
Isabelle M. M. Pau
L.F. Pau

To my father Gus,
with my love and gratitude
C. Gianotti

Acknowledgements

Proper acknowledgements, with thanks, are hereby given to the following companies and persons:

- Digital Equipment Corp., for the permission to reproduce the cover image
- Massimo Ferrando, Fabrizio Scovenna, Torben Tambo for assistance in code development or testing
- Birgit Bruhn, Annett Bergstedt for typing of drafts to some Chapters

We are grateful to the Editor for his support and encouragement.

Contents

3 Knowledge Representation 47

A reader's guide

1 Style of the book

A number of books have appeared which deal with artificial intelligence techniques only, with relations to organizational theory, or with possible applications of expert systems in economics and management (see Bibliography). However, in our volume, we clearly want to give practical "how to do" solutions to real concerns encountered in banking, finance, insurance and economics. The book takes the reader first from a simple case, to the most applicable basic concepts and techniques, followed by a series of real world application-driven topics. The challenges to users as well as an introduction to the contents of the book appear in Chapter 0. The book has three "facets", depending on specific reader interest: a tutorial facet, an application facet and a research facet.

The tutorial dimension of the book relies on illustrations by case studies, and on source code in two of the major artificial intelligence languages.

The application related facet includes an extensive survey of real projects, and a number of throughout methods and tools for tax analysis, technical analysis of securities, information screens, risk analysis in currency trading, and natural language front-ends.

The research related facet highlights novel methods and software for portfolio selection under uncertainty and about fusion in qualitative/quantitative model-based economic reasoning.

The material in this book is extensively cross-referenced. The following conventions are adopted throughout the book:

- references to Sections within a current Chapter are introduced by the keyword "Section", followed by the relevant Section number, without repetition of the Chapter number
- references to Sections outside a current Chapter are introduced by the keyword "Chapter", followed by the relevant Chapter and Section numbers
- references to Figures, Tables and Examples are followed by the relevant Chapter number only if outside a current Chapter.

2 Relevant material for intended audiences

All the material should hopefully be relevant to:

1. Software development groups in/for the financial sector, as well as economic policy bodies
2. Researchers in economics, finance, management science, operations research, and applied artificial intelligence
3. Upper management in most larger companies, investment companies, and banks
4. Academics and graduate students in the above areas

However, readers interested primarily in:

- potential or current applications should start with Chapters 1 and 2
- analyzing approaches selected for a diversity of more complex real world cases should emphasize Chapters 5 through 10
- methods and tools for the purpose of building prototypes should start with Chapters 3, 4, 5, 6
- new research approaches should emphasize Chapters 5 through 12

3 Case studies, applications and examples

Throughout the volume, the reader will find a large number of small examples, all connected to economic/financial applications of the required techniques; these examples are to be located via the subject index. The examples are numbered consecutively within each chapter.

Applications appear as sections directly illustrating related material introduced in the corresponding Chapters.

Finally, there are a few rather extensive case studies, to be considered mostly as small application prototypes.

4 Software code

Software code is liberally used throughout the book to illustrate specific concepts or full algorithms. For quick reference, language primitives used in this code are compiled in Appendix 2, together with indexing to the corresponding definitions. Larger segments of code are in some cases grouped in Appendix 1, while still being explained in the related Chapters.

5 Software implementation configurations

All LISP code has been developed, tested and run on an Apple Computer Corp. Macintosh SE personal computer, using Allegro Common LISP version 1.2.1 by Coral Corp.

Part of the Prolog code has been implemented and tested on an IBM PC-XT, using Expert Systems Intl. Ltd's Prolog 1 and 2. The remaining part from Chapter 9 involved Quintus Prolog version 1.5 running on MicroVax II-GPX/VMS from Quintus Inc.

Although the presented programs have been tested with the outmost care, the authors still take no responsibility for damage, losses and misuse deriving from running these programs.

6 About topics not covered ...

This volume does not cover some topics of relevance to some practical and complete developments of knowledge-based operational applications, including:

- knowledge acquisition from experts
- organizational issues related to project development
- methodology for control of the knowledge-based software development cycle

Likewise, the reader is referred to the Bibliography for introductory or advanced exposés of economic or financial model building as well as many interesting and more sophisticated artificial intelligence, natural language and neural processing techniques.

0 Introduction

0.1 Introduction

This book is about techniques and concepts of strategic importance to banks, insurance companies, financial services, and economic planning units. It addresses the issue of how to turn information technology into a tool whereby to enhance their skills, to increase productivity and promote competitivity. It also makes it possible to go beyond traditional computer mainframe based data base or statistic facilities, to encapsulate and update all types of knowledge. This can be knowledge about the behavior of customers, but also about the markets, about economic or financial instruments, as well as about competitors.

In stating this, we stress that raw data, as often encountered today, are of little value: what counts is the knowledge about how to manipulate them, how to distribute them, and link them together to get a broader more specific picture of a situation, especially in ever changing contexts. The mobility and transaction flows of funds are obvious examples hereof. This ability relies heavily upon replacing fixed procedures with more "adaptative" ones, such as search (Chapter 5), which involves finding all feasible reasoning paths, and not just one. Fundamental to the use of knowledge is the ability to encapsulate heuristics of all sorts, and qualitative judgements, because in the economic and financial fields much information is informal, while coexisting with rigid calculations, accounting or legal requirements. It is here that artificial intelligence theory, but also advanced decision making techniques, have served as an inspiration to this book, although this is certainly not a book about artificial intelligence. Introductory examples are given in Chapter 1, and Chapter 4 gives an introduction to symbolic programming languages in which these concepts are best expressed. Today, however, most embedded applications would use whatever programming language is fitting the user's environment. It is naive to believe that the choice of a programming language is crucial to the final success: more importantly, the availability of suitable software tools is critical for the specification and development time.

Said heuristics include:

- knowledge-based or expert systems, to use knowledge bases to find all possible feasible approaches or solutions to a problem; key to their design is how to "express ideas", called formally knowledge representation (Chapter 3)

- natural language analysis, to screen raw information, or assist the user in his dialogue with a computer system (Chapters 8 and 9)
- search, to generate action plans (Chapter 5)
- learning, to update the systems above on the basis of examples (Chapter 6)

Furthermore, this knowledge can now be decentralized, to serve as a force multiplier to many more sites or employees, to increase their skills by letting them face less routine and more complex issues (Chapters 2 and 8). This also means that more distributed information processing systems can now be introduced into economic, banking, and financial institutions. But where to start and what for ? A wide variety of applications have been developed worldwide as prototypes, and sometimes even as operational systems, in finance, insurance, banking, services, accounting, consulting, organizational strategy, marketing, economics, as evidenced by the list of over 250 such projects in Chapter 2.

The users are fundamentally largely in charge themselves of not only the initiative, but also of the development of knowledge-based systems in the above areas. The first consequence is that the implementations and solutions invariably are merging conventional programming and methods, with the newer techniques and programming languages described in this book (Chapter 4), thus leading to a stepwise improvement. The second consequence of this natural push for solutions to real or new problems, often unsolvable previously, is that application generic or completely specific tools emerge, distributed on a wide commercial basis (Chapter 2, and examples of generic applications in Chapters 7-11).

Even beyond these trends, only knowledge-based processing allows for "data fusion" (Chapters 8 and 10), which is the task of integrating all the information concerning a customer (e.g."customer information files"), investment, or case, so that it can be "cut" in many ways (without unnecessary duplications) to serve the customer, the banker, the management, etc.

0.2 The strategic challenge to banks and insurance

The techniques covered in this volume basically turn money management (deposits, credits), funds transfers, or risk management (insurance contracts, credit scoring) into an issue of creating and updating knowledge bases distributed and kept up to date in a coordinated fashion. With these knowledge bases, customer profiles and needs can be analyzed, marketing can be targeted, back-office operations can be better integrated with all others, and the institution can acquire a "profile" in the competition. Fee structures can be governed by a set of rules made more or less uniform, according to the policy and to other client needs (e.g. real estate, security services, information services, see the didactic examples in Chapters 1 and 4). Another major example hereof is the current fact that fees earned on funds transfers (and possibly currency exchange) are generally below the expenses, reflecting a market share policy and rationalization. The private and business clients will get tailored statements and products, and even will be put in a position to dialogue directly with transaction systems for most routine operations, thanks to the interactive user friendliness of knowledge-based and natural language systems (Chapters 8 and 9). Knowledge pertaining to the marketing of banking services will suddenly be valued much higher than today, and will be distributed according to targeting policies. Likewise, all the knowledge acquired formally will be made available to enhance the efficiency and/or scope of banking or insurance staff training.

0.3 The strategic challenge to financial services

Financial services encompass an ever increasing range of special or dedicated services generally related to such headings as: investment, financial planning, brokerage/trade, portfolio and funds management, accounting, custodial management, marketing research, tax advice. They all basically face competitive pricing mechanisms, planning over time, volatile market/economic/political contexts, advanced security analysis techniques, as well as tight regulatory frameworks. Key is here to develop unique skills and methods, and to cope with volume routine tasks, while at the same time optimizing returns on swaps between vehicles (e.g.the role of money market funds for securities traders). Often, the results of even a simple tool (e.g.information screens, spreadsheets, or simulation) provide surprises.

At the other end, strategic thinking is bolstered by the discovery of why and how exactly decisions are reached and opportunities found. The financial services industry can find in knowledge-based and learning techniques covered here, technology to come up with robust, economic, easily updated software solutions. The capabilities addressed are: bring some order to creative thoughts (Chapter 9), information screening to alert to new goals (Chapters 7 and 8), decision mapping to control the execution of plans (Chapter 5), and policy or management games to play with strategic choices (Chapter 12).

One may wonder if the financial services industry really needs all this wizardry, which contrasts with sometimes highly successful teams who rely solely on clever ideas, people, or technical/fundamental analysis. The fact is, however, that knowledge-based techniques are less wizardry than some quantitative modeling techniques, simply because most knowledge bases can be read and updated in almost plain daily language. Also, all players in the industry rely heavily on on-line information, so that intelligent information screens (even if heavily dependent on knowledge-based processing and man-machine interface techniques) find enthusiastic acceptance provided one can understand and justify how they are "smart": this is provided by the in-built explanation capability of knowledge-based systems (Chapters 1, 5 and 12). Furthermore, some services, e.g.trust and custodial services, basically turn some financial companies into information processing companies, and the high cost of the computing systems required have become a formidable barrier to new entrants. Not to be underestimated, the procedures and policies of monitoring agencies (both internal and external) will have indeed to rely extensively on search and data fusion.

0.4 The strategic challenge to economic analysis and decision making

There are still of course areas where the applications pose significant yet unresolved challenges to knowledge-based techniques and others, such as macroeconomics in a broad sense (Chapter 12), policy analysis, public service policies, legal knowledge, forecasting, and planning with uncertainty (Chapter 10). This is time for e.g. macroeconomic models (usually relying on econometric estimation and statistics) to be coupled with explicit behavioral models for economic agents, with explicit policy rules, and even in some instances with rational expectations models and their extension: "truth maintenance systems" (Chapter 5). It is also time for natural language analysis (Chapter 9), and neural processing or inductive learning (Chapter 6), to generate in a suitable formal way the goals formulated verbally by policy makers. Search, combined with game resolution (Chapters 5 and 12), would also turn a budget planning task into a task of finding an equilibrium between conflicting concerns.

0.5 The strategic challenge for business management

Although business management is not the focus of this book, many of the concepts and techniques will affect the financial, budgetary, and policy components of corporate life. The techniques of price analysis and information screening (Chapters 7 and 8) apply e.g. to commodities or consumer products (Chapter 10). Most budgets will depend on currency hedging (Chapter 11) as forecasting and risk analysis must be carried out on project costs or market prices (Chapter 10). Furthermore, as quasi-money (e.g.prepaid cards) spreads like prairie fire, the limits of money management competence and authority get blurred.

0.6 Conclusion

Today, the proper controlled infusion of knowledge-based techniques covered here, as an ingredient to novel or more efficient solutions to economic and financial practical problems, does offer a significant pay-off. That is why we emphasize here, throughout all chapters, the presentation of techniques in direct relation to a wide variety of small case studies or examples. Also, as many software tools are either proprietary or maladapted, we insist on giving explicit software code (with introductory language notions in Chapter 4), so that the readers may try it out, and thus integrate it into their own user environments.

At the same time, research should not be ignored, out of self-satisfaction, as very major progress still needs to be done especially in reasoning, case analysis, and learning, while reincorporating the often forgotten contributions from economics, social theories, decision systems and finance (see Chapters 2, 10 and 12 for future trends). From the point of view of AI research, this books contains some proven methods, which may appear as well-known as a result (Chapters 3 - 5). They are, however, supplemented by novel concepts and methods (Chapters 5.10, 7, 8, 9 and 10) which fundamentally deal with specific requirements from economics and finance, and which have received only little attention in AI research. Among these requirements are, first highly unstructured goals and knowledge, and next the fact that the elementary objects are transactions between economic agents. These transactions involve a bilateral exchange of goods, risk or information, with conflicting criteria.

Looking ahead, it looks likely that knowledge and information processing outfits will in the future half-own the key parts of the most successful banks and financial companies. Also, this knowledge and its processing will be highly decentralized, thus turning most of the paperwork over to networks of computers. Banks and securities companies are no longer just buying and selling money or securities, and just need a bit of information to do it: they are global information and knowledge companies that also happen to buy and sell. Money is information on the move, and income from it, the knowledge about how to move it.

L.F. Pau and C. Gianotti, April 1990

1 Basic concepts

1.1 Introduction

It is evident even from the most superficial observation that humans are capable of effective (i.e. goal driven) interaction with their environment. A better understanding of the interaction processes would clearly be of great help in enhancing the quality of support to decision-makers faced with ill-defined tasks.

The difficulties arise from the consideration that the environment people are embedded in, is on one hand very complex, being composed of:

- other humans, with competing as well as cooperating attitudes
- physical, legal, financial, institutional and social resources and constraints

from the other hand still not sufficiently understood (e.g. low reliability of forecasting, poor causal models). As opposed to physics, whose object of study is limited to natural phenomena, social sciences suffer from a recognized lack of broadly valid and acknowledged theoretical foundations and previsional capabilities. Economics and related fields (management, finance) are no exceptions: professionals facing broad classes of practical problems have little theoretical, normative basis with wide experimental acceptance to rely upon.

The interaction capability mentioned above, and more practically the different performances of different humans faced with the same somewhat unstructured tasks, are colloquially explained through terms, such as intuition, sixth sense, experience, intelligence, which are only vaguely defined. Nevertheless, they capture, at least *approximately*, the peculiarity of human information processing, and its visible consequences on external behavior, such as rapid adaptation to changes and learning from past failures, which are especially typical of all service activities. At the same time, however, they are also revealing our ignorance.

Artificial Intelligence (AI) is the science studying the principles of intelligent behavior. Our perspective mainly relies upon the concept of *problem-solving* as a unifying framework for understanding the results of the research in AI. By problem-solving is meant the process of achieving a desired situation (goal) starting from predetermined circumstances and procedures and being limited by environmental constraints in the allowable set of actions or decisions. The study of a formal theory of the problem-solving principles, often stimulated by the observation of the human capabilities, is the very core of AI research, and is finalized toward the automation on computers (hence the somewhat improper term of Artificial Intelligence). Computers also provide an invaluable experimental tool for validating (through implementation) theoretical hypotheses, or exploring their consequences. In this respect, AI differs considerably in its methodology from analogous attempts made by psychologists or philosophers.

We shall therefore assume hereinafter Artificial Intelligence to be an experimental science, whose domain of study is the way intelligent entities face problems, and whose purpose is to build an automatic (or interactive) problem-solver with so good performances that it would be judged as intelligent by human observers. Systematic, general-purpose presentations of AI principles can be found in textbooks such as [Barr et al., 1981], [Charniak and McDermott, 1985], [Nilsson, 1976], [Rich, 1983], [Winston, 1984].

This work focuses on the requirements and solutions of AI in economics and finance and shows how some of the ideas developed so far can be applied to the implementation of more flexible computer programs with performances which in some cases are comparable to those of human experts in the same task, or able to replace humans by relieving them from tedious, error prone tasks. Such programs offer good perspectives of tackling successfully many problems which have defeated (or made too expensive) implementations using conventional computer science techniques. A survey of areas of economics and finance where these types of problem-solvers might be considered follows in Section 2, while a more detailed catalogue of actual AI applications is to be found in Chapter 2.

A basic assumption of AI is that intelligent entities are so good in solving problems because they possess *knowledge* about the problem (and in general more about their environment) together with effective mechanisms for representing, organizing and purposely manipulating their knowledge.

The question of how the knowledge should be represented and organized is referred to in AI as the knowledge representation problem. Representing and organizing knowledge means defining a formalism in which knowledge is to be expressed and relationships among pieces of knowledge captured. Similar formalisms are further grouped into classes, the so-called knowledge representation paradigms. There is as for now no widely accepted theory of how intelligent entities (e.g. humans) do represent their knowledge, and even less is known about the feasibility of a computer implementation of such representations; many paradigms have been proposed in the AI literature, without one of them being generally accepted as the right one. Rather, depending on the nature of the problem, one representation paradigm may be better suited than the others, and combinations are frequent, often changing with external circumstances. Knowledge representation is dealt with in Chapter 3.

Knowledge being explicitly coded into AI programs, the need arises for mechanisms capable of retrieving knowledge subsets relevant to the task at hand. Such mechanisms are mostly built upon the ideas of search and heuristics. Both search and heuristics are widely used outside AI (e.g. computer science, Operations Research); their role in human problem-solving has furthermore been extensively treated for example in [Simon, 1957].

Search is the process of exploring alternatives when considering a problem. The motivation behind the choice of search as a principle of problem-solving is that knowledge about complex, unstructured environments is likely to be affected by interactions and uncertainties because of one of the following reasons:

- no reliable theory exists about the factors relevant to a problem and their interaction (lack of a comprehensive causal model)

- a theory is known, but specific information is not practically available, either because it is incomplete, inconsistent, inaccessible, infinite, or too costly (this last point is often crucial in economical applications)

As a consequence, it may be impossible for the decision-maker to produce directly a solution from the problem representation (in other words, the question "What it the best thing to do next ?" cannot be answered a priori). Such uncertainty typically shows up as several, perhaps conflicting courses of actions thought of to be relevant for the same situation. By lacking of further knowledge, or of sufficient resources to get access to such knowledge, commitment to one action must be postponed, and alternatives must be explored, until hopefully the consequences of each decision on the development of the solution have become clearer or further information is available. This is the essence of "search", to be understood as "search for a goal situation" among alternatives whose relative merit is unknown.

Search may seem an attractive problem-solving method because of its generality and conceptual elegance. However, one should take into account the computational resources (memory, time) needed to get a solution: e.g., search can be made very slow by increasing the complexity of the problem to be solved, defined as the number of alternatives to be explored. Unfortunately, in this respect most interesting problems are too complex for search, which is then inapplicable. Consider portfolio selection: its solution by pure search would consist in enumerating all consistent portfolios, and then picking up the best, according to some merit figure. Such enumeration, however, would be practically a never-ending task. Search is a viable problem-solving method only in the case of small problems. Search is extensively explained in Chapter 5.

In order to limit search to possibly small subsets of the overall alternatives, the uncertainty in the problem must be reduced through further knowledge. Hence, unless one disposes of unlimited time and computational capabilities, problem-solving must rely upon knowledge. However, unless one disposes of perfect knowledge about the problem domain, one is compelled by uncertainty to use search. Search and knowledge are in a certain sense complementary.

Heuristics is one kind of knowledge often used to limit search. In fact, heuristic is knowledge about how to solve a problem, i.e. about which alternatives are promising for the desired solution and which alternatives are not. In practical cases, one must cope with the fact that heuristic knowledge may sometimes be misleading (in the sense that is could give a bad evaluation to a good alternative). This has again to do with the uncertainty, inconsistency and incompleteness of the knowledge about complex problem domains and with the inadequacy of the human brain to take into account all causal factors and their interactions. So, one does not aim at infallible heuristics, but rather at heuristics being right most of the time. Promising alternatives are then searched first, the other are discarded, or searched last. Although subject to error, heuristics are mandatory in tackling large problems needing search. Search in connection with heuristics is explained in Chapter 5 as well.

Knowledge (both about a problem and about how to solve it) and search are therefore the key components of AI problem-solvers. To stress the central role played by knowledge, a broad class of AI applications has been named Knowledge-Based Systems (KBS).

Designing intelligent systems based on knowledge entails the need to provide an answer to the following questions:

- how knowledge can be acquired from human experts (knowledge acquisition) or automatically from the environment through given interaction capabilities (learning)

- how knowledge is to be represented (representation)

- how knowledge can be reformulated through inference procedures, that is how new knowledge can be generated not as the result from a direct interaction with the environment, but rather as consequence of the previously present knowledge (reasoning)

- how knowledge can be most effectively manipulated, that is how reasoning can be directed toward the deduction of useful knowledge (heuristics and search)

1.2 Survey of AI applications in finance and economics

This section presents a list of areas where the AI approach to problem-solving may be considered ([Pau, 1986], [Pau, 1987a]).

1. Econometrics:
   - Natural language (e.g.English, or other human-spoken language) explanation of revisions to forecasts
   - Economic/Business model building from policy statements in text form
   - Judgemental forecasting
   - Tutoring in economics
   - Choice of intermediate economic targets

2. Banking:
   - Bank operations and money management
   - Reduce settlement costs
   - Generate/verify money transfer wires
   - Inkasso recovery
   - Credit scoring, granting, authorization
   - Discretionary account surveillance
   - Currency trading
   - Bank tele-marketing

3. Investing:
   - Bond portfolio management
   - Financial planning
   - Stock selection
   - Trading regulations and audit
   - Mortgages and pensions selection
   - Movements in products prices
   - Dealing room desks

4. Insurance:
   - Underwriting advice
   - Claims settlement/processing
   - Insurance vending machines

5. Auditing:
   - Verify balances and match against sector data
   - Financial statements analysis
   - Screening financial disclosure filings
   - Real estate appraisal

6. Tax planning:
   - Personal tax planning
   - Tax code analysis

- Scanning tax forms

7. Personnel:
- Corporate personnel management
- Salary increase equalization
- Personnel selection

8. General management:
- Formulate and justify decisions
- Corporate financing and budgeting
- Financial corporate decision-making tutorials
- Project management integrated with business financial modeling

1.3 Case studies and examples

Throughout this volume, case studies are introduced for didactic or illustrative purposes, and consist in worked-out applications of AI to real (although often simplified) economic or financial problems. They should help the reader to highlight the importance of a given AI technique for economics; furthermore, they are intended to show how the theoretically introduced concepts are transposed into working programs; finally, they should give a feeling of the AI approach to economic problems, as opposed to more traditional approaches (see also Section 5).

Case studies assume the point of view of a professional/expert examining the problem, and show how AI can be useful in implementing a solution. As such, case studies are long enough to deserve a chapter or a section on their own (in fact, the second half of this book is completely dedicated to them: see "A reader's guide" for more details).

Examples are a second place where relationships between AI and economics are often pointed out. Examples, however, are much less complex than case studies; in general, they present elementary applications, chosen so as to clarify the meaning of the concepts being introduced and sufficiently short to be interleaved with the text. Examples are used very liberally all over the book.

1.4 The mortgage loan credit granting case study

The following case study is based on [Pau and Tambo, 1990]. It describes a system for knowledge-based mortgage loan credit granting and risk assessment.

1.4.1 Problem statement

Mortgage credit institutions grant loans in property, both private and commercial, while holding a mortgage in that property for the duration of the loan. Should the debtor be exposed to bankruptcy or similar default, then the mortgage credit institution uses its title in the property to auction it. Normally, the sales price at an auction is not less than the valuation of the property by the public tax assessment body. Nevertheless, the mortgage credit institution can suffer losses due in part to unpaid loan instalments, in part to loss of value at auction sale w.r.t. market price, and finally in legal and other administrative expenses. Such losses are charged against reserves, and exceptionally insurance claims, but they are severely restricted by rules governing the conduct of mortgage credit granting.

The analysis of the mortgage credit application is often carried out first by local agents interacting on the spot with the applicants, and the role of which is to collect data and impressions on the condition of the property. The loan granting decision is thereafter carried out centrally by credit officers who apply a set of selection screens, as well as policy guidelines proper to the institution; they also check past records, including credit data bureaus.

If the screens and guidelines, as well as the application, were easy, then simple, almost mechanistic sorting rules and calculations would suffice. Said calculations would normally require only conventional software, programming languages, and implementation environments. And this indeed applies to most house or apartment mortgage loans.

Nevertheless, the way the judgements should be carried out is far from simple in the case, for example, of so-called mixed property, which combines private housing with business use (e.g. a ground floor store, a workshop, a rented office for private practice, etc.).The loan granting decision then requires to combine all of the following information:

i. market or tax assessment value of the property, or of each part hereof

ii. check on whether rental or other property related income exists and is commensurate with property value

iii. detailed checks on the priority ranking, and amounts, of existing loans with mortgage in parts of the property or its use

iv. cash flow and profit+loss statements for the business conducted on property premises

v. salary or income of owner and lessor of the housing part of the property

vi. condition, quality of property and of its location

vii. individual tax situation of the loan applicant

This involves altogether about 35 items of information, some numerical, some judgemental, finally others binary or finite valued. In the above mentioned case, the requirements on:

- data acquisition and query
- decision-making complexity
- process follow up and validation
- user interface friendliness

are such, that the implementation warrants the use of an expert system approach. This will involve specifying:

i. a knowledge base, which shall contain the evaluation screens, procedures and checks, specified incrementally and independently through so-called rules (Section 4.2)

ii. a search or inference procedure, which shall generate the selection of decision-making alternatives, but also of facts justifying possible choices (Sections 4.3 and 4.5)

iii. a user interface, whereby the loan granting officer will dialogue with the system

iv. an explanation facility, whereby the user can get responses to questions, such as "How?" or "Why?", which he may put to the system at any stage of the loan analysis process (Section 4.6)

Each of the above i.- iv. may again be different between the system development phase and the operational phase. Our presentation will involve presenting the basic contents and syntax of the knowledge base, in order, through an example rule, to present the unification, inference, and expert system architecture.

1.4.2 Knowledge base

A syntactic driven editor, built in the LISP symbolic language, allows to specify in the knowledge base:

- either facts, which are fixed true statements, specified as:

  FACT : (Condition)

  COMMENT : "(Text)"

- or rules, which are elemental reasonings structured as :

  IF : (Hypothesis conditions)

  THEN : (Conclusion condition)

  COMMENT : "(Text)"

  PROBABILITY : (Value)

  DIRECTION : (Forward, backward, or both)

where all conditions are a string of symbols involving constants, variables, logical bindings (AND, OR, NOT), as well as calculation formulae.

Let us take as an example Rule (I), which is typical of a judgement or assessment by a human expert (Fig. 1). In that rule, and with the applicable syntax from the editor:

- symbols in capital letters are either predefined constants (TRUE, FALSE, STORE, INDUSTRY, HANDICRAFT, RENTAL), relations (IF, OR, AND, THEN, PROVABLE, UNPROVABLE, KNOWN, UNKNOWN) or names of other facts or knowledge bases (OTHER-OFFICE-AREA); symbols in lower case are variables, which are quantities or values set through the user dialogue, or by calling other facts and knowledge bases

- calculation or evaluation formulae use operators (=, <=, /, >, + , >=), followed by their arguments in a predefined order, only separated by spaces. For example:

  (+ 1 0 x)

  which is of the format: (operator operand1 ... operandN result), and essentially is an assignment of the value 1 to x

```
RULE (I):        ((IF (OR (AND(= type OFFICE)
                 ( / housing-area office-area x )
                 ( >= x 20 )
                 ( + 1 0 other-office-area )
                 ( + 1 0 housing-fraction))
                 ( AND ( = type OFFICE)
                  (< = total-area 300)
                 ( / housing-area area z)
                 (> z 0.75 )
                 ( + 1 0 other-office-area)
                 ( + 1 0 housing-fraction)))

(THEN            ( OTHER-OFFICE-AREA type office total-area housing-area office-area
                 housing-fraction other-office-area )))

COMMENT:         "Does the rule about small offices/stores be included into those for the
                 housing?")

PROBABILITY:     0.90

DIRECTION:       Backward
```

Fig. 1: Rule (I) obeying the rule syntax for an example of a LISP based expert system shell (CLEOPATRA)

The rule in Fig. 1 says that if the office or store portion of the property is relatively small with respect to the housing use of it, then the property can be processed as if it were a pure residential property. More specifically, the rule tells that if the office-use area represents less than 5% of the residential area, all the property can receive loans according to the same rules as housing; the rule also says that the same holds if the higher floor area is less than 300 sq.m and if at least 75% of the total property is residential.

1.4.3 Unification

Consider again Rule (I). The THEN Conclusion condition starts with a procedure call header OTHER-OFFICE-AREA, whereas the variable "other-office-area" in that condition contains the result (i.e. office or none), and "type", "total-area", "housing-area", "housing-fraction" are parameter values passed onto other rules. That whole procedure in the conclusion condition is treated as a logic condition, or predicate, which must be satisfied.

Assume for the moment that the Conclusion condition has the logic value TRUE; the other cases are discussed in Section 4.5 on inference.

The expert system shell, having verified that the Conclusion condition is TRUE, will search through the IF Hypothesis conditions of the rule to find some parentheses containing variables all found earlier in the THEN condition. Each time an atom is found, that is a string containing sub-condition containing variables appearing in the Conclusion condition (e.g. (= type OFFICE)), the expert system will try to unify the individual symbols. This means that the expert system will test if the variable "type" has the value "OFFICE". If, instead of "OFFICE", there had appeared a variable which had not yet been unified with anything, then this variable would have been assigned the value of "type". If the atom had been instead (/ housing-area office-area x), then the expert system would have tried to unify x with the quotient (housing-area / office-area).

When the unification is attempted on two incompatible variables (e.g. having different values), then the atom has the logic value FALSE. If the unification is possible, then the atom is TRUE. According to elementary logic, one single FALSE condition in a (AND (...) (...)) atom implies that the whole sentence is FALSE. Sentences describing conditions after one which is FALSE, will not be executed. If the condition had been (OR (...) (...)), then the whole sentence would have been TRUE if only one of the atoms had been TRUE. If both the head and the tail of the same rule are TRUE, then it is said that this rule has fired along the search path which first lead to it.

1.4.4 Probability

If there is doubt about the validity of a specific rule, then probability (see Section 4.2) gives the likelihood. These values are combined through sequences of rules as conditional probabilities in agreement with the Bayes rule.

1.4.5 Inference

Direction (see Section 4.2) tells in which sequence rules can be applied, in that forward chaining links rules from Hypothesis conditions to Conclusion conditions, to be unified with Hypothesis of subsequent rules. In backward chaining, the rules are linked from Conclusion conditions to Hypothesis Conditions, to be unified with Conclusion conditions of antecedent rules.

It should be noted that the direction of a rule, but also the unification process with atoms appearing in its conditions, will tell which alternative rules can be unified together.

Moreover, the inference procedure will tell how to select among those rules which do unify in the proper direction with a given rule. There is a variety of such rules, e.g. those who start with the shortest or the longest atom.

1.4.6 Explanations

When inference proceeds as explained above, the user may want to know "How?" or "Why?" a specific sequence of rules was selected. This is done by the so-called explanation facility which essentially prints out in some selectable order the comment texts (see Section 4.2) attached to the rules which have fired:

- in the "Why?" mode, the explanation facility will print the sequence of comments for the rules chaining backward from the rule, the Conclusion condition of which is asking for justification

- in the "How?" mode, the explanation facility will chain forward from the rule, the Hypothesis condition of which is asking for a chain of possible conditions

```
RULE (II):      (( IF ( OR (MEMBER STORE type )
                ( + 0 0 store-fraction)

(THEN (ZERO-STORE-FRACTION type store-fraction)))

COMMENT:        "If the store-fraction is not relevant, it is set at zero"

RULE (III):     ((IF (AND ( MEMBER INDUSTRY type )
                (LOAN INDUSTRY purpose limit principal monthly)
                (/ value-agent value-market ratio)
                ( / earlier-loan value-market ceiling-ratio)
                ( - ratio ceiling-ratio difference)
                ( OR ( AND ( = purpose NEW-CONSTRUCTION)
                                ( + expenses 0 current-need)
                        ( AND ( = purpose IMPROVEMENT)
                                ( + expenses 0 current-need)
                        ( AND ( = purpose OTHER-PURPOSE)
                                ( + expenses 0 current-need))
                        ( AND ( = purpose CHANGE-OWNER)
                                ( * ceiling-ratio purchase-price current-need))
                ( OR ( AND ( < current-need ceiling)
                                ( + current-need 0 loan-proposal))
                        ( AND ( >= current-need ceiling)
                                ( + ceiling 0 loan-proposal ))))

(THEN (CALCULATION type purpose value-agent value-market earlier-loan purchase-
                price expenses current-need ceiling loan-proposal))

COMMENT:        " Calculation of offer for industrial use"
```

Fig. 2: Other mortgage loan credit granting rules

1.4.7 Knowledge acquisition

This is the process, also called knowledge elicitation,whereby a human expert, here a credit rating expert, will explain on the bases of which rules he/she reasons.

As an example, Fig. 2 provides two additional rules to the Rule (I) in Fig. 1.

The first, Rule (II), is just typical of the many system configurations and consistency definitions required; such type of rules are more frequently introduced by an artificial intelligence or software engineer, after consultation with the expert. The MEMBER function checks whether the constant "STORE" belongs to the range of permissible values of the variable "type".

APPLICATION SPECIFIC

KNOWLEDGE BASE

- Evaluation rules (such as (I) (III))
- Configuration and initialization rules (such as (II))
- Loan interest rates and ceilings, for each type of usage of the property
- Calculation rules

USER INTERFACE

- Screen layout and logs generation
- Information retrieval procedure:
  ((IF (AND (RETRIEVE (list of variables))))
  (THEN (CASE (list of variables)))
- Menu dialogue
  ((TOPROVE (QUESTION response-to-question)
  (CHOOSE-ONE (list of choices)))
  COMMENT: "Text of query to user"
- Generate text and graphic layout for the solutions:
  ((IF (AND (WRITELINE "_"))
  (THEN (DISPLAY (list-of variables)))

TOOL

- Symbol list (constants, variables, procedures) and "clear text" explanations of each
- Rule editor

- Selection of goals to be proven
- Graphical/screen generation primitives

INFERENCE ENGINE

- Rule selection strategy
- Search procedure (forward chaining, backward chaining, inductive, etc...)

EXPLANATION FACILITY

- "How?" explanation facility
- "Why?" explanation facility

SYMBOLIC LANGUAGE	DATA BASE INTERFACE	GRAPHICAL GENERATION

Fig. 3: Architecture of the mortgage loan credit granting expert system software

The second, Rule (III), is typical of a complex screen which will sort out hypotheses to find out how a calculation should be carried out. This characterizes administrative regulations and procedures. That rule is set-up as Rule (I), just using new constants and variables.

In practice, most of the rules will, however, be evaluation Rules like (I), which will separately and then jointly, assess the credit worthiness of the loan applicant, and the solidity of the mortgage.

Such a knowledge base, combined with inference, may serve not only the assessment officer, but also the loan applicant through a dialogue aiming at investigating all consequences of alternative loan possibilities. This holds especially as more and more mortgage loans are supplemented by bank loans, or industrial credit loans, the terms of which are all different, esp. with respect to liquidity or tax implications.

1.4.8 Expert system architecture

Fig. 3 illustrates the structure of the mortgage loan credit granting expert system, in its simplest case. It exemplifies the general constituents of such a system as given in Section 4.1.

All items above the thick line are application specific, and must be coded specifically for that case and domain. All items below the thick line are essentially application independent tools and facilities, which can be reused for other cases. At the very bottom appear a symbolic programming language (such as LISP, Prolog, SMALLTALK, OPS-5, etc...), a data base query language and interface, together with a graphic package, which together make possible all the facilities of the expert system.

It is essential to highlight the fact that the knowledge acquisition and knowledge base maintenance, can be developed incrementally by adding rules in any order to the knowledge base. Similarly, each part of the user interface can be updated incrementally. This is due first to the symbolic programming environment used, and next to the unification principle which guarantees that the search will be performed irrespective of the internal organization of the knowledge base.

1.4.9 Risk analysis inference control structure

The simple rule unification of the previous Section 4.3 can handle most cases, but credit granting can be built more solidly using a core control structure specially designed for the type of generic inferences required in that area.

Such a control structure is based on the following qualitative reasoning procedures, with the corresponding editors:

i. comparison relations: which relate the scalar values of a variable with scalar interval codes, on a non-scaled range

ii. context relations: in which the interval boundaries from point 1. above are updated to exogenous or conjuncture attributes, e.g. "tight money" situation, or "money growth" situation, etc.

iii. threshold comparison relations: in which a set of scalar variables must have non-scalar values (such as: "not-acceptable", "low", "acceptable", "strong"), and joint set values on the same range of values (by cross impact tables)

iv. gradient relations: in which variables have a relationship over time, based on the scalar increase or rate of change

v. risk aggregation functions: in which a function of n non-scaled values, maps into the one-dimensional variable representing qualitative risk values or ranks; this apply to credit worthiness (assessed from liquidity, real estates, etc.), as well as bankruptcy risks

1.5 AI and Decision support

It is most interesting to clarify how AI principles compare with more traditional models of decision-making, such as those developed in the framework of Operations Research (O.R.) and Decision support systems (DSS).

AI systems take advantage from the contributions of different research streams of economics, such as decision support and economic theories. They provide basic understanding of the qualitative as well as quantitative decision processes and of the causal relationships among events in the problem domain; hence an essential part of the knowledge and of the knowledge processing techniques required to build up an intelligent system can be captured from them (see Chapter 12.1).

AI stresses the representation and processing of qualitative (i.e.non-numeric) knowledge: elementary data are symbols (e.g. text, nouns, concepts, etc.; numbers are just a particular kind of symbol), relations among symbols are represented as expressions (structured collections of symbols). Furthermore, as explained in Section 1, methods for dealing with incompleteness and uncertainty in knowledge are the core of AI approach to problem-solving.

O.R. support to decision-making is based on:

- linear programming and related techniques (integer programming, stochastic methods)
- probability, for modelling decision-making under risk and to some extent decision-making under uncertainty, as well as forecasting by extrapolation
- utility theory, with the related concepts of standard gamble and risk attitude
- graph theory
- statistics (sampling, error theory)

O.R. is thus mainly concerned with quantitative knowledge: knowledge and constraints are resp. represented as numbers (or variables) and as equations capturing relations among simple data; a whole problem is then described as a set of equations (or sometimes as a set of curves in the geometric space).

The O.R./DSS approach poses two main problems. First, a modelling in the mathematical space assumes the availability of:

- full knowledge of the causal relationships relevant to the domain, in order to calculate the consequences of every decision alternative (i.e. no uncertainty in knowledge other than probabilities)
- a complete definition of a consistent preference system allowing a ranking among alternatives, and hence the choice of the best one

These assumptions (rational model of decision-making) has, however, undergone numerous criticisms, well known from the literature (the satisficing approach, the organizational view, the political view etc.), tending to demonstrate its lack of realism for many, unstructured decision tasks. Second, the advocated decision process is counter-intuitive and not cognitively based: humans in fact scarcely use quantitative knowledge in reasoning. Thus observation of how humans solve difficult problems is of no direct help.

2 Applications of Artificial Intelligence in banking, financial services and economics

This chapter surveys approximately 250 actual applications development projects carried out by companies and institutions, with specifications of the nature of the AI project goals, of the development environments and of project partners (if known). Of course, owing to the fast changes in the field and to implementation experiences, this list cannot be complete nor exhaustive, and can only be up-to-date as of the manuscript completion. The goal is therefore rather to identify methodological as well as software tools needs resulting from the development projects listed. The application areas covered are: banking, finance, insurance, economics, auditing, commodities trading, tax planning, general management.

2.1 The motivations for the use of AI

In the areas of banking, financial services, insurance, economics and related industries the main operational motivation for initiating, and eventually fielding, systems solutions using some significant portion of artificial intelligence (AI) techniques, are the following:

G1: development of computer based solutions allowing for the handling of tasks of a high relative complexity, as measured vs.operator skills, thus leveraging skills/staff, and reducing risks; the complexity involves achieving a compromise between: providing a consistent level of information, a wide range of capabilities promoting specific goals, and providing training capabilities

G2: setting up computer based information services, with user specific information screens, and dialogue functions, offering a time - and/or competitive edge over other actors operating in the same domain, thus pooling knowledge for actions initiated by the user

G3: replacing paperwork, information consolidation and cumbersome control procedures, in rather routine based operations involving usually distributed agents/sources, and where a high consistency is needed reflecting a common policy

G4: outright labour, quality, time and money savings in centralized routine tasks, with reduced errors

G5: ability to upgrade a solution software incrementally with a higher software writing producibililty

As examples of the above motivations, we can mention those presiding in a few case examples:

G1: lending advisors (e.g.Wells Fargo Bank/Syntelligence)

G2: bond portfolio planning and trading systems with market interpretation (e.g.Salomon Brothers)

G3: real estate appraisal for credit granting (e.g.Security Pacific Bank)

G4: money transfer telex conversion into standard formats (e.g.Citibank information resources/Cognitive Systems Inc.; Sumitomo Bank/Digital Equipment)

G5: cash point machines network management and fault diagnosis (e.g.BRED, Bankcontakt Belgium)

The classes of motivations may be further related to the location of the need in terms of the organizational element where the solution is needed; a framework for the location of the solution need is the following (see also [Marmier, 1987]):

L1: front-office services facing the end customer (e.g.pension planning advisory system)

L2: general support functions (e.g.document filing and routing)

L3: product or service specific support functions (e.g.credit card charge authorizer, back office functions)

L4: internal policy making and related information analysis (e.g.matching products to customer needs)

L5: auditing, compliance, and security functions (e.g.accounts auditing)

2.2 Survey of development projects

Whereas a number of studies have tried to survey applications, markets [OVUM, 1988] or generic solutions (e.g.risk management, underwriting), it is the aim here to go back to more technical aspects. The attached tables in Section 2.6 below survey approximately 250 actual applications development projects.

First, we consider each development project as aimed at providing a solution to an actual problem defined by a specific capability to be implemented. This implies that the solution approach and architecture will typically always involve the integration of whatever resources are needed (conventional programming, artificial intelligence tools, databases, user interfaces, computer architectures).

Next, this survey does not deal at a high priority with the AI experience level of the developers and users, nor with the state of actual fielding or testing of the solution.

Next, the projects are grouped by application categories, thus revealing immediately which are the classes of problems resulting in the largest estimated global effort level.There may of course be wide differences between the specific aspects highlighted in different projects within the same category.For example, an investment advisory system running on a mainframe is quite different from a simple one running on a PC.

Last, some entries are incomplete, and a few unchecked, owing to project secrecy, unjustified or excessive publicity, unclear data about their status, etc.; and of course the survey is in no way making any claim for exhaustivity.

2.3 Development and delivery environments

The survey shows a clear trend toward three types of development and delivery principles:

- multi-user applications, which are software packages embodying complex, widely accepted, and open knowledge (e.g.product advisors, self-service sales assistants, personal financial planning systems)
- hybrid environments, which offer integration facilities whereby heterogeneous inference, knowledge representation, languages and database query languages can be blended together, but where no application specific knowledge resides initially
- application generic shell, also called inclination shell, with built-in functions and standard knowledge, but allowing for end user customization of the knowledge (e.g. Lending Advisor from Syntelligence)

In all instances, there is a growing emphasis towards:

- back office/workstation/mainframe integration with the corresponding portability requirements on the development environment
- distributed use over a network with data and knowledge servers (eventually distinct)
- incorporation of validation and software maintenance procedures

  multilingual knowledge acquisition tools or languages
- report generation for results and explanations
- imbedded training modes or facilities
- incorporation of diverse user interface drivers (e.g.terminal drivers, videotext drivers)

- incorporation of menu layout and customization facilities, including the ability to freeze or free some dialogue sequences, and soft key programming features
- parsers for standard economic/financial on-line information services (e.g. various Reuters, Dow Jones, Telerate or Datastream services)
- interface to, or true rule-based spreadsheet capabilities

2.4 Generic domain utilities

Regardless of the development and delivery environments, a number of common calculations, regulatory databases or generic knowledge bases can be identified which must be included in most solutions. They make up upgrades or specific user-developed additions to multi-user application environments, hybrids as well as application generic shells; seen from a different perspective they constitute one major set of capabilities which distinguish environments in economic/banking/finance from other AI applications:

Calculations:

- rates of return
- accounting balance calculations
- tax calculations
- actualization indexes
- time series analysis
- trade commissions/fees

Procedures:

- risk ranking
- account profitability
- protocol verification e.g.for fraud control
- client profiles
- multi attribute scoring
- econometric model re-estimation around a nominal path
- linear programming algorithms
- set-up of search screens, e.g.based on ratios

Knowledge bases:

- trading instruments descriptors (frames), dictionaries of variables applicable in selected industries

- cross-impact tables
- in the future: legal/regulatory knowledge bases
- simple truth maintenance systems
- balanced trade generators, e.g. for swaps or securities/futures trades

Client relation knowledge base (for each client):

- expectations and commitments agreed between the parties
- preferences of each party
- procedures which are agreed between the parties in normal cases
- history of the relationship
- client attributes, incl.risk profile

Furthermore, generic applications at an advanced level may require specific search/inference algorithms, as well as user interfaces with some adaptive features, none of which are found elsewhere (see [Pau, 1986b]).

2.5 Inference control and conflict resolution strategies

Existing AI environment usually provide forward and/or backward chaining to control the search for knowledge elements in the knowledge base. Forward chaining matches these elements with rule antecedents in order to fire consequent actions. Backward chaining matches elements of the knowledge base to rule consequents in an attempt to verify rule antecedents.

Forward chaining from observed facts and backward chaining from goals or likely hypotheses minimize the search space, and are often used in problem types G3, G4, G5. In the other instances, typically for problem types G1, G2, both are used simultaneously, and associated with backtracking, because inference then aims at exploiting the knowledge structure to explore alternatives under control of conflict resolution strategies.

A control resolution strategy produces a subset of knowledge elements with validated antecedents that may be fired. This strategy attempts to select the most applicable inference control strategy in order to reach a solution at the earliest possible time. Some of the conflict resolution strategies are as follows, and are increasingly important in banking/finance/economic applications:

R1: First found: the first applicable knowledge element that is found is used first, which means that it should often be dismissed when knowledge is added incrementally

R2: Least recently used: the applicable knowledge element the least recently used is chosen; this is relevant in e.g. trading systems

R3: Most recently used: counterpart to R2

R4: Antecedent ordered: priorities attached to the antecedents of e.g.rules are used to resolve conflicts. This is helpful when there is a natural or "administrative"ordering of importance amongst the antecedents

R5: Consequent ordered: the same as R4, except that priorities are attached to the consequents of the rules; this is typical of risk assessment

R6: Most complex first: the rule that has the most antecedents or consequent clauses (depending on whether the inference engine is chaining backward or forward,respectively), will be fired first

R7: Simplest first: same as R5, except that the rule with the least number of clauses is chosen; this is typical of applications of type G3, where the solution should process most cases but rare exceptions

R8: Global priority: as well as assigning priorities to the antecedents and consequents of rules, a rule may be assigned a priority as a whole: this happens in most finance and auditing systems

The solution requirements should always specify which of the above or customized conflict resolution strategies should be implemented, otherwise poor user satisfaction and confidence will be the outcome.

2.6 Table of projects

The contents of these tables are explained in Section 2.2. When available, supporting references are given in Section 2.7 below. The sections for these tables are:

AUDITING

BANKING

ECONOMICS

FINANCE

INSURANCE

TAX PLANNING

AUDITING	Balance sheet analysis	ExpertTeam (F)	Production of financial reports, with knowledge-based analyzer and spreadsheet, on Personal Consultant Plus	Finexpro/ Credit Expert/ Finexpert	16
AUDITING	Balance sheet analysis	Bank of France	InterLISP then C on IBM mainframe; balance sheet analysis	COSIE	21
AUDITING	Balance sheet analysis	Coopers & Lybrand	ESE shell		
AUDITING	Balance sheet analysis	Deutsche Kreditgenossenschaft BIK (FRG)	Semantic nets+ Prolog+Basic; balance sheet analysis	Portable adviser	21
AUDITING	Balance sheet analysis	GIPA-Bretagne (F)	GURU environment;		
AUDITING	Business auditing	Univ.Waterloo	Audit planning	CAPEX	
AUDITING	Business auditing	Coopers & Lybrand	Preparation of audit test programmes	EXPERTEST	
AUDITING	Pricing	Data General (USA)	Transfer pricing of parts shipped abroad; in GOLDWORKS shell and MVLISP		
AUDITING	Public contracts	US Air Force/ Intellicorp	Cost analysis on public contracts; use of KEE	AUDIT	16
AUDITING	Report generation	Univ. Erlangen-Nurenberg; DATEV e.G.	Knowledge-based derivation of verbal reports from company data; use of the NEXPERT and HEXE shells	GUVEX/ TYPEX/ BILEX/ FINEX/ CONTREX	20
AUDITING	VAT	Deloitte Haskins and Sells	VAT planning for retailers and control of exposure to points of sale	VOTAR/ POSIS	
BANKING	Account management	SOREFI/ Caisse d'Epargne du Nord; Bull-Cediag	Consolidation of all accounts of each given client, and link to client data	Smertios	
BANKING	Branch analysis	Hypo Bank (Muenchen)	Relative efficiency of 450 branches in terms of returns, productivity, development and scores herefore; hierarchy of branches; Prolog		54
BANKING	Commercial lending	Digital Equipment; State Univ. at Albany; General Electric R&D	GEN-X rule-based shell (Decision Expert);for capital based loans; balance sheet analysis;interface with SuperCalc 4 spreadsheet	CLASS	

BANKING	Commercial lending	Agrileasing(I)/ Artificial Intelligence software	Leasing evaluation; SAVOIR shell	ALVIN	26
BANKING	Commercial lending	Bail Equipement; CIC/ Intellia (F)	Leasing of machines and printing equipment; NEXPERT shell		21
BANKING	Commercial lending	Barclays Bank	Appraisal, compliance and monitoring of corporate lending		
BANKING	Commercial lending	Fed.Caisses populaires Desjardins/ Laval Univ. (CDN)	Structured financial statement analysis via spreadsheets; first GURU then Lotus 1-2-3		20
BANKING	Commercial lending	First National Bank Atlanta	Leasing contract analyzer		
BANKING	Commercial lending	Niederlandsche Middenstandbank (NL)	Lease acceptance; ACQUAINT from Lithp Systems on PC's		21
BANKING	Commercial lending	Oko Bank/ Nokia	Agricultural loans; XiPlus shell and C	MATIAS	21
BANKING	Commercial lending	Standard Chartered Bank N.Y./ Lcexam (NY)	Examining letters of credit for compliance to UCP400 code		
BANKING	Commercial lending	Union Bank of Switzerland (Basel)	Fundamental corporate analysis	FCA	15
BANKING	Credit	Arthur Andersen (Madrid)	Credit card evaluation by neural computing		15
BANKING	Credit	Cullinet	Car loan credit scoring	Application expert	19
BANKING	Credit	Experteam	Consumer loans	Credit Expert	16
BANKING	Credit	Intelligent environments (UK)	CRYSTAL shell; rule-based; inclusion of financial calculations		
BANKING	Credit	Madrid University	Credit scoring; blackboard architecture; backward chaining; Prolog or Lisp+Loops	Risk Evaluation	22
BANKING	Credit	Robson Rhodes Ltd	Loans to small businesses; Xi-Plus shell; 7 knowledge domains about creditworthiness and company management	Corporate lending advisor	23

BANKING	Credit	Technica (NJ)	Credit scoring by decision trees on objects; car loans		24
BANKING	Credit	Univ. Sydney	ID3 learning algorithm for assessing credit card applications by top-down induction of decision trees		25
BANKING	Credit	American Express Co	ART shell and data base interfaces; authorizes credit card charges; use of some Symbolics workstations	Authorizer Advisor	
BANKING	Credit	Apple/ Joy Informatique (F)	Balance sheet analysis of distributors; Plaisir d'Expert shell		16
BANKING	Credit	Banca di San Paolo di Torino/ Digital Equipment	Family credit repayment	SPACE	26
BANKING	Credit	Bank of America/ Helix Technology (UK)	Prolog+Basic+dBaseIII; produces export letters of credit	Letter of credit advisor	27
BANKING	Credit	Banque Hervet/ Evalog (F)	Loan risk	EVENT	26
BANKING	Credit	Barclays Bank (Israel)	C-Prolog		1
BANKING	Credit	British Petroleum/ Soft Computing; GFI	Client risk assessment; use of GURU		16
BANKING	Credit	C.N.Credit Agricole/ CR2A	Nexpert shell for real estate loans		
BANKING	Credit	Cassa di Risparmio di Torino/ Mesarteam	Nexpert shell; personal loan granting	CIP	15
BANKING	Credit	Chase Manhattan/ IBM; Carisma SRL	VM/ Prolog with frames, and discriminant analysis; IBM 3033 host	CRES	2
BANKING	Credit	Credit Agricole (Paris); BRED/ Univ.Paris	SNARK shell	PATRILOG/ CREDEX/ SEAC	3
BANKING	Credit	Credito Italiano/ Olivetti	Use of the Smalltalk based shell PLATO	MOZART	56

BANKING	Credit	Eurotunnel/ MDBS	Manages a line of credit; uses GURU shell	ELCAS	
BANKING	Credit	First Wachovia Bank N.C; Wells Fargo Bank S.F./ Syntelligence; IBM	SYNTEL data flow functional language; MVX (PL/ 1) implementation; forward chaining inference propagating changes across levels in SYNTEL	Syntel/ Lending advisor	4
BANKING	Credit	Kredietbank (B)/ Systems designers (UK)	SAGE shell ; analysis of numeric creditor data; later use of SD Adviser	Loan approval advisor	16
BANKING	Credit	La Craixa/ Tecsidel (SP)	Credit scoring; Intelligence Service shell		16
BANKING	Credit	OKO Bank (SF)/ Nokia	Crystal shell	Oko loan analyzer	16
BANKING	Credit	OKOBANK (SF)	Subsidized agricultural loans grating; XiPlus shell+C on PC's		21
BANKING	Credit	PBS-Eurocard (DK)	Analysis of credit card applications; use of Goldworks		56
BANKING	Credit	Soc. Marseillaise de Credit (CESO, SOFICIM); Barclays Bank; SAVA; Credit Mutuel Mediterraneen/ PROLOGIA	Consumer and house loans; Prolog II based shell OURSE; ORACLE and videotext interfaces	BEST	
BANKING	Credit	Syseca (F)/ Inference Corp.	Credit card authorizer		
BANKING	Discretionary account surveillance	Coopers & Lybrand	Goldworks shell, with mixed chaining		
BANKING	Inkasso recovery	Cybercredit financial systems		Cybercredit	
BANKING	Inkasso recovery	Editions juridiques Lamy (F)/ SEGIN	Object based layered network of rules; distributed by videotext services		
BANKING	Job control	Banca Nazionale del Lavoro/ Mesarteam	Blackboard architecture; scheduling of data processing operations; KEE on Xerox 1186 and data base		

BANKING	Job control	Bayerisches Vereinsbank	Insight-2 shell		
BANKING	Job control	First National Bank Chicago	EDP audit		21
BANKING	Job control	IGIRS Pension fund/ Cognitech (F)	Scheduling work with administrative documents; NL front-end on Sun 260	SAOR	21
BANKING	Job control	Union Bank of Switzerland	Consolidates and prepares all 150000 daily COBOL program scheduling; VM/ Prolog and DEDALE shell	META-PSS	26
BANKING	Marketing	Coopers & Lybrand UK	Advice on pension schemes	CLASP	
BANKING	Marketing	IBM	OPS5 language; financial marketing consultant system; 770 rules in 4 domains; extension with object centered frame representation	FAME	5
BANKING	Marketing	Prophecy dev. corp.	Frame based semantic networks	Profit tool	
BANKING	Marketing	Zentralsparkasse und Kommercialbank Wien	Customer advisory service; first OPS5 then 4GL and TSO; first VAX then IBM mainframe; DB2 interface		21
BANKING	Money transfers	Chase Manhattan			
BANKING	Money transfers	City Bank/ Cognitive Systems	Routing of funds transfers telexes	A-Class	16
BANKING	Money transfers	Generale de Banque/ Deutsche Bank; Cognitive Systems/ Gecosys	Semantic networks and parsers for SWIFT formats; message clarifier; text analyzer; message interpreter; SWIFT formatter; parser identifies frames	Telex Reader/ ATRANS/ Deal Reader	6
BANKING	Money transfers	Generale de Belgique; GECOSYS (B)	SWIFT message formatting for interbank transfers with message scanning , recognition and formatting	Scarbo	
BANKING	Money transfers	SWIFT/ SWIFT			
BANKING	Money transfers	Security Pacific Bank			

BANKING	Money transfers	Sumitomo Bank/ Nihon Digital Equipment	LISP+C+VAX-Scan for text processing on VAX8530 and central access; 80% reliability	TEXPERT	21
BANKING	Money transfers	Union Bank of Switzerland	Automatic processing of payment orders	APOLLO	15
BANKING	Mortgage credit	Polytechnic of Wales	Savoir shell; mortgage valuation		
BANKING	Mortgage credit	Arthur Andersen/ Texas Instrument	Rule-based regulatory assessment of loan features	Mortgage loan analyzer	7
BANKING	Mortgage credit	Caisse d'Epargne/ ACT Informatique	Award of "prêts conventionnés" (controlled loans); LeLisp rule-based shell Antinea	TIPI	8
BANKING	Mortgage credit	Comcap/ Softserv	Savoir rule-based shell; mortgage selection	Mortgage selector	
BANKING	Mortgage credit	Nykredit(DK)/ Tech.Univ.Denmark	LISP based shell Cleopatra; mortgage loan granting on mixed property		9
BANKING	Pricing of services	First National Bank of Chicago	Auditing of data processing service costs		
BANKING	Pricing of services	Midland group	Communications link costing to Thomas Cook		
BANKING	Risk analysis	Univ. Illinois at Urbana-Champaign	Company cash flow model, with Star based induction of risk	MARBLE	20
BANKING	Selecting public funding	Arthur Young	Nexus shell		10
BANKING	Settlement costs	Financial clearing and services			
BANKING	Treasury management	Ambroveneto (I)		E/ G/ I	26
ECONOMICS	Choice of intermediate economic targets	National Bank/ Tech.Univ.Denmark	PROLOG; reallocation of goals amongst endogenous, exogenous and monetary targets		1
ECONOMICS	Judgmental forecasting	Expert Systems Int. (UK)	Economic model building from expectations and factors; Prolog 2+Fortran+statistics	EMEX	
ECONOMICS	Judgmental forecasting	GSI-ECO	Rule-based shell; evaluation of exogeneous variables	ECO/ KARL	20

ECONOMICS	Judgmental forecasting	Kyoto Univ. (J)	Prolog description of causal graph betwen variables		55
ECONOMICS	Judgmental forecasting	Univ. Tilburg (NL)	Qualitative causal model based on chaining the signs of derivatives in macroeconomic models; use of PROLOG		20
ECONOMICS	Judgmental forecasting	Federal Reserve	Dempster-Shafer uncertainty reasoning		
ECONOMICS	Monetary economics	Cognitech (F)	EMICYN and Tigre shells; short term predictions of USD/ FRF exchange rate according to:purchasing power parity, interest rate theory, current account theory; rules about political and social factors	PANISSE	11
ECONOMICS	Monetary economics	Federal Reserve	Prolog; backward chaining from growth targets		12
ECONOMICS	Natural language front-ends to forecasting models	Battelle Institute	Prolog based inference of model relations by NL understanding		1
ECONOMICS	Natural language front-ends to forecasting models	Federal Reserve	Front-end to quarterly model, with judgmental scripts		
ECONOMICS	Risk analysis	Computer Teaching Corp.; Univ. Illinois	Policy goal percentaging analysis in Plato/ Tencore	P/ G analysis	1
ECONOMICS	Risk analysis	Frost & Sullivan	Political risk service for 85 countries		
ECONOMICS	Teaching aids for economics	Digitalk; Univ. Pennsylvania	Smalltalk V	Economics discovery	
ECONOMICS	Teaching aids for economics	ECRC	CAI and explanation facilities		
FINANCE	Bond trading	ICL; Future systems(UK)	Gilts and money market trading	FS-Dealer	
FINANCE	Bond trading	Soft computing	Options on T-bonds; use of NEXPERT shell	X-Options	
FINANCE	Bond trading	Technical Univ. Denmark	Syntactic recognition of price trends, and rule-based trading technical analysis		55

FINANCE	Bond trading	Phillips & Drew (UK)/ IBM	What-if analysis prior to trade	FS-GILTS/ ORBIT	
FINANCE	Bond trading	Salomon Brothers	Reassignment to increase convexity quants in Portfolio		
FINANCE	Bond trading	Telekurs (CH)/ Fininfo (F)	Bond trading and hedging service	Finoblig	
FINANCE	Financial analysis	Cap Sogeti (F)	Ratio interpretation and financial diagnosis; Lotus 1-2-3+Pascal+Prolog; port to Shirka frame based shell	SAFIR	13
FINANCE	Financial analysis	S.Carolina Univ.	Intelligent spreadsheet for balance sheet analysis from ratios; Lotus and MicroProlog	FINEX	14
FINANCE	Financial analysis	Alvey Club ARIES/ Logica	Fundamental analysis and technical analysis	Taurus	
FINANCE	Financial analysis	Central of Risk, Bank of Italy	Interpretation of risk data	SECRETS	15
FINANCE	Financial analysis	Centre formation profession bancaire/ Stratems	Company diagnosis; Argument shell	SEFIA	16
FINANCE	Financial information	Knowledge associates (US)	PROLOG controlled dissemination of financial data	Financial quote system	
FINANCE	Financial information	Knowledge associates (US)	Intelligent trading information screen; Prolog+C on UNISYS/ Centix and workstations	Financial quote system FIQ	21
FINANCE	Financial information	Marubeni (J); Carnegie group	Neural networks		
FINANCE	Financial information	BNP/ CISI (F)	Front office screen for spot prices and swaps; NEXPERT+C	SPEED	
FINANCE	Financial information	Dow Jones	Natural language front-ends to financial databases		
FINANCE	Financial information	National Westminster B./ Intelligent environments; Instant awareness	Integration of Crystal shell, Digilink data logger, and access to:Reuters, Telerate SOP, Extel RTF	City Interface	17

FINANCE	Foreign exchange	Athena group	Hedging or trading on options at opening and closing of trade	FX	18
FINANCE	Foreign exchange	Battelle Institute	Temporal reasoning involving monetary, physical, policy and other assets for foreign exchange in commodities trading		1
FINANCE	Foreign exchange	GECOSYS (B)	Message analysis of FOREX screens	Deal-reader	
FINANCE	Foreign exchange	Property dev. corp.	Rule-based shell	CONTESSA	
FINANCE	Foreign exchange	Chemical Bank	ART shell; FOREX auditing; Symbolics platform	FXAA	58
FINANCE	Foreign exchange	Concepts Logiciels Experts, Paris	Neural network for front-office FOREX activities	Neural Trader's Assistant	
FINANCE	Foreign exchange	Fusion Group (N.Y.)/ Hecht Nielsen Corp.	ANZA Plus neurocomputing environment interfaced to Data Server, and to Sybase data base		
FINANCE	Foreign exchange	Manufacturer Hanover Trust;	Monitoring of worldwide FOREX trading activities	Inspector	57
FINANCE	Foreign exchange	Manufacturers Hanover Trust/ Symbolics	Technical analysis and FOREX reasoning assistant; real-time on Symbolics; GENERA environment; tracks multiple currencies, rates, trading models	TARA	28
FINANCE	Foreign exchange	Security Pacific Ntl. Bank	FOREX predictions	Security	29
FINANCE	Futures trading	Chicago Board of Trade/ Tandem; Apple	Electronic auction for after-hours trading; on TI Explorer with LISP interfaced to Tandem VLX; use of NL interface	AURORA	30
FINANCE	Marketing	Soft Computing (F)	Marketing of financial products; use of NEXPERT shell	MAX	
FINANCE	Mergers and acquisitions	General Electric Corp. R&D	KEE and classification engine	MARS	31
FINANCE	Mergers and acquisitions	ICF Phase Linear systems (Fairfax, VA)	Rule-based matching		

FINANCE	Pension planning	Coopers & Lybrand (London)	Pension scheme selection	CLASP	26
FINANCE	Pension planning	ALKS/ Systems designers	Pension advisor; uses SD-Designer shell	Pension and savings advisor	16
FINANCE	Pension planning	PFA (DK)	Advisory system for pension choice; VP Expert shell and C		56
FINANCE	Portfolio management	ACASTE (F)	Financial analysis+spreadsheet+word processing	Charis	
FINANCE	Portfolio management	Applied Expert systems (Boston)	200 objects; 6000 rules; 125 asset types; forward chaining simulation	PLAN-POWER	32
FINANCE	Portfolio management	Arthur D.Little		PFPS	
FINANCE	Portfolio management	Athena group (NY)		BEST Mix	
FINANCE	Portfolio management	CAP Sogeti; CSELT; Phillips MBLE		ESTEAM Esprit project P316	
FINANCE	Portfolio management	Citymax (UK)		Equus Esprit project	26
FINANCE	Portfolio management	Criterion software (US)	Rating knowledge base	Intelligent market/ equities	
FINANCE	Portfolio management	Helix Financial systems (UK)	Interest rate arbitrage and what-if displays	Opportunity	
FINANCE	Portfolio management	NCR		NCR Planmaster	
FINANCE	Portfolio management	Objective financial systems		Objective F.S.	
FINANCE	Portfolio management	Stanford University	Interview module+forward chaining+algorithmic optimization	FOLIO	33
FINANCE	Portfolio management	Sterling Wentworth (UK)		Planman	
FINANCE	Portfolio management	Univ. Saarbruecken	Rule-based; pre-dialogue to set risk level; use of FranzLisp	GABI	34
FINANCE	Portfolio management	ANZ Bank/ La Trobe Univ.; ISR Corp. (AUS)	Frame and rule-based environment XL	PORT-MAN	20

FINANCE	Portfolio management	Banque de Bretagne/ Arcane	Intelligence service shell	Josephine	16
FINANCE	Portfolio management	C.N.Credit Agricole/ Neuron Data	Personal Portfolio management advisory services; NEXPERT shell	PATRILOG	21
FINANCE	Portfolio management	Caisse d'Epargne Paris/ GSI-Tecsi	Intelligence service shell	SAGE	16
FINANCE	Portfolio management	Canadian Imperial Bank of Commerce	CRYSTAL shell, and DIGILINK data acquisition from Reuters		
FINANCE	Portfolio management	Chase Lincoln First Bank/ A.D.Little	LISP compiler	Personal financial strategies	16
FINANCE	Portfolio management	Generale de Banque/ Cognitive systems; Digital Equipment	Rule-based with knowledge decomposition; stock selection criteria for Belgian market; constraint optimization	Le Courtier/ StreetSmart	6
FINANCE	Portfolio management	Hancock Mutual Life; N.Y. Life insurance; Travellers Inc./ Applied Expert systems; Gold Hill; Fuji Xerox	LOOPS on Xerox workstations	Plan Power/ Client Profiling	35
FINANCE	Portfolio management	Intelligent technology (UK)	Portfolio management services		
FINANCE	Portfolio management	KKB Bank/ Insiders Gmbh (Mainz); IBM	ESE shell on a mainframe, later ADS shell from AION Corp.	RAMSES	15
FINANCE	Portfolio management	Kansallis-Osake-Pankki (SF)	ESE shell+Pascal+Cobol+DB2 on IBM mainframe	Expert-90	21
FINANCE	Portfolio management	Nanceenne Varin Barnier/ Neuron Data	Nexpert shell		16
FINANCE	Portfolio management	National Assn.Investment clubs/ Knowledge Garden		Stock Expert	16
FINANCE	Portfolio management	New York Life	Financial planning of insurance clients		36

FINANCE	Portfolio management	Pierson Heldring Bank/ UNISYS	KEE shell		
FINANCE	Portfolio management	Pregnana Milanese/ Bull (Italia)	Portfolio selection based on macroeconomic factors	INVESTIMAT	26
FINANCE	Portfolio management	Skandinaviska Enskilda Banken (S)/ Epitec			
FINANCE	Portfolio management	Sparda Bank/ GMD (FRG)	Babylon shell in ZetaLisp; 300 rules	EVA	37
FINANCE	Real estate	Security Pacific Corp.	Assessment of real estate assets; Prolog	CBREIS	16
FINANCE	Regulations and audit	Intelligent technology group (UK)	Rule-based shell, and simulation		
FINANCE	Regulations and audit	Moorgate PNL	Logic data base queries; compliance by financial intermediaries	Advisa	16
FINANCE	Regulations and audit	British Treasury/ ICL; Touche & Ross	Detection of fraud in purchases of privatized company shares		16
FINANCE	Regulations and audit	Building societies Expert system Club/ Expertech	Compliance with Financial services act; XiPlus shell		38
FINANCE	Regulations and audit	Equitable Insurance	Selection of business units for audit	TIARA	39
FINANCE	Regulations and audit	NYSE and AMEX/ Arthur Andersen	Company analysis of quoted companies; uses KEE	SEMACS	16
FINANCE	Regulations and audit	New York Stock Exchange	Detect illegal trades and insider dealings	ALERT	
FINANCE	Regulations and audit	S.E.C./ A.D.Little; Arthur Andersen	Natural language parser ELOISE coupled to EDGAR document analyzer		
FINANCE	Regulations and audit	S.E.C./ Arthur Andersen (US)	Analysis of financial filings by EDGAR system, with ratios and notes; KEE on Symbolics	Financial statement analyzer FSA	35
FINANCE	Risk analysis	Univ. California Berkeley	Back-propagation neural network processing; establishement of default risks on bond ratings, such as S&P, on the basis of financial ratios		20

FINANCE	Securities trading	Arthur D.Little	Brokers scratchpad, and traders workstation; GOLDWORKS shell	Traders Assistant/ Equity trader	
FINANCE	Securities trading	Criterion software (US); Financia (UK)	Technical analysis by rules	Breakout/ Intelligent Equities	
FINANCE	Securities trading	GSI (CH); Vanilla (UK)	Off-line trading	Trademaster	
FINANCE	Securities trading	Hewlett Packard Labs Bristol; Lambda Consultants	Rule-based chart analysis	EDWIN	
FINANCE	Securities trading	IBM	Constrained logic programming; tests on options trading		
FINANCE	Securities trading	IBM Research; Monash Univ.	CLP constraint logic programming for option trading, with algebraic combinations, and Black-Scholes model		40
FINANCE	Securities trading	INFORM (UK)	Chart analysis by rules	Traders Assistant	
FINANCE	Securities trading	RTR Software (El Paso)	Trading optimizer exploiting knowledge about economic indicators as well as relative share data v.s. sector; PC based	RTR	
FINANCE	Securities trading	Wagner & Stott (US)	Object based environment on Xerox workstation		
FINANCE	Securities trading	Alvey ALFEX Club/ Expert Systems Int.; Helix Software	Prolog based financial market assessor, and financial sources assessor		
FINANCE	Securities trading	Bankers Trust			
FINANCE	Securities trading	Crédit Suisse	Control of Swiss regulations on brokerages; XiPlus shell		16
FINANCE	Securities trading	Daiwa Securities; Daiwa Computer service/ NEC Central research	Pattern recognition of 1134 TSE stock prices by neural computing in SX-1A supercomputer		
FINANCE	Securities trading	Intelligent int/ Cambridge Consultants (UK)	Intelligent interface to control trade activation and execution in a dealing room		41

FINANCE	Securities trading	Meeschaert-Rousselle (F)	Share trading system		
FINANCE	Securities trading	Morgan Stanley		Autom.securities trading	
FINANCE	Securities trading	Starwood Corp.; AFS Group/ Intelligent technology Group (PA)	Pattern recognition of stock price patterns relative to market	IPM	42
FINANCE	Securities trading	Union Bank of Switzerland; GECOSYS (B)	Natural language understanding of transaction orders and verification	DEAL READER	
FINANCE	Securities trading	Yamaichi Securities (J)/ Global Advanced Technology corp. (NY)	Fuzzy expert system with induction for investment timing	INTEGRAL-25/ IES module	
INSURANCE	Claims processing	CIGNA			
INSURANCE	Claims processing	Lockheed	Medical charge evaluation and control to detect overcharging and fraud in medical insurance; Symbolics host	MEDCHEC	39
INSURANCE	Claims processing	Policy Management systems		ExClaim	43
INSURANCE	Commercial credit	Digital Equipment Corp.	Commercial lines property risk underwriting; classes of business dependent and independent knowledge; VAX-LISP and NEXPERT	CLUE	20
INSURANCE	Credit insurance	Digital Equipment Corp.(Andover)		Commercial lines underwriting	15
INSURANCE	Credit insurance	Sacren; Mutuelles du Mans (F)	Rule-based shell on MacIntosh; connection to IBM mainframe which logs credit insurance applications	SCARON	44
INSURANCE	Fire insurance underwriting	Alvey ARIES Club/ Logica	Assesses fire risks in clothing trade; KEE shell on TI Explorer, then Crystal shell with 8oo rules		45
INSURANCE	Fire insurance underwriting	Protection Mutual Ins.(Illinois)			

INSURANCE	Fire insurance underwriting	Top Center (DK)	Personal Consultant Plus shell and Turbo-Prolog; analysis of site and material dependent risk factors; premium calculation; use of floor geometry	FIRUS	15
INSURANCE	Fire insurance underwriting	Yasuda Fire and Marine Insurance/ Intelligent technology	Knowledge craft shell and Lucid Common LISP on Sun III; 50 rules and 150 input frames		
INSURANCE	Forms processing	New York Life	Queries to requirements necessary to submit a specific policy application		36
INSURANCE	Forms processing	Rentenanstalt/ Plenum Informatik (Zuerich)	Interactive forms editing for life insurance polices		15
INSURANCE	Insurance brokerage	Professional networks (UK)/ Moorgate	Product selection for small brokers; CRYSTAL shell	ADVISA	
INSURANCE	Insurance vending machines	Bank of America			16
INSURANCE	Job control	Prudential Corp.	Batch scheduling system		
INSURANCE	Life insurance underwriting	Cogensys	Use of PARADOCS judgment processing system, which is a dynamic logical model of the relations between judgment states; Pascal and Assembler	PARADOCS	
INSURANCE	Life insurance underwriting	MONY Financial services N.Y./ IBM	ESE shell	CLUES	46
INSURANCE	Life insurance underwriting	Swiss Life	Quintus Prolog		
INSURANCE	Life underwriting	Lincoln National Reinsurance			
INSURANCE	Property and casualty underwriting	AETNA/ Digital Equipment			
INSURANCE	Property and casualty underwriting	AIG; St Paul & Co; Firemans Fund/ Syntelligence; IBM; SRI	SYNTEL data flow model; commercial risk evaluation process knowledge; reduces losses by 20%	Underwriting advisor	47

INSURANCE	Property and casualty underwriting	CIGNA Systems Div. (Philadelphia)	Bond underwriting with financial review of client	Surety aide	48
INSURANCE	Property and casualty underwriting	Equitable Life; CIGNA	ART shell		
INSURANCE	Property and casualty underwriting	Liberty Mutual	Automobile policy renewals		39
INSURANCE	Property and casualty underwriting	Metropolitan Life Insurance	PROLOG		49
INSURANCE	Property and casualty underwriting	Milwaukee Safegard	NEXPERT shell; automotive insurance; RDB data base interface		
INSURANCE	Property and casualty underwriting	Statskontoret (S)/ Epitec			
INSURANCE	Property and casualty underwriting	Transamerica Ins.; Liberty Mutual Ins./ AI Corp.	KBMS shell	KBMS	15
INSURANCE	Reinsurance	Royal Insurance Co;	Selection of reinsurance company and contract		
INSURANCE	Reinsurance underwriting	Copenhagen Reinsurance Co/ Tech.Univ.Denmark	NEXPERT on PC; model information acquisition and analysis process about company risks	REXPERT	56
INSURANCE	Reinsurance underwriting	Kansa Insurance/ MOV Research Oy (SF)			
INSURANCE	Reinsurance underwriting	Skandia Reinsurance; Skandia America Treaty underwriting/ Coopers & Lybrand (NY)	Reinsurance of property risks; LISP+C+dBaseIII	SUE	15
INSURANCE	Reinsurance underwriting	Swiss Reinsurance/ Coopers & Lybrand	Medical underwriting of death risks	TAREX	
INSURANCE	Risk surveys	Tokyo Marine Ins.	Risk survey service accumulating safety and loss knowledge, factory risk surveys		

TAX PLANNING	Business tax	Bradford Univ.	PAYE national insurance contribution tax planning; Prolog interfaced to INGRES data base and COBOL	PAYE	10
TAX PLANNING	Business tax	Cognitive systems		Automated tax assistant	50
TAX PLANNING	Business tax	System software (UK)	CRYSTAL shell for PAYE tax planning	Business taxation advisor	51
TAX PLANNING	Business tax	Coopers & Lybrand	GCLISP rule-based implementation, with forward chaining	Exper-TAX	52
TAX PLANNING	Business tax	Inland Revenue (UK) Univ. Manchester	Advisor for apportionment of close company income	ACCI	14
TAX PLANNING	Forms scanning	Deutsche Kreditgenossenschaft BIM (FRG)			
TAX PLANNING	Forms scanning	US Treasury/ BBN Inc.	Rule-based shell		
TAX PLANNING	International taxation	Coopers & Lybrand (US)		CLINTE	
TAX PLANNING	Personal tax	Expertech	Xi Plus shell, for selection of pension scheme v.s. tax situation	Pension choice	
TAX PLANNING	Personal tax	Legal Knowledge systems	Personal tax form preparation advisor	Tax Payer (DAN)	
TAX PLANNING	Personal tax	Nebraska Univ.	Personal estate tax planning; interactive tool using EMYCIN	Tax Advisor	53
TAX PLANNING	Personal tax	TSB Group (London)	Expatriate taxation		15
TAX PLANNING	Personal tax	US Dept.Treasury	Prolog	Tax consulting system	1
TAX PLANNING	Personal taxation	Coopers & Lybrand (NL); etc..	Rule-based real estate tax advisory system, and social security module; search set up as AND/ OR graphs	Expattax	20
TAX PLANNING	Tax code analysis	US Treasury	Consistency analysis		
TAX PLANNING	VAT	Danish Customs/ CRI	Recoded in C	ESKORT	
TAX PLANNING	VAT	Ernst & Whinney (UK)	VAT validation; Crystal shell and C ; interaction control and recording	VATIA	

2.7 Project references

This bibliography is aimed at giving the numbered references serving as supporting evidence, when available, about the projects appearing in Section 2.6.

1. L.F. Pau (Ed.), Artificial intelligence in economics and management, North Holland, Amsterdam, 1986
2. F. Mariani, CRES, Proc. AICA Annual congress (Italy), 1988
3. S. Pinson, SEAC, in: Economics and AI, J. Roos (Ed.), Pergamon Press, 1986, pp. 153-158
4. Syntelligence's insurance and bank advisors, Expert system strategies, April 1987
5. E. Mays, Organizing knowledge in a complex financial domain, IEEE Expert, Vol. 2, no 3, Fall 1987, pp. 61-70
6. G.Wanet, Proc. 1st Symp. AI and expert systems, Berlin, 18-22 May 1987
7. Texas Instruments AI Letter, Vol. 3, no 12, Dec. 1987
8. TIPI, Expert system user J. , Vol.3, no 2, May 1987, pp. 20-23
9. L.F. Pau, T. Tambo, Knowledge- based mortgage loan credit granting, J. of economic dynamics and control, Spring 1990
10. M.A. Bramer (Ed.), R&D in expert systems, Cambridge Univ.Press, 1985
11. M. Charpin, Proc.Conf. Gottlieb Duttweiler Institute, Rueschlikon, 25-26/4/1986, pp. 159 ff
12. R.T. Chang, IEEE Conf. software tools, 15-17 April 1985, IEEE Computer society press, pp. 57-64
13. F. Rechenmann, Proc. Avignon Expert systems Conf., EC2 Publ., 1987, pp. 949 ff
14. Proc. Avignon Expert systems Conf., EC2 Publ., 1985.
15. Proc. SGAICO Symp. Commercial expert systems in banking and insurance, Lugano, 2-3 May 1989
16. La Lettre de l'intelligence artificielle, no 38, May 1988, pp. 8-12
17. Expert system user J., Vol.3, no 7, Oct.1987, pp. 5 ff
18. R. Reiter, FX, Proc. 2nd Expert systems Conf., Learned Information Publ., London, 1986, pp. 275-276
19. Les systemes experts et la banque, Banque et informatique, no 32 and no 33, 1987
20. L.F. Pau, J. Motiwalla, Y.H.Pao (Eds.), Expert systems in economics, banking and management, North Holland, Amsterdam 1989
21. Bank'AI 1988, SWIFT, London, 22-24 March 1988
22. J. Cuena, Proc. Avignon Expert systems Conf., EC2 Publ., 1987, pp. 981 ff
23. A. Beerel, in: The use of expert systems in finance, London Press center, 24 Nov. 1986
24. P. Makowski, Credit scoring branches out, Credit management J., March 1987, pp. 26-31
25. C. Carter, J. Catlett, Assessing credit card applications using machine learning, IEEE Expert, Vol. 2, no 3, Fall 1987, pp. 71-79
26. Proc.Gottlieb Duttweiler Inst., Lugano, 6-7 June 1988
27. P. Kelly, Expert systems using shells, Data processing (GB), Vol. 28, no 3, pp. 139-40
28. Symbolics Inc., 1989 Annual Report

29. Expert systems J., Vol.1, no 1, July 1984, pp. 9 ff

30. Electronics, May 1989, pp. 43-47

31. S. Dutra, P.P. Bonissone, MARS, to appear in: Computer Science in economics and management J., 1990

32. J.L. Stansfield, PlanPower, IEEE Expert, Vol. 2, no 3, Fall 1987, pp. 51-60

33. P.R. Cohen, Proc. 8th Int. Joint Conf. on Art. Int., 1983, pp. 212 ff

34. Memo 3, Sonderf. bereich 314, Uni. Saarlandes, Nov. 1985

35. Expert Systems J., 1, 2, Oct. 1984, pp. 102 ff

36. J.J. McCormick, Expert systems, Information-WEEK, no 167, 2 May 1988, pp. 24-26

37. J. Bachem, EVA: Experten zur Vermoegensanlageberatung, Gabler, Wiesbaden, 1987

38. Machine intelligence news, Vol. 4, no 9, June 1988, pp. 9 ff

39. D. Leinweber, Knowledge-based systems for financial applications, IEEE Expert, Vol. 3, no 3, Fall 1988, pp. 18-31

40. C. Lassez, Constraint logic programming and option trading, IEEE Expert, Vol. 2, no 3, Fall 1987, pp. 42-50

41. B. Clarke, A KBS interface usable in the hectic stockmarket trading environment, Alvey SIG on intelligent interfaces, Alvey Dir., Oct.1986, pp. 43-58

42. Wall St.Transcript, Vol. C, no 2, 11 April 1988, p.89-113

43. C.Snyder, From research to reality, Insurance software review, 12, 3, 22-24/26-27/30

44. La Lettre de l' intelligence artificielle, no 53, Oct.1989, p.7

45. A.R. Buttler, Expert systems for insurance, Proc.3rd Int.Expert syst. conf., 2-4 June 1987, Learned Information Publ., Oxford, pp. 173-182

46. P.M. Howman, Freeing underwriters for the tough jobs, Best's Review Life/Health ins., 89, 7, pp. 54-56

47. R.O. Duda et al., Syntel, IEEE Expert, Vol. 2, no 3, Fall 1987, pp. 18-32

48. AI Week, 1 April 1988, pp. 5 ff

49. J. Baldwin, J. Inf. Mgt . (USA), 8, 1, Winter 1987, pp. 13-22

50. R. Parker, An expert system for every office, Computer design, Fall 1983, pp. 37-46

51. Expert system user J., Oct. 1987, pp. 6 ff

52. D. Shpilberg, L.E. Graham, H. Schatz, ExperTAX: an expert system for corporate tax planning, Expert Systems, Vol. 3, no 3, 1986, pp. 136-151

53. R.H. Michaelsen, An expert system for federal tax planning, Expert System J., Vol. 1, no 2, 1984, pp. 149 ff

54. U. Guentzer, Informatik Fachberichte 112, Eds.W.Brauer & B.Radig, Berlin, 1985

55. B. Rustem (Ed.), Dynamic modelling and control of national economies, IFAC Proc., Pergamon Press, 1989

56. T. Tambo, Ekspertsystem i gjenforsikring, EMI, Tech. Univ. Denmark, Feb. 1989

57. Proc. IAAI-90, Washington DC, 01-03 May 1990

58. Chemical Bank develops foreign trading ES, AI Week, Sept.15, 1988, pp. 8-9

3 Knowledge Representation

3.1 Introduction

3.1.1 Motivation

Chapter 1 introduced the framework for goal-driven intelligent agents successfully interacting with their environment using knowledge and mechanisms for manipulating knowledge. Similarly, computer programs with problem-solving capabilities (intelligent computer agents) must have specific knowledge about the task they are designed for, and capabilities for efficiently manipulating such knowledge. The following example elaborates on the role of knowledge, and the features of a knowledge-based program.

Example 1: The role of knowledge

In Section 2, we will introduce a case study on the design of a computer-based personal tax adviser. This example highlights the need for knowledge in achieving such a task.

Assume a simple routine is given consisting of a read step, in which a number is read from a given line in the tax form, and of a multiplication. The routine does not contain the following knowledge:

- the input number is supposed to be the total taxable income
- the total taxable income is total income less non-taxable income
- a common case of non-taxed income is income from salaries and wages (taxes directly paid by the employer)
- the multiplication computes the tax amount due
- the tax level depends on the income level, following a table in the tax regulations

Surely such a knowledge was in the mind of the programmer as he implemented the simple routine. Although the routine works properly when faced with a specific computation, the lack of background knowledge makes the following more reasonable behavior impossible:

- when the input number is zero, the routine should return questions such as:

  "Do you confirm that all of your income consists of non-taxable income?" or

  "Does your income only consist of salaries and wages?"

instead of asking meaningless questions like:

"Are you sure?", or even worse: "Invalid input: try again"

- when given an implausible input figure, the routine should exploit its knowledge for issuing user-oriented messages like:

  "I expect a number representing your yearly income; I find it implausible that your income is 0.7 US$ per year. Should I assume your yearly income is 0.7 Millions US$?"

- the routine should accept user questions like:

  "How much taxes must I pay?" and answer, according to its knowledge

  "You should first establish your taxable income" etc.

- the routine should be able to use its knowledge for detecting its own limits, by issuing messages like:

  "I don't have knowledge about the correct tax rate for this income bracket; please refer to the tax regulation", etc.

- the routine should be able to explain its computations, i.e. to answer questions like: "How did you compute this figure?" and "Why do you need this input?"

■

3.1.2 Explicit vs. implicit knowledge

Example 1, Section 1.1 above supports the view that knowledge is essential in producing reasonable behavior of computer programs, and shows how the availability/lack of knowledge determines the responses of the program. In other words, knowledge can be used to explain the program behavior, exactly in the same way as the behavior of a human agent is explained in terms of knowledge he does or does not possess.

AI takes further the view that knowledge be represented explicitly in a program, i.e. there must be a part in it (called the *knowledge base*) in which knowledge is coded; and that knowledge coded in a program be accessible to the program itself. The fact that knowledge is accessible to the program is important, since it makes it possible to build programs which, just like humans, can modify their behavior as new knowledge becomes available, or previous knowledge is removed or changed.
Programs featuring explicit and accessible knowledge are called *knowledge-based programs* (or knowledge-based systems, KBS). Fig. 1 shows the architecture of a knowledge-based system. The reader is also referred to the case study in Chapter 1.4 for a commented example of a knowledge-based system.

Conventional programs possess knowledge as well: in fact, they perform complex and useful tasks. The key difference is, however, that, properly speaking, the only knowledge explicit in conventional programs is the knowledge about which sequence of steps must be executed in order to perform a given task. The domain knowledge relevant to the program design is not included in the program itself, but is either only available as external documentation or, in the worst cases, in the mind of the programmer, i.e. not available at all. Knowledge in either form is not accessible to the program. Therefore changes in the domain knowledge are difficult to map into changes to the code, because one has first to figure out how the previous knowledge affected the design of the sequence of statements, and then modify the sequence of statements according to the new knowledge.

Of course, it is possible to design conventional programs (such as the routine in Example 1) mimicking any given knowledge-based program. However, explicit and accessible knowledge representation has some remarkable advantages, such as:

i. readability: it is easy to find out (sometimes even for to non-programmers) which knowledge the program is based on

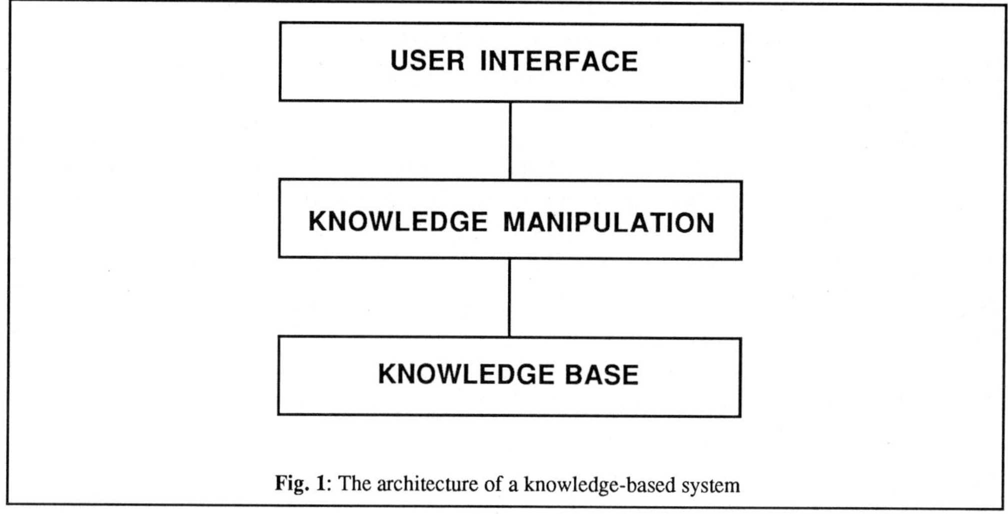

Fig. 1: The architecture of a knowledge-based system

ii. maintenance: it is easy to add/remove/modify a knowledge-based program. Explicit knowledge means that the knowledge must just be coded into the program. Accessible knowledge means that the program automatically accounts for the new/modified knowledge

iii. flexibility: if the knowledge is available explicitly, then it can be used for different situations and types of reasoning. On the contrary, translation of knowledge into a sequence of statements forces in general just one use of the knowledge. This last point is further clarified in the next example

iv. introspection: the knowledge being coded explicitly, the program is in principle able to know what it knows, and therefore to reason about its expertise and limitations, to explain its behavior, etc.

Features i. to iv. are desirable for several reasons.

First, many tasks are so difficult or poorly understood that their complete specification before starting coding is impossible: specifications must be extracted through interaction with experienced professionals (see Chapter 1.1 and 1.4.7). Experts in turn are mostly unable to express their knowledge in an organized, systematic way. As a consequence, a program development methodology is imposed based on a rapid implementation of the experts' knowledge (rapid prototyping), and on incremental refinement by comparison of human and prototype behavior when facing the same set of real-world cases.

Second, AI programs either are problem-solvers, or support tools to problem-solvers. Problem-solvers directly, or through adequate support tools, ultimately interact with humans. Therefore, the man-machine interface design is critical. The appropriate level of interaction with humans is knowledge, rather than program statements. Accessibility of domain knowledge by the program is necessary, among other things, for the design of advanced interfaces (such as natural language front-ends, see Chapter 9).

Example 2: Advantages of explicit knowledge

Refer again to Example 1, Section 1.1 above.

A piece of knowledge such as:

"the total taxable income is the total income less the non-taxable income" can be valuable (together with other knowledge) in all of the following different lines of reasoning:

- to compute the total income from the taxable income and the non-taxable income
- to infer that the total income fully consists of total non taxable income, if the user tells the system that his taxable income is zero
- to trigger a message to the user, in the case he inputs a negative amount of taxable income, reminding him of the definition of taxable income and explaining him why this cannot be negative
- to generate explanations like: "I made the above statement because I know that the total taxable income is the total income less the non-taxable income"

It is easy to see that, if a conventional program with the same behavior is to be implemented, the above piece of knowledge must be translated into different sequences of statements (one for each possible line of reasoning). Yet, this is cumbersome, since really the knowledge underlying the above reasonings is always the same. ■

3.1.3 The knowledge representation problem

The conclusions of the two sections above are:

- knowledge is critical to intelligent behavior of computer systems
- in most cases, it is important to represent knowledge explicitly

As a consequence, the task of designing computer languages just for expressing knowledge is important in AI. Indeed, such a task has received much attention in the AI research and has been given the name of *knowledge representation* (for an account of knowledge representation see [Bobrow, 1977], [Brachman and Levesque, 1985]). Knowledge representation is both difficult and critical to the success of AI applications.

It is difficult because:

- the knowledge representation formalisms, if any, in the human mind are completely unknown
- natural language cannot be directly used as a programming language, since it is not well understood
- no formalism has been developed, which is adequate for all kinds of knowledge
- worse yet, there are no sound criteria for devising a priori an adequate formalism, given a problem domain, or for evaluating competitive formalisms

It is critical, because the design/selection of a representation scheme unable to capture and exploit the constraints and dependencies inherent to the considered domain can make problem-solving very difficult, or even impossible. And, as far as the implementation is concerned, choosing the improper knowledge representation formalism leads to loss of problem-solving capabilities, to an unnecessary knowledge acquisition or data retrieval burden, and to inefficient code.

Practically, the thinking about knowledge representation is usually centered around the following three points concerning the domain knowledge, the knowledge representation language and the inference mechanisms:

i. domain knowledge, i.e. *what* must be represented

ii. knowledge representation language, i.e. *how* should the domain knowledge be represented

iii. inference mechanisms, i.e. *which manipulations* are most adequate for the represented knowledge; these are basically processes whereby new knowledge is derived from the available knowledge, the knowledge relevant to the solution of a specific problem is retrieved and new knowledge is added/removed to/from the already existing knowledge

The rest of this chapter, as well as Chapters 4 and 5, provide a deeper discussion of the above topics.

3.1.4 Knowledge for economic/financial reasoning

A tentative list of categories of objects relevant to the knowledge representation task in economic and financial domains includes:

- real objects (e.g. agents, rates, assets, events) together with their properties or attributes
- psychological states, such as judgements, expectations, assertions, opinions, beliefs, including judgements about the reliability of a given piece of knowledge, i.e. uncertainties
- regulations, corporate policies, work procedures
- contexts, incl. different worlds or assumption sets (Chapter 5.10);
- actions, as well as excluded or forbidden actions
- focused courses of actions, i.e. plans
- time (Section 8)

Relations involving the above objects must be represented as well. Examples are:

- transactions among agents or institutions (Chapter 11)
- hierarchies between objects and classes hereof (Section 7 and Chapter 4.5)
- causality, consistency, analogy among beliefs (see Chapters 5 and 10)
- institutional regulations (constraints) on allowable courses of actions or decisions (see Chapter 4.4)
- temporal relations ("during", "before", "after", etc.) among actions or events (Section 8.1)

3.1.5 Sources of economic/financial knowledge

For economic and financial applications, sources of the above mentioned items are:

- domain experts
- databases containing historical or current data, including past decisions and performances
- manuals, regulations and guidelines
- other natural language sources, such as reports, newsletters, press-agency news, etc.
- more rarely, handbooks and textbooks
- interviews, rumors

The process of translating the knowledge from one of the above locations into one or several formal knowledge representation languages is called knowledge acquisition. Such a process is difficult, and several techniques have been developed for supporting it. Since this book is not concerned directly with knowledge acquisition, interested readers are referred to the specific literature ([Greenwell, 1988], [Diaper, 1989], [Kidd, 1987]).

3.1.6 Knowledge representation languages and formal languages

The word language is used rather vaguely in only this Section, relying on the similarity between knowledge representation languages and human (also called natural) languages, such as English. It should be clear that a knowledge representation language is a set of conventions (allowable words, allowable combinations of words - i.e. sentences -, meaning associated to words and sentences) for representing objects or ideas and expressing relations about them. More exact definitions are to be found in Chapter 4.1 and 4.2.

A knowledge representation language is formal when interpretations and manipulations are defined only in terms of the words and of their relative positions, and therefore independently from the meaning (i.e. the objects or concepts they stand for, not explicitly appearing in the sentence). Of course, representational languages, being designed with the purpose of capturing experts' knowledge, must have an interpretation in terms of the external world: such interpretation is for instance important in selecting an appropriate subset for formal knowledge manipulations, such that their results can be mapped into statements/actions over the environment.

Example 3: Formal vs. not formal knowledge representation

Consider the list of Fortune's 500 companies, ranked by decreasing consolidated turnover:

- the question "find the largest company" is informal; its answer depends on the meaning of the words. The entity processing the question must know that the sequence of letters in the list represents companies names, must interpret the intended meaning of "largest", and so on
- the operation "retrieve the first word in the list" is a formal translation of the above question, since it is defined in terms of an operation, whose specification and result only depend on the shape of the data

■

3.1.7 Segmentation of knowledge types for problem-solving

As an example of the kind of assumptions behind an AI knowledge representation paradigm, consider the following classes of problem-solving knowledge, based on:

i. a domain, i.e. a description of the objects relevant to the problem and of the relations among them (Section 1.4 above), with associated domain knowledge

ii. a set of actions, defined over the described domain, available to an operator (the problem-solver) in order to improve its satisfaction from the objects configurations, with associated knowledge about allowable manipulations

iii. a control strategy for selecting and purposely scheduling the actions (the control strategy may be seen as the abstraction of the actor's reasoning when facing a problem), with associated control knowledge

The purpose of the problem-solver (see also Chapter 1.1) is then to modify, through the allowable actions, the configuration of the domain until a satisfactory state (goal) is reached. The problem-solver then stops.

Example 4: Reasoning about tax regulations

Domain: relevant concepts in the tax regulation (e.g. the tax payer, different kinds of income, expenses and activities, the family status, fines and other penalties, etc.)

	SEMANTIC NETS	RULES	LOGIC	FRAMES
DOMAIN	nodes/links (Section 3.4.2)	facts (Section 3.6.2)	beliefs (Section 3.5.2)	frames (Section 3.7.2)
ACTION	nodes/links or graph manipulation	rules (Section 3.6.3)	sound inference rules (Section 3.6.7)	frames (Section 3.7.2)
CONTROL	nodes/links or graph manipulation	metarules or inference engine (Section 3.6.8 or 3.6.7)	metaknowledge (not covered)	procedural attachment (Section 3.7.3)

Table 1: Knowledge segments and their representation in the basic formalisms

Set of actions: allowable actions are directly specified in the regulations; so it is, for instance, allowed to deduct certain classes of expenses, to pay reduced tax amounts on some incomes, etc.

Control strategy: in this case, the control strategy selects relevant regulations for the question at hand; for example, when facing an income which is a prize, the control strategy would select regulations concerning non-taxable incomes, in order to check if non-taxation is allowed; it would then select regulations concerning standard incomes, if the prize turns out to be taxable. ■

The knowledge classification introduced above underlies, with significant variants, several AI formalisms, but it is by no way limited to the AI community. As a comparison, consider the well-known decision model for management science problems, including a set of variables (decision variables, target variables to be optimized, exogenous/endogenous, instruments/parameters) and relations (equations among the variables) corresponding to point i. above; a list of decision alternatives, uncontrollable events (with uncertainty and risk) and their effects on the variables (point ii. above); a decision criterion, for selecting among alternative decisions/instruments (point iii. above). The similarity is not casual; namely, the three above points provide an answer to the questions an actor involved in a problem-solving process asks himself, i.e. about which objects are relevant, which are the allowable problem-solving actions, and which action is to be selected next (together with reasonable selection criteria).

Peculiar to AI is the fact that the problem-solver (or decision-maker) is itself a computer program: it uses domain knowledge, a set of manipulation rules and control knowledge for achieving a goal. In traditional computer science, on the contrary, programs are formalizations of solutions (algorithms) found by human problem-solvers (or decision-maker). The definition of an appropriate algorithm starting from the client's specifications for the problem is indeed one of the most important tasks in conventional software engineering.

3.1.8 Fundamental knowledge representation formalisms

In Sections 4-7, four standard knowledge representation formalisms will be presented, namely:

- semantic networks (Section 4)
- rule-based or pattern-action representation (Section 6)
- logic (Section 5)
- frames (Section 7)

Differences among them are the consequence of different assumptions on how domain experts acquire, structure, store and use effectively knowledge; a knowledge of the above formalisms is important, since the current trend in knowledge representation is toward conforming to one or more of the above formalisms, but imbricated in a customized way via the world/viewpoints and control knowledge, and resulting in heterogeneous knowledge representation schemes.

The above list of described formalisms is the result of a compromise. At the lower level, there are several possible purely syntactic notations and data structures designs for many of them. Specific computer languages will be discussed at length in Chapter 4. This Chapter only includes the abstract, implementation independent data structures called graphs and trees (Section 3), since they are useful both as didactic tools (e.g. for visualizing relationships) and as a common ground for comparing the alternative representation languages. At an higher level, all of the above formalisms can be extended into knowledge representation languages with the necessary primitives for reasoning about specific problems/environments. Section 8 shows how the knowledge representation concepts behind logic (Section 5) can be extended to support the representation of time and of time-dependent events or actions. Of course, similar extensions are possible for other prototypical reasoning tasks, such as analysis or planning.

Table 1 partly indexes the content of this Chapter by showing for each of the above formalisms how domain, action and control knowledge are represented, and where the corresponding Sections are.

3.1.9 Classification criteria for knowledge representation languages

Section 1.3 stressed the fact that it is often difficult to compare the relative merits of competitive knowledge representation formalisms when coping with a given problem. In general, it can be said that knowledge representation formalisms differ either in the expressive power (i.e. what can be said about the real world) or, in the case of formalisms with comparable expressive power, in the notational efficiency (i.e. the structure and syntax of the representation language). Both of them must be taken into account when selecting a knowledge representation formalism for a specific application area or task. Most often, expressive power and efficiency are conflicting goals, and one must be sacrificed for the other, according to the requirements of the problem to be solved.

Some features dependent on the expressive power of the knowledge representation language are (see [Woods, 1983], [Pau, 1986c]):

- the capability of capturing the relevant distinctions between the concepts being represented
- the capability of expressing the concepts at the desired level of abstraction, or, if so required by the application, of supporting multiple levels of abstraction for the same concepts
- the capability of expressing partial or uncertain knowledge

Hence, expressive power ultimately constraints the kind of knowledge which can be described with the knowledge representation language.

On the contrary, notational efficiency of a knowledge representation language depends on features such as:

- the modularity of the knowledge, where by modularity is meant the decomposability of a system (in this case, a program) into loosely-coupled elements, which can be modified with no unexpected effects on other elements. With "modularity of the knowledge" is meant the capability of modifying (i.e. adding/removing/changing) a data structure in the knowledge base without undesired effects on the other data structures in the knowledge base
- the readability of the formalism
- the efficiency in retrieving knowledge
- the amount of storage required
- the capability of efficiently supporting the knowledge manipulation procedures typical of the task being modelled and of the requirements of the user interface, including explanation mechanisms

This last point clearly hints at the fact that, while distinct, nevertheless knowledge representation and reasoning features do interact.

Whenever possible, a discussion of the relative merits of the standard knowledge representation languages along the lines of expressive power and notational efficiency will follow each presentation. An example of such a discussion, aiming at clarifying the concepts of expressive power and notational efficiency, is presented in Section 1.10 below.

3.1.10 Adequacy of knowledge representation formalisms

Set theory is a well-known example of a formal symbolic language:

- symbols are the elementary data from a specific domain
- a collection of no elements is called the empty set
- symbols are combined into sets (the only allowable data structure) through a set description statement
- a set is a collection of either elementary data or other sets
- the basic property of sets is that sets are equal if they have the same elements, independently from the order of the elements
- sets can be abstracted by naming them and using them as elementary data
- elementary manipulations are provided by the language for operating with sets
- "member": tests if a given element belongs to a given set
- "union": builds a new set containing all elements (each element repeated once) satisfying the "member" test over at least one of the given sets
- "intersection": builds a new set containing all elements (each repeated once) satisfying the "member" test for all given sets
- the "member" test of any element (excepted the empty set) with an empty set always fails; from this fact follows that the empty set has no influence on unions and makes empty all intersections

Sets are just one kind of data structure for working with symbols; actually, pure sets are not used in any computer language because of the property that permutations do not affect sets, which makes their implementation inefficient; however, sets are an appropriate formal structure for capturing the concept of collection (e.g. the set of all U.S. firms), and used extensively in relational database systems.

Example 5: Representing classes with sets

This example shows pros and cons of sets in representing simple knowledge about the economic world.

Classifications: sets can capture classes of entities, and their relationships:

- actors performing economic activities can be grouped into the set of the economic actors
- economic actors which are risk adverse can be grouped into the set of risk adverse actors
- analogous sets can be defined for risk neutral and risk inclined actors
- all economic actors can be further grouped into households, business, government, foreign, etc.
- all the above defined sets are elements of the set of economic actors

Using the primitives of the set language (see above), it is possible to combine classes:

- represent the set of risk-adverse businesses
- represent the set of non-speculative actors (non-speculative: either risk-adverse or risk-neutral)
- find out if a particular actor is member of one or more of the sets defined above
- add to or delete symbols from one of the above sets (through union and intersection)

■

It is possible to represent ordered collections using sets; however the symbolic structures needed for this task are complicated, and the efficiency in the retrieval of an item, given its ordering, is low. Therefore, there is a problem in the notational efficiency.

Example 6: Representing ordered collections with sets

Sets are a cumbersome formalism for representing ordered collections. Consider the following succession of alternative representations, and their limitations:

- the Fortune's 500 companies could be simply represented as elements of a set. *Criticism:* their ranking is not represented
- each company, together with its ranking, could form a set. Then all such sets could be the elements of another set. *Criticism:* the representation is not adequate for retrieving the companies in their order, e.g. of turnover
- sets could be nested one inside the other, with the innermost set representing the first company, its smallest superset the second company, and so on. *Criticism:* the concept of ordered collection is captured, but in an unnatural way: the relation "before", defined over ordered collections, is replaced by the relation "is contained by", in the set language. Furthermore, there is no easy way for directly accessing the "twenty-fourth" company in the list

■

Sets have also limitations in their expressive adequacy. For instance, the primitives of the set language force the assumption that it is always possible to establish if an element belongs to a set. Of course, this is not always true in the real world. So for instance a sentence like: "A large number of financial stocks are going to be split", while a valuable piece of information, could not be represented by a computerized investment adviser based on sets, since the membership of a specific number to the set of "large numbers" is not well-defined. This is the reason why knowledge bases cannot just be data bases in a relational database management system.

3.2 Case study: a tax adviser

The task of building a tax adviser for personal tax planning is used as a joint example all over this Chapter, and in part of the next. There are several motivations for this choice. First, the personal tax adviser is a prototypical task for showing/exploring AI applications to legal reasoning, a broad area with significant implications for the topics addressed in this volume. Second, tax declarations is a widely known problem (in spite of differences in the regulations). Third, building a program for tax advising is a non-trivial task, with some serious implementation efforts (see the table of projects in Chapter 2.6 under heading tax planning, and especially [McRae, 1986], [Michaelsen, 1984], [Sergot et al., 1986], [Shpilberg et al., 1986]). Indeed, for a simple implementation see Chapter 4.4.13.

3.2.1 Structure of a tax form

Tax declaration is a structured task; this structure is mirrored in the outline of the tax form.

A typical tax form is divided into sections, each one pertaining to a different class of incomes, such as salaries, subventions, earnings from land, capital gains, earnings from company activity (profits), etc. Among these income sources, one must distinguish between taxable incomes, non-taxable incomes (e.g.: gifts, exempted bonds, awards), pre-taxed incomes (e.g. salaries in the public and/or private sector). The final tax amount is computed after listing (in a separate form) deductible expenses, such as family expenses, medical care, etc. as well as past credits and debentures vs. the fiscal authority.

Furthermore, usually at the beginning of the form, there are generally a few questions aiming at classifying the tax payer into one of the activity areas: employee, manager, independent worker, etc., and at determining his/her family status. Classifications are important because, depending on the type of activity, on the family status and on the type of income/expense, different sets of prescriptions (sometimes with variants) apply.

The last part of the form is used for summarizing the subtotals, computing the income before taxes, and determining the due amount.

The input/output requirements for a simple tax adviser can be summarized as follows:

- help the taxpayer establish his family situation (first form)
- help the taxpayer establish a correct classification of a given income/expense (to which form does an income/expense item belong)
- given an entry in the tax form, either: query the taxpayer about relevant incomes/expenses, or give him an explanation of the entry, or formulate questions the answers to which are adequate for filling the entry
- perform inferences on the answers from the taxpayer (e.g. infer the main activity from the incomes entered into the tax form, or infer ownership from income)
- check the consistency among entries, subtotals and totals
- optional: signal to the taxpayer dubious interpretations, and give an advice about the less costly alternative
- optional: perform an analysis of the overall consistency of the tax declaration from the viewpoint of the fiscal authority (i.e. a comparison of the income as inductively guessed from the personal assets and the living standard, with the income as declared by the taxpayer) and provide advice on how to fix inconsistencies, if any

3.2.2 Representation guidelines

The following considerations may have an influence on the selection of a representation paradigm:

- basic (default) context: the objects and relations about which the tax adviser must be able to reason (perform manipulations), i.e. the tax form, the tax payer, his family status, his activity, his assets, incomes, expenses, and similar. Regulations can be considered as objects, or as procedures/rules for manipulating objects, or as both

- context switching: the classification of an object may be context dependent, i.e. the same income could belong at the same time (but in different contexts) to the category of land earnings, of partially taxed incomes (e.g. because of tax incentives to agriculture), of incomes from a minor activity of the tax payer, and so on. The representation paradigm must therefore support concurrent contexts and/or context switching (e.g. multiple inheritance, or rule sets, see Sections 7.9 and 7.10)
- even in a given context, categories do not form a partition over the set of objects: in fact, due to ambiguities in the law, a given income may fit into different entries in the forms

3.2.3 Knowledge representation formalisms

Parts of the above case will serve as an illustration of various knowledge representation formalisms to be described formally hereafter.

3.3 The graph and tree data structures

3.3.1 Motivation

This section is a somewhat abstract introduction to graphs and trees, which are used in the specific knowledge representation formalisms.

Graphs and trees are very general structures for organizing concepts about a domain; therefore it should not be surprising that several knowledge representation formalisms can be given a very natural interpretation as graphs or trees. This idea will be further explained and demonstrated in Section 4, where graphs will be used, together with a semantics, to represent domain or actions knowledge about a problem domain. In Section 5, graphs will also be used to represent the control knowledge itself.

Graphs and trees play a key role in many other chapters of this book as well, most notably Chapters 5 (graphs) and 9 (trees).

3.3.2 Graphs

A *graph* consists of a set of *nodes* (or vertexes), and a set of edges each connecting two nodes. In a directed graph, a direction is associated to each edge, which is then called an *arc* (or link).

Fig. 2 shows a directed graph with 9 nodes. Nodes are pictured as small circles, labeled from N1 to N9. Arcs are pictured as arrows between nodes.

Consider the two nodes N1 and N2, connected by an arc (call it A). Then the following statements represent equivalent wordings for expressing the relationship among the two nodes, given the direction associated to A:

- N1 is the father (or parent) of N2
- N2 is the child (or son, or successor) of N1
- A is (N1, N2)
- A is incident from N1
- A is incident to N2
- N1 is the initial endpoint of A

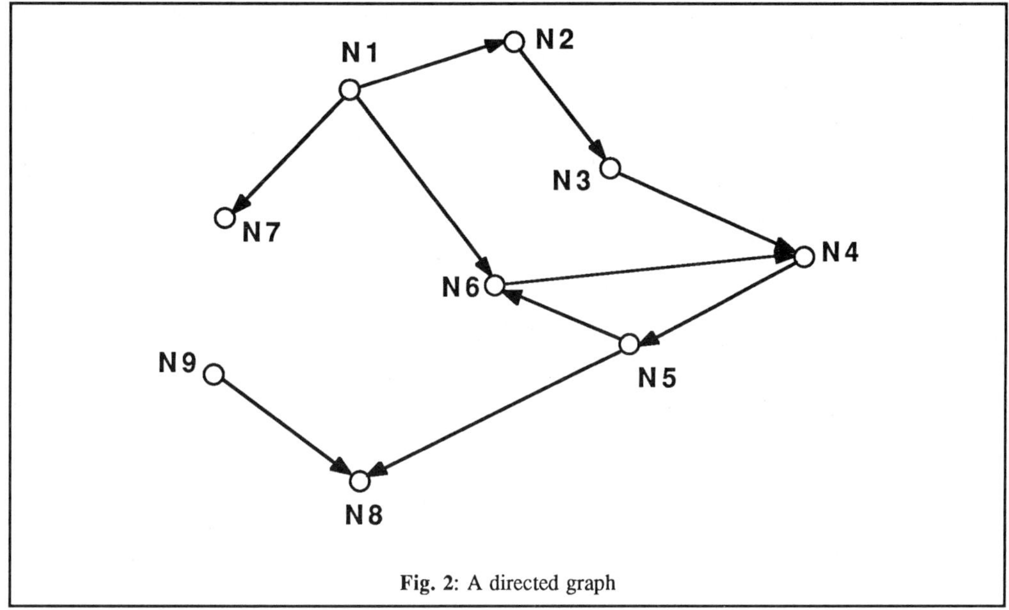

Fig. 2: A directed graph

- N2 is the terminal endpoint of A

Furthermore, a node with no children is called a terminal node, a leaf or a sink, e.g. N8, N7. A node with no fathers is called a root or a source, e.g. N9. Redundant terminology is a consequence of the variety of fields to which graph theory has been applied.
A *path* in a graph is an ordered sequence of nodes, in which any node is the son of the node preceding it in the sequence. By definition, paths are only defined for directed graphs. A path can be seen intuitively as a trajectory in a directed graph, making it possible to move from one node to another through arcs and intermediate nodes. For instance, nodes N1, N2, N3, N4 (in the specified order) form a path, noted (N1, N2, N3, N4). The first node in the sequence is the initial endpoint (or start) of the path, the last node in the sequence is the final endpoint (or end) of the path. For instance, N1 is the start, and N4 is the end of the above path. Conversely, in a graph there is a path between two nodes NA and NB, if there exist a path whose start is NA and whose end is NB (in this order). Obviously, if a path involves a terminal node, then the terminal node must be the end of the path. As a counter example, the sequence N1, N2, N3, N4, N6 is not a path, because N4 is not the father of N6 (the arc is directed the opposite way). A path is elementary if no node appears twice or more in it.

The *cost* of a path is computed as a function (e.g. the sum, the product, the average) of the costs between any pair of successive nodes in the path; the cost of the path N1, N2, N3, N4 in Fig. 2 would be computed (sum is assumed) as the cost from N1 to N2, plus the cost from N2 to N3, plus the cost from N3 to N4. The distance (cost), if any, is an attribute of arcs. If no such attribute is defined, as in the example in Fig. 2, then it is assumed that a unit cost (e. g. 1) is associated to each arc, and that addition is to be used to combine elementary costs. Under such assumptions, the shortest path connecting two nodes among a set of paths with equal starts and ends, is the path with the smallest number of nodes (or arcs). For instance, there are two paths in Fig. 2 between N1 and N6. One of them consists of just the two nodes (N1, N6), has cost 1 and is the shortest. The other one (i.e. N1, N2, N3, N4, N5, N6) has cost 5.

If the start and the end of the path are the same node, then the path is said to be closed, and is called a *circuit*. The path N1, N2, N3, N4, N5, N6, N1 is an example of a closed path. Other examples are the paths N1, N6, N1 and N4, N5, N6. A circuit consisting of just one node is

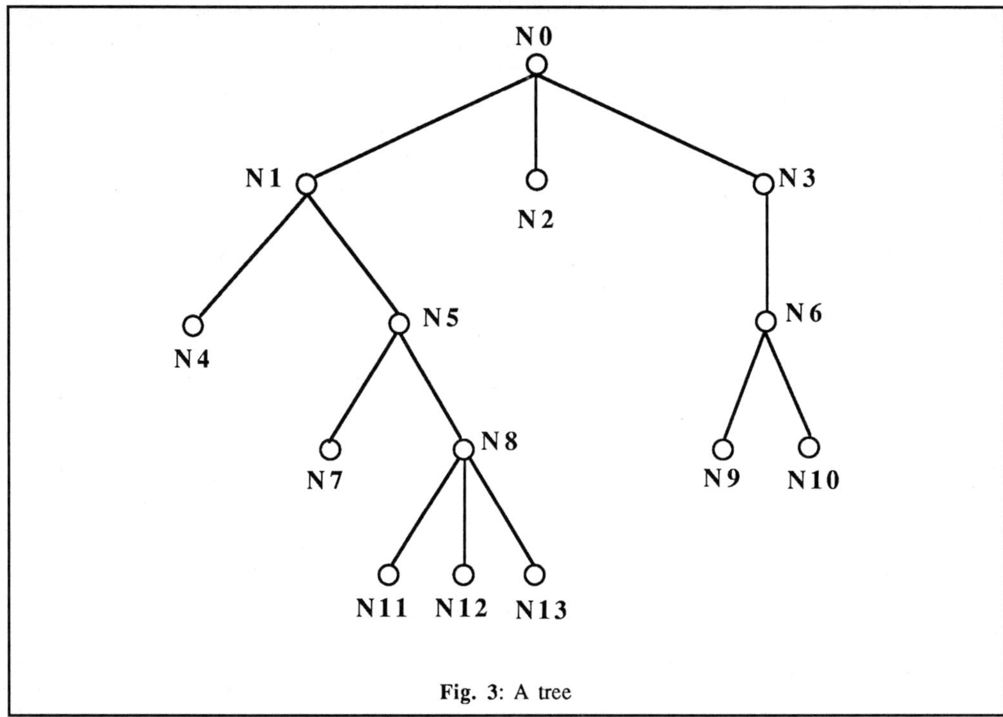

Fig. 3: A tree

called a loop. Graphs with no circuits are called acyclic. In the rest of this book, graphs are supposed to be directed, but not acyclic.

Example 7: City map as a graph

By associating a meaning to graphs, it is possible to understand the above concepts in a less abstract way. Assume that nodes represent cities, and directed arcs represent one-way roads between cities. Then the whole graph can be interpreted as a map.
Assuming this interpretation, the concepts introduced above can be reduced to familiar ones. For instance, a path between two nodes represents a route between two cities; the length of the path is the sum of the kilometers or miles of each street in the above route; the cost of the path can be interpreted, for instance, as the driving time (the mileage may not be an appropriate measure for it, as there could be differeces in speed in the streets along the way), as the gasoline consumption, or as the psychological penalty of driving through a desolated landscape, and so on.

Finally, it is too obvious that our cities are configured as cyclic graphs; probably everyone, when trying to find a way through an unknown city, has had the frustrating experience of finding himself at the same place over and over. ■

3.3.3 Trees

A tree is a special case of graph. A tree, just as a directed graph, consists of nodes, connected by directed arcs called branches. In graphs there are no restrictions in the pattern of nodes and links. On the contrary, a tree is a graph in which each node has just one father, excepted exactly one node, which has no father and is called the *root* of the tree. The resulting structure is shown in Fig. 3, together with some definitions:

- father, child and path are defined as in graphs
- the root is the node with no father: any tree has just one root. The root of the tree in Fig. 3 is the node labelled N0

- the branching factor of a node is the number of its children. The branching factor of the node N8 is 3, since this node has three children (namely, N11, N12, N13). The branching factor of node N2 is zero, since N2 has no children
- a leaf is a node with no children (branching factor = 0): a tree may have several leaves. The tree in Fig. 3 has eight leaves (N2, N4, N7, N9, N10, N11, N12, N13)
- the ancestors of a node are either its father, or the father's father, and so on. The root is the common ancestor of every node in the tree (except itself). The node N5 is the ancestor of only N7, N8, N11, N12, N13. N2 is the ancestor of no node
- the descendants of a node are either its children, or its "grand-children", and so on. Every node in a tree is a descendant of the root. N9 is one descendant of N3

Trees, because of their definition, cannot have circuits. Hence the relationships of ancestors and descendants are meaningful. On the contrary, in cyclic graphs, a node can be at the same time the ancestor and the descendant of another node, because of closed paths.

Nodes in a tree having the same number of ancestors are at the same *level* , i.e. they lie on the same horizontal line in Fig. 3. The reference point for measuring levels in trees is obviously the root, which is the ancestor of all nodes and has itself no ancestors. The maximum level is called the depth of a tree (the tree in Fig. 3 has depth 4, since by convention the root has depth 0). So for instance N1 through N3 are on the same level (level 1), N4 through N6 are on level 2, N7 through N10 are on level 3, N11 through N13 are on level 4.

It is more difficult to define levels in graphs, and the resulting computational expressiveness makes the exact use of levels inefficient; however the level of the node, with respect to a reference node, is the length of the shortest path from a reference node to it.

3.4 Semantic networks

3.4.1 Motivation

A semantic network is a directed graph, in which knowledge is represented by associating to nodes and links (arcs) a meaning or semantics, i.e. an interpretation in terms of objects and entities in the problem domain. For instance, in formalizing knowledge as a semantic network, one frequently used interpretation is:

- nodes are associated to objects (events, concepts) in the domain
- links are associated to relations between objects (events, concepts)

Therefore, two objects in the problem domain are directly related if and only if the two corresponding nodes in the graph are connected through a link. Usually, a labeling facility for nodes and links is included in the formalism, so that different kinds of domain entities and relations can coexist in the same graph without ambiguities. A semantic network fills the "knowledge base" box in Fig. 1, Section 1.2.

As the above considerations suggest, the key feature of semantic networks is that, besides providing a formalism for representing information, they provide at the same time a structure for retrieving it: objects related to a given object in the domain can be found by following the links from the node associated to the given object in the graph. The result is a formalization of the concept of reasoning, i.e. the process of finding (unknown) relationships among entities in the domain, using the available knowledge; in the semantic network representation, reasoning amounts to searching a path between two nodes. Algorithms for searching paths in a graph are extensively discussed in Chapter 5. Any of those algorithms can be used as the basis for implementing a network navigator.

3.4.2 Causality networks

The meaning associated to nodes and links in semantic networks can vary widely depending on the task at hand. Therefore, there is no "standard" way in which semantic networks have been nor can be used. In this section, a very simple kind of network based on just one kind of link is introduced.

An economic model is usually defined through:

- a set of states, each one characterized by a set of variables or attributes with their values
- a set of constraints on the states (mathematical constraints or equations, logical constraints or axioms and inference rules), or relations between these

A model can be easily represented as a semantic network by interpreting nodes as states, and constraints as links. A common example of relationship between entities in an economic model is *causality* (see Chapter 5.10 for a precise definition of causality). A network based on the causal relationship is called a causality network.

A link in a causality network can be interpreted as causal link: "has a direct influence on". Note that the direction of a link is important: the knowledge that A has an influence on B is not the same as the knowledge that B has an influence on A. The direction of the link is defined so that the cause is the father, and the effect is the child.

The advantages of this representation, with respect to the more common mathematical formalization of models, are: adequacy for capturing different levels of incomplete causal knowledge; improved understanding and explanations, either by humans or by programs. These points are motivated in the following example, and addressed in more detail in Chapter 5.10.

Example 8: Causality graphs and economic models:

1. Representation of incomplete causal knowledge:

Consider an unknown coefficient for a variable in a set of equations. The equations cannot be solved; the parametric solution is difficult, especially if the equations are not linear. In general, modelling through equations is only feasible, when the exact mathematical form of the causality can be deduced, guessed or estimated. Causality networks are more flexible, in the sense that they provide the capability of representing incomplete causal knowledge. Namely:

- knowledge about the existence of a causality between two states can be expressed as a link between the two states involved, without any further commitment
- if it is further known which state is the cause (exogenous or not), and which state is the effect (endogenous), a direction can be added to the link

Further information about the causality can be captured as attributes to the causal relationship itself. To this purpose the causality relation can be represented as a node, and attributes can be associated to it. The process of considering a relation or a function as an object is called reification and is quite common in knowledge representation. Fig. 4 shows a graph representation of the knowledge: "a positive variation in the state A causes a negative variation in the state B" (see Chapter 5.10).

2. Improved understanding and explanations:

Equations (constraints in general) do not capture the distinction between the cause and the effect: this is evident from the fact that terms in the left-hand side of an equation can be freely moved to the right-hand side, and vice-versa. Therefore, it is difficult to explain which is the meaning of a solution in terms of the interplay of causalities. Causality networks explicitly represent causality; justifications for the influence of a state on another state can be constructed basing on the path(s) between the two states. Following chains of causal links is much closer to the way problems are solved by humans, and more distant from the mathematical abstraction; hence it is easier to explain the results and to assess their plausibility. ■

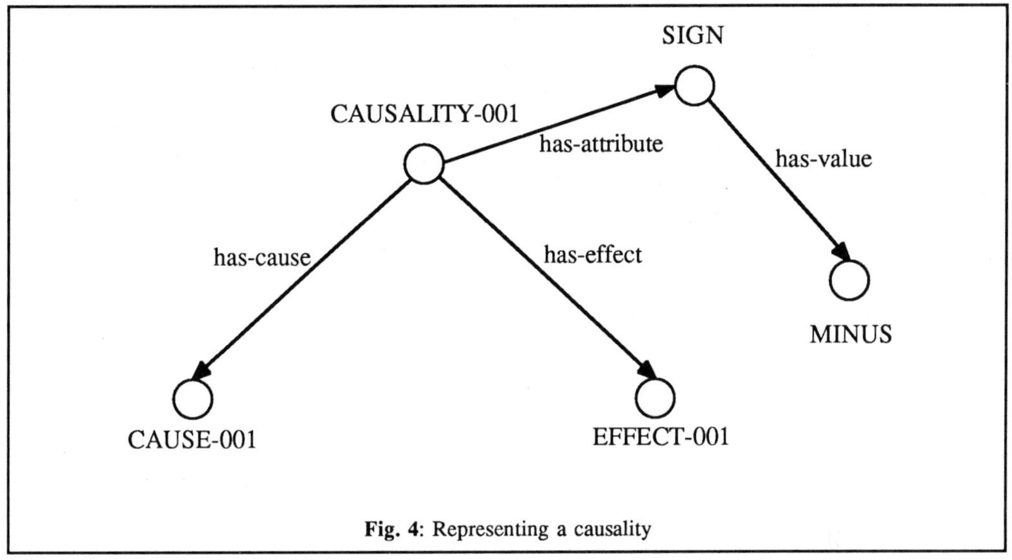

Fig. 4: Representing a causality

3.4.3 Application: a simple economic model

Fig. 5 shows a semantic network capturing a simple, qualitative causal model. The economic model consists of the following states:

- production capacity utilization
- domestic consumption
- salary index
- orders
- service and public sector turnover
- import
- export
- trade balance
- inventory stock level

States are represented as nodes (a sub-model, possibly reduced to one variable or one equation, may be used to describe the state); nodes are labeled, in order to make it clear to which state they refer. Direct causal relationships are represented as arrows connecting related nodes together (the arrow points away from the node playing the role of the exogenous state): links are not labeled, since just one kind of relationship (causality) is involved. There is an indirect causal relation between two nodes, only if there is at least one directed path (see Section 3.1 for a definition) between them.

In a general semantic network, the existence of a path between two nodes does not imply clearly defined (or any) relationship between the objects being represented. In the following example, a path has a clear meaning in terms of dependencies in the domain because of the crucial property of the causal relation of being transitive. A relation is transitive if, from the fatc that it is holds between objects A and B, and between objects B and C, it follows that it holds between objects A and C as well.

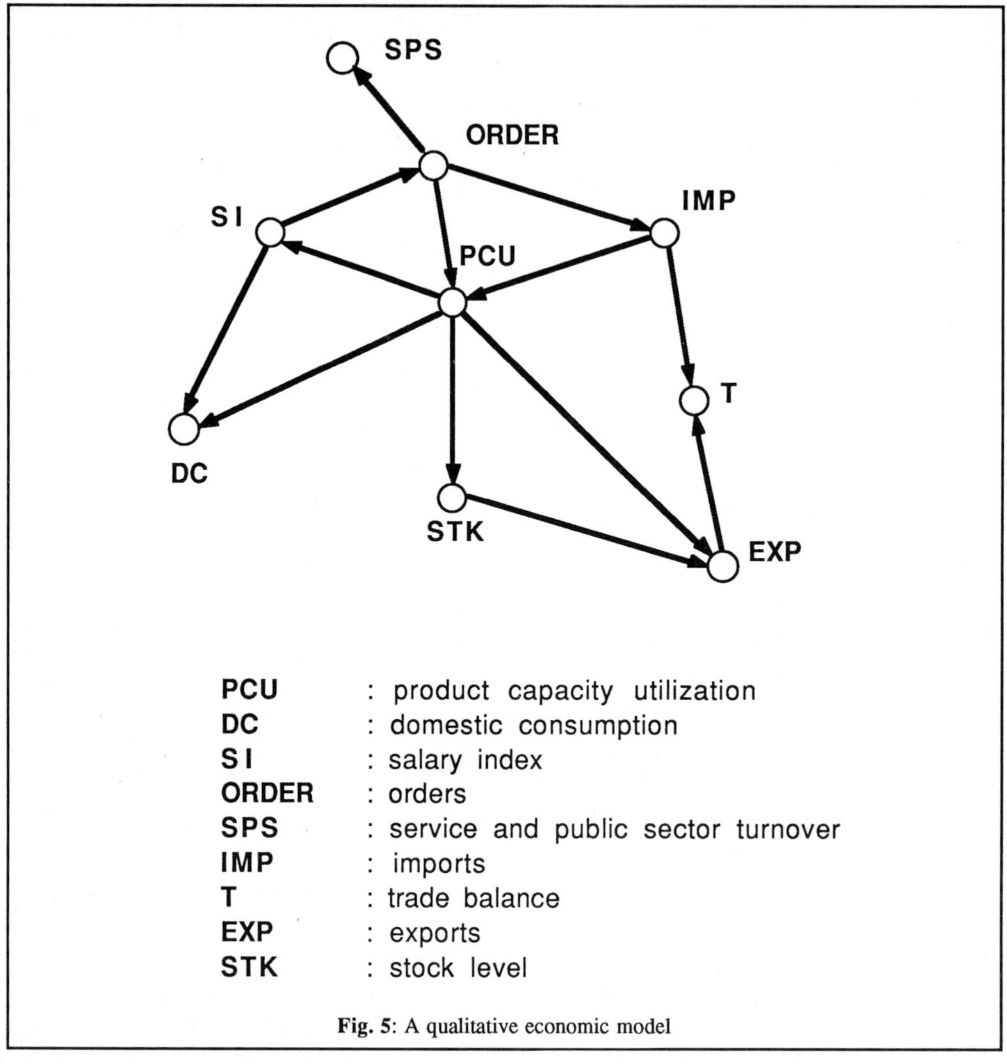

Fig. 5: A qualitative economic model

Example 9: Transitive vs. non-transitive relations

Causality is a transitive relation. Consider Fig. 5: a variation in the state ORDER causes a variation in the state IMPORTS (since there is a link between them), which in turn causes a variation in the state TRADE-BALANCE (because of the link between IMPORTS and TRADE-BALANCE). Therefore, it can be deduced that a variations in the orders causes an indirect variation in the trade-balance. From the same Figure, it is also clear that orders influence the trade balance through a second indirect causal mechanism, involving the production capacity utilization, the stock level and exports.

On the contrary, the relation "near-by" is not transitive. From the fact that a place A is nearby a place B, and that a place B is nearby a place C, it cannot be deduced in general that A is nearby C as well. Therefore although a path exists in the graph between A and C, its meaning is questionable. ■

The above example is an elementary warning that, although reasoning in semantic networks can be seen as "moving around" the graph, one must be careful to "move around" in a way which has a clear interpretation in terms of the domain knowledge. The network in Fig. 5 will be extensively used in Chapter 5 for illustrating search.

3.4.4 Dependency graphs

Semantic networks can be used for capturing general knowledge, not just causality:

- let the nodes represent:
  .objects
  .psychological states
  .propositions
  .assertions
  .and others
- let the links represent relations among two objects, for instance:
  . space: is near to, is far from, etc.
  . time: is before, is after, is at the same time, etc.
  . possession: belongs to, has, etc.
  . classification: is a, is an instance of, etc.
  . collection: is part of
  . action: gives, goes to, etc.
  . assignment: has value, has attribute, etc.
  . expectation: has usually the value, usually causes, etc.
  . and many others

Such a representation is sometimes also called a dependency graph.

Some of the relations listed above occur quite often when representing knowledge, as for instance the basic classification, collection and assignment relations ("instance-of", "is-a", "is-part-of", "has-value"). They are thoroughly discussed, together with the important idea of inheritance, in Sections 7.6 and 7.11 about the closely related frame-based knowledge representation. Section 5.6 highlights the relationship between logic and semantic networks. Section 8 extends logic with primitives for reasoning about time.

3.5 Logic

3.5.1 Motivation

Logic is the study of how to mechanically derive true assertions (beliefs) from given premises. As a knowledge representation language, logic is characterized by the property of being declarative: statements in logic are definitions of true beliefs, instead of being the prescription of actions to be performed in step-by-step plans (as, for instance, are statements in a conventional procedural programming language). For more details about the features of declarative programming, see Section 5.8 below and Chapter 4.2.

In the next three Sections 5.2-5.4, the language of logic (in the notation of first-order predicate calculus) is introduced by presenting model theory (i.e. the meaning of assertions), knowledge representation with logic, inference and resolution (an inference often used in AI programs) respectively. Section 5.6 compares logic to semantic networks. Section 5.7 presents an example of logic as a representation language for legal reasoning. Finally, in Section 5.8 strong and weak points of logic as a knowledge representation language are considered.

For a general introduction to logic see [Mendelson, 1987]. An introduction to logic for knowledge representation can be found in general AI textbooks (e.g. [Nilsson, 1976], Chapter 4, [Rich, 1983], Chapter 5). For a textbook completely dedicated to logic in AI see [Genesereth and Nilsson, 1987].

3.5.2 An introduction to predicate calculus

Predicate calculus is a language for expressing declarative knowledge. For the purposes of representation in predicate calculus, the problem domain must be abstracted as a collection of objects and relations among objects (the kind of abstraction introduced in Section 1.4).

Correct sentences in predicate calculus are called *well-formed-formulae* (shortened wffs). A knowledge base is a collection of wffs. Intuitively, each wff in a knowledge base captures an agent's belief about the domain being represented; a knowledge base contains all relevant beliefs about a given problem domain.

The most simple wff is the assertion that a specific relation exists (is true) among n objects in the problem domain (where n is any positive integer including 0). The following example presents a set of such simple wffs extracted from the Italian tax regulations. A possible interpretation of each of these wffs is suggested in the comments. Each relation is given a name, also called a predicate constant, which is written followed by the objects taking part to the relation, called arguments or object constants, within brackets:

predicate ($argument_1$, $argument_2$, ... , $argument_n$)

Object constants are used to refer to individual objects in the domain (e.g. "John" for referring to a specific person). All over a knowledge base, a given constant must always refer to the same object.

Example 10: Elementary relations in the tax regulation

In the following, interpretation is an informal translation into English of the intended meaning of a wff.

revenue (Mr.X, 1990, s001)

Interpretation: s001 is a revenue of the individual Mr.X imputable to the fiscal year 1990

tax_form (personal_data, family_status, incomes_from_ real_estates, salary_incomes, deducible_expenses, computation_of_tax_amount)

Interpretation: a tax form is a relation among the following kinds of information: personal data, family status, etc. (i.e. the predicate is a rough description of the structure of a tax form).

amount (s001, 15000000)

Interpretation: the amount of s001 is 15000000 (Italian lire!). ■

3.5.2.1 Logic connectives

Beliefs can be connected together into more complex wffs, the truth-values of which are completely determined by the truth-values of the component beliefs, and the definition of the connectives used. So, connectives are constraints among beliefs. The connectives below are the well-known logical connectives:

i. AND (also noted $\wedge$), called logic "and" or conjunction.
Let B_1, B_2, ..., B_N be beliefs. The belief:

$$B_1 \wedge B_2 \wedge ... \wedge B_N$$

is true if and only if all B_i are true, i.e. if asserted it states that the problem-solver believes all propositions B_i to be true

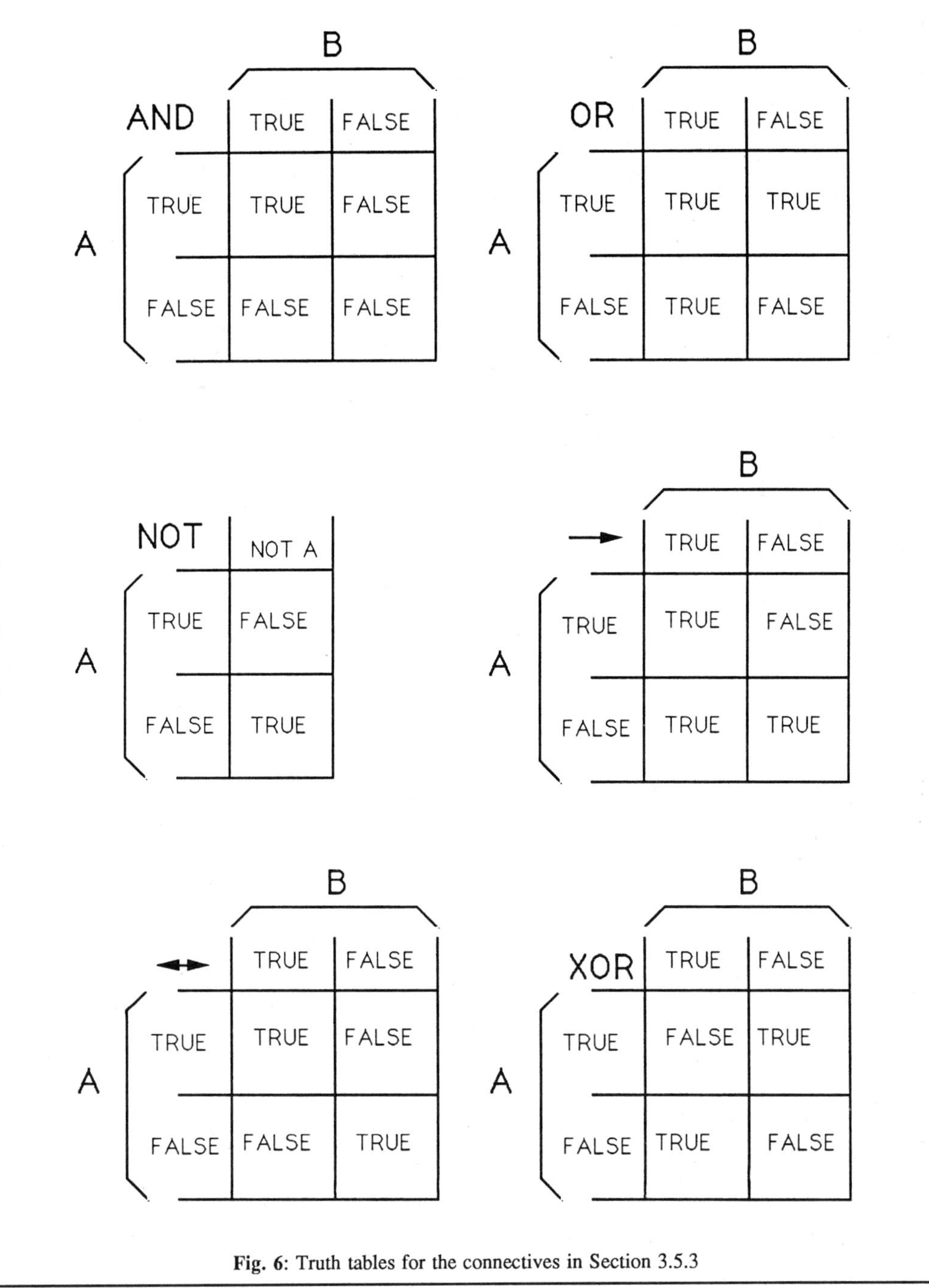

AND (A \ B)	TRUE	FALSE
TRUE	TRUE	FALSE
FALSE	FALSE	FALSE

OR (A \ B)	TRUE	FALSE
TRUE	TRUE	TRUE
FALSE	TRUE	FALSE

NOT (A)	NOT A
TRUE	FALSE
FALSE	TRUE

→ (A \ B)	TRUE	FALSE
TRUE	TRUE	FALSE
FALSE	TRUE	TRUE

↔ (A \ B)	TRUE	FALSE
TRUE	TRUE	FALSE
FALSE	FALSE	TRUE

XOR (A \ B)	TRUE	FALSE
TRUE	FALSE	TRUE
FALSE	TRUE	FALSE

Fig. 6: Truth tables for the connectives in Section 3.5.3

ii. OR (also noted $\vee$), called logic "or" or disjunction.
Let $B_1, B_2, ..., B_N$ be beliefs. The belief:

$$B_1 \vee B_2 \vee ... \vee B_N$$

is true if and only if one or more B_i are true, i.e. if asserted it states that the problem-solver believes that at least one B_i holds, without specifying which one is it

iii. NOT (also noted $\neg$), called logic "not" or negation.
Let B be a belief. The belief:

$$\neg B$$

is true if and only if B is false. If asserted it states that the problem-solver believes that B is false

iv. $\rightarrow$, called implication.
Let A and B be two beliefs. The belief:

$$A \rightarrow B$$

is true if either A is false or B is true
If asserted it states that the problem-solver believes that, whenever A is true, then B is true also, but not necessarily vice-versa.
The wff left of the arrow (in this case A) is called the *premise* (or the left-hand side) of the implication. The wff right of the arrow, B, is called the *conclusion* (or the right-hand side) of the implication (the naming is the same as for rules, see Section 6.3)

v. $\leftrightarrow$, called equivalence.
Let $B_1, B_2, ..., B_N$ be beliefs. The belief:

$$B_1 \leftrightarrow B_2 \leftrightarrow ... \leftrightarrow B_N$$

is true if and only if all B_i have the same truth value (i.e. all true or all false). If asserted, it states that the problem-solver believes that all B_i are equivalent with respect to their truth values, i.e. as far as logic is concerned

vi. TX, called the taxonomic connective.
Let $B_1, B_2, ..., B_N$ be beliefs. The belief:

$$B_1 \text{ TX } B_2 \text{ TX } ... \text{ TX } B_N$$

is true if exactly one belief is true. If asserted, it states that the problem-solver believes in exactly one B_i, without specifying which one is it

The result of combining two wffs with a connective can be described graphically in a table, called truth table. A truth table is a matrix with two columns and two rows. Columns and rows are labelled with the truth values (in classical logic, just true resp. false), and each intersection of columns and rows is labelled with the result obtained by applying the connective. Fig. 6 shows one truth table for each of the above connectives. Truth tables can be used to define new connectives. However, any connective can be decomposed and expressed as a combination of, say, just negations and conjunctions (or negations and disjunctions). So for instance:

$$A \vee B \quad \leftrightarrow \quad \neg(\neg A \wedge \neg B)$$

$$A \text{ TX } B \quad \leftrightarrow \quad \neg(\neg(A \wedge \neg B) \wedge \neg(\neg A \wedge B))$$

$$A \text{ -> } B \quad \leftrightarrow \quad \neg A \vee B$$

Example 11: Computing the truth value of a composed wff

italian-resident (Mr.X, 1990) $\wedge$ total-income (ti040, Mr.X, 1990) $\wedge$ amount (ti040, 7000000) $\rightarrow$
must-file-return (Mr.X, 1990)

Interpretation: if it is true that Mr. X is an Italian resident and his total income (called "ti040") is 7000000 then he must pay taxes (this rule is only partly correct under the current Italian tax regulation; more precise beliefs can be found in Section 5.7)

In specific problem-solving situations, this belief forces some constraints on the truth values of the component beliefs, otherwise contradiction would arise. More precisely, since the implication is known to be true, then either the premise must be false, or the conclusion true (Fig. 6):

¬(italian-resident (Mr.X,1990) ∧ total-income (ti040, Mr.X, 1990) ∧ amount (ti040, 1990, 7000000))
∨ must-file-return (Mr.X)

The premise is a conjunction, and it can only be false if at least one of the component wffs is false (see Fig. 6). Hence the premise is false if:

¬italian-resident (Mr.X, 1990) ∨ ¬total-income (ti040, Mr.X, 1990) ∨ ¬amount (ti040, 7000000)

Inserting into the above wff one obtains the wff:

(¬italian-resident (Mr.X, 1990) ∨ ¬total-income (ti040, Mr.X, 1990) ∨ ¬amount (ti040, 7000000))
∨ must-file-return (Mr.X)

which confirms the equivalence just before the example ■

3.5.2.2 Quantifiers

The previous example lacks generality: in fact the beliefs presented refer to a specific person (Mr. X) and a specific amount of income (7000000).

Obviously, no regulation is concerned with specific people or with specific numbers. Law items are on the contrary quite generic: "Any resident with no dependent relatives whose income only consists of salaries or pensions not exceeding 6602000, is exempt from taxation".

In logic, reference to generic objects in a domain is achieved through the use of variables. Variables may be free or quantified. In this introduction, only quantified variables are considered. Since their names are written immediately after the quantifier symbol, they can be easily distinguished from constants without any need for a specific notation.

i. Universal quantification
Let A be a belief containing the symbol x. Then the wff:

$$\forall x\ A(x)$$

asserts that A(x) is true for any possible substitution of x with any object in the domain

The symbol ∀ is called a *universal quantifier* . The wff following it is said to be universally quantified. The variable written immediately after the universal quantifier can be substituted in the universally quantified wff for any specific object. Were it possible to list all such formulae, then universal quantification would be equivalent to their conjunction.

Example 12: Universal quantifiers

The law item in the above text can be translated into logic as follows:

∀x, year, w, id, y:
italian-resident (x, year) ∧ (∀p ¬depends (p, x)) ∧ (∀z revenue (z, x, year) → is-a (z, salary) ∨ is-a (z, pension)) ∧
total-income (id, x, year) ∧ amount (id, y) ∧ (y < 6602000 ∨ y = 6602000)
→ ¬(must-file-return (x, year)).

Brackets have been added to make clear the scope of the quantification, that is the extent of the wff being quantified. ■

ii. Existential quantification
Let A(x) be any wff containing the symbol x. The wff:
$\exists x\ A(x)$
asserts that there is at least one object in the domain, say object1, such that, if it is substituted for x in A(x), the wff A(object1) is true

The symbol $\exists$ is called an *existential quantifier* . The wff following it (i.e. A(x)) is said to be existentially quantified. The variable written immediately after the existential quantifier can be substituted in the existentially quantified wff for at least one (unknown) object in the domain, such that the substitution preserves the truth of the existentially quantified wff. Would it be possible to substitute the variable for every object in the domain, then the existential quantification would be equivalent to the disjunction of the formulae thus obtained.

Example 13: Existential quantifiers

$\forall$x, year:
italian-resident (x, year) $\wedge$ ($\exists$z, y revenue (z, x, year) $\wedge \neg$(is-a (z, salary) $\vee$ is-a (z, pension)) $\wedge$ amount (z, y) $\wedge \neg$y=0) $\rightarrow$ must-file-return (x, year)

Interpretation: Any Italian resident with at least one source of income different from salary and pension must pay taxes (taxes on salary and pensions are retained by employers resp. the government).

The existential quantifier can also be used to express quantification over a larger number of objects, through the notion of set and cardinality of a set. The sentence: "Less then 10000 Americans have an income higher than 1000000 US$" can be represented as:

$\exists$s set(s) $\wedge$ cardinality(s, y) $\wedge$ y $\leq$ 10000 $\wedge$, $\forall$x (x ε s $\wedge$ total-income(x, z) $\wedge$ z $\geq$ 1000000)

■

Note the following equivalence between quantified predicates:

$$\forall x\ p(x) \leftrightarrow \neg(\exists x\ \neg p(x))$$
$$\exists x\ p(x) \leftrightarrow \neg(\forall x\ \neg p(x))$$

which means that it is possible to rewrite all wffs using just one type of quantifier.

A logic with the ability of quantifying only over domain objects is called a first-order logic. On the contrary, a logic in which a sentence quantifying over predicates like:

$$\forall x\ x(a, b)$$

is a wff, is called a second-order logic. While in principle more useful, second-order logic is not as well understood as first order logic, and is potentially more inefficient, therefore seldom used in AI as a representation language. In the following, we will only be concerned with first-order predicate calculus.

3.5.2.3 Model theory

One of the strong points of logic as a representational language is that it possesses a precise theory for the meaning of wffs with respect to an external world, called a model theory. In fact, under model theory, wffs are taken as assertions about a domain (world). Although model theory finds many applications in mathematics, it is particularly attractive for knowledge representation. From this viewpoint, model theory can be used to understand clearly what is being represented ([Hayes, 1977]).

A wff is given a meaning through an interpretation, i.e. via a mapping from symbols in the knowledge base (relation resp. constants) to a set of relations resp. objects in a world. Depending on the interpretation (i.e. on the chosen domain), a wff may be either true or false. For instance, the wff:

amount (s001, 700000)

may be true under an interpretation in which "s001" is mapped into a specific invoice, "amount" is mapped into the relation associating to each invoice its amount, "700000" is mapped into its amount in dollars, and in which the amount of the invoice referred to by "s001" is 700000 dollars. The same wff may be false under an interpretation in which "s001" refers to a car, "700000" refers to a number, "amount" is the relation between a car and its frame number, but the frame number of the car "s001" is not 700000. Of course, many other interpretations are possible.

A problem domain is described in logic by a set of wffs. Such a set corresponds to the knowledge base box in Fig. 1, Section 1.2. Given a knowledge base, an interpretation under which all wffs in it are true is called a model (of the knowledge base). It is such an interpretation which justifies the claim that a knowledge base written in first order predicate calculus represents something. There are, however, many possible interpretations for a wff. By increasing the number of wffs in the knowledge base, it is possible to restrict the number of models. For instance, adding to the above wff the new wff:

amount (s002, -15)

would prevent both interpretations given above from being models (in fact, neither invoice amounts, nor frame numbers can be negative). In general, it is impossible to add enough wffs to force just one model (the aimed interpretation): it is, however, possible to write enough of them to make all models share a view of the relations and constants introduced corresponding to the view aimed at.

In the next two sections, a set of inference rules deriving new beliefs which are true for all models of a given initial knowledge base is introduced. Roughly, this means that different readers with different models in mind will all find the reasoning process reasonable with respect to their model. However, it also implies that if the knowledge base is too generic, it may account for too many models, and hence it will be impossible to derive all interesting conclusions with respect to the aimed interpretation. As suggested by [Hayes, 1977], model theory supports the attitude of understanding a set of beliefs in terms of imagining a world, and of considering under which circumstances the imagined world is a model or not for it. Most importantly, this mapping from a knowledge base to a domain, and hence the understanding of a logic program, is independent from how the wffs are going to be used. Languages which can be understood this way are said to have a *declarative semantics* , and are called *declarative languages* .

Declarative languages are basically different from conventional programming languages; a conventional program uses statements such as the assignment or iterations, whose meaning is only understandable in terms of the machinery running them. For instance, variable assignment has the effect of changing the configuration of the computer memory, an operation which does not directly apply to the environment. As a consequence, representations in a declarative style are often easier, with the burden of mapping the environment to the computer being taken over by the logic programming language compiler. This happens, however, at the expenses of efficiency.

Note that declarative semantics tells us nothing about how to select objects and relations in order to represent adequately a given problem. Yet this choice is critical, because depending on it some beliefs may not be expressible in the language of first order predicate calculus (see Section 5.4 for an explanation of what "first order" means). The topic is addressed in Section 5.6.

Finally, although logic is a useful formalization for reasoning about beliefs, it is not a theory of how humans represent and understand. For instance, it does not make any assumption (apart from the declarative representation style) about how knowledge should be represented in order to understand spoken or written language (see [Charniak, 1976]): questions concerning the representational primitives, the organization of knowledge, the kinds of inferences best suited for the task are to be answered independently of the choice of logic as a representation formalism.

3.5.3 Guidelines for logic-based knowledge representation

Natural language is the way humans express mostly declarative knowledge. Being declarative, its translation to another declarative formalism understandable by a computer (such as logic) is much easier than its translation to a non-declarative formalism. Since a lot of regulatory knowledge is expressed in natural language, this feature is particularly attractive. However, natural language is much less formalized than logic; for instance, sentences with completely different meanings may have deceptively similar forms. On the other side, natural language is much more powerful than first order predicate calculus. In fact, there are sentences which are not directly representable in the logic introduced here. Typically, however, the following guidelines apply ([Walker et al., 1987], [Sowa, 1984], Chapter 4.4):

- constants refer to objects (Section 5.2)
- predicates represent relationships:

  one-argument predicates represent common names:

  e.g. "Mr.X is a taxpayer" ⇒ taxpayer (Mr.X)

  e.g. "The dollar is a currency" ⇒ currency (dollar)

  e.g. "Share XYZ" ⇒ share (XYZ)

  one-argument predicates also represent adjectives:

  e.g. "The dollar is unstable" ⇒ unstable (dollar)

  e.g. "The red book" ⇒ red(book)

- verbs are represented as predicates, the arguments of which are the subject and the object(s), if any:

  e.g. "it's raining" ⇒ raining () (intransitive, impersonal)

  e.g. "The dollar increases" ⇒ increases (dollar) (intransitive)

  e.g. "The FED lowered the interest rates" ⇒ lowered (FED, int-rate)

  e.g. "Mr.X pays Mr.Y 2000$" ⇒ pays (Mr.X, Mr.Y, 2000)

- verb tenses are best captured by extra temporal arguments (see Section 3.8):

  e.g. "The FED lowered the interest rates" ⇒ lower (FED, int-rate, past)

- quantifiers translate articles and natural language quantifiers:

  indeterminate articles are represented as existential quantifiers:

  e.g. "A client opened an account" ⇒

  $\exists$x,y: client (x) $\wedge$ open (x, y, past) $\wedge$ account (y)

  e.g. "I gave a book to you" ⇒

  $\exists$x: give (me, x, you, past) $\wedge$ book (x)

  "there is", "there exists" and similar are represented as existential quantifiers:

  e.g. "There is an income different from salary or pension"

$\exists$x: income (x) $\wedge$ is-a (x, y) $\wedge \neq$ (y, salary) $\wedge \neq$ (y, pension)

e.g. "There are at least two different incomes"

$\exists$x,y: income (x) $\wedge$ income (y) $\wedge \neq$ (x, y)

"any", "all", "every", "each" and similar are translated as universal quantifiers:

e.g. "Any person must pay taxes" $\Rightarrow$

$\forall$x person (x) $\rightarrow$ must-pay (x, taxes)

- implications represent conditionals (although causality is not part of the definition of logical implication):

the "if" part of the conditional is the premise, but the "then" part is the conclusion:

e.g. "If a man is happy, then he is friendly" $\Rightarrow$

$\forall$x: happy (x) $\rightarrow$ friendly (x)

The fact that universal quantification is appropriate, is shown by the equivalent sentence "Every happy man is friendly", in which the quantifier is explicit, but the conditional is implicit. The logic translation is the same

The reader is encouraged to look retrospectively at the wffs interpretations in the previous sections, and to check the application of the above principles.

Finally, an important issue is reification, i.e. the representation of a relation as an object. This is necessary because first order predicate calculus does not allow one to express beliefs over anything else than objects, and an object is everything that can appear as an argument of a predicate. For instance, it was suggested in the above list to view adjectives as predicates: "the dollar is unstable" was represented as "unstable (dollar)". Since, however, "unstable" is not an object constant, no belief can be expressed about it; the sentence: "such instability is, however, decreasing" is not representable with the above choice. The solution is to make "instability" an object: the above two sentences can be represented as "status (dollar, instability)", "decreasing (instability)".

Another example of reification is the concept of a transaction (see Chapter 12.4). The most natural representation of a transaction is as a relation between two agents in which an agreed amount of, say, a commodity is exchanged for an agreed amount of, say, a different commodity at an agreed time instant:

transaction (agent1, agent2, quantity1, commodity1, quantity2, commodity2, time)

This representation works fine so long as there is no need to represent relations between transactions. For instance, with the above representation it is impossible to express a general rule like: "On all markets, transactions after closing time are not valid". To do that, the concept of transaction must be reified. For instance, one could introduce a predicate:

transaction (p, m)

stating that p is a specific transaction on a specific market. Then the predicate "transaction" defined first, could be decomposed into a collection of more specific predicates. The notion of exchange good has been reified as well, since most markets impose restrictions on the kind of exchange goods admitted for transactions:

agent (p, agent1)	(. agent1 is an agent in the transaction p .)
agent (p, agent2)	(. agent2 is an agent in the transaction p .)
exchange (p, q1)	(. q1 is an exchange good in the transaction p .)
commodity (q1, commodity1)	(. q1 is a commodity .)
quantity (q1, quantity1)	(. q1 is quantifiable .)

exchange (p, q2)	(. q2 is an exchange good in transaction p .)
commodity (q2, commodity2)	(. q1 is a commodity .)
quantity (q2, quantity2)	(. q2 is quantifiable .)
gives-away (p, agent1, q1)	(. in transaction p agent1 gives away exchange good q1 .)
gives-away (p, agent2, q2)	(. in transaction p agent2 gives away exchange good q2 .)
receives (p, agent1, 100, q2)	(. in transaction p agent1 receives 100% of exchange good q2 .)
receives (p, agent2, 100, q1)	(. in transaction p agent2 receives 100% of exchange good q1 .)
time (p, t)	(. transaction p happened at time t .)

One would translate the above regulation as:

$\forall$x,y,t,t1: transaction(x, y) $\wedge$ market(y) $\wedge$ close-time (y, t1) $\wedge$ time (x, t) $\wedge$ after (t, t1) $\rightarrow$ not-valid(x)

Other advantages of the second representation are the capability of representing transactions with any number of agents and exchange goods involved, and in which it is possible to specify which agent receives which proportion of which exchange good. One disadvantage is that a transaction is now a set of wffs potentially spread over the knowledge base (see Section 7.1).

However, it is very important to stress that pure logic is grossly inadequate to represent real transactions, since transactions cause dynamical changes in the truth value of beliefs (e.g. it is no more true that agent1 owns exchange good q1, after the transaction has taken place), and in the logic introduced so far no beliefs can ever be withdrawn: once a belief is true/false, it is true/false forever.

3.5.4 Logic inference

This section deals with techniques for inferring new beliefs from a given set of beliefs, represented as explained above. Such process is called *deductive reasoning* .

There are a number of inference schemata (rules) which can be used to draw inferences. Some of them have the property of deriving only new wffs which are logically implied by the available wffs, and are called "sound" inference rules. A wff is logically implied by a set of wffs (a knowledge base) only if every interpretation satisfying the knowledge base (i.e. making all wffs in it true) also satisfies the newly derived wff. It was explained in Section 5.5 that it is generally impossible to force just one interpretation of a set of wffs. However, if solely "sound" inference rules are used, every observer of the knowledge base, having possibly a different interpretation in mind, will find the results correct from his point of view, since his interpretation will account also for the newly derived beliefs. This is because "sound" inference rules are knowledge independent, relying just on the definitions of the connectives and quantifiers.

Although in the present and the next Section (Section 5.8) we deal solely with "sound" inference rules, this does not imply that inference over a knowledge base in first-order predicate calculus must be sound ([Israel, 1983]).

Given a knowledge base, and a wff, it is often important to answer the question whether the wff logically was derived from the knowledge base. This is the case if a sequence of sound inference rules exists which, if applied to the initial knowledge base, would derive the desired wff. Such a sequence is called a *proof* ; the wff to be derived is called a *theorem* , and wffs in the initial knowledge base are called *axioms* . Problem-solving then can be interpreted as the activity of deriving wffs from a set of axioms describing a problem domain, i.e. as theorem proving. Section 5.8 shortly describes the implications of this view.

i. Modus ponens

Let A and B be two beliefs. Assume known:

$$A$$

$$A \rightarrow B$$

From Fig. 6 it is clear that B must hold as well:

B

This kind of inference is called modus ponens.

ii. Modus tolens

Let A and B be two beliefs. From:

$\neg B$

$A \rightarrow B$

and the truth table in Fig. 6 it follows:

$\neg A$

This kind of inference is called modus tolens.

iii. AND elimination

Let A and B be two beliefs. From:

$A \wedge B$

it can be inferred (see truth table Fig. 6):

A

B

iv. Instantiation of a universal quantifier

Let A(x) be a belief containing the variable x. From:

$\forall x\ A(x)$

it can be inferred that:

$A(object_i)$

where $object_i$ is any specific object in the domain.

This inference follows directly from the definition of a universal quantifier.

The following example shows how the inference rules can be used to deduce if a person must pay taxes, from the general rule in Example 11, Section 5.2.1.

Example 14: A simple inference using the tax law

Suppose that, from a dialogue session with a client, the following information became available:

1. italian-resident ("client nr. 12", 1990)
2. total_income (ti004, "client nr. 12", 1990)
3. amount (ti004, 9000000)

Furthermore, suppose that from the tax law it is known:

4. $\forall$x, year, id, y:
   italian-resident (x, year) $\wedge$ total-income (id, x, year) $\wedge$ amount (id, y) $\wedge$ y> 6602000 $\rightarrow$ must-file-return (x, year)

Are beliefs 1 trough 4 enough for establishing whether the client nr. 12 must pay taxes?

By instantiating the universal quantifiers in 4. (rule iv.), it can be inferred that:

5. italian-resident (ob1, year1) $\wedge$ total-income (id1, ob1, year1) $\wedge$ amount (id1, ob2) $\wedge$ ob2> 6111000 $\rightarrow$ must-file-return (ob1, year1)

where ob1, ob2, year1, id1 are objects in the problem domain. Within the scope of the quantifier (in this case the whole implication), quantified variables with the same name are consistently substituted for the same objects.

Let's now look at the truth value of the premise of the implication. The premise is true if the following four predicates are all true (rule iii.):

6. italian-resident (ob1, year1)
7. total-income (id1, ob1, year1)

8. amount (id1, ob2)
9. ob2> 6602000.

By setting ob1 equal to "client nr.12", and year1 equal to 1990, the first wff can be made equal to belief nr. 1., which is known to be true. By further assuming that id1 is ti004, and retaining the previous values for ob1 and year1, the predicate 7. is true since it is the same as predicate 2., which is known to be true. Finally, by setting the still undetermined ob2 equal to 9000000, also predicate 8. is known to be true (because of predicate 3.). Assuming that the knowledge base contains the elementary axioms of mathematics, it must be possible to show the truth of predicate 9 as well. Hence the premise of the implication is true, for the given set of objects:

10. italian-resident ("client nr. 12", 1990) ∧ total-income (ti004, "client nr. 12", 1990) ∧ amount (ti004, 9000000) ∧ 9000000 > 6602000

Considering 10. and 5., it is easy to see that they form exactly the schema required for modus ponens (rule i.). By applying it, it is possible to conclude:

6. must-file-return ("client nr. 12", 1990)

which answers the question. ■

3.5.5 Clausal logic and resolution

The process of logic inference as sketched above is difficult to automate on computers because of efficiency problems:

- there is a large number of inference rules to choose among (much larger than the five sample rules shown in Example 14 above): often, the process of selecting the best inference rule to prove a wff is tricky, hence difficult to implement on computers
- the same wff can be represented in a number of equivalent ways (see the equivalences among connectives and quantifiers in Sections 5.3 and 5.4): then time is lost during the proof deriving equivalent writings

The two problems are related. By writing wffs in a more constrained format, it is possible to reduce the number of inference rules: e.g. and-elimination (rule iii. in Section 5.7 above) is of no use if conjunction is banned from the set of allowable connectives. On the other side, due to the reduced set of inference rules, proofs can no more derive all equivalent writings for a wff in the knowledge base; then it is important that the language is correspondingly simplified, so that theorems can only be expressed in a constrained format. Usually, logic-based languages (such as Prolog, see Chapter 4.4) restrict their inference methods to just one inference rule, called resolution ([Robinson, 1965]). At the same time, the syntax is limited in the following way:

- the only allowable connectives are negation and disjunction
- only predicates may be negated (i.e. negation must immediately precede a predicate)
- the only quantifier is the universal quantifier

A logic whose wffs comply with such restrictions is called *clausal logic* . Wffs are called clauses. Each wff must be a disjunction of literals. A literal is either a predicate, or a negated predicate (i.e. a predicate preceded by "¬"). Thus:

$$p1 \vee p2 \vee ... \vee pn$$

where $p_1, p_2, ..., p_n$ are literals, is a clause. A knowledge base is a collection of clauses.

It is possible to show that every wff in first order predicate calculus can be translated into clausal logic, although this translation may result in much longer clauses.

v. Resolution

Let $p_1, p_2, ..., p_n, q_2, ..., q_n$ be literals. Given the two clauses:

$$p_1 \vee p_2 \vee ... \vee p_n$$

$$\neg p_1 \vee q_2 \vee ... \vee q_n$$

the clause:

$$p_2 \vee ... \vee p_n \vee q_2 \vee ... \vee q_n ,$$

can be inferred.

In fact, assume that p_1 is true. Then $\neg p_1$ is false, hence one of $q_2, ... , q_n$ must be true. If p_1 is false, then one of $p_2, ..., p_n$ must be true. Hence, the third clause in v. is always true. Mechanically, it is obtained by cancelling literals with opposite truth values from the disjunction of the two clauses containing them.

Example 15: Special cases of resolution

The implication $p \rightarrow q$ is translated in clausal form as follows (see Section 5.3):

$\neg p \vee q$

Let p and q be literals. Assume:

1. p
2. $\neg p \vee q$

Cancelling p and $\neg$p, resolution derives q, i.e. is like a modus ponens for clauses.

Let p and q be again literals, and assume:

1. $\neg q$
2. $\neg p \vee q$

Then resolution can derive $\neg$p, i.e. behave like modus tolens for clauses.

Finally, let p be a literal. Suppose that the knowledge base contains the clauses p and $\neg$p. Such a knowledge base is inconsistent, i.e. there is no interpretation which can make all wffs true at the same time. Then resolution derives the empty clause (a clause with no literals), noted "[]". The empty clause is a mark of inconsistency. ■

Resolution has many interesting properties when used to prove theorems expressed in clausal logic, so the combination of the two is quite popular. When theorem proving is restricted to clausal logic and resolution, its strategy is called proof by refutation: the wff to be derived is negated and added to the set of axioms. If the wff is a theorem, then the new set of axioms is inconsistent. Resolution (this is one of the nice properties) is always able to derive the empty clause from an inconsistent (contradictory) knowledge base.

Example 16: Proof by refutation

Suppose again the same knowledge base as in Example 14, Section 5.4, i.e.:

1. italian-resident ("client nr. 12", 1990)
2. total_income (ti004, "client nr. 12", 1990)
3. amount (ti004, 9000000)
4. ∀x, year, id, y:
   italian-resident (x, year) ∧ total-income (id, x, year) ∧ amount (id, y) ∧ y> 6602000 → must-file-return (x, year)

At first, it is necessary to translate belief 4. into clausal form:

∀x, year, id, y:
¬(italian-resident (x, year) ∧ total-income (id, x, year) ∧ amount (id, y) ∧ y> 6602000) ∨ must-file-return (x, year)

∀x, year, id, y:
¬italian-resident (x, year) ∨ ¬total-income (id, x, year) ∨ ¬amount (id, y) ∨ ¬y> 6602000
∨ must-file-return (x, year)

Second, the wff to be proved (in the following referred as the theorem) must be added, negated, to the knowledge base:

4. ∀x, year, id, y:
¬italian-resident (x, year) ∨ ¬total-income (id, x, year) ∨ ¬amount (id, y) ∨ ¬y> 6602000
∨ must-file-return (x, year)
5. ¬must-file-return ("client nr. 12", 1990)

Resolution is applicable for instance to clauses 4. and 5. In fact, the last disjunct in clause 4. can be made equal to the predicate in clause 4 by letting the variable x stay for the object "client nr. 12", and year for 1990. This is allowed because of rule iv. in Section 5.7 above, provided the same substitution is preserved over the scope of the quantifier, i.e. the whole clause. The result of resolution is:

6. ∀ id, y:
¬italian-resident ("client nr. 12", 1990) ∨ ¬total-income (id, "client nr. 12", 1990) ∨ ¬amount (id, y) ∨
¬(y>6602000)

By resolving 6. with 1. is obtained:

7. ∀ id,y: ¬total-income (id, "client nr. 12", 1990) ∨ ¬amount (id, y) ∨ ¬(y>6602000)

By resolving 7. with 2. (and applying rule iv., Section 5.4):

8. ∀ y: ¬amount (ti004, y) ∨ ¬(y>6602000)

By resolving 8. with 3. (and applying rule iv., Section 5.4):

9. ¬9000000>6602000

If the axioms of mathematics are included in the knowledge base, then resolution can prove:

10. 9000000>6602000

10. and 9. can be resolved together, generating the empty clause. Hence the clauses 1. through 5. were contradictory; since, however, clauses 1. through 4. are consistent, the negated goal must be the reason for the contradiction. Hence, the goal must be true. ■

3.5.6 Logic and semantic networks

While model theory is the essence of logic, there is no need for a syntax like the one introduced in Section 5.2 for predicate calculus. Indeed, a number of formalisms have been devised for expressing declarative knowledge in a way which is more suitable to the problem features than the usual syntax. As often when dealing with problems of information retrieval, semantic nets (see Section 4) are attractive because of their feature of linking (i.e. making directly accessible) all information related to a given node.
One possible mapping of logic into a network is based on the idea that nodes represent concepts, and links relations [Hendrix, 1975]. Relations with more than two arguments must be reified (see Section 5.3 above) and therefore associated to nodes. Fig. 7 shows a representation in form of a semantic network of the the knowledge base about transactions in Section 5.3. The link "instance-of" (shortened "inst-of") does not appear in the knowledge base explicitly: it means that the node is an element of the generic type described by the node pointed at. For a deeper account of this kind

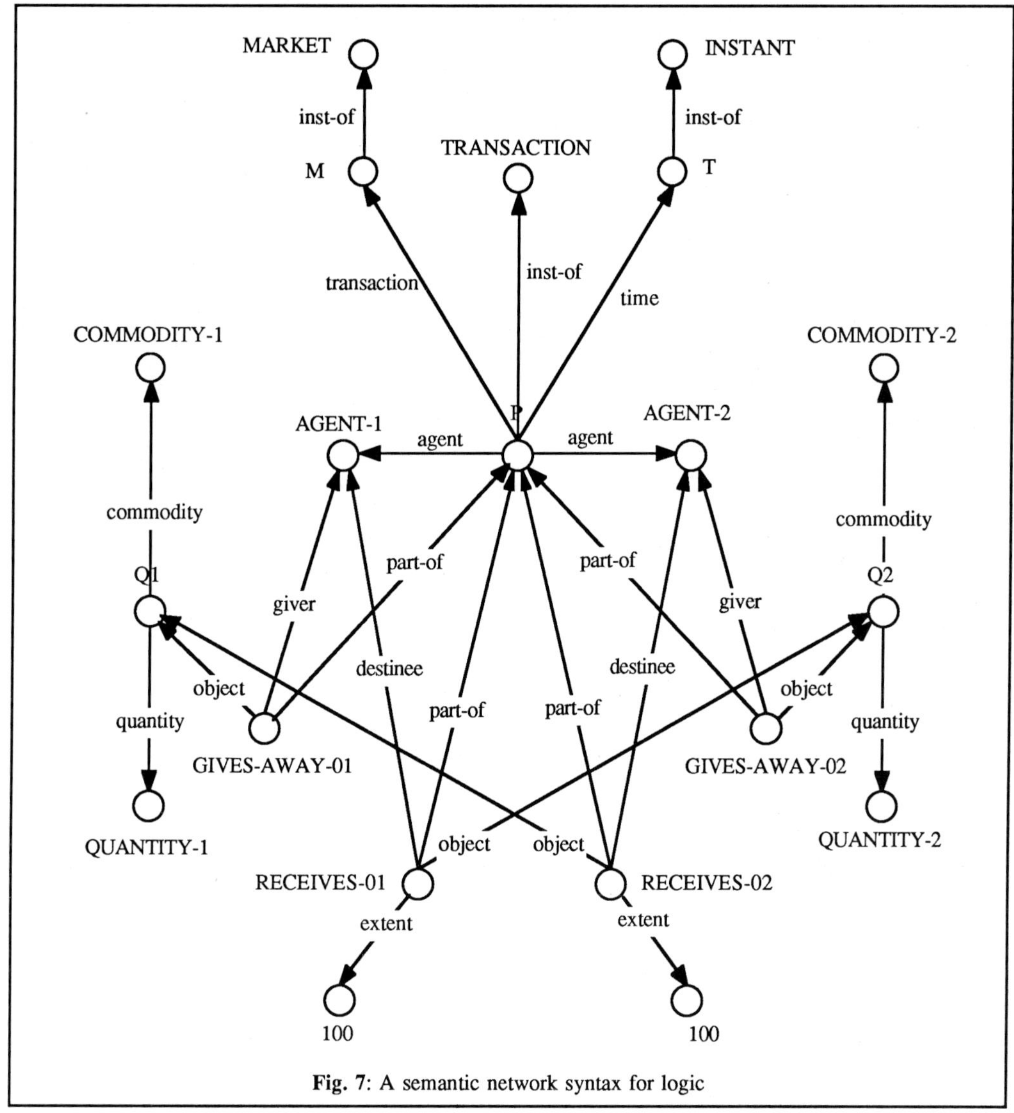

Fig. 7: A semantic network syntax for logic

of link, see Section 7. "GIVES-AWAY-01", "RECEIVES-01" etc. are reification of acts, much alike "transaction" in Section 5.3.

As an example of the increased efficiency for retrieval tasks through the network notation, consider for example the node "P" (i.e., the transaction). Every relation in which "P" is involved is represented as a link either pointing out of, or pointing toward "P". So questions such as: "which concepts are meaningful in the context of a transaction?" can be answered immediately from the very nature of the representation. The same question would require search over all predicates in the knowledge base (a task outside the scope of first order predicate calculus) or an extra rule, explicitly relating a transaction to other concepts. Furthermore, the graph notation is in general easier to read: for instance, it makes dependencies, symmetries and similar information immediately apparent. While attractive for some applications, semantic networks also have limitations: for example, it is not obvious how to directly code disjunctions; at the very end, only binary relations can be pictured; finally, extensions (such as partitioning) are needed to the simple formalism for expressing quantifiers.

Alternative semantic-net equivalents of predicate calculus are proposed in [Shapiro, 1971] and [Sowa, 1984].

3.5.7 Application: representing part of the Italian fiscal regulation

Taxpayers generating any kind of income during the fiscal year have to file an individual income tax return, unless that income is below a given threshold or it completely consists of exempt or pre-taxed revenues. The following rules help taxpayers who are employees decide if they must file the income tax return, according to their revenues, deductible expenses, family status, etc.
In general, taxes on dependent income are directly paid by the employer, and hence the employee does not need to file any tax return; this rule has obviously a lot of exceptions. The rules were extracted from the user's guidelines distributed by the tax authorities together with the tax forms; as a consequence, many non-trivial concepts are undefined. Better coverage and advice could be achieved by referring directly to the tax laws or to the basic state laws (e.g. civil code). Each rule is followed by a plain text interpretation explaining its intended meaning. Apart from slight simplifications, rules closely mirror selected sentences in the guidelines. The rule number at the beginning of each rule has no logical meaning and would be skipped by a theorem prover.

1. Classification of incomes

is-a (salary, dependent-income)
is-a (pension, dependent-income)
is-a (dependent-income, pre-taxed-income)
is-a (pretaxed-income, exempt-income)
is-a (exempt-income, income)

etc., with similar knowledge bases covering deductions, employment status, etc.

The classification rule is then:

∀x, y, z: is-a (x, z) ← is-a (x, y) ∧ is-a(y, z)

2. Sample rules for determining whether dependent workers must file a tax return

[Rule1] ∀x, year: activity (x, year, dependent-work) → ∃ z: revenue (z, x, year) ∧ is-a (z, dependent-income)

Interpretation: if the activity of "x" during "year" is dependent work, then at least one of his incomes must be a dependent income; the rule says nothing about how to conclude if a worker is a dependent worker.

[Rule2] ∀x, year: ¬must-file-return (x, year) ← activity (x, year, dependent-work) ∧ ¬exception (x, year, dependent-work)

Interpretation: if the activity of "x" during "year" is dependent work and "x" is not an exception during said year, then he/she must not file an individual income tax return.

[Rule3] ∀x, year: must-file-return (x, year) ← exception (x, year, dependent-work)

Interpretation: workers which are an exceptions with respect to the dependent worker status must file an income tax return.

[Rule4] ∀x, year: exception (x, year, dependent-work) ←
activity (x, year, dependent-work) ∧
(∀z: revenue (z, x, year) → is-a (z, dependent-income)) ∧
(∃ z: w: z ≠ w, revenue (z, x, year) ∧ revenue (w, x, year)) ∧

$\neg$ ($\exists$ p: ($\forall$z, p: depends (p, x)) $\wedge$
($\forall$z, m, $\exists$ list: revenue (z, x, year) $\wedge$ amount (z, m) $\leftrightarrow$ member (m, list)) $\wedge$
sum (list, result) $\wedge$
result $\geq$ 6602000

Interpretation: a dependent worker, whose yearly returns are all from dependent incomes, with no dependent relatives and with more than one income, is an exception if the sum of incomes is larger than Italian Lire 6602000 (The variable "list" stands for a list, i.e. a sequence of symbols; see Chapter 4.3 or 4.4 for a description of how lists are manipulated in symbolic languages).

[Rule5] $\forall$list, result: sum (list, result) $\leftrightarrow$
(list = [] $\wedge$ result = 0) $\vee$
(sum (b, x) $\wedge$ plus (x, a, result) $\wedge$ cons (a, b, list))

Interpretation: the sum of the elements in a list has value "result" if and only if either the list is empty and the result is 0, or the sum of the rest of the list has value x and result is equal to x plus the first element in the list. "cons (a, b, list)" is a predicate true of a "list" whose first element is a, and the rest is b. "plus" is true if the last argument is the sum of the previous two. Its implementation is not explained here; it could be implemented using the "successor" function or procedural attachment (see Section 7.3).

[Rule6] $\forall$list, x: member (x, list) $\leftrightarrow$ cons (x, b, list) $\vee$ (cons (y, b, list) $\wedge$ member (x, b))

Interpretation: an element is member of a list if and only if either the element is at the beginning of the list, or it is in the rest of the list.

[Rule7] $\forall$x, year: exception (x, year, dependent-work) $\leftarrow$
activity (x, year, dependent-work) $\wedge$
$\neg$($\exists$ z, w: z $\neq$ w, revenue (z, x, year) $\wedge$ revenue (w, x, year)) $\wedge$
($\exists$ k: expense(k, x, year) $\wedge$ is-a (k, deductible-expense) $\wedge$
$\neg$is-a (k, mortgage-loan-deductions) $\wedge$ $\neg$is-a (k, local-tax-on-real-estates))

Interpretation: a dependent worker is an exception if he has just one income and deductible expenses, other than mortgage loan deductions or local taxes on real estate.

[Rule8] $\forall$x, year: exception (x, year, dependent-work) $\leftarrow$
activity (x, year, dependent-work) $\wedge$
($\exists$ z: revenue (z, x, year) $\wedge$ (is-a (z, independent-income) $\vee$ is-a (z, property-income)))

Interpretation: a dependent worker is an exception if at least one of his incomes during the relevant year is an income from independent work or from property.

[Rule9] $\forall$x, year: exception (x, year, dependent-work) $\leftarrow$
activity (x, year, dependent-work) $\wedge$
($\exists$ z, w: revenue (z, w, year) $\wedge$ tutor (x, w))

Interpretation: A dependent worker is an exception if at least one of his income sources during the relevant year is an income from an individual under his tutorship.

etc. (there are about ten more rules like the ones above).

3. "Completing" the knowledge base

The above knowledge base contains one major fault; in fact, it is well possible to conclude, through the application of one of the above rules, that the taxpayer is an exception (and therefore should file his income tax return); however, if no premise of the above rules is true, the system is unable to conclude anything about the status of the taxpayer. The point is that there is no rule telling the system that, if it is unable to show that the taxpayer is an exception, then it can conclude that the taxpayer is not an exception. Unfortunately, the previous sentence cannot be directly translated into logic as it was explained in Sections 5.2 trough 5.4, since it involves a belief about "provability", not about domain objects. However, it is possible to state that a taxpayer is not an exception if none of the preconditions in the above rules is satisfied. If there was just one rule:

$\forall$x, year: exception (x, year, dependent-work) $\leftarrow$ premises

then this could be simply achieved by adding an implication in the opposite direction:

$\forall$x, year: exception (x, year, dependent-work) $\rightarrow$ premises

or also, putting the two together:

$\forall$x, year: exception (x, year, dependent-work) $\leftrightarrow$ premises

In the case, as above, where more than one implication exists with the same conclusion, they must be reduced to just one implication whose premise is the disjunction of the premises from each implication. This implies rewriting the above knowledge base as follows:

$\forall$x, year: exception (x, year, dependent-work) $\leftrightarrow$
(activity (x, year, dependent-work) $\wedge$
($\forall$z: revenue (z, x, year) $\rightarrow$ is-a (z, dependent-income)) $\wedge$
($\exists$ z: w: z $\neq$ w, revenue (z, x, year) $\wedge$ revenue (w, x, year)) $\wedge$
$\neg$ ($\exists$ p: ($\forall$z, p: depends (p, x)) $\wedge$
($\forall$z, m, $\exists$ list: revenue (z, x, year) $\wedge$ amount (z, m) $\leftrightarrow$ member (m, list)) $\wedge$
sum (list, result) $\wedge$
result $\geq$ 6602000) $\vee$

(activity (x, year, dependent-work) $\wedge$
$\neg$($\exists$ z, w: z $\neq$ w, revenue (z, x, year) $\wedge$ revenue (w, x, year)) $\wedge$
($\exists$ k: expense(k, x, year) $\wedge$ is-a (k, deductible-expense) $\wedge$
$\neg$is-a (k, mortgage-loan-deductions) $\wedge$ $\neg$is-a (k, local-tax-on-real-estates))) $\vee$

(activity (x, year, dependent-work) $\wedge$
($\exists$ z: revenue (z, x, year) $\wedge$ (is-a (z, independent-income) $\vee$ is-a (z, property-income)))) $\vee$

(activity (x, year, "dependent-work") $\wedge$
($\exists$ z, w: revenue (z, w, year) $\wedge$ tutor (x, w))) $\vee$

:
premises of the other rules ...

$\forall$x, year: $\neg$must-file-revenue (x, year) $\leftarrow$
activity (x, year, dependent-work) $\wedge$ $\neg$exception (x, year, dependent-work)

$\forall$x, year: must-file-revenue (x, year) $\leftarrow$ exception (x, year, dependent-work)

The technique of making a predicate either true or false, but never unprovable, with respect to a knowledge base is called *completion*.. In legal applications, completion returns correct inferences if the knowledge base can be guaranteed to contain all rules relevant to the completed predicate. This is so because most state laws establish explicitly that, in case of a lack of regulation, the citizen is entitled to the course of decisions the most favourable to him. So, for instance, if the above knowledge base contained all ruled exceptions to the general exemption rule for dependent workers, and a specific worker did not fit any of the ruled exceptions, then the system would correctly conclude that the worker should not pay taxes.

3.5.8 Pros and cons of logic

Logic has some important advantages as a representation language:

1. Declarative semantics

The semantics of logic provides a formal account of what it means to express knowledge about the world (see Section 5.5). This is the very purpose of knowledge representation, and logic provides a clean way to deal with it. So, if one wants to know what he is saying about a problem domain, he may well use logic as a tool for making precise his own formalism and validating it.

2. Declarative programming style

Being declarative, programs in logic contain explicit knowledge (Section 1.2). A good example is the predicate "member" (Rule 6, 5.7.2 above). The predicate is just a definition of what the relation "member" among two domain objects (of which one must be a list) means, i.e. in which cases it holds. The check on membership is performed automatically by the theorem prover, since it can be proved, like a theorem, from the definition together with the inference rules. No loop scanning the list and comparing each element in the list to the given element must be designed, nor is it necessary to specify the length of the list, the datatype of the list elements etc. Such a general definition would take several lines of code in a procedural programming language, beside being difficult to program and to understand (for another discussion of this same topic, see Chapter 4.3.7; further examples of a declarative programming style are to be found in Chapter 4.4).

The assertions in a knowledge base being expressed independently from their use, the resulting representation formalism is very flexible: the same "member" definition can be used to test whether a given element is member of a given list, which unknown element satisfies the membership relation within a given list, and to build a list from a description of which elements are members, etc.

3. Deduction

Logic is a theory of deduction, i.e. about which beliefs are derived from others. If deductive reasoning is an important part of the task (as for instance in tutoring a taxpayer), the approach of logic might be appropriate.

4. Modularity

Knowledge is expressed in logic as a collection of predicates, grouped into beliefs. Each belief is an assertion. The tasks of adding, removing and changing beliefs is trivial, because of the independence among beliefs. Also, a belief is always defined independently from its use. Therefore logic is adequate for incremental development.

5. Incomplete knowledge

Logic is well suited to represent incomplete knowledge [Moore, 1982]. Logic primitives logic for representing imprecise information are essentially: disjunction, negation, existential and universal quantification. More precisely:

- disjunction enables one to express that at least one belief must be true, without specifying which one
- negation enables one to distinguish among true beliefs, false beliefs and beliefs whose truth value is unknown
- universal quantification enables one to state that a wff holds for all objects, without the need of knowing all of them
- existential quantification enables to express that a wff is true of at least one object, without knowing which

The above primitives can be combined to express different degrees of incompleteness. For instance, the TX connective (see Section 5.2.1) can be used to assert that exactly one of the component wffs is true, without knowing which.

While the above advantages are important, the limitations of logic as a representation language are also important.

1. Limitations in expressive power

First order predicate calculus alone is not enough for expressing knowledge about the world. Some extensions needed are reasoning about multiple agents and contexts; expressing possibility, time, belief; capturing limitations in the deductive power of the modeled agents.

Several extensions to classical logic have been proposed to overcome (or try to overcome) the above-mentioned limitations: e.g. temporal logic for expressing beliefs whose truth changes with time (Section 8), reasoning based on assumptions possibly subject to later revisions, such as default logics [Reiter, 1980], [McCarthy, 1986], and reasoning about knowledge and beliefs [Kripke, 1971]: although many of the above proposals are interesting and worth studying, they are, nevertheless, quite complicated and not sufficiently settled, and therefore skipped from this volume.

2. Combinatorial explosion

Reasoning even over a small set of clauses with resolution can be very inefficient [Charniak, 1976]. This is because the number of reasoning lines (i.e. proofs) increases combinatorially with the depth of the search (see Fig. 9, Section 6.6 for a visualization of this kind of problem in a different context). This problem is shared by all mechanically reasoning systems which, faced with a choice of what to do next, cannot decide for just one action, and leave the decision open (or, which is the same, take into account all alternatives). At the following reasoning step, still more indecision will be faced, since the results of the previous reasoning are only partly known and some other causes of indecision may reside at the current step. The overall effect is called "combinatorial explosion", meaning that, from a small set of possible choices, subsequent combinations cause a large amount of possibilities at the end. Combinatorial explosion is essentially a problem of insufficient control knowledge [Minsky, 1975] and of insufficient exploitation of the problem structure.

4. Imprecise knowledge

Logic deals well with exact data or beliefs (e.g. true/false, equal/not equal, match/no match etc.), but it cannot capture less sharp-cut ideas like similarity, uncertainty and fuzziness, which seem empirically to be important characteristics of how humans perceive and use knowledge. Some important reasoning methods, such as analogy, are fundamental in human reasoning, yet are not easily coupled with using logic.

5. Contradiction

A belief and its negation (or another belief incompatible with it) cannot coexist in the same knowledge base, because logic inference will be unable to derive (and hence believe) any formula, i.e. will become useless; humans on the contrary are able to maintain contradictory hypotheses without impairing their rational capabilities. Here again, logic seems to be too "clean" for describing real-world environments.

6. Changes

Humans deal with an ever-changing environment; it is natural that mechanisms of revision of beliefs play an important role in human reasoning. Classical logic cannot accommodate beliefs revision (see Section 5.3). In logic inference, newly derived beliefs never change the truth value of the set of axioms from which they were derived.

3.6 Rules

3.6.1 Motivation

In many practical cases, knowledge is naturally expressed by human experts as a collection of situation descriptions, each associated to a set of appropriate, situation-dependent actions. This consideration strongly suggests the idea that:

- a data structure (we'll call it *fact*) is needed for formalizing situation descriptions
- another data structure, basically a situation-action pair, might be adequate for capturing expert responses to situations: such a pair is called a *rule*

A knowledge base then consists in a collection of facts and rules, until possibly the whole set of problem domain configurations and actions is covered. An early example of such a way of formalizing knowledge was presented in the case study in Chapter 1.4 (refer in particular to Chapter 1.4.2). Systems representing knowledge as facts and rules are called *rule-based system* (or *production system*). Most traditional expert systems are rule-based, although expert behavior can be achieved with other knowledge representation formalisms as well.

3.6.2 Facts

A fact is the unconditioned expression of an assertion about the world. Formally, a fact can be represented as any collection (a list, a tree, a record, etc.) of symbols.

In many cases, facts state values of objects attributes; for instance, the belief "the amount of inflation is 4%" can be interpreted as meaning that the attribute "magnitude" of the object "inflation" has value 4% (refer to Section 5.3 for similar guidelines). Such a structure for facts has a special name, object-attribute-value triple. In some systems (such as OPS5, see [Browston et al., 1985]), attributes pertaining to the same object may alternatively be collected into unique structures, similar to those of frames (see Section 7).

Depending on the domain, however, the object-attribute-value scheme may be extended: e.g. assertions need not be true or false, most often they are uncertain; hence an attribute "uncertainty" and a measure for it are often added. Sometimes, the time at which the assertion was made is important. Finally, completely different kinds of structures closer to the domain knowledge may be used (e.g. specification of primitive curve segments in the application discussed in Chapter 7). Although it is easy to recognize the object-attribute-value formalism in some of the facts in the next example, the presentation adopted, inspired by the discussion in the previous Chapter, is to represent facts as predicates. This representation is consistent with the view in Section 1.4.

Example 17: Facts about fiscal regulations

The following facts could be derived by the system at run-time by questioning the user:

```
activity (mr.x, employee)
taxable-income (mr.x, 9984000)   (. taxable income in Italian liras .)
has-spouse (mr.x, dependent)      (. a dependent spouse .)
has-children (mr.x, dependent, 2)  (. two dependent children .)
has-children (mr.x, independent, 1) (. one independent child .)
has-relatives (mr.x, dependent, 0)  (. no dependent relatives .)
```

The following facts could have been put into the knowledge base by an expert, and capture parts of the tax regulations:

exemption (dependent-spouse, 552000) (. tax exemption for dependent spouse .)
exemption (dependent-child, 48000) (. tax exemption for dependent child .)
exemption (dependent-relative,0) (. tax exemption for dependent relative .)

The following fact could be derived by running part of the knowledge base (shown in Example 18, Section 6.3 below):

gross-taxes (mr.x, 1380000)

etc. ■

The collection of all facts in the knowledge base makes up a description of the current situation of the world. Referring to a terminology which is commonplace in system theory, the collection of facts is also referred to as the state of the world, since it conveys all the information available to the problem-solver about the environment. In the following, "collection of facts" and "state" are used as synonyms.

3.6.3 Rules

Rules (or productions) are again data structures following a highly constrained syntax. In most rule-based languages, rules take the following form:

IF <condition> THEN <action>

where "IF" and "THEN" are reserved symbols of the representation language, chosen to improve readability.

Rules are therefore condition-action pairs, where:

- the <condition> part (or left-hand side, or premise) describes configurations of the state enabling the execution (firing) of the rule. In general such configurations are expressed as constraints on a subset of the problem state: it is well possible that different condition parts of different rules be satisfied in a given state, or conversely that the condition part of the same rule be satisfied in different states
- the <action> part (or right-hand side, or conclusion) describes one or more actions, whose effects generally also include a change to the problem state

A rule can be fired whenever the condition part is fully satisfied by the current state. Firing a rule means performing the actions coded in its right-hand side. Because of the state-changing actions in the rule conclusion, after the execution of a rule the computer agent faces a slightly modified environment. This in turn causes the condition parts of some rules to be no longer satisfied, and the condition parts of other rules to become satisfied by the new environment. The computer agent solves a problem by repeatedly firing applicable rules, until the state satisfies some goal conditions (in which case, the agent stops). Sections 6.5 and 6.6 below further elaborate on this point.

The next example shows some rules about tax reasoning. Premises are expressed as conjunctions of simple facts (see Section 5.3): hence a premise is satisfied only if all facts in the premise are true in the current state (not-mentioned facts are irrelevant for the firing of the rule). Most systems also allow disjunctions or negations in the rules premises.

Relation arguments beginning with a capital letter are variables. Relations containing variables as well as constant arguments are satisfied (*matched*) by any relation in the collection of facts with the same name, number of arguments, and the same constant arguments in the same positions. The constant arguments in the fact must be thought of as taking the place of the variables in the corresponding position. Once a constant is substituted for a variable, all occurrences of that same variable within the rule are substituted for the same constant. However, variables with the same name in different rules need not be bound to the same entity. Other example rules with a more realistic structure allowing for commentaries and uncertainty, where presented in Figs. 1, 2 and 3 of Chapter 1.4. For an account of uncertainty, see Chapter 10.

Example 18: Rules

[Rule 1]
IF activity (X, employee) THEN activity (X, dependent-worker)

[Rule 2]
IF activity (X, retired) THEN activity (X, dependent-worker)

[Rule 3]
IF has-spouse (X, dependent) AND exemption (dependent-spouse, Amount) THEN taxpayer-exemption (X, dependent-spouse, Amount)

[Rule 4]
IF has-children (X, dependent, Number) AND exemption (dependent-child, 48000) AND Amount = Number * 48000
THEN taxpayer-exemption (X, dependent-children, Amount)

[Rule 5]
IF has-relatives (X, dependent, Number) AND exemption (dependent-relative, 96000) AND Amount = Number * 96000
THEN taxpayer-exemption (X, dependent-relatives, Amount)

[Rule 6]
IF activity (X, dependent-worker) AND taxable-income (X, Amount) AND Amount > 11000000
THEN taxpayer-exemption (X, dependent-work, 552000)

[Rule 7]
IF activity (X, dependent-worker) AND taxable-income (X, Amount) AND Amount ≤ 11000000
THEN taxpayer-exemption (X, dependent-work, 732000)

[Rule 8]
IF activity (X, Y) AND Y ≠ dependent-worker
THEN taxpayer-exemption (X, dependent-work, 0)

(. other exemptions are provided for low-income independent-workers, but they will not be listed in this sample knowledge base .)

[Rule 9]
IF taxpayer-exemption (X, dependent-spouse, A) AND taxpayer-exemption (X, dependent-children, B) AND taxpayer-exemption (X, dependent-relatives, C) AND taxpayer-exemption (X, dependent-work, E)
AND Result = A + B + C + D + E
THEN tax-exemptions (X, Result).

[Rule 10]
IF net-taxes (X, Amount) AND Amount ≤ 0
THEN must-not-file-return (X).

[Rule 11]
IF gross-taxes (X, Amount) AND tax-exemptions (X, Ex-amount) AND Result = Amount - Ex-amount
THEN net-taxes (X, Result).

■

Example 19: Firing a rule

Consider Rule 1:

IF activity (X, employee) THEN activity (X, dependent-worker)

Its premise consists of just one fact, "activity (X, employee)". "X" is a variable, while "employee" is a constant. For the premise of the rule to be satisfied, there must be in the knowledge base at least a fact of the form:

activity (..., employee)

where the first argument of the predicate can be any entity (i.e. constant).

The fact collection in Example 17, Section 6.2 above effectively contains such a fact:

activity (mr.x, employee)

Then the premise of [Rule 1] is satisfied if the variable X stands for mr.x. The rule is fired, the result being that the system believes the rule conclusion:

activity (mr.x, employee)

The scope of a variable is the rule itself: while the variable "X" in the conclusion of Rule 1 must stand for the same object as the variable "X" in the premise of the same rule, the object the variable "X" stands for in, say, Rule 4, is unspecified. ■

3.6.4 Rules as a knowledge representation formalism

From a knowledge representation viewpoint, rules support a representation of the environment as a collection of elementary and self-contained pieces (called "chunks") of knowledge.

A rule is self-contained in the sense that all preconditions for the applicability of a rule are coded locally in the rule left-hand side. In a given context, the applicability of a rule can be assessed simply by comparing its condition part to the state of the system, hence independently from the other rules in the knowledge base. This also implies that rules in a knowledge base must be correct (i.e. represent practically useful <condition> <action> pairs) on their own, independently from which other rules are present. The attachment to the rule itself of rule application conditions is the basis for modularity in rule-based systems. Modularity suggests that a knowledge base be seen as an unstructured collection of facts and rules: many rule-based languages (such as OPS5, see [Browston et al., 1985]), support this view. This approach to modularity is somewhat debated. However, one clear advantage is that it makes it possible to add/remove rules and facts to/from the knowledge base without affecting other rules; this in turns is again the prerequisite for the incremental development of programs, a feature which is of paramount importance in AI programming (see also Sections 1.2 and 5.6).

A rule must be elementary from the point of view of the problem domain features, in order to achieve the desired granularity (i.e. level of detail in representing knowledge). If rules were too specific, then their condition parts would become complicated, their applicability would narrow down, their number would increase (in the limit case, one rule for each possible configuration of the problem domain), and finally they would require heavy upgrades in the case of a change in the problem state definition. Moreover, complicated rules are not easily readable. If rules were too generic, e.g. rules coding the background principles of the economic theory, then probably only a small set of rules would be required, but at the expense of an increased reasoning effort for bridging the gap between the very abstract principles, their instantiation and interplay with the environment. Beside inefficiencies, such an approach violates the spirit of rule-based representations, which is not that of capturing the basic axioms ruling the domain, but rather the first-hand, rule-of-thumb experience of top-performing professionals.

3.6.5 Applications of rule-based representation

The rule-based formalism described in Sections 6.2 and 6.3 above, is flexible enough to make it possible to represent naturally the knowledge in several domains. In the following, four such domains are considered: representing knowledge about actions, logic-based reasoning, data analysis and classification, stimulus-reaction models.

1. Representing knowledge about actions

Knowledge about actions basically consists in specifying the correct preconditions and postconditions to an action. Preconditions are constraints on the environment which must be satisfied for an action to be executable. Preconditions must be tested before performing the action. Postconditions are modifications to the environment caused by the execution of an action. From the viewpoint of an observer of the environment, an action is accomplished when all its modifications have taken place. Postconditions must be enforced after the successful termination of an action.

Using rules for representing actions, preconditions account for the left-hand sides of the rules, while postconditions fit the right-hand sides.

Example 20: Preconditions as rule premises

Assume that knowledge about the action "sell an amount x of the stock XYZ at time t on the stock market z" must be represented.

One precondition is that the seller holds at least an amount x of stock at time t (or, for the sake of completeness, enough assets to satisfy margins requirements for an uncovered position). Another precondition is that the actor be willing to sell at the current price in the stock market (it is assumed that the amount sold can be small, and that the stock be liquid).

There are essentially two postconditions to this action: first of all, the agent's long position on stock XYZ must be reduced by the amount sold; second, the agent's money balance must be increased by the sale income. Under the assumption of small trade amounts, the current price on the stock market can be considered unchanged at the end of the transaction and needs not be included as a postcondition. The rule is coded as follows:

```
IF (amount of XYZ is y) AND (sell (amount of XYZ is x)) AND (sell (price of XYZ is w)) AND
   (price of XYZ is j) AND (y > x) AND (j > w)

      THEN  retract (sell (amount of XYZ is x))
            retract (sell (price of XYZ is w)
            retract (amount of XYZ is y),
            assert (amount of XYZ is (y - X)),
            retract (amount of my-balance is z),
            assert (amount of my-balance is z + (x * w)).
```

Interpretation: IF the amount of stock XYZ held is y and there is a desire to sell an amount x of stock XYZ at price w and the current stock market price is j, and j is larger than w, and y is larger than x, THEN (unexpressed: perform the sell) adjust the amount held, adjust the money balance and remove the sell goal and related information.

j, x, y, w, z are variables whose values are retrieved from the facts in the knowledge base.

"retract" and "assert" are primitives of the rule-based languages for respectively removing/adding facts in the knowledge base. "retract" is used to prevent, "assert" to enable the firing of rules.

Given a knowledge base with the following facts:

```
(amount of XYZ is 1000)
(sell (amount of XYZ is 200))
(sell (price of XYZ is 2.5$))
```

(price of XYZ is 2.6$)
(amount of my-balance is 760$)

then the rule fires since all its conditions are satisfied. By comparison with the facts, variables are assigned the following values:

y = 1000, x = 200, w = 2.5, j = 2.6, z = 760.

Firing the rule results in the new system state:

(amount of XYZ is 800)
(price of XYZ is 2.6$)
(amount of my-balance is 1280$)

Note that, since the fact assessing the desire to sell has been retracted from the knowledge base, the rule at the beginning of this example cannot be fired again, until other rules "assert" again a sale plan. ■

Preconditions and postconditions (together with timing and possibly uncertainty) are what is basically needed to simulate the effects of a strategy over the environment. The actual actions can either be simply omitted (as in the above example), or enclosed at the beginning of the conclusion part of the rule as calls to an external program (e.g. for computer trading).

2. Theorem proving

A common pattern of logic inference is "modus ponens" (see Section 5.4), in which:

A is true
If A is true, then B is true
follows: B is true.

Assume that A denotes the left-hand side of a rule. If the state of the system is such that it is satisfied (is true), then the rule can be fired, and B (an assertion) can be added to the knowledge base. By restricting the allowable contents in the condition and action parts of the rules, it is then possible to use rules as implications (see Section 5.3), and the firing mechanism as modus ponens. Hence, rule-based systems can be written to act as theorem provers. Prolog (see Chapter 4.4) is such an example.

3. Data analysis and classification

Data analysis is the process of formulating explanatory hypotheses about the observed behavior of a set of indicators/measurements. Here, the occurrence of known patterns in the data triggers the formulation of one or more explanatory hypotheses. In a rule-based paradigm, knowledge for data classification is captured according to the scheme:

IF <pattern> THEN <hypotheses>.

A special case of recognizing given patterns among a set of data is the classification problem, in which an individual, described through a set of features, must be assigned to a class of individuals, again characterized through a set of feature values. Knowledge about classification can be captured by rules following the scheme:

IF <features> THEN <class>.

where <features> should be a specification of sufficient conditions for concluding the membership to the class mentioned in the right-hand side; it is not mandatory that those conditions be both necessary and sufficient, although by doing so the reasoning efficiency can be improved. Reasoning about data analysis and classification is typically affected with uncertainty, due to several factors, including noise in the data, incompleteness in the available information (i.e. the left-hand side cannot be fully satisfied), uncertain characterization of patterns or classes (i.e. the conditions are not sufficient), etc. For a more specific presentation for this same kind of reasoning see Section 7.8.

4. Stimulus-action

In this paradigm, knowledge is expressed as a set of stimulus-action pairs, in which a set of actions is associated to a given pattern in the data:

IF <pattern> THEN <action>

This paradigm is similar to both the action representation formalism in point 1. above and the data analysis formalism in point 3. above, except that the emphasis is not so much on the logical organization of actions (point 1.) nor on the interpretation of data (point 3.), but rather on the monitoring of the environment for detecting anomalous configurations. One example of a typical application is the implementation of complex alarms, whose activation is not only threshold-sensitive, but also depends on the behavior of the parameter under control and of related parameters.

3.6.6 Reasoning with rules

A very appealing feature of rule-based systems is reasoning by chaining rules, a method which, in many circumstances, provides similar results to humans developing lines of reasoning while solving problems ([Newell and Simon, 1972]). Besides any psychological consideration, such a feature is attractive whenever systems must heavily interact with the users.

Rule chains are caused by the fact that the execution of the conclusion part of a rule modifies the state of the problem so that the premises of different rules are satisfied; one of them is in turn fired, causing other changes in the set of facts, which in turn enable a different rule to fire, and so on, until either a desired state has been generated, or no rules exist in the knowledge base whose premises are satisfied by the reached state. This technique of chaining is called forward chaining, since the computer agent moves through rule application from its current state toward a goal state (in the above case, the state containing the fact "must-not-file-return (mr.x)").

Example 21: Forward chaining of rules

From the knowledge base in the Examples 17 and 18, Sections 6.2 and 6.3, the following chain can be used to reach the conclusion that "mr.x" should not file the tax return:

STEP 1	The initial set of facts (state S1) satisfies the preconditions of Rule 1. Applying it, it is concluded that: activity (mr.x, dependent-worker). The new state S2 consists of all facts in S1 plus: activity (mr.x, dependent-worker).
STEP 2	S2 satisfies the preconditions of Rule 7. Applying it, it is concluded that: taxpayer-exemption (mr.x, dependent-work, 732000). The new state S3 is S2 plus: taxpayer-exemption (mr.x, dependent-work, 732000).
STEP 3	S3 satisfies the preconditions of Rule 4. Applying it, it is concluded that: taxpayer-exemption (mr.x, dependent-children, 96000). The new state S4 is S3 plus: taxpayer-exemption (mr.x, dependent-children, 96000).
STEP 4	S4 satisfies the preconditions of Rule 3. Applying it, it is concluded that: taxpayer-exemption (mr.x, dependent-spouse, 552000). The new state S5 is S4 plus: taxpayer-exemption (mr.x, dependent-spouse, 552000).
STEP 5	S5 satisfies the preconditions of Rule 5. Applying it, it is concluded that: taxpayer-exemption (mr.x, dependent-relatives, 0). The new state S6 is S5 plus: taxpayer-exemption (mr.x, dependent-relatives, 0).
STEP 6	S6 satisfies the preconditions of Rule 9.

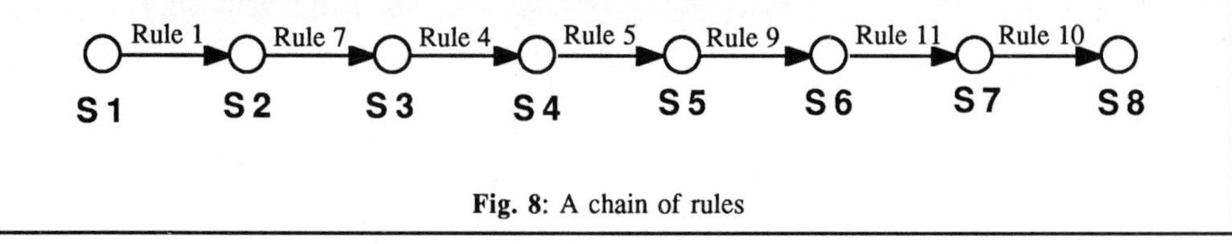

Fig. 8: A chain of rules

Applying it, it is concluded that: tax-exemptions (mr.x, 1380000).
The new state S7 is S6 plus: tax-exemptions (mr.x, 1380000).

STEP 7 S7 satisfies the preconditions of Rule 11.
Applying it, it is concluded that: net-taxes (mr.x, 0).
The new state S8 is S7 plus: net-taxes (mr.x, 0).

STEP 8 S8 satisfies the preconditions of Rule 10.
Applying it, it is concluded that: must-not-file-return (mr.x).

■

The dynamics implicit in the knowledge base of a rule-based system can be pictured using graphs and trees (see Section 3 for an introduction to graphs and trees): states (i.e. collections of facts) are represented as nodes, and rules as directed arcs (allowable transitions between states). A node "A" is the father of a node "B" if there is a rule whose premises are satisfied in state "A" and whose actions modify the state "A" into the state "B". With this representation, lines of reasoning are represented as paths in a graph. The task of reaching a desired state is then again a problem of path finding.

Fig. 8 shows a simple graph-representation of the above reasoning line (links are labeled with the rule numbers as in Example 18, Section 6.3 above).

Fig. 9 shows a graph in which all possible chains of length 3 (i.e. all chaining of 3 rules) in the described knowledge base are pictured. The number of the children of a node is equal to the number of rules which can be fired in the state represented by that node. As is clear from Fig. 9, even in the most simple cases the number of possible chains is very large (this is another instance of the problem of combinatorial explosion, introduced in Section 5.11); often, in real-world applications, only a few of them lead to the desired conclusion.

Alternatively, it is also possible for the computer agent to devise a (partial) description of a desired state, and then to search for a set of one or more rules whose conclusions enforce that state. If such rules can be found, then the problem shifts to finding another set of rules whose conclusions force a state, satisfying the premises of at least one of the rules previously found. This process can be repeated until either the current state of the world is derived, or no rules are found whose conclusions enforce a given state. This chaining method is called backward chaining, since the computer agent moves through rule application from the desired state back to the current state.

Example 22: Backward chaining

The same conclusion reached through the line of reasoning in Fig. 4 can be found by reasoning "the other way around" (numbers in the left column refer to tasks):

0 To show: "must-not-file-return (mr.x)", look for either a fact, or a rule concluding it. Rule 10 is such a rule. The conclusion can be asserted if the premises of Rule 10 are true. Hence the next step is to show that: "net-taxes (mr.x, Amount) AND Amount $\leq$ 0" is true, i.e. that:

- "net-taxes (mr.x, Amount)" is true (TASK 1)
- "Amount $\leq$ 0" is true (TASK 2).

1 To show: net-taxes (mr.x, Amount), look for either a fact, or a rule concluding it. Rule 11 is such a rule. The conclusion can asserted if the premises of Rule 11 are true. Hence the next step is to show that:

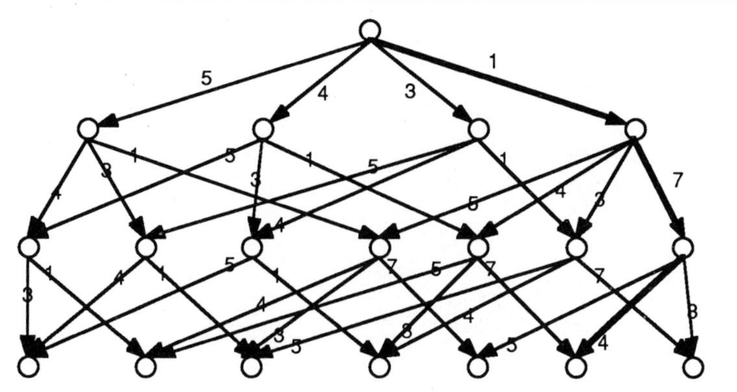

Fig. 9: All possible chains of three rules (link numbers refer to rule numbers in Example 18, Section 3.6.3)

- "gross-taxes (mr.x, Amount)" is true (TASK 1.1)
- "tax-exemptions (mr.x, Ex-amount)" is true (TASK 1.2)
- "Result = Amount - Ex-amount" is true (TASK 1.3).

1.1 To show: gross-taxes (mr.x, Amount), look for either a fact, or a rule concluding it. There is such a fact: gross-taxes (mr.x, 1380000), i.e. Amount = 1380000.

1.2 To show: tax-exemptions (mr.x, Ex-amount), look for either a fact, or a rule concluding it. Rule 9 is such a Rule. The conclusion can asserted if the premises of Rule 9 are true. Hence the next step is to show that:

- "taxpayer-exemption (mr.x, dependent-spouse, A)" is true (TASK 1.2.1)
- "taxpayer-exemption (mr.x, dependent-children, B)" is true (TASK 1.2.2)
- "taxpayer-exemption (mr.x, dependent-relatives, C)" is true (TASK 1.2.3)
- "taxpayer-exemption (mr.x, dependent-work, E)" is true (TASK 1.2.4)
- "Result = A + B + C + D + E" is true (TASK 1.2.5).

1.2.1 To show: taxpayer-exemption (mr.x, dependent-spouse, A), look for either a fact, or a rule concluding it. Rule 3 is such a Rule. The conclusion can asserted if the premises of Rule 3 are true. Hence the next step is to show that:

- "has-spouse (mr.x, dependent)" is true (TASK 1.2.1.1)
- "exemption (dependent-spouse, Amount)" is true (TASK 1.2.1.2)

1.2.1.1 To show: has-spouse (mr.x, dependent), look for either a fact, or a rule concluding it. There is such a fact, so this task is accomplished.

1.2.1.2 To show: exemption (dependent-spouse, Amount), look for either a fact, or a rule concluding it. There is such a fact: exemption (dependent-spouse, 552000), i.e. Amount = 552000.

1.2.1 Since all subtasks have been accomplished (i.e. all premises satisfied), the conclusion can be asserted: taxpayer-exemption (mr.x, dependent-spouse, 552000).

1.2.2 To show: taxpayer-exemption (mr.x, dependent-children, B), look for either a fact, or a rule concluding it. Rule 4 is such a Rule. The conclusion can asserted if the premises of Rule 4 are true. By the same method used for task 1.2.1, it can be shown that all premises are satisfied. Hence the conclusion can be asserted: taxpayer-exemption (mr.x, dependent-children, 96000).

1.2.3 To show: taxpayer-exemption (mr.x, dependent-relatives, C), look for either a fact, or a rule concluding it. Rule 5 is such a Rule. The conclusion can asserted if the premises of Rule 5 are true. By the same method used for task 1.2.1, it can be shown that all premises are satisfied. Hence the conclusion can be asserted: taxpayer-exemption (mr.x, dependent-relatives, 0).

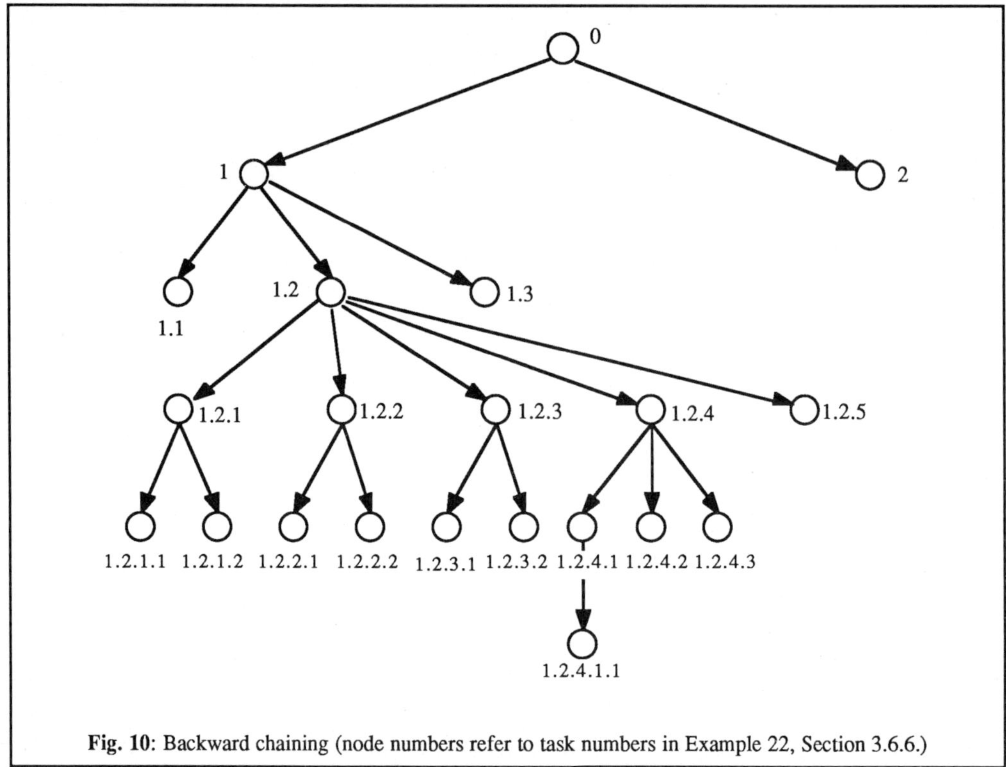

Fig. 10: Backward chaining (node numbers refer to task numbers in Example 22, Section 3.6.6.)

1.2.4 To show: taxpayer-exemption (mr.x, dependent-work, E), look for either a fact, or a rule concluding it. Contrary to the previous cases, there are three rules (from no. 6 to no. 8) concluding the asserted fact. Suppose that one first tries to use Rule 6. The conclusion can then be asserted if the premises of Rule 3 are true. Hence the next step is to show that:

- "activity (mr.x, dependent-worker)" is true (TASK 1.2.4.1)
- "taxable-income (mr.x, Amount)" is true (TASK 1.2.4.2)
- "Amount > 11000000" is true (TASK 1.2.4.3)

1.2.4.1 To show: activity (mr.x, dependent-worker), look for either a fact, or a rule concluding it. As in the previous case, there is more than one relevant rule no. 1 and no. 2) concluding the asserted fact. Suppose that Rule 1 is tried first. The conclusion can then be asserted if the premises of Rule 1 are true. Hence the next step is to show that:

- "activity (mr.x, employee)" is true (TASK 1.2.4.1.1)

1.2.4.1.1 To show: activity (mr.x, employee), look for either a fact, or a rule concluding it. There is such a fact, so this task is accomplished.

1.2.4.1 Since all subtasks have been accomplished (i.e. all premises satisfied), the conclusion can be asserted: activity (mr.x, dependent-worker).

1.2.4.2 To show: taxable-income (mr.x, Amount), look for either a fact, or a rule concluding it. There is such a fact: taxable-income (mr.x, 9984000), i.e. Amount = 9984000.

1.2.4.3 To show: Amount > 11000000, simply use the primitive comparison operation, with the value for Amount as retrieved in TASK 1.2.4.2. However it is false that 9984000 > 11000000. Therefore TASK 1.2.4.3 fails.

1.2.4 Attempt to show: taxpayer-exemption (mr.x, dependent-work, E) using Rule 6 has failed. The task however has not yet failed, since there were two other Rules with the desired conclusion. So one of them (e.g. Rule 7) is picked up. The new premises to satisfy are:

- "activity (mr.x, dependent-worker)" is true (TASK 1.2.4.1)
- "taxable-income (mr.x, Amount)" is true (TASK 1.2.4.2)
- "Amount < 11000000" is true (TASK 1.2.4.3)

The first two are again satisfied as indicated above in the corresponding tasks. Hence, Amount has the same value. Since the direction of equality has changed in the last premise, now TASK 1.2.4.3 is satisfied. Hence the conclusion: taxpayer-exemption (mr.x, dependent-work, 732000) can be asserted.

1.2.5 To show: Result = A + B + C + D, simply use the primitive definition for addition, and the values for the variables as computed by the subtasks:
Result = 552000 + 96000 + 0 + 732000 = 1380000.

1.2 Since all subtasks have been accomplished (i.e. all premises satisfied), the conclusion can be asserted: tax-exemptions (mr.x, 1380000).

1.3 To show: Result = Amount - Ex-amount, simply use the primitive definition for addition, and the values for the variables as computed by the subtasks 1.1 and 1.2:
Result = 1380000 - 1380000 = 0.

1 Since all subtasks have been accomplished (i.e. all premises satisfied), the conclusion can be asserted: net-taxes (mr.x, 0).

2 To show: Amount $\leq$ 0, simply use the primitive comparison operation, with the value for Amount as retrieved in TASK 1. The comparison is satisfied.

0 Since all subtasks have been accomplished (i.e. all premises satisfied), the conclusion can be asserted: must-not-file-return (mr.x).

■

Fig. 10 shows how backward chaining can be represented graphically as a tree. Each node in the tree is labeled with the corresponding task number in the above example. A task is solved if and only if all children of the associated node are solved. A leaf node is solved by a fact in the knowledge base (or by querying the user). Chapter 5 is completely dedicated to the problem of finding paths in graphs, i.e. of chaining.

3.6.7 The inference engine

Refer to Fig. 1, Section 1.2: facts and rules are the two components of the knowledge base box; this Section describes the knowledge manipulation box, which in the case of rule-based languages is called the *inference engine* . The inference engine is an algorithm (see Chapter 5) determining which rules are applicable to the given state and, in the case that more rules are enabled by the same state (i.e., there is a conflict), deciding which of them to fire (conflict resolution). Other tasks of the inference engine are to test the current state and stop the system when the desired final state has been reached or computational resources have been exceeded.

The inference engine automatically builds rule chains such as those introduced in Section 6.6 above, discards irrelevant chains, and tries to generate a chain (a path) between the current state and a desired state. Such a path is a solution to the problem in the sense that, if an agent applies the rules associated to the links in the path in the right order, he can modify its current situation into a situation he is more satisfied with.

To start a session about a specific problem with a production system, the user must then supply the initial state of the environment (i.e. a set of facts), as well as a specification of what is a satisfactory final state (also called a goal state). The goal can be specified by either (partially) describing the facts making up a satisfactory state, or by defining a set of constraints to be satisfied by an a priori unknown state. The inference engine tries to achieve a goal state by repeatedly applying rules to the current state. Since each rule causes a modification in the state, chances are that possibly a state satisfying the goal description will be generated. More in detail, the inference engine works in three steps:

1. Match: the right-hand sides of the rules are compared with the current state. Those rules whose condition parts match the current state, build up the conflict set

2. Select: one rule is selected for firing from the conflict set

3. Act: the rule is fired, causing some changes to the state

The cycle is repeated from step 1. with the new state, until a goal state is reached.

One problem of an inference engine as sketched in this section is that it works without exploiting control knowledge (see Section 1.7), i.e. expertise on how to solve classes of problems. In the following section, it is shown how this additional kind of knowledge can be captured within the frame of a rule-based representation.

3.6.8 Metarules

By metaknowledge is meant knowledge about knowledge. Many rule-based paradigms make it possible to include a certain amount of metaknowledge as a part of the rule definition (see the rule syntax introduced in Chapter 1.4.2). For instance, consider the following rule syntax:

IF <condition> THEN <action> RULE-SOURCE: <name>

enabling a rule to be associated to with its source (this information is often useful in the development phase). The rule author can be seen as a piece of metaknowledge, since it is knowledge about the rule (who suggested or wrote it), not about the domain.

The following example [Pau, 1989], shows another piece of metaknowledge useful in economic-oriented rule-based systems.

Example 23: Knowledge about economic theories

Many conclusions in economics depend on the theory adopted. This suggests labeling rules with the theory inspiring them:

IF <condition> THEN <conclusion/action> UNDER <theory>

IF imports to (B) from (A) are (increasing)
THEN currency (A) may increase over next (3) months
UNDER (theory is balance of payment equilibrium)

Here, the advantage of isolating the motivating theory from the other conditions in the rules left-hand side is to set a higher-level context in which sets of rules, instead of single rules, can be taken into account. This technique permits an efficiency similar to nested IFs in conventional programming languages:

IF theory = balance of payment equilibrium
THEN IF imports to (B) from (A) are (increasing)
        THEN currency (A) may increase over next (3) months

while preserving modularity among the single rules.

It is equivalent to a metaknowledge of the kind: "If the current theory is: balance of payment equilibrium, then the compatible rules are ..." ■

As metaknowledge gets more complex than the simple examples introduced above, it becomes less appropriate to represent it simply by making the rules syntax richer. Moreover, not all metaknowledge is rule-specific, as is the knowledge about each rule author or inspiring economic theory. Finally, the language of metaknowledge needs objects and relations such as "rule", "length of the condition part", "fire before", which are not part of the problem domain, but of the knowledge representation formalism itself. A kind of metaknowledge very important in knowledge-based system is control metaknowledge [Davis, 1980], i.e. knowledge about which piece of domain knowledge to use next in order to get closer to the problem solution. Control knowledge is important because it is critical to the efficient use of large amounts of knowledge, and hence to the solution of large problems. At the same time, it is knowledge related to the context of use of the rules, rather than to the single rules.

As shown in Section 6.7 above, the only way to embed control knowledge into a rule-based system is by coding a suitable algorithm into the "Select" step of the inference engine cycle. This implies that control knowledge is not explicit and accessible to the inference engine itself. From a human expert point of view, however, control knowledge captures domain-specific problem-solving strategies, also called heuristics (see Chapter 1.1 and Chapter 5.11), which are explicitly available. Exactly the same reasons supporting the use of an explicit knowledge representation language for domain knowledge (see Section 1.2), can be invoked to justify the use of a knowledge representation language for metaknowledge, and of problem-solving techniques for reasoning about metaknowledge.

Furthermore, in general it is desirable to have a single formalism for domain and metaknowledge. This design choice increases the expressive power of the language, since the metaknowledge can be seen in turn as the "object-level knowledge" for higher level knowledge: as an example, knowledge for selecting the most appropriate strategy among a set of competitive strategies can be represented as first-level metaknowledge of a knowledge base about strategies. The formalism being uniform, it is irrelevant that the knowledge about strategies is in turn metaknowledge with respect to the object-level knowledge. More generally, any number of metalevels can be implemented with no additional effort. A single formalism is also useful for increasing the notational efficiency of the representation language, since the knowledge support tools (e.g. editors, debuggers, knowledge acquisition and maintenance packages, etc.) developed for the object-level knowledge can be used with virtually no modification for the metalevel knowledge as well. In particular, it is possible to make use of the same interface and explanation facilities.

For the above reasons, metaknowledge is implemented as rules in rule-based systems. The data structures capturing metaknowledge are called metarules. Metarules have the same syntax as object-level rules, except that the language of metarules is extended to enable reference to the content of lower-level rules. The following example shows several kinds of control metaknowledge.

Example 24: Types of metaknowledge

1. Ordering metaknowledge

This kind of metaknowledge is used to explicitly order the firing of rules while trying to achieve a goal. It does so by specifying which subset of rules should be considered first, and which should be considered last. An example of a rule of this kind could be:

IF <the task is to find out deductible expenses>
THEN
<use first the rules referring to work-related expenses>
<use next the rules referring to other expenses>

Tax exemptions in most of the cases have to do with working activities; it would be surprising for the user to be asked for some exotic deductible expense before being asked how much he did pay for gasoline during the last year. Conversely, if the user's deductible expenses are all of the conventional type, he will exhaust his itemization without any need to know about, say, deductions to support sheep breeding in depressed areas (for an example of how ordering metaknowledge can be included in a Prolog program, see Example 57, Chapter 4.4.12).

2. Pruning metaknowledge

In some cases, it is possible completely to exclude a set of rules, since they are definitely not useful in given situations. So, for instance, in looking for exemptions for high-income taxpayers, it is a nonsense to consider family exemptions, because family exemptions are mostly suppressed for high-income individuals:

IF <the task is to reduce the tax amount>
  AND <the taxpayer's income is larger than ...>
THEN
  <all rules referring to the family status will not be useful>

3. Prototypical metaknowledge

The two above types of metaknowledge can be interpreted as defining a kind of reasoning triggered by prototypical situations. So, if one prototype has been recognized, certain rules can be postponed or suppressed, or the tax adviser could assume default values, and then direct its interaction according to the discrepancy between the expected and the returned value (see Section 7.8). Thus, it is easy for the tax adviser to form an expectation about the amount of deductible expenses for a given taxpayer, given his/her activity, family status and residence area. A mismatching of the expectation, could trigger a set of rules for validating the claimed deductions, or for taking into account less common items:

IF <current prototype = middle-class taxpayer>
  AND <deductions much larger than the expected default-deductions>
THEN
  <use first the rules for validating deductions>
  <set prototype = high-expenses tax payer>

■

Metarules in general address the important question of how to retrieve just the relevant (i.e. useful) knowledge for the current problem or subproblem, instead of all context-compatible knowledge. A common extension to metarules in this direction is knowledge base decomposition into rule-sets: a rule-set is a kind of small knowledge base containing only those rules relevant to the solution of a specific subproblem. The advantage of rule-sets is to break down the knowledge base, and therefore reduce the search time for the inference engine. So, for instance, rules in a tax adviser devoted to consistency checking over the final tax return form are definitely different from rules establishing the correct classification of a specific income, and can be easily put into separate knowledge bases.

3.6.9 Rules vs. procedural programming

Sometimes, rules can be viewed as IF - THEN statements in procedural programs (see Chapter 4.1.5). The latter, however, are always executed in a fixed order, pre-defined by the programmer; rules on the contrary do not explicitly transfer control amongst them, and their order in the knowledge base is therefore irrelevant.

Rules can also be viewed as procedures not called by name, but by pattern (i.e. when some preconditions are satisfied). The programmer is no longer responsible for putting the right subroutine call in the right place of the program, since the subroutine itself has coded inside it the conditions under which it should be active (this viewpoint is also useful for understanding procedural attachment in frame-based systems, see Section 7.3).

The real difference between the two paradigms is that conventional programs do not nearly exhibit the same level of modularity: data, operations and control are not separated in the traditional programming languages, and modifications to the problem representation (data and operators) or to the control strategy require heavy manipulation of the computer code. On the other side, since control information in a conventional program is passed from each statement to exactly one other (pre-defined) statement, conventional programs turn out to be very efficient, and do not suffer from the problem of combinatorial explosion.

3.6.10 Rules vs. logic

Logic and rule-based systems share modularity based on the independence of assertions. Rules in many rule-based systems are directly translatable to logic (although the rule format is generally more readable). Differences essentially consist of three points:

- rule-based systems are more oriented toward managing change: facts only describe the current situation of the objects in the world, and can be changed as a consequence of the actions of the problem-solver. Logic forces the view of a problem-solver as a theorem prover, deducing new beliefs from assumptions, whose truth is obviously not modified by the deductive activity: hence a primitive like "retract" (see Example 20, Section 3.6.5) is incompatible with the viewpoint of logic
- allowable data structures for facts and rules are a subset of those possible with logic (e.g. not all rule-based systems support lists, sets and other complex structures)
- rules are sometimes coupled with procedures, and in general most rule-based languages support procedural attachment to rules. This is generally not the case with logic

3.6.11 Concluding remarks

The above sections have highlighted several features of rule-based representation, the key ones being modularity (see Section 6.4), explicit knowledge, flexibility in accounting for procedural knowledge. However, rule-based systems also have weak points:

- a flat knowledge base of rules and facts is inadequate to represent the structured nature of many domains
- local context encoding in the rule premise is inefficient from the point of view of both storage requirements (possibly a long list of constraints over the domain must be encoded for each rule) and of retrieval of the relevant knowledge (the inference engine must in principle take into account every rule in the knowledge base)
- a knowledge base can generate a huge number of lines of reasoning: it is impossible for the programmer to be aware and to test all of them. There is no computationally acceptable method to prove that a rule-based system does not contain an invalid chain
- in some applications, more explicit ways of passing control among rules are needed. Pure rule-based systems do not allow a rule to call explicitly another rule, so this is generally achieved by having one rule assert a token which is in the premise of just another rule. By such a programming approach, however, the knowledge base becomes messy, and modularity is reduced

A relief to some of the above problems, is often found in combining rule-based representation with hierarchical representations (such as frame-based, see Section 7 below) for organizing rule premises into a taxonomy, or in using metarules for reducing search over the knowledge base.

3.7 Frames

3.7.1 Motivation

Both logic and rules (see Sections 5 resp. 6) force an organization of knowledge around primitive assertions, were each statement is essentially a relation among concepts or the specification of an action (rules); modularization is achieved by keeping those statements independent as long as possible, making it feasible in principle to add/delete/modify a single piece of knowledge without affecting the rest of the knowledge base.

However, objects in the environment (in the generic sense explained in Section 1.4) are naturally perceived as a complicated set of possibly interdependent attributes, called a pattern. Often the essence of an object does not lie in a single attribute-value pair, but in the fact that a specific group of attributes interact in a given way. It seems then natural to associate structured descriptions to objects in the environment, made up of those attributes which experience or theory have shown as relevant in a given problem domain (of course, other attributes might be relevant when dealing with the same object but in different circumstances, see the Example 25 Section 7.2 below).

Consequently, new formalisms have been proposed ([Minsky, 1975]), featuring a pattern- or object- (rather than assertion-) centered approach to knowledge representation. These formalisms, generally referred to as frame-based languages, share the following characteristics:

- the basic representation unit (called frame, unit or concept) is a collection of the features (attributes, physical properties etc.) relevant to the description of an object (see Section 7.2)
- representation units are organized by capturing relations among them, the most important being generality, by which frames are partially ordered into chains connecting more general entities to their specializations (see Section 7.5)

Because frame-based representation languages provide extensive support for organizing knowledge, and hence improve notational efficiency while preserving modularity, it is common to see hybrid knowledge representation paradigms being developed by incrementing rules or logic with frames [Intellicorp, 1988], [Brachman et al., 1983], [Aikins, 1983], [Hewitt et al., 1980]. In a rule-based system using frames, for instance, the knowledge that the current situation is a special case of a more general one may lead to the selection of plausible rules, even if no rule left-hand side explicitly matches it.

3.7.2 Frames, slots and facets

A *frame* is a data structure for storing and organizing pieces of knowledge. At the same time, the frame is also the representational unit. A knowledge base is a collection of frames. A frame corresponds to the description of either a specific object, or a concept encompassing many specific domain objects (e.g. the concept of income). In the first case, a frame it is called an *instance* ; in the latter, a *class* or a *concept* (see also Section 7.5). Attributes characterizing the frame are represented as *slots* .

Example 25: The concept of corporation

The concept of "corporation" may be defined to include specifications of:

name
legal status
state
county
nationality
partners
duration
board of directors
president
aggregate number of shares
registered agent

Of course, other descriptions are possible depending on the context: in screening corporations for good investment opportunities, relevant features would probably include the corporation main activity, its market share, equity and its distribution, management, financial data such as turnover, debt and key ratios, number of employees, etc. The "corporation" frame looks as follows:

```
CLASS corporation
      name:
      legal status:
```

state:
county:
nationality:
partners:
duration:
board of directors:
president:
aggregate number of shares:
registered agent:

where each indented identifier is the name of a slot. ■

The above frame does not represent a specific corporation, but rather collects the relevant features of any corporation from the viewpoint of the given problem domain: it is therefore labeled as a class. All of the slots in the above example had no values associated to them. According to the analogy suggested by the term "slot", a slot with no value is said to be empty. Similarly, the value associated to a slot is called the slot *filler*.

It is convenient for a frame slot to be in turn structured. Although the exact structure of a slot may vary among different frame-based systems, most of them admit at least the following properties (also called *facets* or aspects):

i. the value

ii. the value-restriction

iii. the cardinality

iv. other specific facets for associated procedures (see Section 7.3 below)

Fillers for all of the above facets, with the exception of iv., are again frames or collections of frames in the knowledge base. In fact, in an object-oriented paradigm, the only way to describe an object is to relate it to other objects, each of them accounting for a specific feature (suggested by the slot name) of the object to be described. While assertion-based representations focus on elementary statements which are true about the environment, object-oriented paradigms stress to importance of (structured) interconnections among domain concepts. By filling slots with other frames, such interconnections are made explicit and put into perspective. Furthermore, by having fillers defined in terms of the same classes or instances, slot values can be shared among objects. Finally, fillers being frames can be specialized to reflect the specialization of the concept associated to the frame: this point is clarified in Section 7.5 below.

Fillers for the value facet of a slot are any instances in the knowledge base. For example, all corporations are legally registered as such. The slot "legal status" in the above example can then be filled by the value "incorporated", assuming that in the knowledge base there is a concept for "incorporated" (if not, "incorporated" can simply be interpreted as an instance of the generic concept of string, but in this way the user has no further clues about what "incorporated" means).

The slot value-restriction is any expression denoting a set of objects, among which the filler(s) for the facet value must be chosen. So, the slot value restriction may be a class, and the slot value an instance of that class; or the slot value restriction may be a logical disjunction of several instances, and the slot value one of the disjuncts. For instance, the value for the "president" slot in the above example could be restricted to be an instance of the class "person", or better to an instance of the class "adult person", where in "adult person" the value of the "age" slot must be larger than, say, eighteen. Alternatively, a class "president" could be defined which, beside sharing the slots of the class "person" and the value restriction of the class "adult person", includes specific attributes, such as benefits, past experience, years-to-retirement, etc. Then the facet value of the "president" slot could be restricted to an instance of the "president" class.

Value restriction is a powerful method for generating new concepts from existing ones. For example, the class of "large corporations" can be derived from the more generic class "corporation" by adding a turnover slot and restricting its value to amounts larger than 10 million US$ (the number of employees may also be considered). In this case, the set of objects in the knowledge base to which the slot's value must belong is a collection of integer numbers, i.e. of instances of the class "integer number".

Finally, the cardinality facet constrains the number of values a slot may be filled with. For example, the cardinality of the slot "person" is one, since corporations only have one chairman. On the contrary, the "board" slot in the "corporation" class is an example of a slot with more values: its value restriction can be filled with "person", while its cardinality is set to the allowable number of people in a board (for instance, larger or equal to three). A slot whose cardinality includes zero may be left empty, without violating the essence of the concept being described. The following example shows again the "corporation" class together with the filled slots properties. This is the case of the "registered agent" slot.

Example 26: Filling the slots of the corporation class

```
CLASS corporation
        name
                value restriction: string
                cardinality: 1
        legal-status
                value: incorporated
        state
                value restriction: a US-state
                cardinality: 1
        county
                value restriction: geographic-entity
                cardinality: 1
        nationality:
                value restriction: one of ("domestic", "foreign")
                cardinality: 1
        partners
                value restriction: a person
                cardinality: ≥ 3
        duration:
                value restriction: one of ("perpetual", "limited")
                cardinality: 1
        board of directors
                value restriction: a person
                cardinality: ≥ 3
        president
                value restriction: a person
                cardinality: 1
        aggregate number of shares
                value restriction: a share
                cardinality: > 0
        registered agent
                value restriction: a person
                cardinality: 0...1
```

■

Frames as discussed in this section provide a structure for organizing relationships among domain objects, and hence for expressing beliefs about a problem domain.

The difference with a conventional set of beliefs (see Section 5.2) is that frames add contexts to the beliefs, suggesting when their use is appropriate. For instance, from the "corporation" frames the system knows that "president" is an appropriate attribute when describing a corporation, and would possibly query the user (or a database) about it. However, this attribute is not appropriate when describing a sole-proprietorship, and would therefore not be included in its frame. Furthermore, "president" may make sense, but embody slightly different relevant features, when used in connection with, say, a state. The appropriate definition of president being local to each context (i.e. frame), the system correctly would not consider president when reasoning about a sole proprietorship, and would not ask the same questions when reasoning about a corporation and a state.

3.7.3 Procedural attachment

Most frame-based systems have facilities for integrating procedures into frames, for instance by associating them to the frame itself or to one or more facets. A procedure corresponds roughly to a piece of program in a conventional programming language (such as COBOL or FORTRAN), or, in a few systems, in a rule-based formalism [Aikins, 1983].

Motivations for admitting procedures within frames are:

- to define monitors or demons, i.e. procedures which are automatically run by the system when some changes in the data occur [Bobrow and Winograd, 1977]. Demons are a way to convey control knowledge, since they essentially prescribe what to do next (see the examples at the end of this Section)
- to define methods for carrying out operations on a given object, i.e. procedures which are explicitly invoked when some computation is needed (see Chapter 4.5, Object-Oriented Programming)
- to define constraints among slots or frames. Most frame-based knowledge representation languages lack an explicit formalism for defining complex constraints among parts of the system, to be enforced as soon as enough data become available [Fikes, 1981]. As shown by the two examples below, procedures can be used to this purpose
- to express knowledge about processes whose description in terms of declarative knowledge could be difficult (e.g. setting up a communication line)
- to improve efficiency, by coding purposely in a program knowledge which could be otherwise deduced from the frames represented [Winograd, 1975]

Consistently with knowledge decomposition based on domain objects, procedures relevant to operate on a given object are associated (attached) to the frame representing it, or to one or more slots in said frame. Procedures can then be triggered (called for execution) either when given conditions are satisfied, or whenever other parts of the system (or the user) ask the frame to start a process described procedurally: in the first case one speaks of pattern-directed execution, a technique already met in Section 6.6.

Conventional programming languages are based on an opposite view about modularization, with procedures as the representational units, and within them different behaviors according to the objects they must operate on (i.e. according to the arguments). The calling mechanisms are different as well: in a conventional programming language, procedures are called by their name at a specific execution step indicated by the programmer; in frame-based languages (as well as in rule-based languages) they are automatically invoked when their invocation conditions match the current program status.

The following examples show two typical procedures used in frame-based systems. They are interesting because the result of using them is to turn frames into active data, i.e. data reacting to changes in other parts of the system.

Example 27: "If-needed" facet

A procedure is typically attached to the "if-needed" facet of slots, to be invoked whenever the system tries to retrieve a value from an empty slot. The procedure implements a specific process for computing the slot's value, either from related values in the knowledge base, or by querying external sources. For instance, an "if-needed" procedure associated to a slot "amount-to-be-paid" could compute the desired slot value by retrieving from other slots the taxable income and the applicable rate, perform the multiplication, and fill the result into the "amount-to-be-paid" slot. ■

Example 28: "When-changed" facet

Sometimes it is useful to define a facet "when-changed", to be filled by a procedure specifying a computation which is run whenever the slot value is modified by either the system or the user. For instance, a "when-changed" procedure could be associated to the slot "taxable income" of the frame describing the profile of a specific tax payer. As this amount is changed, the procedure first checks if the relevant tax rate is still the same, then recomputes the value of the slot "amount-to-be-paid". Hence, "when-changed" procedures are often used for maintaining information in the knowledge base in a consistent state. Such procedures are also useful as monitors: e.g. in many frame-based commercial systems, "when-changed" procedures update charts on the screen whenever the value of the variables being plotted changes. This is an attractive feature for the design of friendly, real-time user interfaces. ■

Example 29: Attaching procedures to the "revenue" frame

Consider the frame "revenue", describing a generic revenue, whose definition includes two if-needed procedures:

```
CLASS revenue
        IS-A:
        type:
                value restriction: transaction
        amount:
                value restriction: instance of (number ≥ 0)
        date:
                value restriction: instance of (date)
        source:
                value restriction: person or institution
        fiscal declaration:
                value restriction: one of (true, false)
                if needed: fill with (self.type).fiscal declaration
                -- "self.type" retrieves the value of the type slot in this frame. Such a value is
                  a frame whose "type" slot contains the value to be copied.
        reference:
                value restriction: legal-document
                --put here reference to invoices, legacies etc.
                if needed:
                - put here a query to the appropriate database
        remarks:
                value restriction: text
                --a text with observations
```

■

3.7.4 Interpretations of frames

An important question is: what does a frame exactly represent ? Depending on how frames are used in the system, two basic answers are possible [Brachman, 1983]:

1. Definitions

A class can be formally defined through a list of attributes (and attributes properties), objects belonging to the class must comply with. More precisely, the collection of attributes is such that it contains all attributes shared by objects of that class (so called necessary attributes), and all attributes which, if possessed by an object, would imply its membership to that class (so called sufficient attributes). From another point of view, such frames can be seen as implicitly defining a set of individuals [Stefik, 1979].

Formal definitions are typical of artificial concepts, as are many of those met in legal reasoning (not all of them: e.g. public interest, prevalent activity, etc.). So, for instance, it is precisely defined what a taxpayer is. Knowing that a person is a taxpayer, one can infer a set of attributes and restrictions it must comply with; conversely, given a person, there exists a set of attributes and restrictions to be checked such that, if satisfied, one can definitely conclude that the person in question is a taxpayer.

2. Prototypes

The problem with the above clear-cut definitions is that they are not available for most natural concepts humans deal with. For instance, it is not possible to represent in this way the concept of middle-class taxpayer. This is not really a definition, rather an abstraction a tax adviser might find useful in reasoning about his clients: the set of features characterizing members of this class is not well established, restrictions might be violated in special cases, but it is still important to be able to represent this idea as a frame.

Then the collection of slots in the middle-class taxpayer frame has rather the meaning of typical attributes and typical values restrictions which hold for a typical representative of the middle-class taxpayer group. The typical individual may not exist in reality, and only be an abstraction refined through experience; or it may be a peculiar individual, which is used as model for his class.

However, the important point is that with this interpretation it is no longer possible, knowing that an individual is a middle-class taxpayer, to infer which are his attributes and his attributes values, but only that typically he would share (part of) the attributes and values in the class definition. Conversely, knowing the frame representing an individual, it is no longer possible to infer by definition its membership to the class, but only to compare the individual and the class frames for similarities and differences and, depending on the result of the comparison, derive an estimate of the compatibility between the two concepts. The domain expert will help point out those attributes and values critical in the comparison, and those less important. In the AI literature, the term stereotype is often found: stereotypes are prototypical frames representing situations.

Example 30: A prototype of the middle-class tax payer

```
CLASS middle-class-taxpayer
        total income:
                value restriction: number ≥20000 US$ and ≤50000 US$
        status:
                value: married
        children:
                value restriction: umber ≥1 and ≤3
        houses:
                value restriction: number ≤ 2
        car:
                value restriction: number ≤ 2
```

■

3.7.5 Taxonomies

In representing knowledge about a domain, it often happens to face definitions/assertions like:

"a deductible expense is an expense which can be subtracted from the taxable income"

"Mr. Jones is a taxpayer".

Both of the above pieces of knowledge, although different in several respects [Brachman et al., 1983], share the use of generality (or specialization) as a way to relate knowledge to other knowledge. In the first case, the term "deductible expense" is defined relying on the definition of the more general term "expense". In the second case, Mr. Jones, a specific individual, is asserted to be one of the domain objects sharing the property of being taxpayers.

Generality/specialization relations are so useful, because concepts related through them exhibit common features. For example, the frame for "deductible expense" and "expense" can be expected to have common features (for instance, a key common attribute of any expense is its amount). Similarly, if it is known that "Mr. Jones is a taxpayer", then the attributes in the "taxpayer" frame can be assumed to be true of Mr. Jones as well. Assume taxpayers have monetary incomes larger than a floor amount: then the above assertion indirectly expresses the fact that Mr. Jones has as well a monetary income larger than the floor amount.

An organization of entities according to generality (or specialization) is called a taxonomy. Automatically, such an organization forces the distinction already introduced in Section 7.2 above between classes or concepts, representing collections of objects (see Section 7.4 above), and instances, standing for specific objects in the domain: while it does make sense to specialize a class into, say, a subclass (e.g. "expense", "deductible expense"), the specialization of instances is meaningless: instances are the most specific entities in a taxonomy.

Correspondingly, two different kinds of taxonomic links are distinguished:

- specialization links relate classes to subclasses (more specific concepts): it must account for the possibility that a sub-concept be defined by a set of attributes, attribute properties and/or procedural attachments which is different (usually, more focussed) from the one defining the concept (see also the Example 31 below)
- instantiation links relate classes to instances: by the very nature of instances, instantiation only admits filling or modification of slot values, while keeping unchanged the set of slots, their value restrictions and procedural attachments

Example 31: Specialization

The concept "deductible expense" differs from the more general concept "expense" because:

- deductible expenses belong to specific fields in the tax form;
- deductible expenses can be used to reduce the taxable income;
- there are usually restrictions on the maximum deduction for given expenses.

The first difference involves a change in the procedure attached to the frame taking care of displaying part of the frame content at the appropriate place inside an electronic tax form on the screen. The second difference involves the addition of a new procedure for computing the difference. Finally, deductible expenses need possibly two slots for holding the deductible amount with and without itemizations. ■

In order to make more generic concepts accessible from the most specific ones, frame-based systems define a built-in slot, called "is-a" or "superclasses" or similar in the case of classes, and "instance-of" in the case of instances, whose values are the names of the classes of which the current frame is a specialization: such classes are called superclasses.

Example 32: A taxonomy

In a knowledge base dealing with fiscal regulations, a prize can be seen as a special case of deductible income; deductible income is in turn a special case of income; income is in turn a special case of a generic revenue, etc. This example shows how generality relations are captured in a frame-based system. The first frame to be defined is the most general one, "revenue":

```
CLASS revenue
        IS-A:
        type:
                value restriction: transaction
        amount:
                value restriction: instance of (number ≥ 0)
        date:
```

```
                value restriction: instance of (date)
        source:
                value restriction: person or institution
        fiscal declaration:
                value restriction: one of (true, false)
                if needed:
        reference:
                value restriction: legal-document
                if needed:
        remarks:
                value restriction: text
```

"income" is a "revenue" with a compulsory fiscal declaration required. As a consequence, a new attribute called "taxable" is added to the concept, while the value of the slot "fiscal declaration" is set to "true":

```
CLASS income
        IS-A: revenue
        type:
                value restriction: transaction
        amount:
                value restriction: instance of (number ≥ 0)
        date:
                value restriction: instance of (date)
        source:
                value restriction: person or institution
        fiscal declaration:
                value: true
        taxable:
                value restriction: one of ("yes", "no", "special")
        reference:
                value restriction: legal-document
                if needed:
        remarks:
                value restriction: text
```

A further specialization step leads to the concept of deductible-income:

```
CLASS deductible-income
        IS-A: income
        type:
                value restriction: transaction
        amount:
                value restriction: instance of (number ≥ 0)
        date:
                value restriction: instance of (date)
        source:
                value restriction: person or institution
        fiscal declaration:
                value: true
        taxable:
                value: "no"
        reference:
                value restriction: legal-document
                if needed:
        remarks:
                value restriction: text
```

A prize is a kind of deductible income, since prizes are (in general) not taxed:

```
CLASS prize
        IS-A: deductible income
```

```
        type:
                value restriction: transaction
        amount:
                value restriction: instance of (number ≥ 0)
        date:
                value restriction: instance of (date)
        source:
                value restriction: person or institution
        fiscal declaration:
                value: true
        taxable:
                value: "no"
        reference:
                value restriction: legal-document
                if needed:
        remarks:
                value restriction: text
```

Finally, prize XYZ is a specific prize

```
INSTANCE XYZ
        INSTANCE-OF: prize
        type:
                value: donation
        amount:
                value: 100000
        date:
                value: 1/1/90
        source:
                value: Award Inc.
        fiscal declaration:
                value: true
        taxable:
                value: "no"
        reference:
                value: law nr. 757
        remarks:
                value: "second edition"
```

■

3.7.6 Hierarchical networks

The structure of a frame knowledge base with a generality relation can be interpreted as a directed, acyclic graph (see Section 3.2).

Fig. 11 shows such a network for classifying expenses (another similar figure is Fig. 17, Chapter 4.5, showing a taxonomy for accounts receivable): nodes correspond to frames, links to generality relations. There are no arrowheads on the links, since it is assumed that they connect subclasses (or instances) to their superclasses and vice-versa. Links are labeled with "is-a" if they connect two classes, "instance-of" if they connect an instance to a class. The key property of the generality relation making it so useful is transitivity, i.e.:

if concept A is more general (specific) than concept B

and concept B is more general (specific) than concept C

then it is also true that concept A is more general (specific) than concept C.

This means that it is possible to give a useful interpretation to paths of "is-a" links: one node is a specialization of another node if there exists a path from the first to the second; correspondingly, path finding algorithms can be seen as implementing taxonomic reasoning, since they can be used

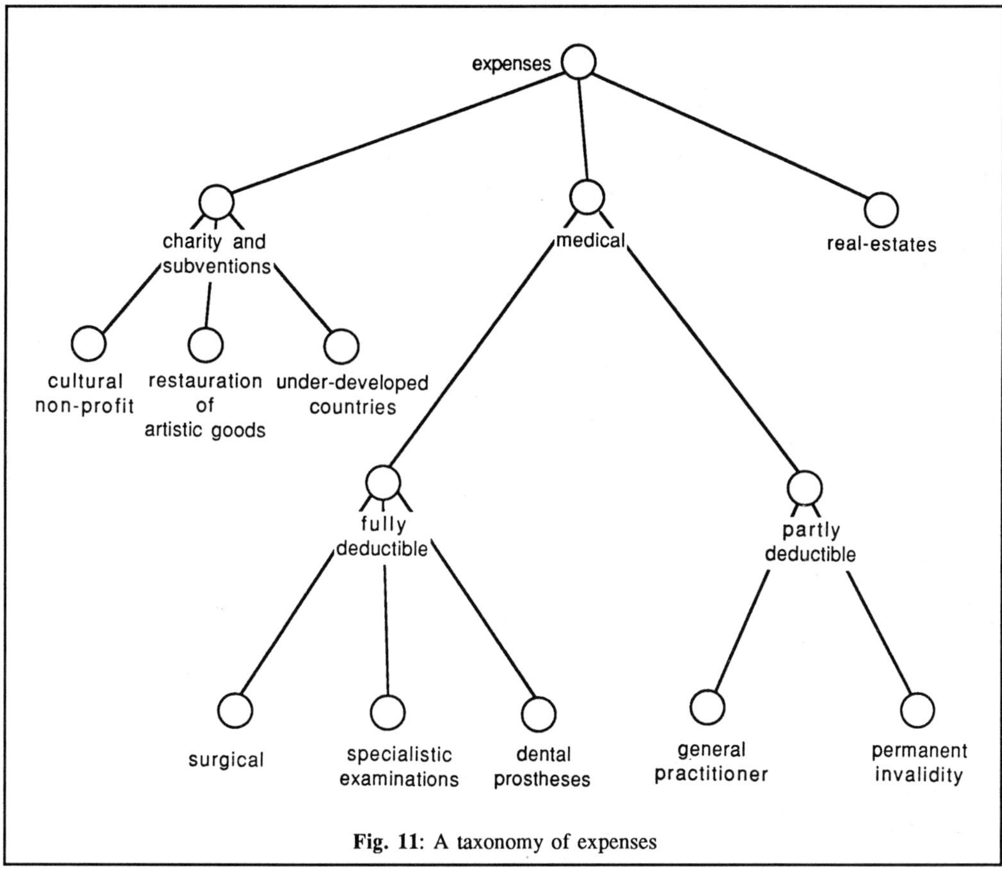

Fig. 11: A taxonomy of expenses

to derive new generality relations using transitivity together with the relations initially specified by the expert. Because of transitivity, taxonomies enjoy the property that all concepts more general than a given concept are accessible from it.

Of course, not all frames in the knowledge base can be related through generality/specialization to every other frame: e.g. it does not make sense to establish a generality relation between the unrelated concepts of taxpayer and of income, apart from the fact that both of them are specializations of the class "concept", representing a concept.

3.7.7 Other relations among frames

The "is-a" ad "instance-of" relations are not the only ordering criteria among domain objects. Useful extensions to the taxonomic relations are:

- partition: the subclasses form a partition of a class when an object which is an instance of the class must belong to one and just one subclass. When this is the case, a particular case of the "is-a" relation can be used to capture this knowledge. A typical example is the specialization of the frame "day" into the subclasses "Monday" through "Sunday"
- exclusion: two or more subclasses of the same class can be mutually exclusive, in the sense that if an object belongs to one subclass, then it cannot belong to the other(s). For instance "night-shift" and "holiday" are mutually exclusive, although they do not form a partition, since there are many days in which a worker is neither on a night shift nor on holiday

- conjunction: a subclass is a specialization of more than one superclass

For a large selection of primitives for organizing and relating frames/slots see for instance the system described in [Brachman and al., 1983].

3.7.8 Comparative descriptions

Associating representational units to entities, and collecting all knowledge about entities into the associated unit, turns out to be an advantage in capturing several important methods in human knowledge processing and organization. For example, it normally happens to describe new objects (concepts, situations, events) by comparing them to related, known objects and pointing out common, different or new features.

A typical example from financial textbooks is the description of a future as "a kind of contract", followed by a description of its peculiarities. In the frame terminology, this is equivalent to the assertion that "future" is a subclass (specialization) of "contract". From his previous knowledge of a contract, the reader expects the writer to mention attributes such as the parties involved, the commencement and expiration date, provisions for termination, penalties for violation of the terms, and perhaps an arbitration clause. He also expects the writer to explain the peculiarities and values of the above attributes in a futures contract. The following example further elaborates on this point.

Example 33: Description by comparison

In section 5.7, the rules (laws) for deciding if an Italian resident must file an income return were coded in first-order predicate calculus.

The obligations for a foreign resident can be simply described as being the same as for of an Italian resident, limited to the part of income imputable to activities in Italy.

By this way of reasoning, a similarity has been established between the concepts of Italian and foreign resident, together with some restriction to the applicability of the similarity. The concept of Italian resident is used as a kind of prototype for understanding, from a certain point of view, the concept of a foreign resident. ■

The process opposite to definition by comparison is recognition, in which a partially specified set of attributes is compared with the frames in the knowledge base to recover the associated entity. Recognition is sometimes referred to as understanding.

Refer to the Example 30, Section 7.4 above, in which a prototypical frame for a middle-class taxpayer has been defined. When examining the specific case of a married man with two children and an income of 40000 US$, a recognition procedure could activate the prototype "middle-class-taxpayer", although this information is still very partial. As a consequence of that, the computer agent can form some expectations about the tax payer, e.g. he would guess that the number of cars does not exceed two. If this turns out to be false, and if the number of cars is a critical attribute, the failure may be used to trigger a control procedure, whereas the type of violation may help direct the control strategy, or to try a different recognition.

The above discussion strongly suggests considering recognition when thinking about consultation models, i.e. the rules of interaction of intelligent support programs with clients. In a consultation model based on recognition, after collecting a first set of client's attribute-value pairs, the support program compares those data with a collection of clients' prototypes in its knowledge base. Such prototypes can be derived from market surveys, from feature extraction over past cases, from statistical data, etc. Prototypes matching the partial user data are activated, and direct the subsequent flow of questions, by gathering information about the compatibility of the user's situation with their key attributes. If the result disconfirms the initial matching, then the prototype is abandoned and a different one is selected (sometimes, associated to the abandoned prototype, there is a procedure for helping in this choice); if the dialogue confirms the matching, then decision rules specific to that user category are retrieved from the prototype and run.

In [Heuer and al., 1988], such a consultation model is adopted in designing an adviser for personal investors. Other applications are possible in credit assessment, leasing, and related fields.

3.7.9 Inheritance

Inheritance is a mechanism by which classes or instances automatically "inherit", i.e. share, the attributes and corresponding properties in their generalizations without a need for rewriting them.

Example 34: A taxonomy with inheritance

Consider again the Example 32, Section 7.5 above.

Given the definition of "revenue" (repeated here for convenience), inheritance makes a much shorter description of its specializations or instances possible:

```
CLASS revenue
        IS-A:
        type:
                value restriction: transaction
        amount:
                value restriction: instance of (number ≥ 0)
        date:
                value restriction: instance of (date)
        source:
                value restriction: person or institution
        fiscal declaration:
                value restriction: one of (true, false)
                if needed: fill with (self.type).fiscal declaration
        reference:
                value restriction: legal-document
                if needed:
        remarks:
                value restriction: text

CLASS income
        IS-A: revenue
        fiscal declaration:
                value: true
        taxable:
                value restriction: one of ("yes", "no", "special")

CLASS deductible-income
        IS-A: income
        taxable:
                value: "no"

CLASS prize
        IS-A: deductible income

INSTANCE XYZ
        INSTANCE-OF: prize
        type:
                value: donation
        amount:
                value: 100000
        date:
                value: 1/1/90
        source:
                value: Award Inc.
        reference:
                value: ID700
        remarks:
```

value: "second edition"

So, the fact that prize XYZ is not taxable is true in the above knowledge base because "XYZ" inherits from the class "prize", which inherits from the class "deductible income" the slot "taxable" with value "no". From the definition of the class "income", it can be seen how inheritance makes it possible to add new slots (in this case, the slot "taxable") during specialization simply by writing them with the specialization, and to modify values/values restrictions in inherited slots simply by rewriting the slot definition. ■

Inheritance increases notational efficiency because attributes need to be stored in only one place, i.e. with the most general concepts: all specializations/instances automatically share that attribute. Hence, the programmer writes less code, and modifications are limited to one specific place in the knowledge base.

More importantly, inheritance helps the programmer focus on the distinguishing aspects of a class with respect to its superclasses, i.e. on description by comparison: only new attributes, or modifications to properties of already existing attributes, must be coded at the subclass level; attributes of the superclasses need not be coded again. In order to take full advantage from inheritance, it is convenient to store attributes with the most general concept such that all of its specializations share them, or a modification to them.

Finally, recognition is made more efficient: starting with the most general object in the knowledge base, and continuing with its specializations, the attributes of the frame to be recognized are compared to the attributes of the available frames, until the most general frame matching all attributes is retrieved. The advantage is here that, if a frame contains an attribute which is not part of the description to be recognized, then all its specializations (and the specializations of specializations, etc.) can be discarded, since they will all inherit the "wrong" attribute: hence it is possible to exclude early from the search a whole subgraph, rather than a single frame.

Example 35: Features of inheritance

In defining the concept of "taxpayer", the programmer must only concentrate on the specific features making a generic person a taxpayer. These features are essentially the age, the income during the previous year, and the fiscal domicile.

Some of these attributes (e.g. the age) are inherited from the more general concept of "person"; only a new value restriction is added to the "taxpayer" frame. Some other concepts (e.g. the income during the previous year) must be added also.

However, the programmer needs not to recall that a taxpayer also has a "marital status", since this attribute is already part of the definition of "person", of which "taxpayer" is a specialization. The same consideration apply with all personal data (family name, first and middle name, sex etc.) which are part of the concept of "person", and should therefore be defined at that level to be inherited thereafter. ■

The general functioning of inheritance is simply understood in terms of the graph representation of taxonomies (Section 7.6 above): it consists of an algorithm, recovering more general concepts from a given concept through path finding in a graph, an inspecting nodes on the path to verify if they contain the attribute/value required from the original concept.

Although the idea of inheritance is a powerful one, there is a lot of freedom in the more precise specification of how strict inheritance should be, as for example the possibility of selectively applying inheritance to certain attributes only. From a knowledge representation point of view, inheritance has no meaning at all, but is simply a coding convenience. Therefore, inheritance must be suited to fit the desired interpretation of a frame and of the generality relationship. Section 7.10 below deals with these issues.

3.7.10 Inheritance mechanisms

Depending on which interpretation of the interpretations of a frame in Section 7.4 is appropriate for the application at hand, the meaning of the specialization/instantiation relations is changed (and of hence the inheritance mechanism).

1. Definitions

If frames are definitions, then subconcepts essentially stand for subsets, and instances for set elements. Under the simplifying assumption of no dependency among slots, the slot values must be inherited without changes, while value restrictions may either be inherited without change, or may be further tightened. An advantage of this interpretation is the sound classification (or recognition) procedure: since the listed attributes are sufficient and necessary, any "entity" featuring the set of attributes of a known frame can be immediately recognized as a specialization/instance of that frame.

2. Prototypes

Inheritance must necessarily be less strict in this case, since attributes and attribute properties in the prototype frame are just typical, and hence not binding for its specializations. Here the meaning of inheritance can be best understood within the framework of default reasoning, the most important reasoning activity over taxonomies of prototypes.

A *default* is a piece of knowledge assumed to be true about an entity due to the lack of more precise information. In taxonomic reasoning, it is natural to consider as default values for an object the values stored in its prototypes: lacking knowledge about an object is automatically filled through inheritance with the prototypical values for the class the object is an instance (or specialization) of. So, a tax consultant with no more precise information can base his tax-plan advice assuming by default that his client is a prototypical middle-class man, or an employee can schedule his plan for the next morning by assuming that his car will work properly. Reasoning based on default assumptions is called reasoning by default.

The point with defaults is that, while allowing possibly interesting conclusions to be derived even in the case of incomplete information, such conclusions are nevertheless subject to revision as soon as more specific information is available. In taxonomic reasoning, belief revision is made possible by admitting exceptions (called cancellations or overriding) to inheritance. An elegant way to achieve this, is by associating "inheritance roles" to slots in class definitions; inheritance roles establish ways in which subclasses or instances inherit slot specifications/values from a class. Inheritance roles make a precise customization of the generic inheritance principle possible, at the cost of an often difficult interpretation of the reasoning processes in terms of the problem domain. So, for example, if the inheritance role is "override", then slots must be inherited, but slot values or values restrictions might be changed in subconcepts; the inheritance role "not critical" mahes it possible for subconcepts not to inherit a slot; the inheritance role "unchanged" might be used to force inheritance of a slot and its properties without modifications.

3.7.11 Frames and semantic networks

Frames and semantic networks are closely related paradigms. In Section 7.6 above it was shown how taxonomies naturally lend themselves to a network based representation. A typical way of translating frame-based systems into a graph formalism is to associate nodes to frames, and to use links both for representing slots and for capturing the taxonomic ordering. Links representing slots can be labelled with the slot name; taxonomic links follow the labeling in Section 7.6. Indeed, the "is-a" and "instance-of" links are among the most commonly used in semantic networks.
Alternatively, instead of defining a new link for each conceptual relation in the system, slots can be associated to nodes. This is the representation used in the following Example 36 and in Fig. 12. The link "has-attribute" is used to connect a concept with its slots; other links are introduced to

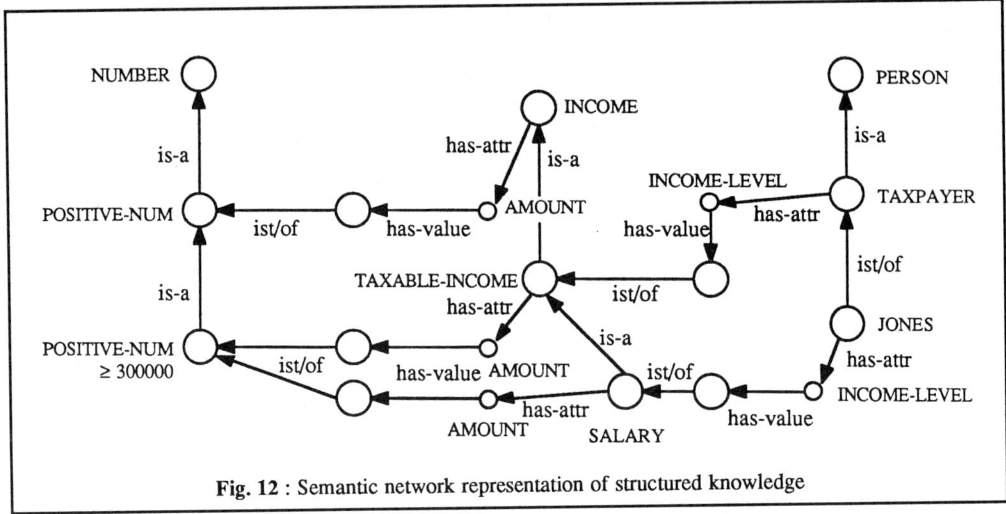

Fig. 12 : Semantic network representation of structured knowledge

connect the slot to its filling concepts, a different link for each slot property: an example is the link "has-value", connecting the slot to the concept containing its value. Inheritance is easily implemented as suggested in Section 7.9. Most network manipulators support inheritance.

Example 36: Dependency graphs and tax law representation

Fig. 12 shows a semantic network representation of the knowledge:

> Jones is a taxpayer
> taxpayers have income larger than zero
> salary is a kind of income
> Jones' income is salary

The knowledge: "Jones is a taxpayer", is captured by introducing a node (labeled Jones) representing the entity Jones, a second node (labeled taxpayer) representing the category of taxpayers, and a link from Jones to taxpayer, representing the classification relationship "instance-of".

The knowledge: "Taxpayers have income" is represented by a link "has" from the node taxpayer to the new node "Jones". The value restriction on the income is represented as a constraint associated to an attribute.

The knowledge: "Salary is an income" is captured by the specialization link "is-a" from the new node salary to the node income.

The knowledge: "Jones has salary" is captured by a link "has" from the node Jones to the node salary". ■

3.7.12 Frames vs. logic

For the first interpretation of frames in Section 7.4, there exists an equivalent representation in first-order predicate calculus [Hayes, 1979].

To this purpose:

- the frame is considered as an unary belief, for example "corporation(x)" is the property of an object x of being a firm
- slots are predicates for a binary relation, for example "president(x,y)", where x satisfies "corporation(x)", and y satisfies "person-of-age(y)", according to the associated value-restriction in the Example 26, Section 7.2 above

Assuming that attributes (slots) "s_i" in a class frame "c" express necessary and sufficient conditions for membership to the class, the frame can be represented in a logic-based paradigm by the following formula:

$$\forall x\ c(x) \leftrightarrow \exists\ y_1, y_2, \dots, y_n\ s_1(x, y_1) \wedge s_2(x, y_2) \wedge \dots \wedge s_n(x, y_n)$$

Generalization hierarchies are translated into logic by formulae of the kind:

$$\forall x\ subc(x) \rightarrow c(x)$$

where "subc" is the name of a subclass of the class "c". This formula also ensures that attributes not mentioned at the subclass level are inherited from higher levels. Since, in the above interpretation, the expressive power of frames is a subset of the expressive power of logic, the choice of using frames is simply one of notational efficiency.

A logic interpretation of frames as containers for default (prototypical) attributes is more difficult, since belief revision (a key idea in default reasoning) is not consistent with the viewpoint of standard logic (i.e. the logic introduced in Section 5). However, extensions to standard logic have been proposed to this purpose [Reiter, 1980].

3.8 Temporal reasoning

3.8.1 Introduction

The issue of representing times and actions arises continuously in almost all areas of economics and finance. The problem domain at hand, and the intended use of the representation dictate the requirements on the model for time and action: it should be powerful enough to capture the semantics and distinctions between the actions (as e.g. in planning) and moreover, the formalism should be a useful representation for action reasoning (e.g. for resource allocation).

The basic temporal reasoning approaches fall into three categories:

i. point-based theories, where the primitive object is an instantaneous time instant, corresponding to the intuitive notion of start or end of an action occurrence

ii. time interval theories, based on the primitive object of time-interval corresponding to the duration of an action occurrence [Allen 1983] [Allen and Koomen, 1983] [Allen, 1984] [Allen and Hayes, 1985]

iii. subjective or rational temporal constraint theories, based on the primitive object of allowed transitions in the (time x action) space, and corresponding to the intuitive notion of temporal goals [McCarthy and Hayes, 1969], [Sandewall, 1986]

In all three cases, temporal relationships between times need to be represented. In i. and ii., the $\leq$ relation between endpoints of a time-interval is used, allowing for overlap between intervals, and for multiple relations between a given time-point and different intervals. In iii., the relation is between time-points or intervals, where a given action allows or not to achieve a specified goal.

Because of similar temporal relationships, i. and ii. are often merged, as below in Section 8.3, on the basis of a temporal logic (Section 8.2), whereas subjective temporal constraint reasoning will be treated separately (Section 8.4).

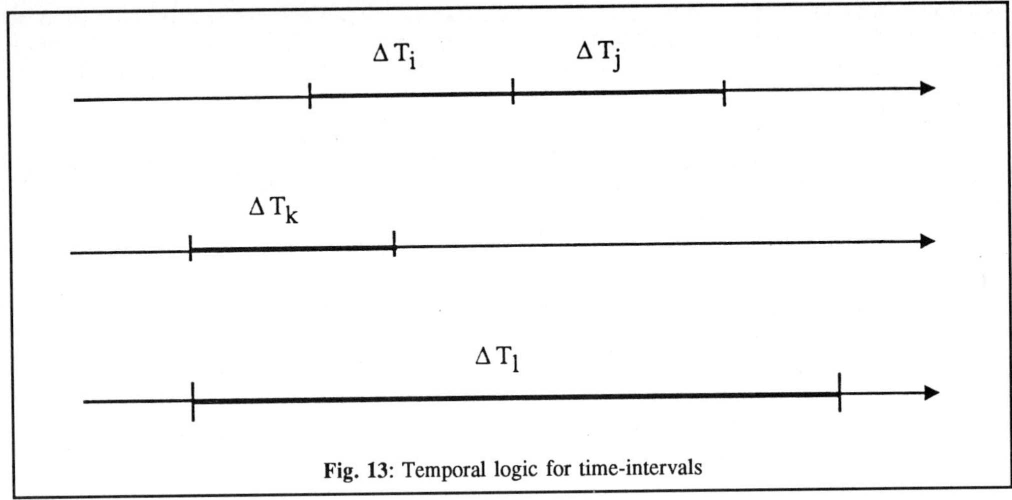

Fig. 13: Temporal logic for time-intervals

3.8.2 Temporal logic

Temporal logic describes properties holding over time, and actions occurring over time, with a time interval Δ T predicate as a primitive object, and time-instants predicate t as a special case.

The logic predicate primitives used will be:

$\neg$	negation
$\wedge$	conjunction
$\vee$	disjunction
$\rightarrow$	implication
$\leftrightarrow$	equivalence
XOR	exclusive OR

The following object classes are defined

time-intervals	TIME-INT
time-instants	INSTANT

A basic requirement on time intervals ΔT is that two such intervals can follow one-another, i.e. there is no time between them, and they have no time-instant in common. The primitive predicate Next (ΔT_1, ΔT_2) expresses the previously stated condition, where ΔT_1, ΔT_2 are two time-intervals; an equivalent notation is "ΔT_1 Next ΔT_2".

Other time-interval relations defined below in terms of Next, are: Before, Overlaps, Starts, Ends, During, Contains, After, Next-by. Amongst these, obvious transitivity or non-transitivity dependencies exist.

Here, each time-interval is a time segment which has at least two subintervals, one which starts, and one which ends the time-interval, while both subintervals are fully contained in the later (Fig. 13). This definition allows for an equivalence between time-intervals and time-instants, where both subintervals are empty and identical.

Time-intervals, time-instants and their relations satisfy a set of basic axioms listed below.

$\forall$ i, j $\in$ TIME-INT:

1. $\Delta T(i) \leftrightarrow \exists$ k, l, m, n $(\Delta T_k$ Next $\Delta T(i)$ Next $\Delta T_l) \wedge (\Delta T_k$ Next ΔT_m Next ΔT_n Next $\Delta T_l)$
2. $(\Delta T_i$ Before $\Delta T_j) \leftrightarrow \exists$ k $\in$ TIME-INT $(\Delta T_i$ Next ΔT_k Next $\Delta T_j)$
3. $(\Delta T_i$ Equal $\Delta T_j) \leftrightarrow \exists$ k, l $\in$ TIME-INT $(\Delta T_k$ Next ΔT_i Next $\Delta T_l) \wedge (\Delta T_k$ Next ΔT_j Next $\Delta T_l)$
4. $(\Delta T_i$ Overlaps $\Delta T_j) \leftrightarrow \exists$ k, l, m, n $\in$ TIME-INT
   $(\Delta T_k$ Next ΔT_i Next ΔT_m Next $\Delta T_n) \wedge (\Delta T_k$ Next ΔT_l Next ΔT_j Next $\Delta T_n)$
5. $(\Delta T_i$ Starts $\Delta T_j) \leftrightarrow \exists$ k,l,m $\in$ TIME-INT
   $(\Delta T_k$ Next ΔT_i Next ΔT_l Next $\Delta T_m) \wedge (\Delta T_k$ Next ΔT_j Next $\Delta T_m)$
6. $(\Delta T_i$ Ends $\Delta T_j) \leftrightarrow \exists$ k, l, m $\in$ TIME-INT
   $(\Delta T_k$ Next ΔT_l Next ΔT_i Next $\Delta T_m) \wedge (\Delta T_k$ Next ΔT_j Next $\Delta T_m)$
7. $(\Delta T_i$ During $\Delta T_j) \leftrightarrow \exists$ k, l, m, n $\in$ TIME-INT
   $(\Delta T_k$ Next ΔT_l Next ΔT_i Next ΔT_m Next $\Delta T_n) \wedge (\Delta T_k$ Next ΔT_j Next $\Delta T_n)$
8. $(\Delta T_i$ Next-by $\Delta T_j) \leftrightarrow (\Delta T_i$ Next $\Delta T_j)$
9. $(\Delta T_i$ After $\Delta T_j) \leftrightarrow (\Delta T_j$ Before $\Delta T_i)$
10. $(\Delta T_i$ Contains $\Delta T_j) \leftrightarrow (\Delta T_j$ During $\Delta T_i)$
11. Axiom of uniqueness of meeting-place (1):

    $\exists$ k $\in$ TIME-INT $(\Delta T_i$ Next $\Delta T_k) \wedge (\Delta T_j$ Next $\Delta T_k)$
    $\rightarrow (\forall$ l $\in$ TIME-INT $(\Delta T_i$ Next $\Delta T_l) \leftrightarrow (\Delta T_j$ Next $\Delta T_l))$
12. Axiom of uniqueness of meeting-place (2):

    $\exists$ k $\in$ TIME-INT $(\Delta T_k$ Next $\Delta T_i) \wedge (\Delta T_k$ Next $\Delta T_j)$
    $\rightarrow (\forall$ l $\in$ TIME-INT $(\Delta T_l$ Next $\Delta T_i) \leftrightarrow (\Delta T_l$ Next $\Delta T_j))$
13. Ordering axiom:

    $\forall$ l, k $\in$ TIME-INT $(\Delta T_i$ Next $\Delta T_j) \wedge (\Delta T_k$ Next $\Delta T_l)$
    $\rightarrow$ 1. $((\Delta T_i$ Next $\Delta T_l)$ XOR
    2. $(\exists$ m $\in$ TIME-INT $(\Delta T_i$ Next ΔT_m Next $\Delta T_l))$ XOR
    3. $(\exists$ n $\in$ TIME-INT $(\Delta T_k$ Next ΔT_n Next $\Delta T_j)))$
14. Existence axiom:

    $\exists$ l, k $\in$ TIME-INT $(\Delta T_k$ Next ΔT_i Next $\Delta T_l)$
15. Union axiom:

    $(\Delta T_i$ Next $\Delta T_j) \rightarrow \exists$ k, l, m $\in$ TIME-INT
    $(\Delta T_k$ Next ΔT_i Next ΔT_j Next $\Delta T_l) \wedge (\Delta T_k$ Next ΔT_m Next $\Delta T_l))$

3.8.3 Time-interval reasoning

Time-interval reasoning is achieved, by casting into the previously described basic temporal logic formalism, three types of generic predicates (see Fig. 14):

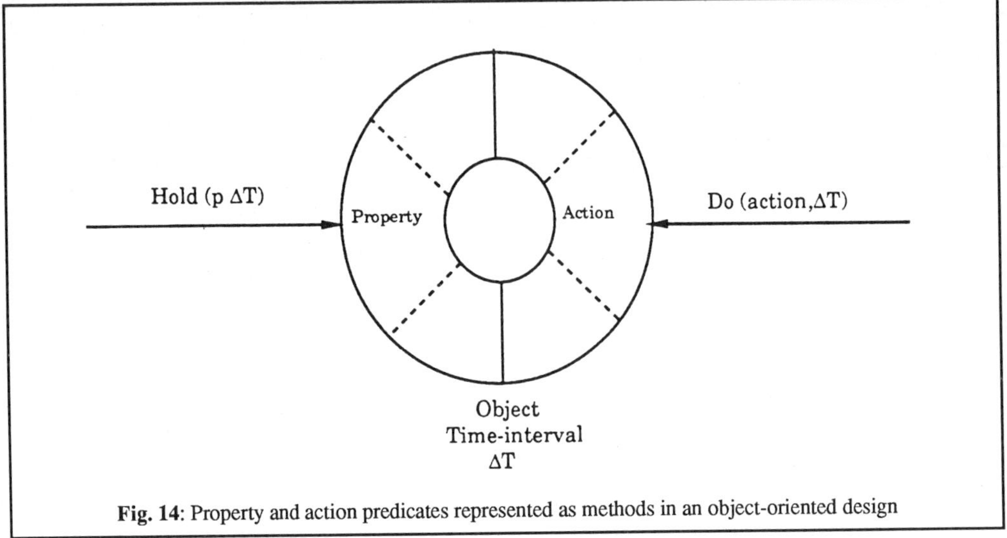

Fig. 14: Property and action predicates represented as methods in an object-oriented design

i. Property predicates Hold (p, ΔT)
These predicates state that the property p holds in the time-interval $\Delta T \in$ TIME-INT

Examples:
Hold (Price, ΔT_i), $\Delta T_i = [t_i, t_i]$ expresses that a price Price holds, at time t_i
Hold (Pay-back, ΔT_i) expresses that the pay-back period for a loan is ΔT_i.

It results from the temporal logic that any property p holds homogeneously during a time interval, or only during some subintervals, where such conditions must be spelled out explicitly (see iii. below). All logic predicates AND, OR, NOT, etc. apply of course to the predicate Hold (p, ΔT).

ii. Action predicates Do (action, ΔT):
These predicates state the action "action" holds in the time-interval $\Delta T \in$ TIME-INT.

Examples:
Do (Buy, ΔT_i), $\Delta T_i = [t_i, t_i]$, states that a purchase was made at time t_i
Do (Insure, ΔT_i) expresses that an asset is insured over the time interval ΔT_i.

An action may apply homogeneously during a time-interval, or only during some subintervals hereof, and all logic predicates apply to the predicate Do (action, ΔT).

iii. Temporal classes Class (ΔT, $\Delta T_1 \cdot \Delta T_2 \dots \cdot \Delta T_n$)
These predicates serve the purpose of creating time interval classes and subclasses, where $\Delta T_1, \dots, \Delta T_n$ are (expressed in list form) subclasses related to ΔT in that the subclasses inherit the properties of ΔT. The time interval ΔT may itself relate to properties or actions. At the same time, the subclasses $\Delta T_1, \dots, \Delta T_n$ may have other properties or actions than ΔT

Class	Asset class
1.	Monetary assets
2.	Physical assets
3.	Policy assets
4.	Service or information assets

Table 2: Asset classes applicable to all properties or actions

Examples:

Class (Year, 1Q·2Q·3Q·4Q) states that a budget year is tied to four quarters to which properties of the Year apply equally.

Class (Long-term-plan, $\Delta T_1 \cdot \Delta T_2$) states that, attached to a long-term planning horizon, there are intermediate planning targets ΔT_1, ΔT_2 which may or not be subintervals of the original planning horizon.

3.8.4 Temporal constraints

The basic object in temporal constraint reasoning is the couple (time, action) or (time, property), and the primary concern is to represent bindings between conditions to be met prior to a real state, conditions at the time of the state, and conditions to be met afterwards. It can be formalized as a stack predicate describing permitted transitions between pairs of time-intervals and actions or properties:

Stack ((ΔT_1, action-1), (ΔT_2, action-2))
Stack ((ΔT_1, property-1), (ΔT_2, property-2))

where (ΔT_1, action-1) is a pre-condition for (ΔT_2, action-2), and likewise for the properties.

However, in economics and management, there are already some known and more precise (although not formalized) temporal constraints which find their justification on one hand in law, and on the other in business and decision-making processes [Pau, 1986a] [Wilensky, 1983]. This is based on a classification of the Property and Action variables of Section 8.3 according to the four asset types involved (Table 2).

Properties and actions are to be always supplemented by the asset class involved, and transitions applicable to the couples (time, action) or (time, property) correspond to transactions between asset types. Table 3 gives the 10 classes of transactions, regardless of the specific assets which are considered but who must belong to one of the 4 asset classes. It is then obvious that temporal constraints apply to such transactions, due to prescribed or imposed sequences between legitimate transaction classes.

Besides the asset types involved (Table 3), a transaction is characterized by the following attributed:

i. settlement terms: immediate, fixed time interval, futures, hedges, options, delayed

ii. constraints on transaction duration

(i,j) Asset types	1	2	3	4
1	Financial			
2	Investment	Barter		
3	Aid	Legal Control	Negotiation	
4	Access	Insurance	Assistance	Intellectual

Table 3: Transactions between asset classes (at corresponding prices or utilities)

iii. transaction costs, expressed for each transaction as an array with one component for each of the 4 asset types by which the costs are payable

Temporal constraint reasoning, subjective or rational, therefore involves the following steps:

i. specify true/allowed sequences or scripts of transaction types from Table 3, using the temporal logic operation After:

$$\text{Asset-type}_l \quad \text{AFTER} \quad \text{Asset-type}_i$$

ii. classify all actions "action" and properties "p" by Asset-type, resulting in the fact bases Asset-type (action, i) and Asset-type (p, l), i, l = 1,..., h

iii: generate the constrained transitions in the (time, action) or (time, property) spaces by validation of the predicates:

Asset-type (action-1, i) Asset-type (action-2,j) After (j,i) $\rightarrow$
Stack ((ΔT_1, action-1), (ΔT_2, action-2))

iv. validate the transactions i. in terms of all attributes described above, and evaluate the cost array.

This hypothesis refinement procedure allows for meeting and chaining together all constraints on transactions, properties and actions, while complying with temporal logic.

3.8.5 Feature extraction in the time domain

When temporal constraints cannot be expressed explicitly, or when causal factors govern trends, one must carry out a feature extraction in the time domain; examples are financial company time series, accounting data, trends of financial ratios [Pau and Valstorp, 1977].

Such feature extraction can be either categorical or not. Categorical feature extraction is carried out by e.g. discriminant analysis [Altman, 1968], and is based on labeling the evolutions used as

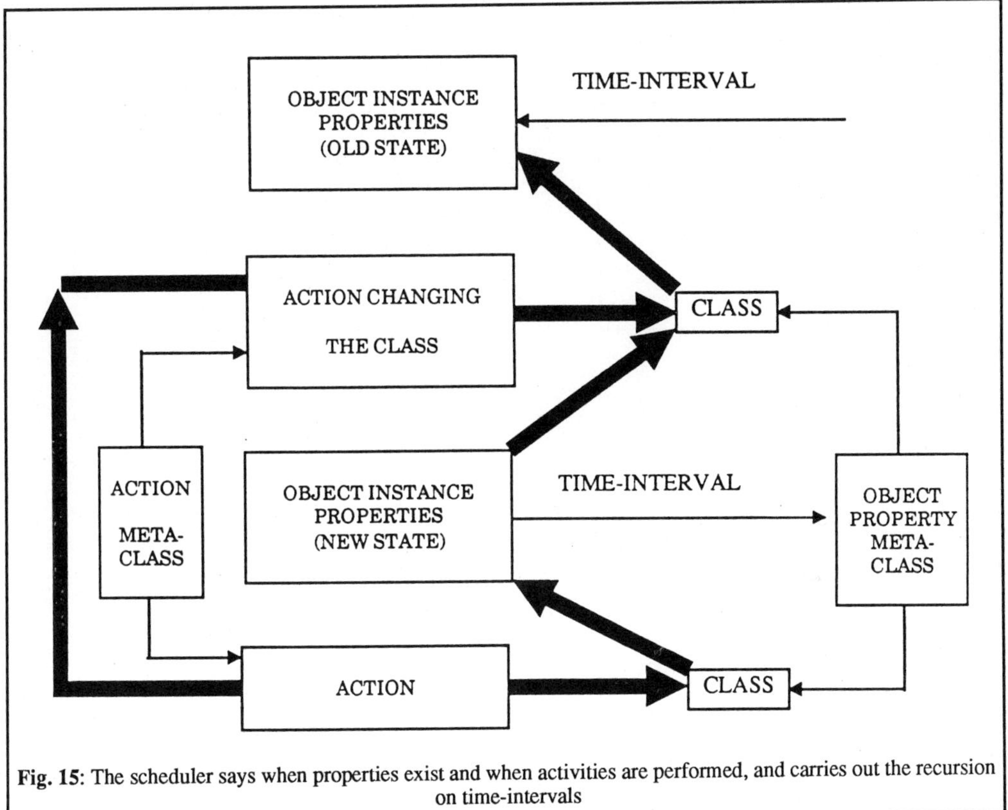

Fig. 15: The scheduler says when properties exist and when activities are performed, and carries out the recursion on time-intervals

learning data, into either of known classes. Non-categorical feature extraction relies on normalized principal component analysis, correspondence analysis [Pau and Valstorp, 1977], or by Markov chains revealing preferences [Fogler, 1974]. Feature extraction of both types is addressed also in Chapter 6.

Correspondence analysis and component analysis involve decomposing the temporal evolutions with respect to a vector base of orthogonal basis evolutions (principal components in the (attribute x time) space. These basis evolutions are the causal factors governing the trends.

3.8.6 Temporal inference

After a proper representation of the temporal reasoning has been selected and implemented, one more level applies, namely the selection of the scheduling procedure (see Section 6.7 and Chapter 5) which involves event scheduling (Fig. 15):

- forward chaining generates action plans, with corresponding transaction costs and choices
- backward chaining generates properties to be met to satisfy planning goals
- more general inference procedures

In all cases, attribute values are calculated by external procedures or knowledge bases (accounting, econometric estimation, risk analysis, clustering); and explanation facilities are added to the inference engine (Fig. 16).

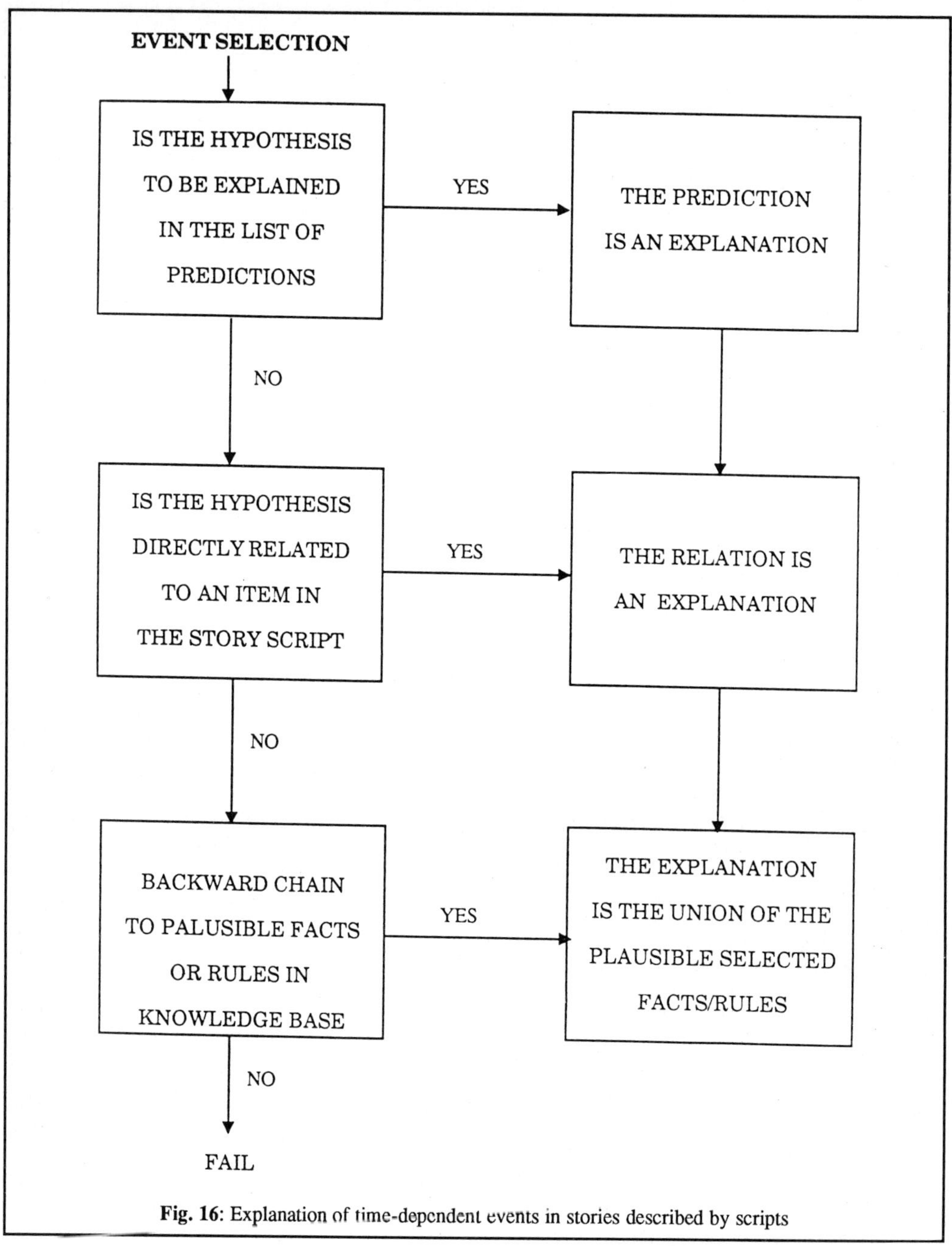

Fig. 16: Explanation of time-dependent events in stories described by scripts

Examples involve: business planning, project scheduling, currency rate adjustments [Pau, 1986a], signal clustering [Pau and Valstorp, 1977].

4 Artificial Intelligence Programming Languages

4.1 Introduction

4.1.1 Syntax and semantics

Programming languages are formalisms for describing problems or solutions to problems in a way understandable (i.e. executable) by computers. A programming language is defined through its *syntax* and *semantics* .

In natural languages (e.g. English), the syntax specifies which words are part of the language and how words can be combined into correct sentences; in programming languages the syntax plays exactly the same role, only it is much simpler. Also note that in formal languages (and hence in computer languages) words are often referred to as *symbols* , sentences as *expressions* .

A precise formalism for describing the syntax of a broad class of languages is introduced in the next section. Such a formalism is important for two reasons:

- syntactic analysis of expressions has many potential applications to economics (see Chapter 7 for an application)
- it is useful for describing programming languages, as in Sections 3 - 6 of this Chapter

Semantics deals with the meaning associated to sentences (expressions) and words (symbols).One way whereby to describe semantics of a language is to translate it into a language whose semantics is known. In the following section, the meaning of the programs will be informally stated in English. This approach to semantics is adequate for the purposes of this work, although this is not theoretically acceptable, due to the ambiguities inherent in any natural language.

4.1.2 AI programming languages

In Chapter 3 it was stressed how the complexity of real-world problems stimulated the development of paradigms for knowledge representation. Computer languages of interest to AI encompass one or more of such knowledge representation criteria.

Since knowledge representation paradigms are very heterogeneous, AI programming languages do not share as many features as, say, COBOL-type languages. However, two characteristics are common to most of them. First, they use symbols as the basic data type. Second, they are interactive. Each of these topics is briefly addressed in the two following paragraphs.

4.1.3 Symbols and symbolic expressions

A *symbol* is the representation in a formal language of an elementary entity (an object, a concept, and so on) in the problem context; symbols are not decomposable.

Example 1: Symbols

American-currency
A33
gfwystr

are all symbols. In computer languages, symbols are usually defined as strings of characters and numbers. Although the first symbol has a clear interpretation in English, this interpretation is irrelevant for the execution of formal manipulations. ■

Languages based on symbols (so-called *symbolic languages*) include methods for *symbolic manipulations* . Typical elementary manipulations on symbolic structures are:

- creation, deletion or modification of symbolic structures of varying complexity
- retrieval, addition, substitution or deletion of substructures or in case symbols from the structures
- comparison between structures or substructures (this problem has a special relevance in AI and is called *pattern-matching*)
- "ad-hoc" processing of particular symbols (e.g. arithmetic operations on numeric symbols, logical operations on the symbols "true" and "false")

Different knowledge representation formalisms make different hypotheses on how symbols should be combined into structures and about the kind of manipulations allowed over the structures (corresponding to different hypotheses on how intelligent entities acquire, store and effectively use knowledge, see Chapter 3.1); the programming languages are designed to support the different symbolic structures and manipulation methods.

4.1.4 Interactivity and language interpreters

A language is *interactive* if it is designed so that expressions are executed as soon as they are entered by the user. An interactive language consists of an *interpreter* , i.e. a program which reads an expression typed in by the user or from a file, evaluates it, returns the result to the user, and waits for a new expression. All languages described in this chapter are interactive.

Example 2: A simple formal symbolic language

Consider the following toy formal symbolic language:

i. allowable symbols are English words (for instance, all words listed in the English dictionary). Such symbols have obviously no meaning to the language interpreter. To stress this fact, symbols are enclosed in double quotes in the rest of this example

ii. the language supports just one symbolic structure (structured collection of symbols): the sequence. Any number of symbols can be grouped into a sequence simply by putting blanks between the symbols. The blank (" ") is said to be a *reserved symbol* of the language, i.e. a symbol having a special meaning to the interpreter

iii. primitive manipulations are associated to reserved symbols, e.g. "remove-first", "remove-second", etc., "delete-first", "delete-second", etc. When the interpreter is presented one of them, it performs a predefined computation transforming a sequence of symbols into another sequence of symbols

iv. finally, the reserved symbol ":" is used to separate a reserved symbol for symbolic manipulation from the sequence to be transformed. It tells the interpreter to apply the symbolic manipulation specified left of the ":" to the sequence right of the":"

Correct sentences (i.e. sentences accepted by the interpreter) are either a single symbol, or a sequence of symbols, or one of the reserved symbols for sequence manipulations, followed by ":", followed by any correct sentence to which the manipulation must be applied.

The behavior of the interpreter is described by the following two *rules* , which specify the value to be returned to the user for each correct sentence he may input:

a. if the interpreter is given a symbol or a sequence, it simply returns that symbol or that sequence

b. if the interpreter is given a sequence containing a ":", it applies the computation specified left of the ":" to the result of interpreting the expression right of the ":".

Rules do not make any reference to the meaning associated with symbols, and can be correctly applied by simply analyzing the external "shape" of the user input. Therefore the language is formal.

It is now possible to use this primitive language for symbolic manipulations. In the following, the user input is labelled "U>", interpreter answers are labelled "O>". To save space, comments are written on the same line as the intepreter output, separated by a semicolon.

```
U> "doctor"                ;the interpreter recognizes a symbol (i.)
O> "doctor"                ;according to rule a., the interpreter returns the input

U> "doctor"" ""Jones"      ;the interpreter recognizes a sequence (ii.)
O> "doctor"" ""Jones"      ;according to rule a., the interpreter returns the input

U> "return-first"":""doctors"" ""pay""taxes"
                           ;colon found, the interpreter recognizes a manipulation (iii.)
O> "doctors"               ;manipulation is performed, returns first element in the sequence (rule b.)

U> "delete-second"":""delete-second"":""students"" ""do"" ""not"" ""pay"" ""taxes"
                           ;colon found, the interpreter recognizes a manipulation (iii.)

O> "students"" ""pay"" ""taxes"
                           ;rule b. is first applied to the sequence left of the first colon, then the first element
                           ;of the sequence is applied to the result
```

Here, "delete-second" is assumed to mean: delete the second element of the sequence. Note how a negation has been removed from a sentence in a purely formal way. ■

Since in interpreted languages there is heavy interaction between the user and the computer, the interpreter is often embedded in a programming environment. Environments have been developed for all the languages in this chapter, and in some cases (such as SMALLTALK, see Section 5), the environment is part of the language specification.

Interactivity is important in AI languages because it supports:

- incremental programming, i.e. a technique for building complex programs by adding more functionalities to simpler programs
- prototyping, i.e. a methodology for software development based on the implementation in short time of a program solving part of the problem, and on successive refinements or redesign until the whole solution is implemented (see Chapter 3.1.2)

Interactivity is achieved, however, at the expense of efficiency; interpreters are slow because they cannot optimize (e.g. each time a procedure is executed, its code must be retrieved from memory). Hence compilers have been made available for practically all AI languages. Typically, short modules of software are developed and debugged interactively, and compiled at a later point, when the code is more stable.

4.1.5 A classification of programming languages

From an AI viewpoint, it is convenient to classify programming languages according to the knowledge representation criteria which inspire them. The following classes can be defined:

- procedural languages (e.g. PASCAL, FORTRAN, COBOL)
- functional languages (e.g. LISP, see Section 3)
- logic-based languages (e.g. Prolog, see Section 4)
- rule-based languages (e.g. OPS5 [Browston et al., 1985], see Chapter 3.6)
- frame-based languages (e.g. partly SMALLTALK, see Section 5)
- hybrid languages (e.g. KEE [Intellicorp, 1988])

Fig. 1 organizes the concepts introduced so far: rows contain programming paradigms, columns the basis for the abstraction.

"Procedural abstraction" means that the knowledge about how to operate on data is local to the procedure ("procedures manipulate data"); "object-oriented abstraction" means on the contrary that the knowledge about how to operate on data is located in the data definition itself ("data responding to requests to perform operations").

The languages mentioned are by no way all available languages. Bold fonts highlight languages described in this Chapter.

As a last remark, note that O.R./MS assumes that it is possible to extract a mathematical representation from the reality of a decision problem, and provides mathematical methods for solving the model: thus just one representation formalism is adopted (mathematics) and any procedural or functional language is adequate. Hence the reason why procedural/functional programming languages have been (and still are) so heavily used for implementing economic and financial problems.

	procedural abstraction	object-oriented abstraction
procedural	Pascal, Fortran, Ada, Cobol	**Smalltalk**, C++
functional	**Lisp**, APL	Loops, CLOS, Flavors
logic	**Prolog**	Omega
rule-based	OPS family	Yaps
hybrid		Nexpert, Kee

Fig. 1: Classification of programming languages [M. Colombetti, personal communication]

4.2 Language syntax and parsing

4.2.1 Language syntax

The *syntax* (or *grammar*) of a language describes the way allowable language symbols (*terminal symbols*) can be grouped together into sequences. In natural language, terminal symbols are all *words* included in the vocabulary for that language; sequences of symbols assumed grammatically correct are called *sentences* . The grammar partitions all possible sequences of symbols into two subsets: the sentences (which are part of the language) and the incorrect sequences (which are not part of the language). A grammar is a complete description of a language (or of allowable sequences of words) in the sense that, given any sequence and a known grammar, it is possible to decide whether the sequence is a correct sentence (is part of the language) or not. Such a decision may , however, take infinite time.

Example 3: Sentences vs. non-sentences

The sequence of terminal symbols:

"recessions cause a rise in unemployment"

is a sentence obeying English grammar because it is syntactically correct. On the contrary sequences like:

"recession inflation is unemployment"
"recessions causes a rise in unemployment"

are syntactically incorrect in English and therefore are not part of the English language. ■

Syntax and semantics are distinct, yet interact in several ways. A sentence like "recessions cause a rise" is syntactically correct (in the sense that there is a subject, a verb consistent with the subject, and a complement), but does not have a clear meaning. On the other side, syntax is helpful in determining the semantics in the potentially ambiguous sentence "recession causes unemployment", since it states that the subject must come before the predicate. In languages with a less constrained ordering of the words, the interpretation of unemployment as being the cause of a recession would be possible. The syntax, by establishing the structure of a sentence, helps gain insight into its meaning. Finally, a sentence like "recessions cause a rise in employment" is correct from both a syntactic and semantic point of view, although most economists would disagree with its truth. The problem of formally establishing the truth of a sentence with respect to a pre-existent set of sentences and given semantics is addressed by logic, while the problem of assessing the truth of a sentence from observations and experimentations is the task of scientific inquiries. Thus a set of sentences (a discourse) can be analyzed on at least four different levels of abstraction: syntactical, semantical, logical, empirical. In this section we will describe a formalism for expressing the syntax of languages.

The concept of *non terminal symbol* is useful in describing the syntax of a language. Non terminal symbols are symbols which do not appear in the language, but refer to abstract syntactic constructs, whose realization in the language may invoke alternative sequences of terminal symbols. In the following sections, by convention we write terminal symbols in lowercase, non terminal symbols in uppercase.

Example 4: Non terminal symbols

SENTENCE is a non terminal symbol, representing any allowable sequence of terminal symbols. Similarly, PREDICATE and VERBAL-PHRASE are other non terminal symbols denoting collections of terminal symbols. ■

A set of production rules (also called productions, see Chapter 3.6) specifies substitutions (or rewritings) of non terminal symbols into non terminal symbols, terminal symbols, or a combination of both. Each production rule specifies one type of substitution. Starting from an *initial symbol* and through repeated substitutions of non terminal symbols, and finally with terminal symbols, it is possible to generate all correct sentences in the language (cfr. rule chaining in rule-based knowledge representation, Chapter 3.6.6).

Example 5: Production rules

A sentence in English is decomposable into a nominal phrase and a verbal phrase; this grammatical decomposition can be captured by a substitution rule for replacing the non terminal symbol SENTENCE by the two (simpler) non terminal symbols NOMINAL-PHRASE and VERBAL-PHRASE. Another rule in the grammar can be used to capture the substitution of VERBAL-PHRASE into the two non terminal symbols VERB and PREDICATE. Finally, there could be rules for substituting VERB into terminal symbols, that is into the verbs actually used in the language. ■

Ideas introduced above can be easily formalized for the purposes of automatic computation. A formal grammar G is defined as:

$$G = (V_T, V_N, P, S)$$

where:

V_T	is the set of terminal symbols
V_N	is the set of non terminal symbols
P	is the set of productions
S	is the initial symbol

A language can be either described explicitly by listing all sentences or implicitly through its grammar.

Substitution rules are written in a special language, called the *Backus-Naur Formalism* (BNF) purposely developed for describing the syntax of computer languages. Like any other formalism, BNF has its own syntax and semantic. BNF is a language for talking about the syntax of other languages. The following is a list of terminal BNF symbols; they are selected not to conflict with symbols in the language to be examined, in order to avoid ambiguities. Their meaning is introduced informally:

::= separates the left-hand side from the right-hand side of a production rule; it means "can be substituted/rewritten into"

NAME a non-terminal symbol. For instance SENTENCE is a non terminal denoting a sentence, while VERBAL-PHRASE is a subset of it

a b	the sequence of the two symbols a and b
a|b	the vertical bar stands for an exclusive OR, i.e. "either a or b, but not both"
[a]	square brackets stand for the repetition of the enclosed symbol zero, or one time
{a}	curly brackets denote zero, or more repetitions of the enclosed symbol

Example 6: A grammar for simple economic sentences

Consider the following grammar G for analyzing simple economic sentences:

S = SENTENCE

V_T = (the, dramatic, impressive, unexpected, inflation, recession, unemployment, causes, explains, reduces, slows-down, accelerates)

V_N = (SENTENCE, NOMINAL-PHRASE, NOMINAL-PHRASE-1, VERB-PHRASE, TRANSITIVE-VERB-PHRASE, ADJECTIVE, NAME, TRANSITIVE-VERB, INTRANSITIVE-VERB)

P:

G-1: SENTENCE ::= NOMINAL-PHRASE VERB-PHRASE

G-2: NOMINAL-PHRASE ::= [the] NOMINAL-PHRASE-1

G-3: NOMINAL-PHRASE-1 ::= [ADJECTIVE] NAME

G-4: ADJECTIVE ::= dramatic | impressive | unexpected [ADJECTIVE]

G-5: NAME ::= inflation | recession | unemployment

G-6: VERB-PHRASE ::= TRANSITIVE-VERB-PHRASE | INTRANSITIVE-VERB

G-7: TRANSITIVE-VERB-PHRASE ::= TRANSITIVE-VERB NOMINAL-PHRASE

G-8: TRANSITIVE-VERB ::= causes | explains | reduces

G-9: INTRANSITIVE-VERB ::= slows down | accelerates

The rule for ADJECTIVE is an example of a recursive rule: a production is recursive if the right hand side contains the symbol in the left hand side. Recursion is an easy way to account for an infinite number of correct sequences with a finite number of production rules. In our case, any sentence containing a list of any length of adjectives in the appropriate position is correct. The same rule could also have been defined without recursion using curly brackets:

ADJECTIVE ::= dramatic | impressive | unexpected {dramatic | impressive | unexpected}

■

Production rules can be given a tree representation. Fig. 2 shows for instance an AND/OR tree containing part of the information in the rules in the example (for an exact definition of an AND/OR tree, see Chapter 12.8). For the purposes of tree representation, rules involving alternatives must first be decomposed. Thus the rule:

NOMINAL-PHRASE-1 ::= [ADJECTIVE] NAME

is decomposed into two rules, one for each possible alternative implied by the square brackets notation:

NOMINAL-PHRASE-1 ::= NAME

NOMINAL-PHRASE-1 ::= ADJECTIVE NAME

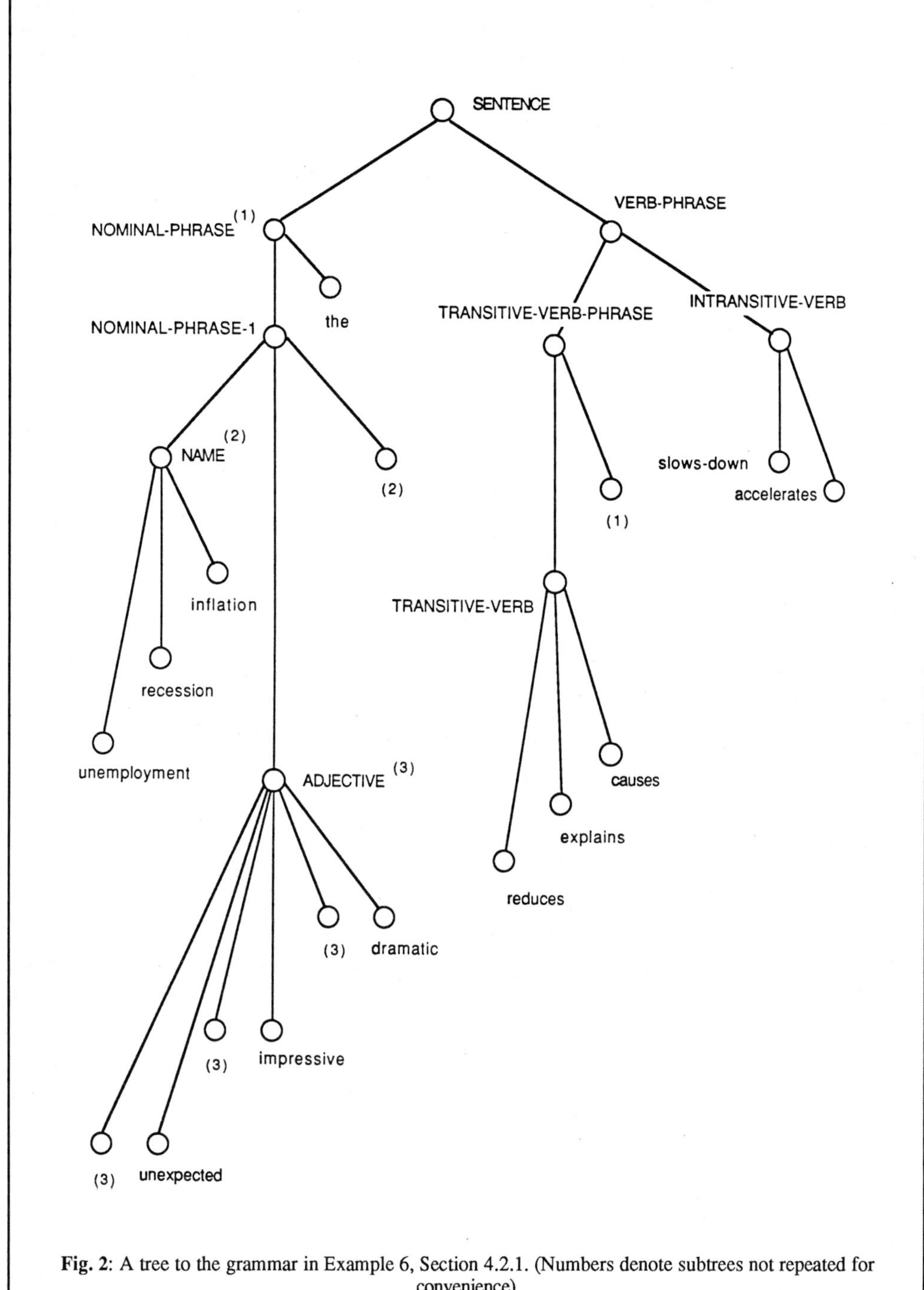

Fig. 2: A tree to the grammar in Example 6, Section 4.2.1. (Numbers denote subtrees not repeated for convenience)

The substitution for ADJECTIVE implies an infinite number of alternatives, which are not representable within a finite tree. Fig. 2 represents only alternatives up to a single recursive call, and therefore does not convey exactly the same information as the set of production rules. It is, however, interesting because it shows how the rules are chained together to obtain a set of links between the initial symbol S and the terminal symbols in the language.

4.2.2 Language parsing

Given a formal language (described through G), *parsing* a language sentence means finding the ordered sequence of substitutions (production rules) either transforming the start symbol into the sentence (by replacing the right side of the rules with the left side), or alternatively transforming the sentence into the start symbol (by looking at the rules from the right to the left). A program for parsing sentences is called a *parser* . Parsing is possible either top-down (from the start symbol to the sentence) or bottom-up (from the sentence to the start symbol). The reason for these names should be clear from Fig. 2: top-down parsing means descending the tree in Fig. 2 from the top node down to the terminal symbols; a bottom-up parser works the other way around. In the following example a simple sentence is parsed top-down, and the resulting parse tree is shown, that is the tree describing the production rules able to generate that specific sentence (as explained in Fig. 2).

Example 7: A parsing problem

Given the language defined in Section 2.1, parse top-down the sentence:

"the dramatic unexpected recession causes impressive unemployment". ■

The basic ideas behind the parsing process are pattern-matching and search. Pattern-matching is necessary to find chains of substitutions, from the initial symbol down to the terminal symbols in the sentence. Consider, for instance, the rewriting rule G-1:

SENTENCE ::= NOMINAL-PHRASE VERB-PHRASE

Both symbols in the right-hand side are non terminal, therefore rewriting rules having in their left hand side the patterns NOMINAL-PHRASE and VERB-PHRASE must exist; there are indeed two rules for each pattern:

NOMINAL-PHRASE ::= NOMINAL-PHRASE-1
NOMINAL-PHRASE ::= the NOMINAL-PHRASE-1
VERB-PHRASE ::= TRANSITIVE-VERB-PHRASE
VERB-PHRASE ::= INTRANSITIVE-VERB

The parser can choose among several matches (there are four possible combinations). Therefore, in the case of failure of a combination, it must explore the other alternatives before concluding that the sentence is not part of the language; how this can be done is explained in Chapter 5, dealing with search. For instance, choosing the match:

NOMINAL-PHRASE ::= NOMINAL-PHRASE-1
VERB-PHRASE ::= TRANSITIVE-VERB-PHRASE

does not lead to a solution, since there are no rewritings for NOMINAL-PHRASE-1 and TRANSITIVE-VERB-PHRASE consistent with the terminal symbols in the given sentence (specifically, there is no match for the symbol "the"). However the match:

NOMINAL-PHRASE ::= the NOMINAL-PHRASE-1
VERB-PHRASE ::= TRANSITIVE-VERB-PHRASE

does indeed lead to the solution. The parsing stops when either the top or the bottom of the tree is reached. If the succession of terminal symbols does coincide with the sentence, then the parsing has succeeded. However, should this not be the case, the parser will try first to use all possible sequences of substitutions, and then possibly reject the sentence.

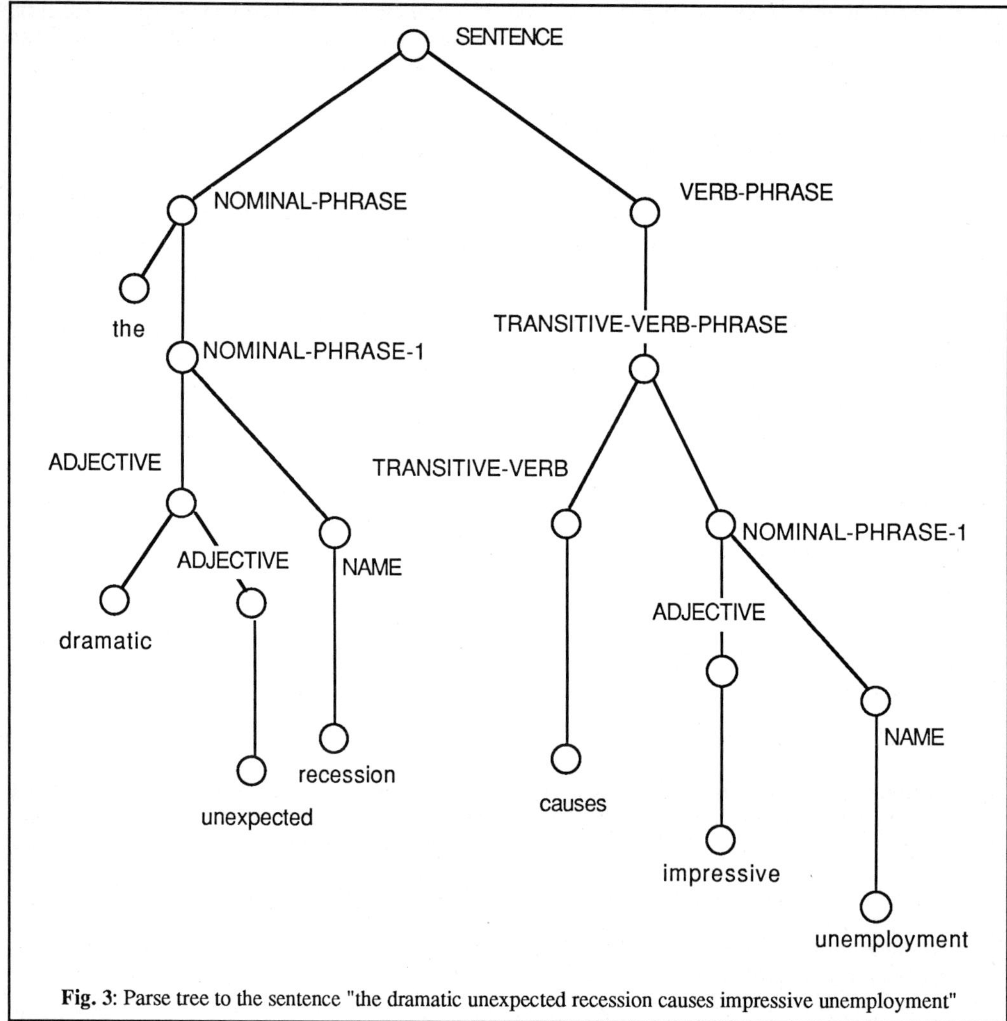

Fig. 3: Parse tree to the sentence "the dramatic unexpected recession causes impressive unemployment"

Fig. 3 shows a parse tree, a simple way of visualizing parsing, for the problem in Example 7 above. It shows how the sentence to be analyzed can be obtained by chaining the rewriting rules. The tree is invariant with respect to top-down or bottom-up parsing. The different steps of the top down parsing of the above sentence are shown in the order they would be generated by a depth first parser (e.g. Prolog, see Section 4.11).

4.2.3 Context-free and context-sensitive languages

Up to now it was implicitly assumed that the languages G = (V_T, V_N, P, S) were **context-free**. In context-free languages all rewriting/production rules have the following form for any non terminal symbol A belonging to V_T:

A ::= SEQUENCE

That is, in a *context-free* language the substitutions prescribed by the productions are applicable to a symbol independently from the other symbols surrounding it (the context). Most languages however are not context-free, and are called *context-sensitive* . English is clearly context–sensitive.

Example 8: Context-sensitive substitution

Referring to the grammar in Section 2.1, the correct substitution for VERB depends on the form of NAME; singular names require verbs in the singular form, whereas plural names require verbs in the plural form. Therefore the simple substitution:

TRANSITIVE-VERB ::= causes | explains | reduces

is not appropriate. The correct substitution must instead be conditioned (i.e. more than one term on the left-hand side of the rule):

recession TRANSITIVE-VERB ::= recession causes | explains | reduces
recessions TRANSITIVE-VERB ::= recessions cause | explain | reduce

Indeterminate articles "a", "an" are yet other examples of a context-sensitive feature in English. The correct substitution depends on the beginning letter of the following adjective, adverb or noun ■

The BNF language is limited to context-free grammars. Since programming languages are generally context–sensitive, BNF captures only a context-free approximation of the real syntax of a programming language. It is, however, very convenient to use, since programming languages are relatively simple (about one hundred productions are required for describing most of them). Moreover, there exist programs accepting a BNF description of a language as their input and automatically generating a parser for that language; Prolog is one example (see Section 4).

4.3 LISP

LISP is a widely used general purpose language for Artificial Intelligence programming.

The purpose of this section is not an exhaustive or formally precise introduction to the LISP language, but rather an explanation of the basic concepts, enough to understand the LISP code in the rest of the book. Although many important LISP features have been left out (most notably, macros and advanced data structures), the LISP subset presented in this Section is expressive enough to make it possible to develop non-trivial applications (see the code in Chapter 5).

The LISP syntax presented in this section and in all examples is that of CommonLISP. A more detailed description of CommonLISP, its implementation and its applications can be found in [Steele, 1984], [Winston and Horn, 1989], [Allen, 1978] and [Wilensky, 1988]. For an excellent introduction to LISP and programming in general, see [Abelson and Sussman, 1987].

4.3.1 A first look

When a LISP interpreter is started, typically a prompt is displayed at the beginning of a line. The prompt is a special character (">" in this section) displayed by the interpreter when it waits for the programmer to input an expression.

Indentation is free in LISP, with the only limitation that at least one blank is required between symbols. By default, the expression typed by the user, in this case the addition "(+ 5 6)", is written on the same line as the prompt, while the *value* (computed by the interpreter) is printed on a new line. Immediately after that, the interpreter prints the prompt again, since it is ready to process a new expression:

```
> (+ 5 6)
11
>
```

4.3.2 Atoms and lists

LISP words are called *atoms* . An atom is a string of any number of characters, except zero. Some characters (e.g. brackets, blanks) are not allowed within atoms, because they have a special meaning to the LISP interpreter. Atoms are either *symbols* or *numbers* . Numbers are defined as in other languages (they may be signed, etc.). Atoms which are not numbers are symbols. For instance, the present sentence consists of 14 atoms, 11 symbols and 3 numbers.

Example 9: Numbers and symbols

5
11
- 55.234

are numbers.

+
aBc33
hello
American-currency

are symbols. ■

LISP sentences are called *expressions* . Expressions consist either of a single atom, or of a *list* . A list is a sequence of expressions within brackets:

EXPRESSION ::= ATOM | LIST
ATOM ::= SYMBOL | NUMBER
LIST ::= ({EXPRESSION})

Example 10: Sample lists

```
(+ 5 6)                                     ;a list of 3 elements, one symbol and two numbers
(this is an introduction to LISP)           ;a list of six symbols
()                                          ;a list with no elements, called the empty list
(profit ((income less expenses) less taxes)) ;a list containing other lists
```

In the last list, the first element, "profit", is a symbol. The second is the expression:

((income less expenses) less taxes)

This last expression is a list with three elements; the first element is a list "(income less expenses)", the remaining are symbols. ■

Lists enclosed in other lists are said to be *nested* ; in the last list of the previous example, there are two levels of nesting.

The LISP interpreter accepts expressions, tries to find/compute a value associated to them using a set of *evaluation rules* , similar to, though more complex than, the evaluation rules in Example 2 Section 1.4 above. Then the interpreter returns the computed value. The fact of knowing LISP means to understand the evaluation rules used by the interpreter for computing the value of an expression, and to learn a set of expressions which are part of the definition of the language.

4.3.3 Evaluation rules for atomic expressions

Atomic expressions are expressions consisting of just one atom; when the interpreter is given an atomic expression, it evaluates it obeying the following rules:

1. if the atom is a number, its value is the number itself:

```
>15
15
>
```

2. if the atom is a symbol, the interpreter considers it as a variable, and returns the value associated to it (e.g. through a previous assignment, see Section 3.10 below). If there is no value associated to that symbol, then an error message is issued (compare with uninstantiated variables in high-level languages).

4.3.4 LISP functions

Any list typed to the interpreter is seen as a function; this section describes functions and their evaluation rules.

A mathematical function is a rule associating (mapping) to each element in a set (the domain) one element in another set (the range). One says that the function is applied to an element in the domain and computes the associated element in the range. Mathematics provides a formalism for defining and naming functions, and for applying functions to specific elements, called the arguments.

LISP functions are in many respects similar to mathematical functions. The first element of a list typed to the interpreter is considered to be the function name (*functor*), the other elements the arguments. Suppose that a LISP function has been defined (in a way to be explained later) under the name "f" and with two parameters. The expression:

(f a b)

is then a function *call* , i.e. the mapping rule defining the function f is applied to the arguments "a" and "b"; the result, returned by the interpreter, is called the **value** of the function:

(FUNCTION-NAME ARGUMENT$_1$ ... ARGUMENT$_N$)
FUNCTION-NAME ::= SYMBOL
ARGUMENT1 ::= EXPRESSION
ARGUMENTN ::= EXPRESSION

The functor refers to a sequence of expressions called the *function body* (analogy with procedural languages: a procedure or subroutine name refers to a sequence of statements). When evaluating a function, the interpreter first searches for a function body associated to the functor. This association is either defined by the user through a kind of "declaration" (analogy: procedure or subroutine declaration) or is predefined as a part of the LISP language. Predefined (or built-in, or primitive) functions are directly executable by the interpreter.

Example 11: Function call

```
> (+ 5 6)  ; this is a function call
11
>
```

"+" is the functor of a built-in function (users do not need to define the addition); 5 and 6 are the arguments of the call. The interpreter evaluates the function body associated to "+" and returns the result. ■

DEFUN is one primitive function for defining new functions. Alternatively, functions can be defined anonymously (i.e. without specifying the name) using the primitive **LAMBDA**:

(**DEFUN** FUNCTION-NAME PARAMETER-LIST

FUNCTION-BODY)

(**LAMBDA** PARAMETER-LIST
FUNCTION-BODY)

FUNCTION-NAME ::= SYMBOL
PARAMETER-LIST ::= (PARAMETER$_1$ ... PARAMETER$_N$)
PARAMETER1 ::= SYMBOL
PARAMETERN ::= SYMBOL
FUNCTION-BODY ::= EXPRESSION

Parameters are place takers for values. When a function is called, the value of a parameter is made equal to the value of the argument in the corresponding position in the function call (analogy: passing values to a procedure or a subroutine). This process is called *parameter binding* . LISP uses *call-by-value* for passing values to functions: i.e. no operation, such as assignment, inside the function body altering the value of the parameters can ever affect the value of the arguments in the function call. Conversely, there is no way to modify the value of the parameters in order to convey information back to the calling environment; the only information returned is the value of the function. Anonymous functions are used to define functions not referenced again at a later time. The expressions:

```
> ((LAMBDA (a b) <foo-body>) argument1 argument2)
result
```

and:

```
> (DEFUN foo (a b) <foo-body>)
foo
> (foo argument1 argument2)
result
```

produce the same results, with the difference that no new function was defined in the first case. The first expression is so common that the primitive **LET** has been introduced:

(LET ((parameter$_1$ argument$_1$)
(parameter$_N$ argument$_N$))
<body>)

being equivalent to:

((LAMBDA (parameter$_1$ ... parameter$_N$) <body>) argument$_1$ ... argument$_N$)

Programs in Chapter 5 contain many examples of LAMBDA definitions and LETs. LETs are commonly used to define local variables for blocks of statements within functions.

The evaluation rules in Section 3.3 above can now be augmented with the following steps for handling the named functions:

3. the first element in the list is considered to be the function name

4. a function definition is searched corresponding to the function name (either the function is a primitive, or was previously defined through a call to DEFUN)

5. the remaining elements of the list are evaluated, using the evaluation rules, and the results are bound to the parameters in the function definition (step 4.)

6. the expressions in the function body are evaluated

7. the value of the last expression in the function body is returned as the result

8. parameters are unbound upon exit from the function. If a parameter had the same name as another symbol in the calling environment, the value of that symbol is restored

4.3.5 Functional composition and abstraction

LISP retains the traditional approach to programming as a collection of simple user-defined functional procedures. Building blocks of LISP programs are the built-in functions. Programming in LISP basically consists in combining simpler functions into more complex functions. The most important technique, well known from mathematics, is functional composition: the value (or result) of one function is fed as the argument to another function.

Functional composition would be of little use without abstraction. Abstraction is the technique of using user-defined functions as if they were built-in; this is simply achieved by naming the functions obtained as a combination of built-in functions. The primitive supporting abstraction is the already mentioned **DEFUN**.

Example 12: Functional composition and abstraction

```
> (DEFUN relative-variation (X Y)        ; this is a function for computing the relative variation
      (/ (- X Y) Y))
relative-variation
> (relative-variation 5 3)
0.66667
> (relative-variation 2 (square 2))
- 0.5
>
```

In the first call, X was bound to 5, Y to 3; the function body was then evaluated. In the second call, X was bound to 2, and Y to the result of evaluating (square 2), i.e. 4. "Square" can be simply defined as:

```
> (DEFUN square (X) (* X X))
square
>
```

■

4.3.6 Application: computing elasticities in economics

Let's look at a slightly more complex example of functional composition and abstraction. First, we will define a function for computing the percentage-variation using the already defined relative-variation as a building block (abstraction).

Example 13: Percentage variation

```
> (* 100 (relative-variation 9 3))
200
>

> (DEFUN percentage-variation (X Y)
          (* 100 (relative-variation X Y)))
percentage-variation
> (percentage-variation 9 3)
```

```
200
>
```

■

Percentage-variation and relative-variation can in turn be used as building blocks in many interesting computations, such as elasticities.

Example 14: Elasticity

```
> (DEFUN elasticity (Q1 Q2 P1 P2)
        (- (/ (relative-variation Q1 Q2) (relative-variation P1 P2))))
elasticity
> (elasticity 5 4 3 4)
1
>
```

■

As a next step, let's compute arc elasticity. Here we have to define some more building blocks, namely arithmetic-average and variation-to-average.

Example 15: Arc elasticity

```
> (DEFUN arithmetic-average (A B)
    (/ (+ A B) 2))
arithmetic-average
> (arithmetic-average 4 6)
5

> (DEFUN variation-to-average (A B)
    (/ (- A B) (arithmetic-average A B)))
variation-to-average

> (DEFUN arc-elasticity (Q1 Q2 P1 P2)
    (- (/ (variation-to-average Q1 Q2) (variation-to-average P1 P2))))
arc-elasticity
> (arc-elasticity 5 4 3 4)
0.778
```

■

To appreciate the power and elegance of abstraction, compare the above definition of arc elasticity with the following, rather confusing definition, which uses primitive functions only:

```
> (DEFUN arc-elasticity (Q1 Q2 P1 P2) (- (/ (/ (- Q1 Q2) (/ (+ Q1 Q2) 2)) (/ (- P1 P2) (/ (+ P1 P2) 2)))))
```

4.3.7 Functional vs. procedural programming

The above sections stressed the analogies between procedural and functional programming paradigms. This section highlights some differences.

Procedural languages use statements (instead of functions) as primitives; programs and procedures consist of sequences of statements. Functions, on the contrary, are defined in terms of other, primitive functions. Some of the statements in a PASCAL-like language are functional (e.g. IF ... THEN ... ELSE ...). Others, however, are not. Among them:

- assignment, since its purpose is to modify the environment (exactly the opposite of what a function is supposed to do). In a (pure) functional programming style, assignment is not allowed, since it can cause subtle consequences: for instance, the same piece of code (with the same local variables), called at different times during execution, may return different results, because of an assignment modifying the value of a free variable in between

- control statements, such as "goto", "callsub" etc. These statements are used to modify the sequential execution of a program. Functional programming is non-sequential, being based on nested functions, and in principle has no control statements.

The next example is purely functional, and shows very clearly some of the strengths of a functional programming language over a procedural one.

Example 16: Expenditure calculations as inner product

Problem: Given two vectors of the same length, multiply corresponding elements and sum the results [Backus, 1978].

For instance, one vector (unitary-cost) could represent the unitary costs of a set of transactions, the other vector (quantity) the quantity of each transaction. Then the inner product is the total expenditure. In LISP, vectors can be simply represented as lists.

PASCAL-like:

```
total-expenditure := 0;
FOR i := 1 TO n DO
 total-expenditure := total-expenditure + unitary-cost[i] * quantity[i]
END;
```

LISP:

```
(APPLY '+ (MAPCAR '* unitary-cost quantity))
```

* and + are primitive functions, having obvious mathematical meanings (for the moment, forget the quotes). MAPCAR and APPLY are primitive as well. They accept functors as arguments (* is an argument of MAPCAR, + of APPLY) and modify their behaviors:

- **MAPCAR** causes the multiplication to be repeatedly executed over elements in corresponding positions in the two lists (the first element of unitary-cost times the first element of quantity; the second element of unitary-cost times the second element of quantity and so on). The results are packed in an output list;
- **APPLY** causes the elements in a list to be passed as arguments to the function +; the returned result (i.e. total-expenditure) is therefore the sum of all elements in the vector computed by MAPCAR.

MAPCAR and APPLY are just examples of functions modifying the behavior of other functions. This is another way of combining functions.

Note that LISP computation is independent of the length n of the vectors; this makes the program at the same time more general and easier to understand; furthermore, neither loop nor counter were needed. ■

Example 17: Functional composition

PASCAL-like:

```
proc1 (arg1 arg2 temp1)
proc2 (arg3 temp1 temp2)
proc3 (temp1 temp2 result)
```

Additional arguments (called temp1, temp2 and result) must be added to the procedures in order to store partial results. The procedures are called sequentially one after the other, and the additional argument is passed each time. temp1, temp2 and result must be known outside the procedures and hence affect the environment, potentially causing undesired interactions with other parts of the code.

LISP-like:

```
(funct3  (funct1 arg1 arg2)  (funct2 arg3 (funct1 arg1 arg2)) )
```

Functions return values, hence can be combined: "funct1" and "funct2" return respectively temp1 and temp2, the two arguments of funct3; funct3 then computes the result. The example also shows one source of inefficiency in purely functional programming: funct1 is computed twice with the same arguments; this is one case in which an assignment could help. ■

4.3.8 Boolean functions, IF and COND

A Boolean function is a function whose value is one of true (**T**) or false (**NIL**). **T** and **NIL** are two built-in atoms for expressing Boolean truth values, with special evaluation rules: evaluating **T** returns **T**, evaluating **NIL** returns **NIL**. Later (see Section 3.9), a second interpretation for NIL will be introduced.

Boolean expressions take some kind of data as argument(s) and return a Boolean result. These include:

- expressions for testing and comparing numbers (EVENP, ODDP, ZEROP; =, /=, <, >), with the obvious meaning (/= stands for different). The final P is a mnemonic for predicate
- expressions for testing and comparing atoms (NUMBERP, INTEGERP, ATOM; EQUAL, EQL), with their obvious meaning (so e.g. ATOM returns true if the argument is an atom). Roughly, given two arguments, EQUAL is an equality test in the sense of the structures, while EQL tests for equality w.r.t. the same physical location in the computer memory
- expressions for testing special values of other datatypes (LISTP, NULL), where LISTP returns true if the argument is a list, and NULL returns true if the argument is the empty list

Logical connectives are Boolean functions taking as arguments T, NIL or other Boolean functions, and returning T or NIL, following the usual rules of logic (see Chapter 3.5.2.1). When a Boolean value is expected, but the function is not a Boolean function, the interpreter considers any returned value different from NIL as being T.

Example 18: Boolean functions

```
> (< 6 7)
T
> (AND (+ 5 6) (- 8 3))
T
> (AND (+ 5 6) NIL)
NIL
>
```

■

Boolean expressions are often used in connection with **IF** and **COND**, the LISP functions for conditional branching:

(**IF** BOOLEAN-EXPRESSION EXPRESSION$_1$ EXPRESSION$_2$)

BOOLEAN-EXPRESSION ::= EXPRESSION
EXPRESSION$_1$ ::= EXPRESSION
EXPRESSION$_2$ ::= EXPRESSION

(**COND** (BOOLEAN-EXPRESSION$_1$ EXPRESSION$_1$)
(BOOLEAN-EXPRESSION$_2$ EXPRESSSION$_2$)
(BOOLEAN-EXPRESSSION$_N$ EXPRESSION$_N$))

BOOLEAN-EXPRESSION$_1$ ::= EXPRESSION

BOOLEAN-EXPRESSION$_N$ ::= EXPRESSION
EXPRESSION$_1$ ::= EXPRESSION
EXPRESSION$_N$ ::= EXPRESSION

IF is evaluated as follows:

BOOLEAN-EXPRESSION is evaluated first; if it is T (or can be interpreted as T), EXPRESSION$_1$ is evaluated and its value is returned as the result of the IF; otherwise, EXPRESSION$_2$ is evaluated and its result is returned as the result of the IF. Contrary to the general evaluation rule, only the Boolean test is evaluated at function call time, but not EXPRESSION$_1$ and EXPRESION$_2$; depending on the result of the test, only one of them is evaluated.

Example 19: "IF"

```
> (DEFUN tax-status (income)
      (IF (< income 6000)
            'no-taxes
            'normal))
> (tax-status 3400)
no-taxes
> (tax-status 6000)
normal
>
```

■

COND is evaluated as follows:

The Boolean expressions are evaluated in their order, until one succeeds; the corresponding expression is then evaluated, its value is returned, and the COND is terminated. If no Boolean expression succeeds, the COND returns NIL. Note that only the first successful Boolean test found is ever considered.

Example 20: "COND"

```
> (DEFUN tax-level (income)
        (COND           ((income < 6000)    0)
                ((income < 10000) 10)
                ((income < 50000)  20)
                ((income < 80000)  40)
                (T                  50)))
tax-level
> (tax-level 4000)          ; all Booleans in COND would succeed, but the COND terminates after the first one
0
> (tax-level 11000)
20
> (tax-level 100000)
50
>
```

The last Boolean in the COND always succeeds, since it is T, and is called a *catch-all* condition (analogy: ELSE or OTHERWISE in similar statements in procedural languages). Catch-all conditions must always be at the end of a COND, otherwise they would shield the other tests. A catch-all condition as the above may cause unexpected answers:

```
> (tax-level 'this-is-not-a-valid-income)
50
>
```

■

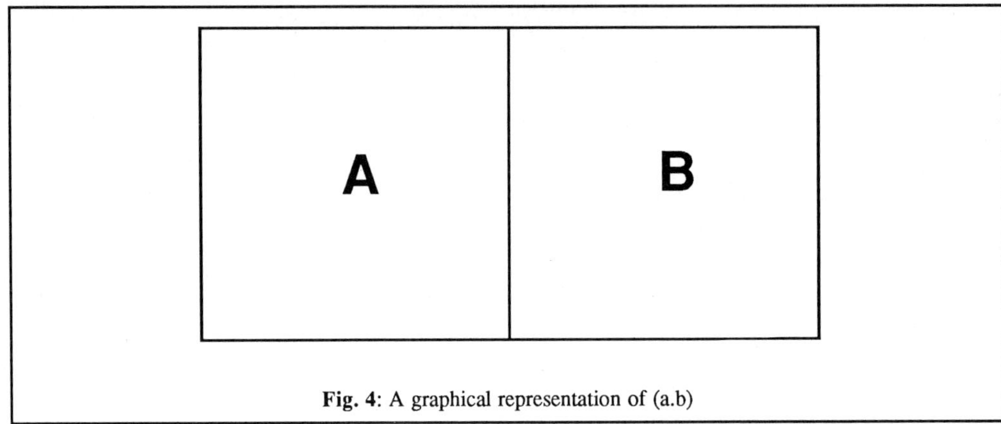

Fig. 4: A graphical representation of (a.b)

4.3.9 Symbolic data structures

All above examples were numeric; however the essence of AI programming languages is their capability for manipulating symbols. LISP provides a simple way for building symbolic data structures of any complexity. The elementary data, as explained in Section 3.2 above, is the atom. Atoms can be grouped into *pairs* . The primitive functions **CONS, CAR** and **CDR** are used for building resp. retrieving elements from pairs:

(**CONS** ARGUMENT_1 ARGUMENT_2)

(**CAR** PAIR)

(**CDR** PAIR)

ARGUMENT_1 ::= EXPRESSION
ARGUMENT_2 ::= EXPRESSION
PAIR ::= EXPRESSION

CONS takes two expressions and packs them into a pair; **CAR** retrieves the first element of the pair; **CDR** retrieves the second element.

Example 21: "CONS", "CAR", "CDR"

```
> (CONS 'a 'b)
(a . b)
> (CAR '(a . b))
a
> (CDR '(a . b))
b
>
```

■

The interpreter prints a pair enclosed in brackets, with a dot separating the two elements. Fig. 4 displays a simple way to imagine a pair, as a collection of two squares representing the symbols (again, the meaning of the quote before the atoms will be explained later).

Pairs can in turn be combined to form sequences (*lists*) of any length: the second element in each pair is assumed to be a pair itself; the empty pair (or list) is indicated with **NIL**. Fig. 5a shows a list containing the symbols a, b, c. Its LISP representation would be:

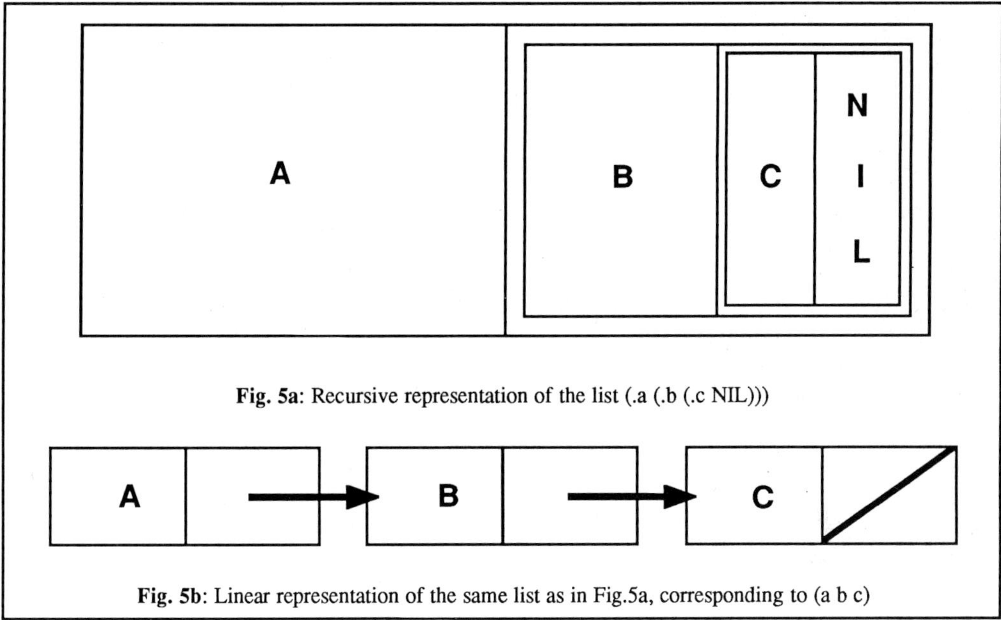

Fig. 5a: Recursive representation of the list (.a (.b (.c NIL)))

Fig. 5b: Linear representation of the same list as in Fig.5a, corresponding to (a b c)

(a . (b . (c . NIL)))

An equivalent representation, closer to the actual implementation, is shown in Fig. 5b. The resulting notation is much simpler than the notation shown above, and therefore used as the standard notation for lists:

(a b c)

Intuitively, **CONS**, **CAR** and **CDR** can still be used for building and decomposing lists. Obviously, just as lists are nested pairs, so **CONS**es, **CAR**s and **CDR**s (defined over pairs) must be nested when used over lists.

NIL, beside being an atom (the Boolean value false), is a list as well (the empty list). Therefore **NIL**, or (), which is an equivalent notation, is the only LISP object being an atom and a list at the same time.

In addition to **CONS**, **CAR** and **CDR**, LISP provides a number of primitive functions for manipulating and testing lists. Among them:

LIST returns a list of the arguments

```
> (LIST 'a 'b)
(a b)
> (LIST 'a 'b '(a b c))
(a b (a b c))
```

APPEND connects together two or more lists

```
> (APPEND '(a b) '(c d))
(a b c d)
> (APPEND '(a b) '())
(a b)
```

REVERSE returns a list with arguments in opposite order:

```
> (REVERSE '(a b c d))
(d c b a)
```

LENGTH returns the length of a list

```
> (LENGTH '(a b c d))
4
```

Furthermore, remember the predicates LISTP and NULL, already introduced in Section 3.8 above.

Since lists are the very core of LISP, a useful set of predefined functions is available, which takes as arguments another function and one or more lists, and repeatedly applies the function to each element of the lists provided (see Section 3.10 below for hints on how to pass functions as arguments to other functions). A first example was MAPCAR, introduced in Section 3.7. A second class of such functions are filters:

(<filter-name> <predicate-name> <list>)

where predicate-name must be a Boolean function. Such functions return a list filtered for elements satisfying (or not satisfying) the predicate. REMOVE-IF and REMOVE-IF-NOT are two primitives for building filters, the expected filtering being achieved by defining an appropriate predicate.

4.3.10 Assignment and evaluation of the data

An atom can be associated to a value through an assignment statement. Although the assignment is not functional, it has been retained in LISP because it is difficult to do without it in large programs (reassigning a set of variables is a way of implementing the idea of a change in a state). Moreover, assignment is a way of naming complex data so that they can be used as if they were simple, i.e. to support data abstraction. An often used built-in function for performing the assignment is **SETQ**:

(**SETQ** VARIABLE VALUE)

VARIABLE ::= SYMBOL
VALUE ::= EXPRESSION

which is equivalent to assignment in conventional programming languages. The expression is evaluated by the interpreter and the result is assigned to the variable. The evaluation rule for SETQ does not follow the general evaluation rule for functions: e.g. VARIABLE is not evaluated by the interpreter (it would return an error, if the atom had no value associated to it).

Example 22: Assignment

```
> option1
error: unbound atom
> (SETQ option1 (FORD 50 July call))
(FORD 50 July call)
> option1
(FORD 50 July call)
>
```

When at first option1 is evaluated, fail is returned, because no value is associated to it. Through an assignment, however, a value is associated to the atom. As the atom option1 is evaluated again, it will return its value. ■

A crucial function in connection with the use of assignment is **QUOTE**:

(**QUOTE** DATA)

DATA ::= EXPRESSION

QUOTE is used so often, that a shorthand notation exists:

'EXPRESSION ::= (**QUOTE** EXPRESSION)

When evaluating QUOTE, the interpreter uses again a special evaluation rule. The argument is not evaluated, and the value returned is the argument itself.

```
> (QUOTE a)
a
> 'a
a
```

So, when evaluating a list, the interpreter looks for a function definition associated to the CAR of the list (see Section 3.4). When the list is intended to be a collection of data (as in Section 3.9 above), it must be quoted:

```
> (a b c)
error: no function definition for atom a
>'(a b c)
(a b c)
```

The notions of assignment and quoting help to clarify the relation between DEFUN and LAMBDA expressions introduced in Section 3.4: DEFUN can be viewed as an assignment of a LAMBDA expression to an atom, which then becomes the name of the function:

(DEFUN foo (a b) <body>) is equivalent to

(<assignment statement> foo '(LAMBDA (a b) <body>))

<assignment statement> is not simply SETQ, because CommonLISP (as opposed to some other LISP dialects) does not store the function definition of an atom exactly in the same way (and the same place) as its value. The primitive function **FUNCTION** must be used to retrieve the functional definition of a symbol. In some circumstances, however, it is useful to store and retrieve a function as the value of an atom. One common example is passing functions as arguments to other functions. Another common example is storing functions as fields in data structures (e.g. as properties, see Section 3.11 below). Consider the function:

(DEFUN foo (a b error-printer) <body with detection of error conditions>)

"error-printer" must be a function to be used within foo body to print out error conditions. Assume the user has defined a function:

(DEFUN my-error (error) <body>)

to customize error printing. Then he would call foo as follows:

```
> (foo arg1 arg2 'my-error)
```

whereby error-printer is bound to the value of my-error. Quoting is necessary because, from the viewpoint of CommonLISP, my-error is unbound, since the function definition is not stored at the same place as the atom value. The function **FUNCALL** does the job of retrieving the function definition, i.e. foo must contain an expression like:

```
(DEFUN foo (a b error-printer)
        < ... (IF error (FUNCALL error-printer error)) ... >)
```

Recall the definition of REMOVE-IF in the previous Section 3.9. The following function filters all expired options from a list of available options:

```
>(DEFUN option-filter (option-list current-date)
        (REMOVE-IF #'(LAMBDA (x) (BEFOREP (CADDR x) current-date)))
```

where BEFOREP is a function for comparing dates, and each option in option-list is supposed to be represented as a list of the form (<security> <strike-price> <date> <option type>). #' is a special kind of quote enforcing lexical scoping rules.

As a final remark on assignment, note from Example 22 above that the same atom, evaluated before and after the execution of the assignment, returns different results: this means that the execution of **SETQ** has left a permanent change in the environment, also called a *side-effect*. The change above was made purposely; however, in more complicated contexts, assignment may cause unwanted effects which may be difficult to detect.

4.3.11 Properties and association lists

Two important ways of organizing data are properties and association lists. Since they are heavily used in the code later in this book, they are briefly introduced here. *Properties* are named slots which can be attached to atoms and filled with a value. They are useful for representing information relevant to the atom (such as comments to be printed by the system, pointers to other elements, etc.)

The functions **SETF** (a generalization of SETQ) and **GET** are used for modification-initialization properties and for retrieving them, respectively:

> (**GET** VARIABLE PROPERTY)
> VARIABLE ::= EXPRESSION
> PROPERTY ::= EXPRESSION
>
> (**SETF** PROPERTY NEWVALUE)
> PROPERTY ::= EXPRESSION
> NEWVALUE ::= EXPRESSION

GET takes two arguments (whose evaluation must return two symbols, the atom and the property name) and computes the property value; if there is no property with that name it returns **NIL**. **SETF** uses **GET** to retrieve the old value (or **NIL**) and replace it by the second argument.

Example 23: Properties

Consider how to express the rating of bonds as a property. Then:

```
>(SETF (GET 'IBM 'rating) 'AAA)
AAA
>
```

adds a property called rating to the atom IBM and instantiates it to AAA.

```
>(GET 'IBM 'rating)
AAA
>
```

retrieves the property value. Any number of properties is allowed:

```
>(SETF (GET 'IBM 'volume) 400000)
400000
>
```

To change a property simply use SETF again:

```
>(SETF (GET 'IBM 'duration) 4)
4
>(GET 'IBM 'duration)
4
>
```

■

Association lists are lists in which each element is a list. The first element of each sublist is assumed to be the key, and the rest of the sublist some information associated to the key. Since association lists are nothing but lists, they are built and modified in the usual ways (see Section 3.9 above). However, the primitive **ASSOC** is provided for returning the first sublist containing the key.

Example 24: Association lists

The list:

((\$ 15000) (DM 30000) (£ 2000))

can be viewed as an association list.

In the following we store this list in a property of the client Jones:

```
> (SETF (GET 'Jones 'currency-portfolio) (($ 15000) (DM 30000) (£ 2000)))
(($ 15000) (DM 30000) (£ 2000))
> (ASSOC 'DM (GET 'Jones 'currency-portfolio))
(DM 30000)
>
```

■

One problem with association lists is that it is difficult to change the information in them. An often used trick is to add a new sublist with the same key and the new information at the beginning of the association list. Since ASSOC returns the **first** sublist containing an occurrence of the key, the proper sublist will be retrieved. The following example updates the amount in DM of Mr. Jones' portfolio:

Example 25: Changing information in association lists

```
> (SETF (GET 'Jones 'currency-portfolio)
        (CONS (DM 35000) (GET 'Jones 'currency-portfolio))
((DM 35000) ($ 15000) (DM 30000) (£ 2000))
> (ASSOC 'DM (GET 'Jones 'currency-portfolio))
(DM 35000)
>
```

■

4.3.12 Dynamic data typing

Variables in PASCAL and similar languages are rigidly typed, i.e. the set of values which can be assigned to a variable is established through a declaration and never modified during the program. In LISP only data objects (constants) are typed, but variables can be assigned any value of any type (see Section 3.8 above for a collection of predicates testing the type of data objects). Dynamic typing is crucial for implementing high level functions and generic operators (operators working on a broad class of different types).

Example 26: Generic operators

Generic addition for numbers or data pairs, such as (price, volume):

```
(DEFUN generic-add (Number1 Number2)
        (COND ((NUMBERP Number1)
                (IF (NUMBERP Number2)
                   (+ Number1 Number2)
                   (CONS (+ Number1 (CAR Number2)) (CDR Number2))))
            ((NUMBERP Number2)
                (CONS (+ (CAR Number1) Number2) (CDR Number1)))
            (T   (CONS (+ (CAR Number1) (CAR Number2))
                          (+ (CDR Number1) (CDR Number2))))))
```

■

4.3.13 Identity of programs and data

In Section 3.2 above it was explained that lists are expressions; accordingly, in Sections 3.3, lists were viewed as functions. However, in Section 3.9 above, lists represented data structures. There is no contradiction among these views, since LISP does not distinguish between statements and data. This is evident from the fact that functions are LISP expressions, just like lists.

Two functions are crucial in switching the interpretation between data and expressions: **QUOTE** (see Section 3.10 above) and **EVAL**.

(EVAL EXPRESSION)

Example 27: Programs as data

```
> (arc-elasticity 5 4 3 4)
0.778
> (CAR '(arc-elasticity 5 4 3 4))
arc-elasticity
> (CDR '(arc-elasticity 5 4 3 4))
(5 4 3 4)
> (CONS 'elasticity (CDR '(arc-elasticity 5 4 3 4))
(elasticity 5 4 3 4)
>
```

The last expression shows how programs can be decomposed into pieces and then rebuilt using CAR, CDR, CONS, QUOTE: a program computing arc-elasticity is transformed into a program computing elasticity by replacing the CAR of the list. ■

EVAL is a function of one argument performing a user controlled call to the interpreter; it returns the evaluation of its argument. EVAL forces data to be interpreted as expressions: it is often necessary to use EVAL when executing the results of data manipulations as programs.

Example 28: "EVAL" function

```
> (EVAL  (CONS 'elasticity (CDR (arc-elasticity 5 4 3 4)))
1
>
```

■

The identity of programs and data makes it possible to use programs as inputs and results of other programs. This is useful for implementing parsers, evaluators and interpreters.

4.3.14 Application: computing compound interests by recursion

A function is recursive when it is defined by expressions involving the function itself. In this sense, recursion can be seen as a special kind of functional composition. For instance, consider a function for computing the amount of capital after a n years investment at a fixed interest rate; this is also called the terminal value of the investment. This calculation involves compound interests. A recursive definition for such a function is:

```
> (DEFUN terminal-value (capital interest-rate years)
    (IF (= years 0)
          capital
        ( * (+ 1 interest-rate) (terminal-value capital interest-rate (- years 1)))))
```

If the number of years is zero, the terminal value is the capital itself. Otherwise, the return at the end of the k-th year is (1 + interest-rate) times the terminal-value at the end of the previous year.

Note that terminal-value (the function to be defined) appears in its own definition. At first, it may seem that the interpreter would get caught in an infinite loop, jumping forever back and forth between function definition and function call. The best way to find out that this is not the case, is to follow step-by-step the evaluation of the call:

```
>(terminal-value 1000 0.06 3)
```

1. The body of the function is evaluated with parameters bound to the arguments values.

Since years is not 0,

```
( * (+ 1 0.06) (terminal-value 1000 0.06 (- 3 1)))))
```

is evaluated. To do this, the interpreter must first evaluate the multiplication. Hence, the interpreter searches for a function definition for terminal-value (and finds it in the above DEFUN) and calls it with the new arguments:

```
(terminal-value 1000 0.06 2)
```

The value returned from this call is used to compute:

```
(* 1.06 (terminal-value 1000 0.06 2))
```

whose result is the result of the original call. Hence the initial problem has been reduced to the problem of evaluating:

```
(terminal-value 1000 0.06 2)
```

2. Analogously to step 1., the result of the multiplication:

```
(* 1.06 (terminal-value 1000 0.06 (- 2 1))
```

cannot be computed until the interpreter evaluates:

```
(terminal-value 1000 0.06 1)
```

This is a new function call, and is treated in the next step.

3. By the same reasoning, the result of:

```
(terminal-value 1000 0.06 1)
```

is the result of:

(* 1.06 (terminal-value 1000 0.06 (- 1 0)))

Therefore the new function call is:

(terminal-value 1000 0.06 0)

4. When executing the body of terminal-value with **0** as the number of years, the test in the IF statement succeeds. Hence the **first** expression after the test is executed, and the value of the capital is returned. Thus this call **succeeds** and returns the result 1000.

3'. With the result of the call, the multiplication in step 3. can now be evaluated:

(* (1 + 0.06) (terminal-value 1000 0.06 0))

which returns:

(* 1.06 1000) = 1060

Hence:

(terminal-value 1000 0.06 1) = 1060

2'. Similarly, the multiplication in step 2. can be computed:

(* (1 + 0.06) (terminal-value 1000 0.06 1)) = 1123.6

Hence:

(terminal-value 1000 0.06 2) = 1123.6

1'. Finally, the interpreter can compute the multiplication in step 1.:

(* (1 + 0.06) (terminal-value 1000 0.06 2)) = 1191.016

Hence:

(terminal-value 1000 0.06 3) = 1191.016

and this is the returned result.

Therefore:

```
> (terminal-value 1000 0.06 3)
1191.016
>
```

As it is clear from the above discussion, the essence of recursive definitions is that the function is defined in terms of a modified (usually simplified) call to itself. Recursion terminates because of the termination test (which is part of every recursive definition), i.e. a test which will surely be satisfied (after an unknown number of calls) returning a computable result independently of the function being defined. In the above example, the IF statement provides a non-recursive definition for terminal-value when the value of years is 0. The test in the IF will surely be satisfied, since at each call the years are decreased by 1.

4.4 Prolog

The basic idea of declarative programming is to express programs as a set of assertions (in the following referred to as *beliefs*) in some kind of declarative language (usually logic or some simplifications thereof). A few languages have been designed to incorporate concepts of logics into their data structures. The most popular among them is Prolog, shortly introduced in this section.

References for further study are [Clocksin and Mellish, 1987], [Giannesini et al., 1986]. Interesting programming examples can be found in [Walker, 1987], [van Caneghem and Warren, 1986].

[Clocksin and Mellish, 1984] is also the reference work for the syntax assumed here. For a different syntax, see [Giannesini et al., 1986].

4.4.1 Beliefs in Prolog

Prolog is a programming language based on a subset of the clausal form of logic (see Chapter 3.5.5). In clausal form, wffs (i.e. sentences) of the language are called *clauses* . A clause is a disjunction of literals, were each literal is either a predicate (see Chapter 3.5.2) or a negated predicate. Disjunction and negation were explained in Chapter 3.5.3. Furthermore, the only allowable variables are universally quantified variables (see Chapter 3.5.4). In Prolog, for efficiency reasons, wffs are a restricted kind of clauses, in which there is at most one unnegated literal. Such clauses are called *Horn clauses* (see [Kowalski, 1979]). In other words, if p_1, ... , p_N are predicates, then:

p1 ∨ ¬p2 ∨ ... (other negated literals) ... ∨ ¬pN

is a Horn clause. By rewriting clauses as implications (see Chapter 3.5.3), a Horn restriction is equivalent to imposing conclusions consisting of just one predicate:

p1 ∨ ¬p2 ∨ ... (other negated literals) ... ∨ ¬pN

p1 ∨ ¬(p2 ∧ ... ∧ pN)

p2 ∧ ... ∧ pN –> p1

p1 <– p2 ∧ ... ∧ pN

The last wff is a rearrangement of the preceding one, with the conclusion put in evidence. Apart from notational conventions (which may in turn vary among different Prolog implementations), the above Horn clause corresponds to a Prolog *rule* (see Section 4.3 below). Note that, using implication, negation no longer appears explicitly.

Two special cases of Horn clauses are worth noting. First, a Horn clause consisting of just one non-negated literal:

p <–

is called a *fact* (see Section 4.2): it expresses the belief that p is true. Secondly, a Horn clause with just negated literals, i.e.:

<– p2 ∧ ... ∧ pN

is called a *goal* (see Section 4.5), and is equivalent to a negated conjunction.

4.4.2 Facts

The syntax of Prolog defines the way in which beliefs can be expressed. Prolog assumes that beliefs are described within a framework which is the same as that of first order predicate calculus:

- constants give a name to objects and relations. In the Prolog syntax used here a constant is a sequence of alphabetic characters or numbers, beginning with a lowercase letter
- variables refer to objects without naming them. The clausal form of logic allows only universally quantified variables (see Chapter 3.5.5). In Prolog, a variable is a sequence of alphabetic characters or numbers, beginning with an uppercase letter. The quantifier is dropped, since no confusion can arise. Because of the first order restriction of logic (see Chapter 3.5.4), variables cannot be used in the place of predicates or structures (Section 4.10), but only as arguments in relations. Variables with the same name but in different clauses may denote different objects

A fact is then a wff:

predicate_name($Term_1$, ..., $Term_N$).

where predicate_name is a constant naming a relation, and terms are object constants, or variables, or object structures. As any wff in Prolog, facts must be terminated by a full stop.

A *predicate* (i.e. a relation) is defined through a collection of facts, one for each combination of objects among which the relation holds. The arity of a predicate is the number of terms involved in the predicate. The predicate_name and arity completely identify a predicate. Predicates with the same predicate_name but different arity are different predicates.

Example 29: Representing knowledge about currencies

Suppose there are five currencies (dollar, yen, deutschmark, pound, ruble). The following is a collection of Prolog facts which might be relevant to the task.

```
inflation.                          /* there is something called inflation */
                                    /* inflation has arity =0, i.e. is a belief not involving objects */

currency(dollar).                   /* the dollar is a currency */
currency(yen).                      /* the yen is a currency */
convertible(deutchmark).            /* the deutchmark is convertible */
not_convertible(ruble).             /* the ruble is not convertible, at least for the moment */
                                    /* currency, convertible and not_convertible are predicates of arity=1*/

exchange_rate(yen, dollar, 157).    /* the exchange rate of the yen to the dollar is 147 */
exchange_rate(yen, pound, 227).     /* the exchange rate of the yen to the pound is 227 */
                                    /* exchange rate has arity=3; it involves two currencies and a number */

exchange_rate(X, X, 1).             /* this is a fact with variables. It expresses the belief that the exchange */
                                    /* rate of a currency to itself is always 1 */
```

■

Example 30: Facts about a transaction

In Chapter 3.5.3 a set of beliefs relevant to the representation of transactions was introduced. The same set of beliefs, with minor syntactic changes, is a correct Prolog program consisting of just facts:

```
transaction(p).                     /* object p is a transaction */

agent (p, agent_1).                 /* agent_1 is an agent in the transaction p */
agent (p, agent_2).                 /* agent_2 is an agent in the transaction p */

commodity (q_1, commodity_1).       /* q_1 is a commodity */
```

```
commodity (q_2, commodity_2).          /* q_2 is a commodity */

exchange (p, q_1).                     /* q_1 is an exchange good in the transaction p */
exchange (p, q_2).                     /* q_2 is an exchange good in transaction p */

quantity (q_1, quantity_1).            /* q_1 is quantifiable */
quantity (q_2, quantity_2).            /* q_2 is quantifiable */

gives-away (p, agent_1, q_1).          /* in transaction p agent_1 gives away exchange good q_1 */
gives-away (p, agent_2, q_2).          /* in transaction p agent_2 gives away exchange good q_2 */

receives (p, agent_1, 100, q_2).       /* in transaction p agent_1 receives 100% of exchange good q_2 */
receives (p, agent_2, 100, q_1).       /* in transaction p agent_2 receives 100% of exchange good q_1 */

time (p, t).                           /* transaction p happened at time t */
```

■

4.4.3 Rules

Being logical implications, *rules* are constraints about the truth values of predicates, according to the truth table in Fig. 6, Chapter 3. Basically, they allow abstraction (i.e. the definition of new predicates in terms of old predicates), as described in Section 3.5. A Prolog rule has the form:

```
predicate_name(<terms>) :-
        predicate_name1(<terms>),
        :
        predicate_nameN(<terms>).
```

":-" denote implication "<–", and separates the conclusion from the premise. The premise may consist either of a conjunction (noted with comma, ","), or a disjunction (noted ";") of predicates, or of just one predicate. <terms> is any sequence of terms, separated by a comma, as explained in Section 4.2 above. Syntactically identical terms denote the same objects or structures. Commas as separators between terms should not be confused with commas between predicates in rule premises, nor with the logical meaning of AND. Since a rule is a Prolog sentence, it must be ended by a full stop.

Example 31: Two rules for the exchange rate of currencies

```
exchange_rate(Currency_1, Currency_2, Z) :-
        exchange_rate(Currency_1, Currency_3, X),
        exchange_rate(Currency_3, Currency_2, Y),
        Z is X * Y.
```

/*If the exchange rate between any currency and another currency is x, and the exchange rate between that other currency and a third currency is y, and z is x times y, then the exchange rate between the first currency and the third currency is z */

```
exchange_rate(Currency1, Currency2, X) :-
        exchange_rate(Currency2, Currency1, Y),
        X is 1 / Y.
```

/*If the exchange rate of a currency to another currency is y, then the exchange rate of that other currency to the first currency is 1 over y */

Variables are used in rules to express generic constraints among objects. ■

Table 1 summarizes rules 1 and 2 in the above example, as well as facts similar to those in Example 29, Section 4.4.3 into an elementary knowledge base about currencies. This knowledge base will be used later to show some problems related to coding logic into Prolog.

```
exchange_rate(yen, dollar, 147).            /* fact1 */
exchange_rate(lira, dollar, 1400).          /* fact2 */
exchange_rate(lira, yen, 9.5238).           /* fact3 */
exchange_rate(dollar, pound, 1.5).          /* fact4 */
exchange_rate(lira, pound, 2100).           /* fact5 */
exchange_rate(X, X, 1).                     /* fact6: the exchange rate of any currency to itself is 1 */

/* Rule1 */
exchange_rate(Currency1, Currency2, Z) :-
                    exchange_rate(Currency1, Currency3, X),
                    exchange_rate(Currency3, Currency2, Y),
                     Z is X * Y.

/* Rule2 */
exchange_rate(Currency1, Currency2, X) :-
                    exchange_rate(Currency2, Currency1, Y),
                     X is 1 / Y.
```

Table 1: A knowledge base about currencies (bugged !)

Example 32: Validity of transactions

Example 30, Section 4.3 presented a simple database of facts about a transactions. One criterion for transaction validation is correct transaction timing. An implementation of temporal logic (see Chapter 3.8) would be needed to express full time constraints; however, in this Example, the simple implication at the end of Chapter 3.5.5 is translated into Prolog.

Logic:

$\forall$x,y,t,t1: transaction(x, y) $\wedge$ market(y) $\wedge$ close-time (y, t1) $\wedge$ time (x, t) $\wedge$ after (t, t1) –> not-valid(x)

Prolog:

```
not_valid(X) :- transaction(X, Y), market(Y), close-time(Y, T1), time(X, T), after(T, T1).
```

The above comparison makes explicit the elimination of the quantifiers and the different syntactic conventions. ■

A collection of facts and rules is called a knowledge base or database. A knowledge base is a Prolog program. Prolog provides two built-in (predefined) predicates for adding/removing beliefs to/from the knowledge base: **assert** and **retract**:

assert(Clause).

retract(Clause).

If Clause is a rule, it must be enclosed within brackets. **assert** and **retract** are generally not used to enter clauses into the program knowledge base (much better editors are available for this task), but are needed for implementing predicates causing changes in the program's state (the knowledge base).

Example 33: Knowledge about actions

In Example 20, Chapter 3.6.5, an IF -THEN rule was defined for transactions.

Its translation in Prolog involves, as the original rule, the use of "assert" and "retract".

```
transaction(Stock, Owned_amount, Sale_amount, Goal_price, Market_price) :-
        amount(Stock, Owned_amount),
        amount_for_sale(Stock, Sale_amount),
```

```
Owned_amount ≥ Sale_amount,
goal_price(Stock, Goal_price)),
current_price(Stock, Market_price),
Market_price ≥ Goal_price,
retract((amount(Stock, Owned_amount))),
retract((amount_for_sale(Stock, Sale_amount))),
retract((goal_price(Stock, Goal_price))),
Remaining_amount is Owned_amount - Sale_amount,
assert((amount(Stock, Remaining_amount))),
retract((balance(Old_balance))),
New_balance is Old_balance + Market_price * Sale_amount
assert((balance(New_balance))).
```

■

4.4.4 Goals

Prolog, as LISP, is an interactive language.

Being based on logic, the Prolog interpreter works like a theorem prover (see Chapter 3.5.5). The programmer writes a set of *axioms* (i.e. a program) in clausal form, assessing relations in the problem domain. Prolog programs are not executed in the usual sense. Instead, the user *queries* the interpreter. Allowable queries concern the *truth* of a predicate or of a conjunction or disjunction of predicates. A query is sometimes called a *goal* , and a predicate in a compound query a *subgoal* . The interpreter tries to derive the truth of the query from the facts and rules in the program. After the interpreter has answered a question, the user may ask another question, or leave the program.

To show a goal, the interpreter uses *resolution* and proof by *refutation* (Chapter 3.5.5). The goal is negated and temporarily added to the knowledge base. Hence the prompt displayed by the interpreter when it is ready to accept a question (e.g. "?-") has the logical meaning of a *negation* of what follows. If the goal is logically implied by the knowledge base (i.e. it is true), its negation is inconsistent with it, and the interpreter is able to derive the mark of inconsistency, i.e. the empty clause. On the contrary, if the goal is not implied by the knowledge base (i.e. no empty clause can be derived), the interpreter *assumes* it is false. Practically, the interpreter is able to prove a predicate goal if:

- there is a predicate in the knowledge base matching it (i.e. syntactically identical to, through substitutions of variables for terms, see Section 4.7 below)
- the corresponding assertion can be derived from the knowledge base, i.e. there is a rule the conclusion of which matches the goal, and the premise of the rule, taken as the goal, can be shown

If the user enters a conjunction of goals, it succeeds if *each* goal in the conjuntion succeeds. If the user enters a disjunction of goals, it succeeds if *at least one* goal in the disjunction succeeds, according to the usual meaning of conjunction and disjunction.

Since queries are clauses, they are terminated by the full stop.

The following example explains how resolution works.

Example 34: Resolution

Consider the following knowledge base:

```
/* fact 1 */   exchange_rate(yen, dollar, 147).
/* fact 2 */   exchange_rate(yen, pound, 227).
/* rule 1 */   exchange_rate(dollar, yen, 0.0068) :- exchange_rate(yen, dollar, 147).
/* rule 2 */   exchange_rate(dollar, pound, 1.5436) :- exchange_rate(dollar, yen, 0.0068).
```

Then:

?- exchange_rate(yen, pound, 227).
yes

which means that the goal is true. The interpreter derives the truth of the goal since it finds an assertion (fact 2) syntactically identical to it. More technically, the negated goal is added to the knowledge base and then resolved with fact 2 producing the empty clause. Consider now:

?- exchange_rate(dollar, yen, 0.0068).
yes

Although there is no fact equal to the goal in this case, its truth is derived through the following steps:

1. The negated goal is added to the knowledge base:

¬exchange_rate(dollar, yen, 0.0068).

2. The negated goal is resolved with rule 1 (this is the special case in which resolution works as modus tolens, see Example 15, Chapter 3.5.4). From:

¬exchange_rate(dollar, yen, 0.0068).
exchange_rate(dollar, yen, 0.0068) :- exchange_rate(yen, dollar, 147).

it follows:

¬exchange_rate(yen, dollar, 147).

which, being negated, can be seen as a new goal.

3. The new goal succeeds because a matching fact is available in the knowledge base.

As a further example, consider the following:

?- exchange_rate(dollar, pound, 1.5436).
yes

The interpreter is able to derive the truth of the goal as follows:

1. The goal matches the conclusion of rule 2, hence the rule premise becomes the new goal:

?- exchange_rate(dollar, yen, 0.0068), exchange_rate(yen, pound, 227).

2. According to the definition of conjuntion, this query is true if *every* goal in it is true. Their separate truth was proved above. Hence the conjunction succeeds.

Finally, consider:

?- exchange_rate(pound, yen, 0.0044).
no

i.e. the goal fails ('no' is the output of the interpreter in such a case). In fact, since the interpreter is unable in this case to derive the empty clause, it assumes that the belief is false. Although, for the intended interpretation of the above knowledge base, the queried belief should be true (0.0044 is the converse of 227, the exchange rate of the yen with respect to the pound), the programmer forgot to put enough axioms to make derivable this true belief. ■

What was said above is a simplification applicable to goals and knowledge bases with no variables. The generalization to the case with variables is explained in Section 4.8 below.

4.4.5 Structured objects: tuples, lists and trees

Any expression referencing objects is called a term. Up to now, two different types of terms were introduced: constants (i.e. references to specific objects through their names), and variables (references to *all* objects in the domain).

There is, however, a further need to express relations involving collections of objects, over which beliefs can be expressed as if they were individual terms. For instance, LISP supports such a process by providing the pair (see Section 3.9) as the basic data structure, and recursion to build up from it structures of any complexity. Similarly, Prolog objects can be aggregated into *structures* or *tuples* , which encompass, but are more general than, pairs.

The syntax of a structure unfortunately is the same as that of a predicate (see Section 4.12 below). As in the case of facts, arguments must be terms; however, since structures are terms, structures can have arguments which are other structures. Hence, as in LISP, recursion can be used to build compound data of any complexity. To highlight the recursivity, the BNF definition of a term is:

```
TERM ::= CONSTANT | VARIABLE | STRUCTURE
STRUCTURE ::= FUNCTOR [ ( [ARGUMENT {, ARGUMENT}] )]
FUNCTOR ::= ATOM
ARGUMENT ::= TERM
```

Example 35: Options as complex data

Consider expressing knowledge about options in financial markets. Constants are not a good choice for representing options, since the essence of an option is in a collection of data fields which cannot be evoked by a single name. A solution is then to define a tuple, whose functor is the atom "option", and whose arguments identify a particular option:

```
option(Asset_name, Expiration, Price, Type, Premium, Position, Contracts)
```

"Type" is either "put" or "call", "Position" is either "long" or "short", "Contracts" is the number of contracts owned. Predicates can be introduced as if an option would be an elementary object. For instance a bull spread could be defined as a relationship between two options having the same owner:

```
bull_spread(option(Asset, Exp, Price, call, P1, long, C),
   option(Asset, Exp, Price, put, P2, short, C)).
```

Syntactically equal variables and constants insure that both arguments of the spread relation are options, and that the underlying asset, expiration and exercise price, while not specified, are the same for both options involved. C, the number of spread contracts, is the smaller of the numbers of option contracts part of the spread. The following predicate implements the usual understanding for the minimum relation:

```
min(A, B, A) :- A ≤ B.
min(A, B, B) :- B < A.
```

■

Example 36: Dates

Another possible application for tuples is the representation of dates. A date is a complex object, consisting of a month/day/year indication. In a knowledge base, it is quite natural to have relations involving dates. So the fact:

```
transaction(p, t).
```

specifying the time t of a transaction p (see Example 30, Section 4.4.2) can be expressed as follows with a tuple if the time is a date:

```
time(p, date(4, 23, 90)).
```

■

A tuple is the most general kind of structured object. Prolog also provides primitives for handling a special kind of tuple called *list*. Lists are defined exactly the same way as in LISP. The only difference is that while LISP uses the functions CONS, CAR and CDR as constructors resp. selectors, Prolog uses predicate names and the syntax of structures. Section 4.10 presents a set of useful recursive predicates for manipulating lists.

Prolog	**LISP**	**Description**
.(a, b)	(CONS 'a 'b)	builds a pair
[]	NIL	the empty list
.(a, [])	(CONS 'a NIL)	builds a list
[a, b, c]	(a, b, c)	non-recursive notation for lists
[H | T]	(SETQ H (CAR a-list))	H is the first element in the list
[H | T]	(SETQ T (CDR a-list))	T is the rest of the list

Example 37: A knowledge base about financial options

An alternative, more general way to define an option is through a predicate, "contract", between one object, the contract type (i.e. option, stock, bond, etc.), a list collecting all information to completely identify a specific contract, the asset, expiration, striking price, type of option, a list collecting all information about the current state of the contract (number of contracts, current premium, position), a list collecting all historical information relevant to the contract (e.g. purchase date and price), and finally a list containing the description of the contracts involved (in the case of synthetic contracts):

contract(option, [ford, date(july, _, 1990), 50, call], [10, 3, long], [date(1, 7, 1990), 2], []).

This representation is however a bit confusing because of the effort required by the programmer to remember which element in the list corresponds to which definition.

■

The following example shows three alternative ways for defining trees (see Chapter 3.3.3) by tuples. Only the last one, using nested lists, has a direct correspondence to LISP (at least, to the small subset of LISP introduced above).

Example 38: Representing a tree

Consider the tree in Fig. 11, Chapter 3.7.6, used to classify expenses. The three representations are:

1. The relation "is_son" explicitly captures the hierarchy among concepts ("is_son" is equivalent to the "is_a" relation introduced in Chapter 3.7.5):

```
is_son(charity, expense).
is_son(cultural, charity).
is_son(restauration, charity).
is_son(under_developed, charity).
is_son(medical, expense).
is_son(fully_deductible, medical).
is_son(surgical, fully_deductible).
is_son(specialist, fully_deductible).
is_son(dental, fully_deductible).
is_son(partly_deductible, medical).
is_son(general, partly_deductible).
is_son(invalidity, partly_deductible).
is_son(real_estates, expense).
```

```
more_general(X, Y) :- is_son(X, Y).
```

2. The tuple "tree" captures the structure of a tree; adequate rules must be defined to navigate through it. A drawback of this approach is that empty lists must be added to ensure that each structure has the same number of arguments:

```
tree(expenses,
        tree(charity,
                tree(cultural, [], []),
                tree(restauration, [], []),
                tree(under_developed, [], []))
        tree(medical,
                tree(fully_deductible,
                        tree(surgical, [], []),
                        tree(specialist, [], []),
                        tree(dental, [], [])),
                tree(partly-deductible,
                        tree(general, [], []),
                        tree(invalidity, [], []),
                        tree([], [], [])),
                [])
        tree(real-estates, [], []).

more_general(X, Y, tree(Y, tree(X, _, _), _, _)).
more_general(X, Y, tree(Y, _, tree(X, _, _), _)).
more_general(X, Y, tree(Y, _, _, tree(X, _, _)).
more_general(X, Y, tree(R, L, M, Right)) :- more_general(X, Y, L).
more_general(X, Y, tree(R, L, M, Right)) :- more_general(X, Y, M).
more_general(X, Y, tree(R, L, M, Right)) :- more_general(X, Y, Right).
```

3. This is the usual LISP representation, based on nested lists, whose first argument is the tree root, while the rest of the list contains the children of the root. Since lists (as opposed to tuples) are variable-length structures, it is no longer necessary to ensure a fixed pattern:

```
tree([expenses,
        [charity,
                [cultural],
                [restauration],
                [under_developed]],
        [medical,
                [fully_deductible,
                        [surgical],
                        [specialist],
                        [dental]],
                [partly_deductible,
                        [general],
                        [invalidity]]],
        [real_estates]]).
more_general(X, Y, [Y|Rest]) :- is_on_top(X, Rest).
more_general(X, Y, [Z|Rest]) :- more_general(X, Y, Rest).
is_on_top(X, [[X|_ ]|_ ]).
is_on_top(X, [H|T]) :- is_on_top(X, T).
```

■

The *underscore* ("_"), first used in the above example, is the sign for a special variable, called anonymous variable. While named variables, once associated to a term, can be used to retrieve it, the underscore cannot be used for future reference to the term. Hence, it is used in the place of a term one is not interested in (something like: "I don't care which term is in this position"). Underscores in the same clause may well correspond to different terms. Anonymous variables help avoid inventing names for variables which are not used later; furthermore, they make programs more readable, by signaling that certain terms are not relevant; finally, when used in

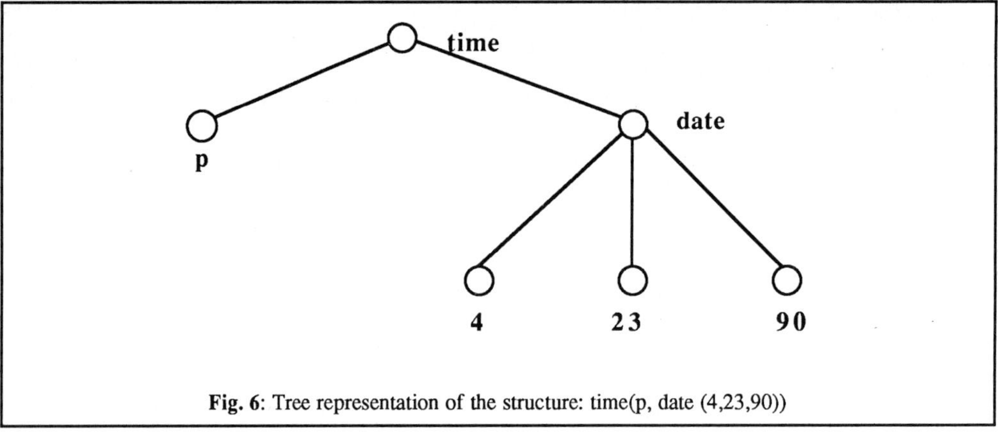

Fig. 6: Tree representation of the structure: time(p, date (4,23,90))

queries, anonymous variables do not cause the display of the associated value (see Section 4.8): hence they are helpful in suppressing irrelevant information from answers.

4.4.6 Parse trees of Prolog expressions

A parser for Prolog decomposes expressions (and structures) into trees, having the functor as root (predicate name or function name), and whose leaves are either constants or variables. Intermediate nodes correspond to the functors of structures. Because of the first order restriction, variables are not allowed in nodes other than leaves.

Since everything written in Prolog can be seen as a tree, Prolog is often viewed as a language for building (Section 4.6), comparing (see Section 4.8) and manipulating (Section 4.10) trees, alike LISP with lists.

Example 39: Tree representation

Fig. 6 shows the tree associated to the Prolog expression:

```
time(p, date(4, 23, 90))
```

■

The tree structure of rules and goals can be easily obtained by rewriting them in the equivalent form:

```
':-' (c, ','(p1, ','(p2, ','(p3, ... ','(pN-1, pN)...)))).

'?-' (','(g1, ','(g2, ...','(gN-1, gN)...))).
```

The parse tree for the goal:

```
?- g1, g2, g3, g4.
```

is given in Fig. 7.

Functors defined so that they can be written before, between or after their arguments are called resp. prefix, infix, and postfix operators. Among the operators already met, the '?-' is a prefix, while ':-' is an infix. In some Prolog implementations, programmers are given the facility to define operators (through a built-in predicate). Operators improve the readability of programs.

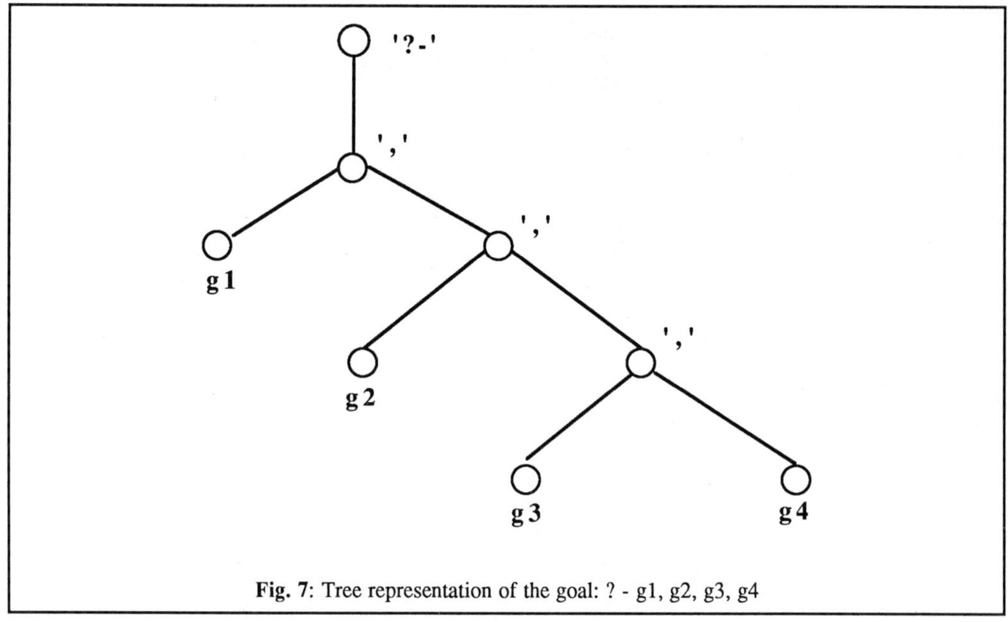

Fig. 7: Tree representation of the goal: ? - g1, g2, g3, g4

4.4.7 Pattern-matching and unification

Pattern-matching is a comparison operation between symbolic structures. *Unification* is the extension of pattern-matching to the comparison between structures, both involving variables. Pattern-matching and unification are important for resolution, which involves the cancellation of matchable resp. unifiable predicates in different clauses (Chapter 3.5.5). The unification algorithm, embedded in the Prolog interpreter, consists of two steps:

1. the parse tree of each expression is derived (Section 4.6 above)
2. the parse trees are compared.

Hence a parser, together with the matching conditions for nodes in the parse trees, completely specify unification.

If the expressions to be matched only contain constants, then the comparison criterion is equality between corresponding nodes in the parse trees. In other words, the parse trees must be equal. Matching between constant expressions returns either success or failure. Example 34, Section 4.4, showed proofs involving matching of expressions with no variables.

Example 40: Pattern-matching with no variables

Given the fact:

```
option(option1, [ford, july, 50, call, 3, long]).
```

and the negated goal:

```
¬option(option1, [ford, july, 50, call, 3, long]).
```

the interpreter succeeds in deriving the empty clause, i.e. in proving the goal. The corresponding trees, shown Fig. 8, can be superimposed. Note that for the purposes of tree representation, lists must be re-converted to the recursive notation with the dot functor. ■

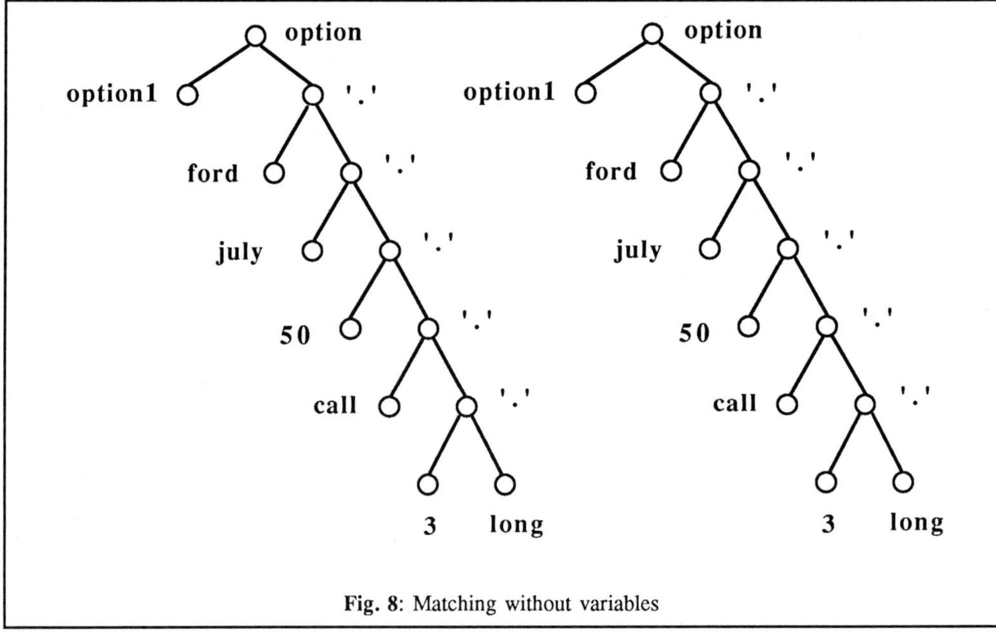

Fig. 8: Matching without variables

A slight generalization of the previous case is the comparison of two expressions, one of which may contains variables. Variables can be seen as *place-takers* for terms. A variable with a term associated to it is said to be *bound* to that term. When a variable is bound to a term in a clause, that term should be imagined as replacing any occurrence of that variable within that clause. Matching of a structure containing no variables with a structure containing variables succeeds if the unbound variables can be associated with terms such that, when replaced for the variable, they make the parse trees for the two expressions equal; if some variables are already bound, then the associated terms must be consistently substituted for the purposes of the matching.

There is no way in Prolog to give a constant value to a variable through an assignment; variables can only be bound as a consequence of previous pattern-matchings or unifications. A difference between binding and assignment is that binding can be undone, if so needed by the interpreter.

Example 41: Pattern-matching with lists

A common case of pattern-matching is pattern-matching of variables with lists. Consider the following two structures:

[ford, july, 50, call, 3, long]

    [A|B|C]

Fig. 9 shows the corresponding trees, and associations between them. The match is successful, and the returned bindings are:

    {A, ford}, {B, july}, {C, [50, call, 3, long]}

On the contrary, the above expression cannot be matched with:

    [A, B|C|D|E|F|G]

since the list has only six arguments. ■

The most general case, in which both expressions to be compared contain variables, is handled by the unification algorithm of the Prolog interpreter. New cases to be resolved involve the comparison of two variables. If both variables are unbound, the most general condition ensuring the unifiability of the structures is that the two variables be constrained to be place takers for the

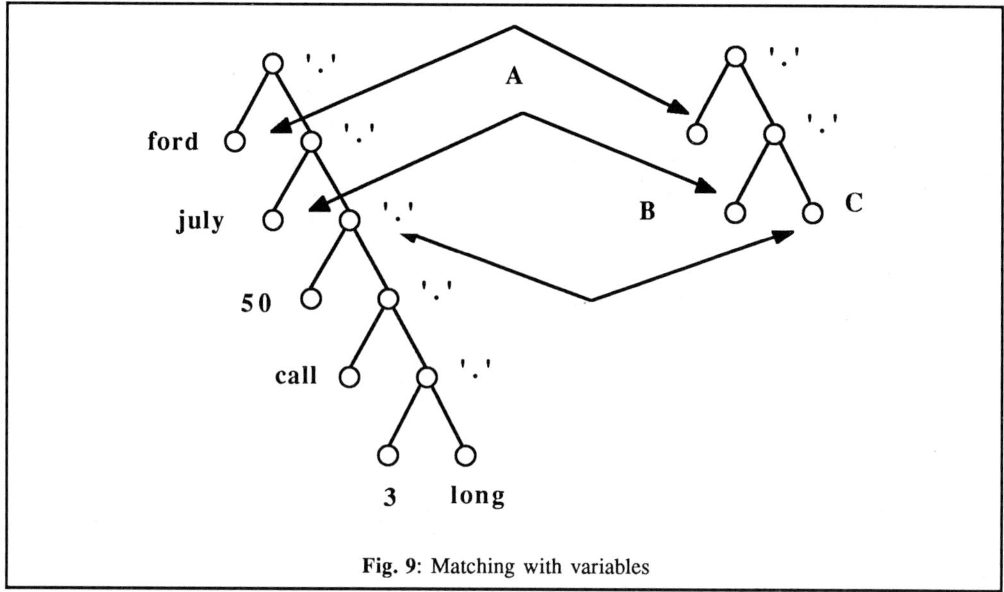

Fig. 9: Matching with variables

same term, without committing them to any specific term for the moment. Technically, two such variables are said to *share*. If in the rest of the proof one gets a binding, then all sharing variables get the same binding. On the contrary, if one of the variables is bound, then the other variable is bound to the same term.

The output of unification is either success/failure, or a list of bindings for each variable, including a list of sharing variables.

Example 42: Unification

Recall Table 1, with a set of beliefs about currencies. Consider the simple query:

```
?- exchange_rate(yen, pound, Y).
Y = 220.5
```

The interpreter first matches the goal with the conclusion of Rule 1, and produces the following binding list:

{Currency1, yen}, {Currency2, pound}, {Y, Z}.

The last pair, featuring two variables, means that the variables share. Then the interpreter tries to prove the conjunction of goals in the right hand side of the rule (bindings have been substituted for variables), to see if all of them match:

```
exchange_rate(yen, Currency3, X), exchange_rate(Currency3, pound, Y), Z is X*Y.
```

In the line above, which is a clause, the variable Y was named in the knowledge base and holds only within that line/clause, although being the same letter as in the user query: the scope of a variable is just the clause. The first subgoal matches with Fact 1; as a result, the following list of bindings is produced:

{Currency3, dollar}, {X, 147}

With these new bindings, the remaining subgoals in the conjunction become:

```
exchange_rate(dollar, pound, Y), Z is 147*Y
```

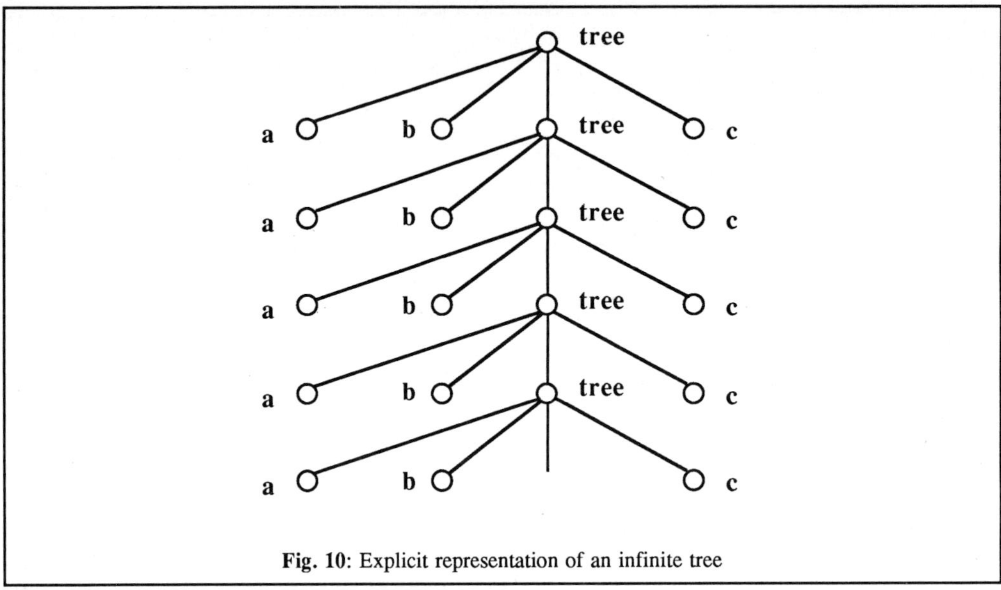

Fig. 10: Explicit representation of an infinite tree

Fact 4 is a match for the first subgoal, hence:

{Y, 1.5}

The last goal is a *primitive* predicate. It succeeds if Z is the result of the multiplication 147*1.5, which is 220.5. Therefore:

{Z, 220.5}

Since, however, Z and the Y in the user query shared, the binding of Z also becomes the binding of Y. Hence the user query is true if Y is bound to 220.5, and this is the result returned by the interpreter. ■

Prolog provides the infix operator "=" (see Section 4.7) for calling the unification algorithm. Hence, for any two structures:

S1 = S2

succeeds only if they are unifiable, in which case it returns either success, or establishes a list of bindings.

4.4.8 Infinite trees

An interesting feature of unification is that it may generate terms which are more complex than those in the input, or even infinite. Consider:

X = trec(a, b, X, c)

The binding:

{X, tree(a, b, X, c)}

causes a substitution for X in the right hand side of the equality, with the following effect:

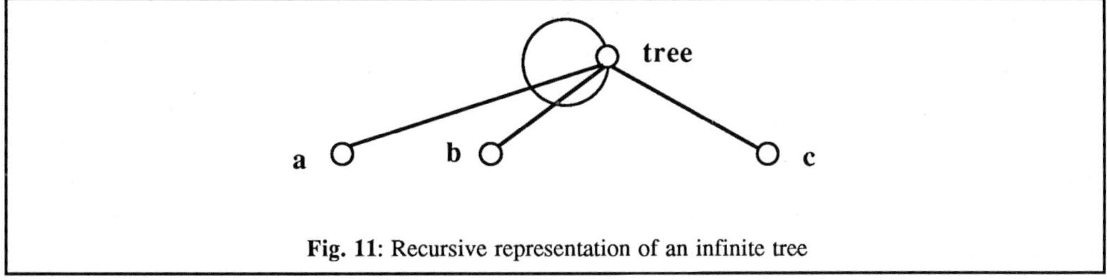

Fig. 11: Recursive representation of an infinite tree

```
tree(a, b, X, c)                         /* substitutes X for its binding */
tree(a, b, tree(a, b, X, c), c)          /* substitutes X for its binding */
tree(a, b, tree(a, b, tree(a, b, X, c), c), c) /* substitutes X for its binding */
```

Fig. 10 shows graphically the result: unification causes an infinitely growing tree.

Many Prolog systems, when facing a unification like the one above, enter into a loop, keeping on substituting until the structure becomes so large that memory overflows. Others (most notably, Prolog II [Giannesini et al., 1986]), recognize that the infinite tree in Fig. 10 can be represented in a finite way as a graph (Fig. 11) with a circuit. They provide facilities also for printing such a graph. Finally, some systems offer the capability to preliminarily check for unifications leading to an infinite structure. This check is implemented as a routine controlling whether a variable is being unified with a structure containing itself, or a sharing variable, or a structure with sharing variables. Unfortunately, this check is inefficient, and it can be optionally switched off after debugging is completed.

4.4.9 Recursion

Like any language supporting recursive data structures (LISP), recursion is a basic programming technique in Prolog. There are two ways in which to understand recursion in Prolog; the first one, used in this Section, relies on the declarative interpretation of programs, the second one (see Section 4.11 below) traces the inference engine at work.

The key idea of recursion is to define a problem as a simplified copy of itself, until the problem becomes so simple, that its solution can be given directly (see Section 3.14). In Prolog, recursive predicates are recognized because they appear both in the left and the right-hand side of the same rule, or in the right-hand side of rules defining predicates used in the definition of the recursive predicate. The following examples show predicates to manipulate lists (see Section 4.6).

Example 43: The predicate member

"member" was already defined in predicate calculus in Chapter 3.5.7. Its one-to-one Prolog translation is:

```
member(X, List) :- List = [X|T] ; (List = [H|T], member(X, T)).
```

where ";" is the disjunction operator (see Section 4.4).

However, a rule containing a disjunction can be written as two different rules:

```
member(X, List) :- List = [X|T].
member(X, List) :- List = [H|T], member(X, T).
```

Finally, both rules can be simplified as follows, yielding the standard Prolog definition:

```
member(X, [X|_]).
   /* X is member of a list if it is the first element of the list, or */
member(X, [H|T]) :- member(X, T).
   /* X is member of a list if X is member of the rest of the list */
```

Procedurally, member is effectively defined as a simplified copy of itself: the list argument to "member" in the right-hand side of the rule is the rest of the list in the left-hand side, i.e. is shorter by one element. So, every time the current goal is matched against the left-hand side of the rule, a new goal is created (the right-hand side of the rule), which is simpler, until either the element searched after surfaces, in which case the fact matches and recursion is stopped, or the list gets empty, and the goal fails ([] can never be unified with [H| T]).

The declarative reading of the predicate is given in the commentaries. ■

Example 44: The predicate length

"length" checks or computes the length of a list. Intuitively, "length" can be described as follows:

1. the length of an empty list is 0
2. the length of a list is equal to one plus the length of the tail of the list

which leads to the following behavior:

```
?- length(L, 0).          /* Which L has length 0 ? */
L = []                    /* Point 1. in the above definition can answer this query */
?- length([], X).         /* Which is the length X of the empty list ? */
X = 0                     /* Point 1. in the above definition can answer this query */
?- length([a, b, c], 4).  /* Is it true that the length of [a, b, c] is 4 ? */
no                        /* Points 1. and 2. in the above definition can answer this query */
?- length(L, 3).          /* Which list has length 3 ? */
L = [_11, _12, _13]       /* Returns a list of three variables */
```

The Prolog implementation is:

```
length([], 0).
length([H|T], N) :- length(T, M), N is M + 1.
```

As before, the second clause, the rule, feeds the recursion by decomposing the original problem into two simpler ones (i.e. find the length of a shorter list, add 1 to the result). The first clause, the fact, stops the recursion when the problem has been sufficiently simplified.

"is" is a built-in operator (see Section 4.7). It succeeds if, after computing the expression to its right, the result matches with the term to its left. In the above program, it is used to bind the variable N to the result of M + 1. ■

Example 45: The predicate append

"append" checks or computes if the constraint "concatenation" holds among three lists, i.e. if the third list can be seen as the first list with the second list appended to its end. "append" can be defined as follows:

1. if the first list is empty, the concatenation of the second list to the first results in the second list
2. otherwise, the first element of the concatenation is the first element of the first list, and the rest of the concatenation is the concatenation of the second list to the rest of the first list

From the above definition the following queries should be understandable:

```
?- append([], [a, b, c], L).                 /* Which is L being the concat. of [] and [a, b, c] */
L = [a, b, c]                                /* Point 1. in the definition can answer this query */
?- append(L, [a, b, c], [a, b, c]).          /* L such that if [a, b, c] is concatenated to it. The result is [a, b, c] */
L = []                                       /* Point 1. in the definition can answer this query */
?- append([a, b], [c, d, e], [a, b, c, d, e])  /* Is it true that [a, c, d, e] is the concat. of [a, b] and [c, d, e] ? */
yes                                          /* Points 2. and 1. in the definition can answer this query */
?- append([a, b], L, [a, b, e, g]).          /* Which is L such that, if concatenated to [a, b], yields [a, b, e, g] */
L = [e, g]
?- append(L, M, [a, b, c]).                  /* Which are L, M such that, if concatenated, they yield [a, b, c] */
L = [], M = [a, b, c];                       /* ";" means: other solutions ? */
L = [a], M = [b, c];                         /* Other solutions ? */
L = [a, b], M = [c];                         /* Other solutions ? */
L = [a, b, c], M = [];                       /* Other solutions ? */
no
```

Here is the Prolog implementation:

```
append([], L, L).
append([H|T], L, [H|R]) :- append(T, L, R).
```

■

Example 46: The predicate reverse

"reverse" checks or computes if a list is the reverse of another list. Declaratively, it means:

1. the reverse of a list of one element is the list itself
2. the first element of a list is the last in its reverse; the rest of the list must be reversed and the first element appended to its end

Therefore:

```
reverse([A], [A]).
reverse([H|T], L) :-
   reverse(T, R),
   append(R, [H], L).
```

The above implementation is rarely used, because of its inefficiency. The following is a better one, though perhaps a bit less intuitive:

```
reverse(A, R) :- reverse3(A, [], R).
reverse3([], R, R).
reverse3([H|T], P, R) :- reverse3(T, [H|P], R).
```

Here a new argument (to be called top of the empty list) is added. As the list to be reversed is scanned, each element is added at the top of the new argument. The last argument returns the result. ■

Example 47: The predicate permute

"permute" checks or computes if a list is one of the possible permutations of a given list. It finds some application, together with the predicates above, in the processing of user input. "permute" is most easily (but inefficiently) defined in terms of "append". Declaratively, it can be understood as follows:

1. the permutation of an empty list is the empty list
2. the permutation of a list is obtained by selecting a random element from it, and putting it on top of the permutation of the rest of the list

In Prolog:

```
permute([], []).              /* termination for recursion */
permute(L, [H|T]) :-
   append(V, [H|U], L),       /* an element from L is put on top of the permutation */
   append(V, U, W),           /* the rest of L is built */
   permute(W, T).                     /* the rest of L is permuted */
```

■

Example 48: Computing interest rates

This example is the same as the one used in Section 4.3.14 for explaining recursion in LISP. For convenience, the LISP code is reported here:

```
> (DEFUN terminal-value (capital interest-rate years)
    (IF (= years 0)
          capital
        ( * (+ 1 interest-rate) (terminal-value capital interest-rate (- years 1)))))
```

The same function, implemented in Prolog, looks like:

```
terminal-value(Capital, _, 0, Capital).
terminal_value(Capital, Rate, Years, Value) :-       terminal_value(Capital, Rate, Years1, Value1),
```

```
Years is Years1 + 1,
Increment is Rate + 1,
Value is Value1 * Increment.
```

■

4.4.10 The inference engine

This section as well as the following one explain how logic is turned into a working programming language, i.e. we introduce the Prolog interpreter. It consists basically of a parser *and* an inference engine:

- the syntax checkings made by the parser relate to formal BNF syntax of a specific Prolog implementations
- the *inference engine* , the part of the interpreter responsible for inference activities, consists in a unification algorithm (Section 4.7) and in a search procedure

This Section deals with the inference engine. Because a goal is a predicate, the inference engine tries to prove it as follows:

1. Match: the knowledge base is searched, until the first clause (either a fact or a rule conclusion) unifiable with the goal is found. If no clause is found, the goal fails
2. Act: if the matching clause is a fact, the query succeeds. If the matching clause is a rule conclusion, step 1. is repeated with the rule premise as the new goal, and variables are bound or shared according to the binding list from the previous unifications
3. Backtracking: whenever a goal fails, the inference engine tries to recover from the failure by reconsidering the way the goal immediately before the failed goal was matched earlier. If a different match can be found, bindings/sharings derived from the previous match are undone, and the bindings/sharings from the new match are added to the list of bindings. The failed goal then is tried again, with the new list of bindings. If no different match can be found, then the goal before is tried again, etc. Only if no different match is found up to the first goal, does the query fails

In practice, the conflict set (see Chapter 3.6.7) is not computed in Prolog, being replaced by the fixed strategy of always using the first matching clause found in the database. Alternative matchings are taken into account only upon failure of the proof, in the order they appear in the database. The process is repeated until the proof is successful, or no more matching clauses are found. Code for the backtracking algorithm is given in Chapter 5.8.

The price to be paid is, however, high. First, since the conflict set is never computed, selection criteria different from the ordering in the knowledge base cannot be directly implemented, unless the knolwedge base itself is decomposed or restructured dynamically. Second, as opposed to pure logic, one must be most careful in terms of the arrangement of the clauses; whereas pure backtracking should produce the same (reordered) set of results regardless of the clause/goal ordering, different results can occur if the primitives "not" or "!" appear in the goal clauses (see Example 54, Section 4.11)

When facing a conjunction of goals, the inference engine proves it by proving one goal after the other, from the left to the right. Variables bindings/sharings set up during the proof of early goals in the conjunction must hold for subsequent goals. If a goal, with the bindings from the previous matches, fails, Prolog backtracks to the previous goal, i.e. to the goal left of it. If an alternative match is found, it moves to the right, and tries to satisfy the failed goal with the newly computed bindings. If no alternative bindings can be found, Prolog backtracks further to the left. In the case of success, it moves again to the right, etc. A conjunction succeeds when the inference engine reaches and proves the rightmost goal. The conjunction fails when the leftmost goal cannot be (re)satisfied.

The output of the unification algorithm is also the output of the query. If a goal succeeds, the interpreter outputs either "yes" (no variables bound or shared) or a list of bindings. The user can type ";" (Prolog symbol for disjunction) to start backtracking and see if different solutions can be found. If a goal fails, the interpreter outputs "no".

Example 49: The predicate sublist

"sublist" checks or computes if a list is the sublist of another list:

```
sublist([], _).                 /* fact 1: the empty list is the sublist of any list */
sublist([X|M], L) :-            /* rule 1 */
        list_member(X, L, LL),  /* generate a candidate sublist, i.e. one starting with the same
                                   element as the searched sublist */
        test(M, LL).            /* test the candidate sublist */

test([], _).                    /* fact 2 */
test([H|T], [H|R]) :- test(T, R).   /* rule 2: check/compute if list begins with sublist */
list_member(X, [X|T], T).               /* fact 3 */
list_member(X, [_|L], M) :- list_member(X, L, M). /* rule 3: return the sublist after a given element */
```

Consider the following query:

```
?- sublist([a, b, c], [d, a, b, f, a, b, c]).          /* goal 1 */
yes.
```

The proof runs as follows:

First, the goal is matched against the knowledge base. The first matching clause is the conclusion of rule 1. The matcher computes the binding list and the premise of rule 1 (with the variables substituted for the just computed bindings) becomes the new goal:

{X, a}, {m, [b, c]}, {L, [d, a, b, f, a, b, c]}
list_member(a, [d, a, b, f, a, b, c], LL), test([b, c], LL).   /* goals 2-1 and 2-2 */

Conjunctions are tried from the left to the right. The leftmost conjunct is matched against rule 3. To prove it, the new subgoal:

{LL, M}
list_member(a, [a, b, f, a, b, c], M)   /* goal 3-1 */

is issued. The inference engine scans the knowledge base, until the first match, fact 3, is found:

{X, a}, {T, [b, f, a, b, c}, {M, T}
list_member(a, [a|[b, f, a, b, c]], [b, f, a, b, c])

Because of {LL, M}, LL gets the same binding as T. Hence the first conjunct is proven (in the following, proven subgoals are stroke):

~~list_member(a, [, b, f, a, b, c], [b, f, a, b, c]~~), test([b, c], [b, f, a, b, c]).   /* goal 2-2 */

To prove the "test" goal, rule 2 is used first. Unification with its conclusion causes the following bindings to be established, together with the new goal (the premise) to be proved:

{H, b}, {T, [c]}, {R, [f, a, b, c]}

test([c], [f, a, b, c]). /* goal 3-2 */

This goal fails; of the only two clauses with the test predicate, fact 2 (the first found) expects an empty list as its first argument, and rule 2 expects the first element of the lists in the first and in the second argument to be the same. Hence Prolog backtracks to the last satisfied goal. The variables H, T and R are unbound, and Prolog tries to resatisfy the goal:

test([b, c], [b, f, a, b, c]). /* goal 2-2 */

The interpreter searches again from rule 2 to the end of the knowledge base for a matching clause, but none is found. Prolog backtracks further, and reconsiders the goal:

list_member(a, [a, b, f, a, b, c], M) /* goal 3-1 */

previously matched against fact 3. This time, upon scanning the knowledge base from fact 3, Prolog finds an alternative match, rule 3. The following bindings and new goal are computed:

{X, a}, {L, [b, f, a, b, c]}, {M, M}
list_member(a, [b, f, a, b, c], M). /* goal 3-1' */

Rule 3 is again used as a match for goal 3-1', and a new goal is generated:

{X, a}, {L, [f, a, b, c]}, {M, M}
list_member(a, [f, a, b, c], M). /* goal 4-1' */
Upon further use of rule 3:
{X, a}, {L, [a, b, c]}, {M, M}
list_member(a, [a, b, c], M). /* goal 5-1' */

This time, the first matching clause is fact 3. This match proves the goal for the following bindings:

{X, a}, {T, [b, c]}, {T, M} hence {M, [b, c]}
~~list_member(a, [a, b, c], M).~~ /* goal 5-1' */

Goal 5-1' being proved, goal 4-1' can be proved, and thereafter goal 4-1', goal 3-1'. Bindings must be consistently substituted for the variables:

{X, a}, {L, [f, a, b, c]}, {M, [b, c]}
~~list_member(a, [f, a, b, c], [b, c]).~~ /* goal 4-1' */
{X, a}, {L, [b, f, a, b, c]}, {M, [b, c]}
~~list_member(a, [b, f, a, b, c], M).~~ /* goal 3-1' */

As a consequence, goal 2-1 is also proved. Its new bindings cause a change in goal 2-2:

{LL, M}, {M, [b, c}
~~list_member(a, [a, b, f, a, b, c], [b, c])~~, test([b, c], [b, c]). /* goal 2-2' */

The first matching clause for it is rule 2, which causes the following bindings and new goal:

{H, b}, {T, [c]}, {R, [c]}
test([c], [c]). /* goal 3-2' */

By matching again with rule 2:

{H, c}, {T, []}, {R, []}
test([], []). /* goal 4-2' */

Goal 4-2' succeeds (because of fact 2). Hence also goals 3-2', 2-2' can be proved:

~~test([], [])~~. /* goal 4-2' */
~~test([c], [c])~~. /* goal 3-2' */
~~list_member(a, [a, b, f, a, b, c], [b, c])~~, ~~test([b, c], [b, c])~~. /* goal 2-2' */

and, consequently, goal 1. ■

The next example shows the differences between Prolog and logic, by showing two cases in which Prolog inference engine is unable to derive logically implied beliefs.

Example 50: Looping due to the selection strategy

Recall the knowledge base about currencies (Table 1). This knowledge base works for some queries (see Example 42, Section 4.8). However, it is a concentrate of potential problems due to the way in which Prolog inference engine works. Two types of looping are shown:

1. Consider the query:

```
?- exchange_rate(pound, yen, X).
```

The first matching rule is rule 1. The resulting bindings and new goals are:

```
{Currency1, pound}, {Currency2, yen}, {X, X}
exchange_rate(pound, Currency3, X), exchange_rate(Currency3, yen, Y), Z is X * Y.
```

The leftmost goal ("exchange_rate(pound, Currency3, X)") is first examined. It matches with fact 6. The match causes the following bindings and new goal:

```
{Currency3, pound}, {X, 1}
exchange_rate(pound, yen, Y)
```

which corresponds exactly to the initial query. In proving it, Prolog will repeat all the above steps over and over, and it will enter an infinite loop.

The knowledge base is not logically incorrect: facts and rules may well reflect those of an expert. It is the way the inference engine uses the rules that causes it to loop.

In pure logic, although some inference rules may cause the same belief to be derived over and over, nevertheless all other provable beliefs are always derivable as well. In Prolog, in similar cases, the proof strategy implemented cannot derive other beliefs, since it loops forever.

2. The following case is based on a subset of Table 1, consisting of just rule 2 and fact 1:

```
exchange_rate(Currency1, Currency2, X) :-
                              exchange_rate(Currency2, Currency1, Y),
                              X is 1 / Y.
exchange_rate(yen, dollar, 147).
```

Note the ordering, with the fact after the rule. Now the query:

```
?- exchange_rate(yen, dollar, W).
```

causes the system to loop. The reader can try to trace the inference engine at work and discover why. This kind of error is a consequence of the "wrong" ordering of the clauses. In fact, it is simple to check that, with the fact before the rule, no loop would have occurred (for the specific query). For similar reasons, in all examples of Section 4.10 above the fact stopping recursion was always written before the rules.

In pure logic, the order of the beliefs does not matter: if a belief can be derived from a knowledge base, then it can be also derived from any permutation of it. ■

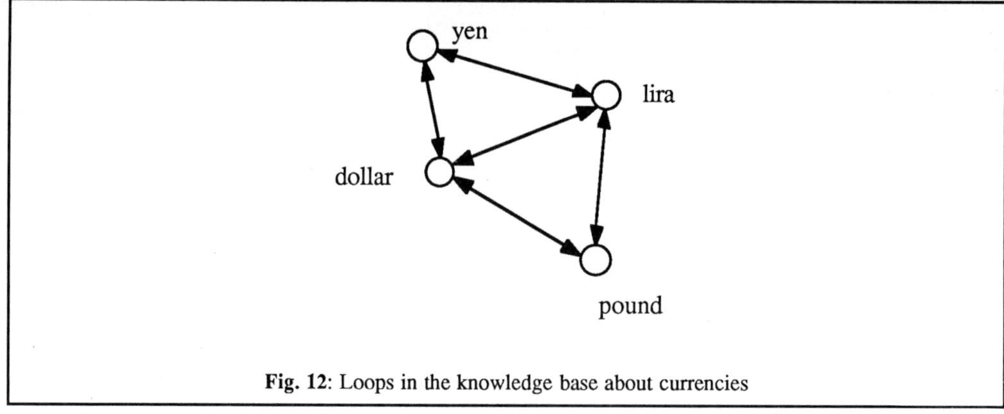

Fig. 12: Loops in the knowledge base about currencies

In Fig. 12, the representation of the exchange rate relation is a graph with circuits (see Chapter 3.3), where the Prolog strategy gets lost (as would any other strategy based on depth-first search without check for loops). Circuits essentially are consequences of the transitivity of the relation "exchange_rate". In Chapter 5, several search strategies (inclusive the one for Prolog) over graphs with circuits are explained extensively. One of them could be used to implement a different inference engine (see Section 4.11).

Table 2 takes a different approach: facts, rules about symmetry and rules about transitivity have been separated by introducing three different predicates. It shows how recoding of the knowledge in a less intuitive way can solve the above problem. Furthermore it will return all possible ways of computing the exchange rate for all possible currencies.

4.4.11 Controlling backtracking: !

Sometimes, it is useful to control backtracking. The *cut* is a primitive predicate (written '!') defined to this purpose. Its behavior in a conjunction of goals is the following:

- the first time the inference engine tries to prove the cut, it succeeds
- if the inference engine tries to resatisfy the cut (because of backtracking), it fails, causing the whole conjunction to fail. More precisely: if the conjunction is a query, the query fails; if the conjunction is the right-hand side of the rule, the predicate in the left-hand side fails, i.e. the interpreter does not try to resatisfy it by looking for other matches in the database

Example 51: Behavior of the cut

Consider the following clauses:

```
estate_income(Value).                          /* fact1 */
estate_income(Value) :-                        /* rule1 */
        write('Input estate income of land property'),
        nl,
        ask(estate_income, Value, [real(Value)]).
```

Here the idea is that, as long as the fact is not present in the knowledge base, the only way to satisfy "estate_income" is to satisfy the rule, which triggers a question to the user about its "estate_income". As soon as the fact is known, the program asserts it to the database before the rule. Whenever Prolog needs such information again, it retrieves the fact first, which returns the needed information. In principle, there is no need to run Rule1 again.

However, assume now that a proof involving "estate_income" fails. Prolog tries to backtrack over "estate_income" and finds a way to resatisfy it using rule1. Unfortunately, this causes the tax adviser to ask twice the same question, which is not a totally reasonable behavior. Many solutions to this problem are

```
has_change(yen, dollar, 147).
has_change(lira, dollar, 1400).
has_change(lira, yen, 9.5238).
has_change(dollar, pound, 1.5).
has_change(lira, pound, 2100).

change(X, Y, Z) :- has_change(X, Y, Z).
change(X, Y, M) :- has_cahnge(X, Y, Z), M is 1/Z.


exchange_rate(X, Y, Z) :- change(X, Y, Z).
exchange_rate(X, Y, Z) :- change(X, W, Z1),
                          exchange_rate(W, Y, Z2),
                          Z is Z1 * Z2.
```

Table 2: Correct version of the knowledge base in Table 1

possible; one of them is to tell Prolog that backtracking should not try to resatisfy the fact "estate_income". This is the role of the cut. When the user first answers the question about "estate_income", the program asserts a cut as well, resulting in the following database:

```
estate_income(Value):- !.                    /* rule0 */
estate_income(Value) :-                      /* rule1 */
        write('Input estate income of land property'),
        nl,
        ask(estate_income, Value, [real(Value)]).
```

Now, once the inference engine looks for a matching to "estate_income", it finds rule0, and runs through the cut in the right hand side. Should Prolog ever try to resatisfy it, it would immediately fail, because of the cut. Rule 1 can never be reached again, unless the fact is removed from the database.

■

The cut "!" together with "fail", is a common technique which causes the failure of a predicate, without Prolog trying to resatisfy it. "fail" is a zero-argument predicate, with no matching facts or rules; i.e. by convention Prolog programmers never put clauses of the form "fail." or "fail :- ..." in their knowledge bases. "fail" (without cut) can be used to force Prolog to start backtracking.

Example 52: A knowledge base about the Italian fiscal regulation

In Chapter 3.5.7, a set of logic beliefs representing part of the Italian fiscal regulation was introduced. The idea behind them was the following: in general, a dependent worker must not file an income tax return, since taxes on salary are directly paid by the employer; exceptions were, however, listed.

One possible implementation in Prolog uses the predicate "not_exception" (this implementation is not part of the Appendix 1.1). The definition of "not_exception" is based on the exception criteria in Chapter 3.5.7; as soon as one such criterion is satisfied (i.e. the taxpayer is indeed an exception), "fail" causes "not_exception" to fail. The cut prevents backtracking, which would cause "not_exception" to be satisfied by the catch-all clause. If *no* rule is applicable, then "not_exception" is true; otherwise, "not_exception" fails , preventing the predicate "must_not_file_return" from being applied.

```
must_not_file_return(X, Year) :- activity(X, Year, dependent_work), not_exception(X, Year, dependent_work).
not_exception(X, Year, dependent_work) :-
        revenue(Z, X, Year), is_a(Z, Type), not(Type /= dependent_income),
        revenue(W, X, Year), ≠(Z, W),
        not(depends(p, x)),
        findall(M, (revenue(R, X, Year), amount(R, M)), list),
        sum_list(List, Result), Result ≥ 6602000, !, fail.
not_exception(X, Year, dependent_work) :-
        revenue(Z, X, Year), revenue(W, X, Year), ≠(Z, W),
        expense(K, X, Year), is_a(K, deductible_expense),
```

```
        not(is_a(K, mortgage_loan_deductions)), not(is_a(K, local_tax_on_real_estates)), !, fail.
not_exception(X, Year, dependent_work) :-
        revenue(Z, X, Year), (is_a(Z, independent_income); is_a(Z, property_income)), !, fail.
not_exception(X, Year, dependent_work) :- revenue(Z, W, Year), tutor(X, W), !, fail.
not_exception(X, Year, dependent_work).    /* catch all */
```

The predicate "not" is explained later in this section.

"findall" is a built-in predicate with three arguments, the first being a variable, the second any expression containing that variable, and the third a list. The list is bound to all possible occurrences in the database of the variable in the first argument in the expression of the second. ■

"not" is a primitive predicate which simplifies programs similar to the one in the above example. It implements a kind of negation called *negation as failure* , i.e. the view that a goal is false if it cannot be proved:

```
not(A) :- call(A), !, fail.   /* if A provable, then not(A) fails */
not(A).                       /* if A not provable, then not(A) succeeds */
```

"call" is a built-in predicate, whose argument is treated by Prolog as a goal to be proved. So "call(A)" should be read as: prove A.

Example 53: Reordering the knowledge base about fiscal regulations

Let's define a predicate "exception", instead of "not_exception". The knowledge base in Example 52 above can then be rewritten as follows:

```
must_not_file_return(X, Year) :- activity(X, Year, dependent_work), not(exception(X, Year, dependent_work)).
exception(X, Year, dependent_work) :-
        revenue(Z, X, Year), is_a(Z, Type), not(Type /= dependent_income),
        revenue(Z, X, Year), revenue(W, X, Year), ≠(Z, W),
        not(depends(p, x)),
        findall(M, (revenue(Z, X, Year), amount(Z, M)), list),
        sum_list(List, Result), Result ≥ 6602000.
exception(X, Year, dependent_work) :-
        revenue(Z, X, Year), revenue(W, X, Year), ≠(Z, W),
        expense(K, X, Year), is_a(K, deductible_expense),
        not(is_a(K, mortgage_loan_deductions)), not(is_a(K, local_tax_on_real_estates)).
exception(X, Year, dependent_work) :-
        revenue(Z, X, Year), (is_a(Z, independent_income); is_a(Z, property_income)).
exception(X, Year, dependent_work) :- revenue(Z, W, Year), tutor(X, W).
```

■

Note the improved readability of the latter program: for instance, it contains no cuts. In namy cases, not is helpful in making programs easier to understand. However, negation as failure is different from logic negation (Chapter 3.5.2.1), as Example 54 below clearly shows, and may cause an unexpected behavior.

Example 54: A problem with not

Consider the following clauses:

```
g(a, b).
g(a, a).
g(d, e).
?- g(X, Y), not(g(X, X)).
g(d, e);
no
?- not(g(X,X)), g(X, Y).
no
```

The two arguments of "not" are unbound in the second query. "call(g(X, X))" in the definition of "not" succeeds, with {X, a}; hence "not" fails, with no possibility for backtracking.

In the first query, "not" is called with bound arguments; although it fails first for {X, a}, because "g(d, e)" is retrieved after backtracking, the goal succeeds. Needless to say, in pure logic the order of the conjuncts can never affect the truth of the conjunction. ■

4.4.12 Identity of data and programs

As in LISP, programs are data in Prolog as well. The built-in predicate:

clause(A, B)

is provided to this purpose. Given a clause of the form:

Conclusion :- Premise.

"clause" unifies the Conclusion with A, and the Premise with B (if the clause is a fact, B is set to "true"). The next example shows how "clause" makes it possible to design a Prolog program describing other Prolog programs.

Example 55: Prolog interpreter in Prolog

The following is a well-known Prolog interpreter, consisting of just three clauses. The interpreter is not complete, in the sense that it does not account for built-in predicates. However, it accounts for the top-down, left-to-right proof strategy.

```
interpret("true"):- !.                          /* the clause "true" succeeds */
interpret((A, B)) :- !, interpret(A), interpret(B).   /* left-to-right order in interpreting conjunctions */
interpret(A) :- clause(A, B), interpret(B), !.        /* top-down order in interpreting clauses */
```

■

The following examples show simple variations to the above interpreter. Both are potentially useful for building consultation programs, as used in advisory services.

Example 56: A Prolog interpreter querying the user

The following is a Prolog interpreter with the capability of querying the user, if it cannot prove a goal (the standard interpreter would fail in such case). If the user answers that the goal is true, then the goal is added to the knowledge base. This simple strategy may be inappropriate in some cases (e.g. consistency problems with other clauses). The interpreter below is a simple version of the interpreter in Appendix 1.1.

```
interpret("true"):- !.                          /* the clause "true" succeeds */
interpret((A, B)) :- !, interpret(A), interpret(B).   /* left-to-right order in interpreting conjunctions */
interpret(A) :- clause(A, B), interpret(B), !.        /* top-down order in interpreting clauses */
interpret(A) :- query-user(A, Answer), !, process(A, Answer).
process(A, true) :- assert(A).                  /* if the clause is true, it is added */
process(A, false) :- fail.                      /* if the clause is false, the predicate fails */
```

■

Example 57: A Prolog interpreter with user-ordered proof

There often is more than one clause with the same conclusion. As we have seen, Prolog tries them in the order they appear in the knowledge base.

Sometimes, however, the user may have a clue about which clause is better for proving a goal. For instance, in a tax consultation program different kinds of expenses may be deductible: the user may know which ones are relevant to him, and therefore suggests the order in which the clauses should be examined. The details of the interpreter-user dialogue are hidden in the predicate "reorder_by_query". Alternatively, the predicate "reorder_by_query" could perform some reordering automatically, through inspection of the candidates list ("List") and consultation of a model of the user stored in the knowledge base. The returned result ("Odered-list") should distinguish rules meaningful to the user, to be queried, from other rules, to be skipped or interpreted in the conventional way. "reorder_by_query" is an example of a predicate capturing metaknowledge (see Example 24, Chapter 3.6.5).

```
interpret("true"):- !.                               /* the clause "true" succeeds */
interpret((A, B)) :- !, interpret(A), interpret(B).  /* left-to-right order in interpreting conjunctions */
interpret(A) :- findall(B, clause(A, B), List),      /* see Section 4.11 for a definition of "findall" */
            reorder_by_query(List, Ordered_list),
             prove(A, Ordered_list).
prove(A, [H|T]) :- interpret(H), !.
prove(A, [H|T]) :- prove(A, T).
prove(A, _) :- query_user(A), !, process(A, Answer).
process(A, true) :- assert(A).                       /* if the clause is true, it is added */
process(A, false) :- fail.                           /* if the clause is false, the predicate fails */
```

■

4.4.13 Application: a Prolog knowledge-based tax adviser

The Prolog programming language as described above, together with additional development tools as found in most professional versions of Prolog, can be used to develop large-scale programs performing significant mostly symbolic tasks difficult to code otherwise.

The code in Appendix 1.1 shows an expert system tax adviser along the guidelines presented in Chapter 3.2. This knowledge-based tax adviser is designed to perform the following tasks:

- help the user in filling the tax forms, by coding knowledge of all required items of information needed to complete a tax form (or a subset of it), and about how such items are related to each others, or about how they depend on simpler, well-known items, which are then queried to the user when needed
- help the user to keep his answers consistent
- help the user to detect when a tax form is properly and completely filled, and stop the session if the status is such that a full and consistent completion is no longer possible
- help the user understand how results depend on previous assertions, and return information about the performed inferences

Architecturally, the program can be understood as being organized into the following components:

- a database, where domain facts and rules are stored
- a control database, including all rules implementing different inference strategies
- an input/output component, where to each fact relevant to a section of the tax form, appropriate rules are attached in order to help asking specific questions and performing control about the acceptability of the user's answers
- an explanation module, which enables the user to ask "how" questions and to synthetize appropriate answers, by retrieving the rules involved in the derivation of the information queried

Each rule left-hand side has the structure:

```
#(fact_name, fact_value, inferential_tag, rule_identifier)
```

where:

fact_name this is the name of the fact derivable through the considered rule.

fact_value this is the value associated to such a fact

inferential_tag

this is a field whose value can be fw, bw, or not instantiated; it is used by the inference engine to know how the rule is to be included in the inferential process. If such a field is instantiated fw/bw then the rule is to be used only in reasoning forward resp. backward. If the field is not instantiated, then both forward and backward modes are allowed.

Typical backward rules are rules querying the user, as well as rules involving side effects (e. g. leaving the program) in their right hand side.

Typical forward rules include rules enforcing consistency among propositions, whereas a given configuration of the knowledge base triggers the inference of incompatible facts to be immediately rejected and never queried. A further class of forward rules is responsible for deriving basic facts from more complex assertions made by the user. Using such rules the other way around would produce the unreasonable behavior of asking complex questions to infer basic facts

rule_identifier

this is an instantiated identifier naming each rule uniquely. Such a field is of no use to the final user, but is useful for bookkeeping purposes

The rules right hand side consists of a conjunction of facts. Each fact has the structure:

```
fact_name(fact_value)
```

The control component is a collection of rules implementing three different inference procedures.

Backward reasoning derives facts from a chain of rules ending with elementary facts.

Forward reasoning completely searches the knowledge base for all possible consequences of asserted facts. This strategy, while inefficient in other application domains, is reasonable in a personal tax adviser because of the modularity of the task. The forward reasoning engine gives the user an opportunity to volunteer information. Its task is to derive logical consequences from such information, so that it never triggers useless questions to the user. The forward engine is invoked immediately after a deduction or a user volunteered information is asserted.

The *forward-fail* engine is also invoked each time a new fact is asserted: it scans the right hand side of the rules in the knowledge base, and marks all rules whose premises depend on a fact which is in contradiction with the newly asserted fact, i.e. all rules which are inconsistent with the specific user configuration. Incosistent rules can never fire, since assertions, once made, cannot be retracted. Furthermore, if there is no other way to infer a fact but through inconsistent rules, then the forward fail engine asserts the negation of the fact to the knowledge base. This is a consequence of the rather specialized nature of tax form filling, which makes it reasonable to assume that the program contains all possible derivations for a conclusion. It may also be motivated with "default" principles embedded usually in legislations, by which, for instance, none is guilty until there is a proof of it. In fact, if the program is indeed complete with respect to all possible "derivations" for a fact, the negation of the fact itself must follow from the confutation of all proofs.

The explanation-based consistency check component is invoked when the user tries to input a fact already available in the knowledge base. It returns the asserted fact, together with its value, as well as the derivation which lead to the assertion of such a fact. If the fact was asserted by the user previously, then the returned answer highlights the contradiction. Should the already existing fact be derived by one of the inference engines, then the returned answer includes a list of the facts involved in the premises of the last used rule in the derivation process. Of course, the user can recursively enquire about such premises, in order to obtain a justification for them as well.

The program as listed in Appendix 1.1 is limited in its capabilities in several ways. In fact, it does not fully meet the requirements listed in Chapter 3.2.1.

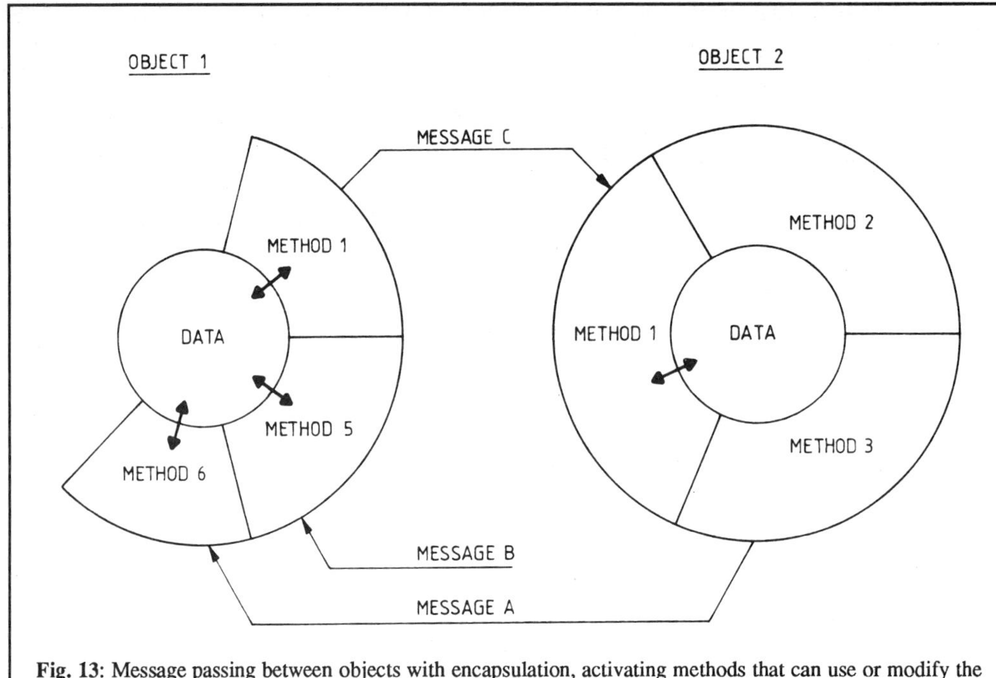

Fig. 13: Message passing between objects with encapsulation, activating methods that can use or modify the data within their object

First, it cannot adapt its behavior to the user's proficiency level: the program would ask the same questions to both the layman and the expert. To avoid this, some programs have the capability of maintaining or inferring an explicit user model, which is then updated as the user's proficiency level changes. The tax advisor presented here has not this capability. Note, however, that a sort of primitive adaptation to the user's level is achieved as a side-effect of the combined action of the backward and forward inference engines. Namely, if a user directly asserts that he has some estate-property income, the forward inference engine would infer land ownership (a more elementary fact) without need for further questions. Furthermore, the user is always given the chance to early terminate backward reasoning by volunteering more complex information.

A second important limitation is the lack of a mechanism for retracting assumptions. This means that the user cannot assume different scenarios for deductions, expenses etc. and compare the results. It also implies that the user cannot change his mind, or try to exploit ambiguities in the tax law by committing to the most favourable interpretation. Although this is a serious flaw in the present program, refer to Chapter 5.10 for a mechanisms allowing retraction of beliefs.

Finally, the system is limited in the kind of consistency checks it can make by lack of commonsense knowledge. It can easily infer cases in which the form is incomplete or inconsistent (wrong totals, etc.), but it cannot infer situations in which the form is simply not plausible. For instance, the system has not the knowledge to compare owned properties with generated income. Similarly, it cannot compare job position with life style. Partly because of this, many silly errors (missing zeros in a figure) simply cannot be detected.

4. 5: Object-oriented programming

4.5.1 Introduction

Object-oriented programming, and the corresponding languages or environments, are widely used in AI because:

- they reflect many ideas of the frame-based knowledge representation paradigm (see Chapter 3.7), such as concentrating in a single data structure, called an *object*, properties related to the same entity, while separating data from procedures
- they support the structuring of knowledge into hierarchies of related concepts (see Chapter 3.7.6), through a mechanism called *inheritance* (see Chapter 3.7.9)
- the programming is highly modular, the modularity being achieved through mechanisms called *message passing* and *encapsulation* ; this helps in prototyping when the requirements are unknown, specifications are wrong or incomplete, and designs must be executable. The goals addressed are understandability, modifiability and reusability

Some of the major object-oriented programming languages are Smalltalk [Goldberg and Robson, 1983], C++ [Stroupstrup, 1986], KEE [Intellicorp, 1988], Actors, even ADA in some respects. Most languages come along with programming environments, enhanced with also large graphics capabilities; some are interpreted while others can be compiled and linked to assembly code.

4.5.2 Object-oriented programming concepts

Each object is a functionally complete description of the entity it represents, including the *data* necessary to define its state and the *methods* necessary to define its behavior.

Example 58: Representing a client's portfolio

The entity "client's portfolio" is an object, with e.g. the balances of securities in it as data, while the trading instruments, priorities and rules are methods ■

Object-oriented design relies on encapsulation, message passing, dynamic binding and inheritance; current object-oriented languages implement these techniques to a varying extent. In the following each of these concepts is briefly explained.

i. Encapsulation

Encapsulation means that data are encapsulated inside an inviolable shell along with the methods required to use it. The only way to reach the data is through these particular methods (see Fig. 13).

ii. Message passing

Message passing means that, in order to use one of the methods on the data, one must send a message to the object telling it to perform a certain function (see Fig. 13). The message is independent of the method it requests.

Example 59: Messages to the object "client's portfolio"

When a message tells the object "client's portfolio" to execute a trade on a specific bond, for instance, the message contains no information about where the object stores the securities data, or about the type of methods which updates the balance of that bond holding. ■

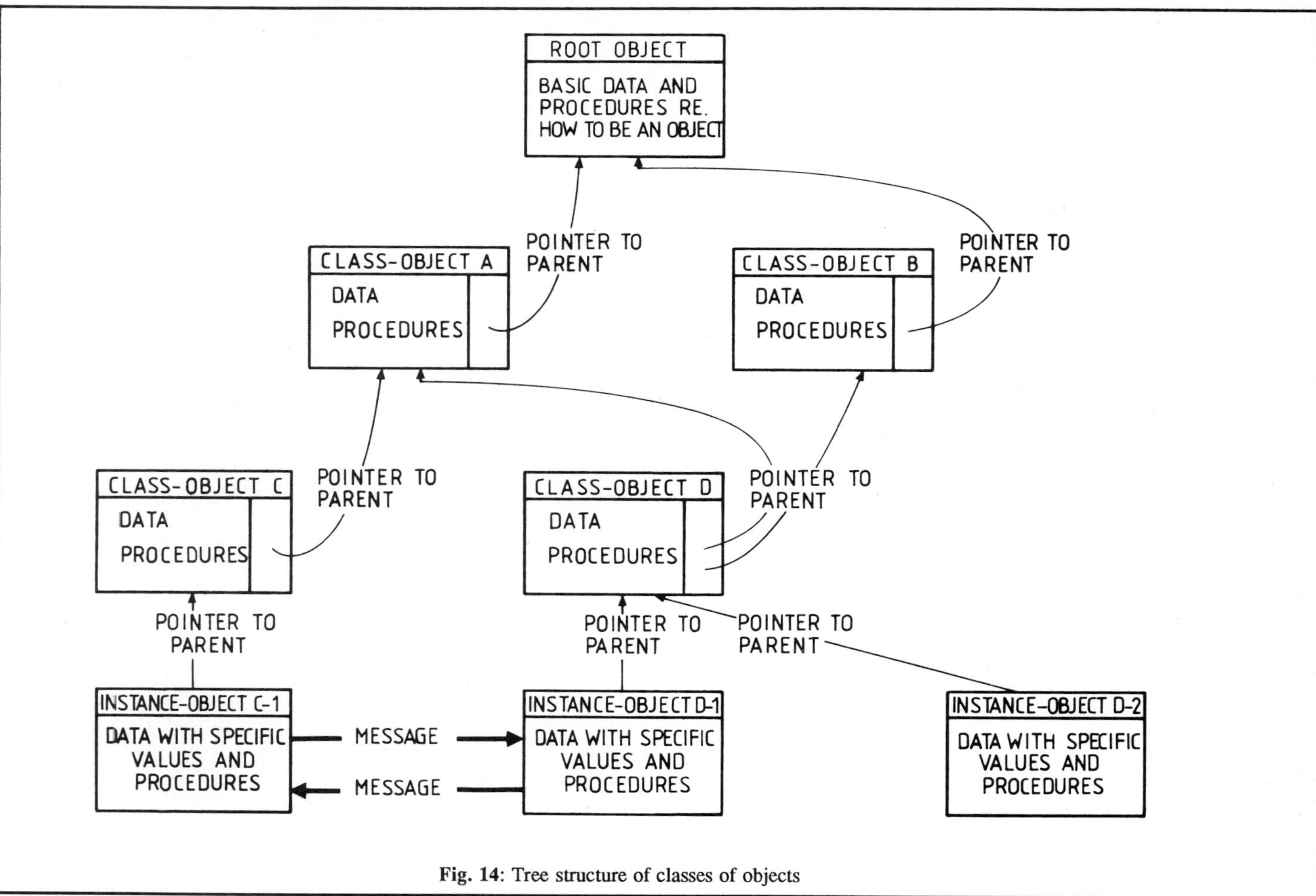

Fig. 14: Tree structure of classes of objects

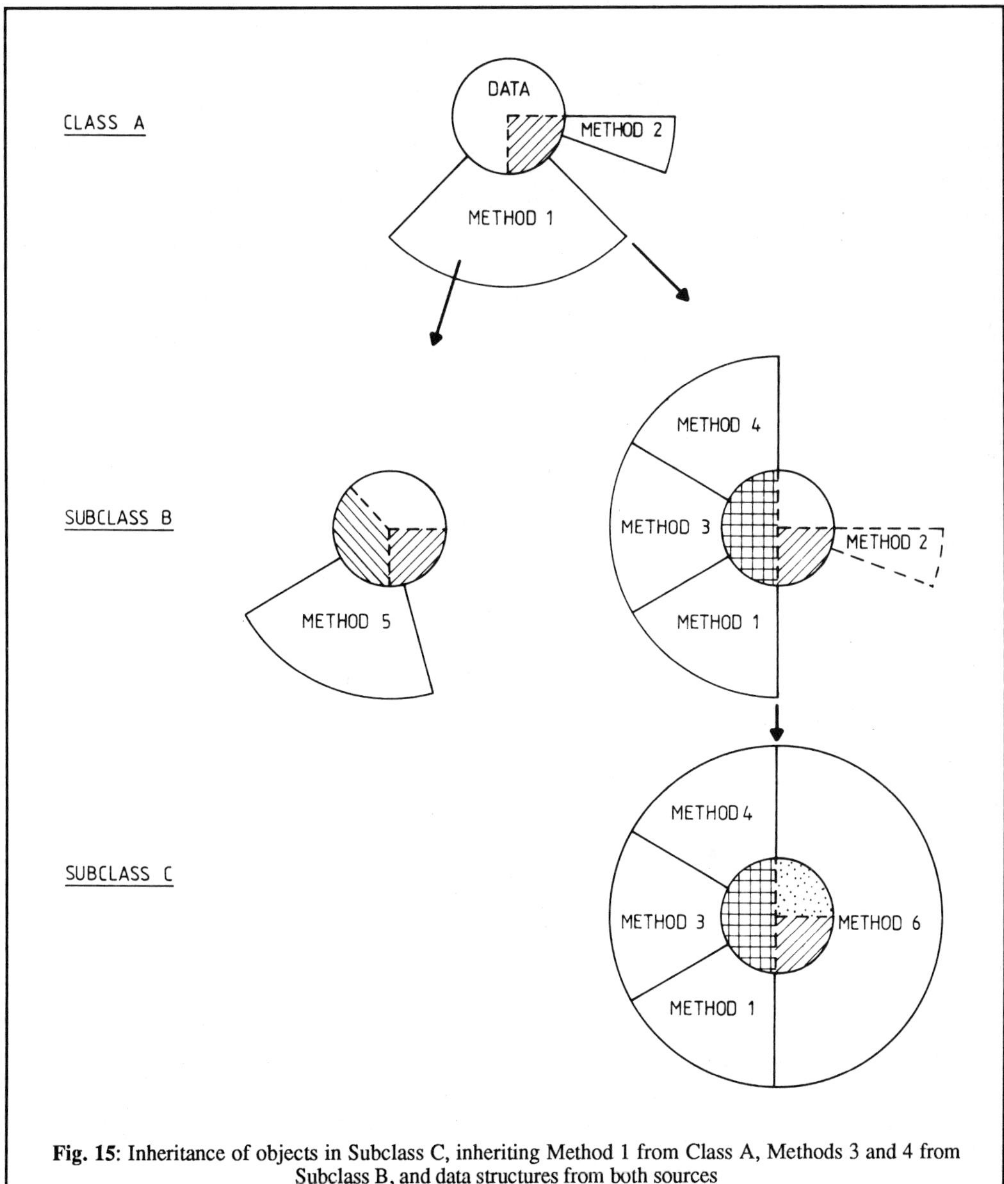

Fig. 15: Inheritance of objects in Subclass C, inheriting Method 1 from Class A, Methods 3 and 4 from Subclass B, and data structures from both sources

iii. Dynamic binding

Dynamic binding refers to putting together the methods and the data on which they will operate. Since messages are independent of data or objects, when an object receives a message the language searches the object class to find the correct method for that message. But the relationship between message and procedure is established only at run time. This implies that all but the very lowest classes are independent of data type, which ensures code reusability; even, the data type of a variable can change if necessary during execution.

iv. Inheritance

Inheritance builds a tree structure of classes of objects (Fig. 14). At the top, is a general class, e.g. "client's portfolio"; within this class are subclasses that define the fundamental objects in the object, like "share balance", "bond balance", " liquidity", "margin loans". Within each of these subclasses are classes that define important functional parts, such as "round-lot orders", "margineable securities", etc. With inheritance, an object not only contains the data and methods of its own class, but has access to, or inherits, the methods and some data from all its superclasses (Fig. 15 and 16).

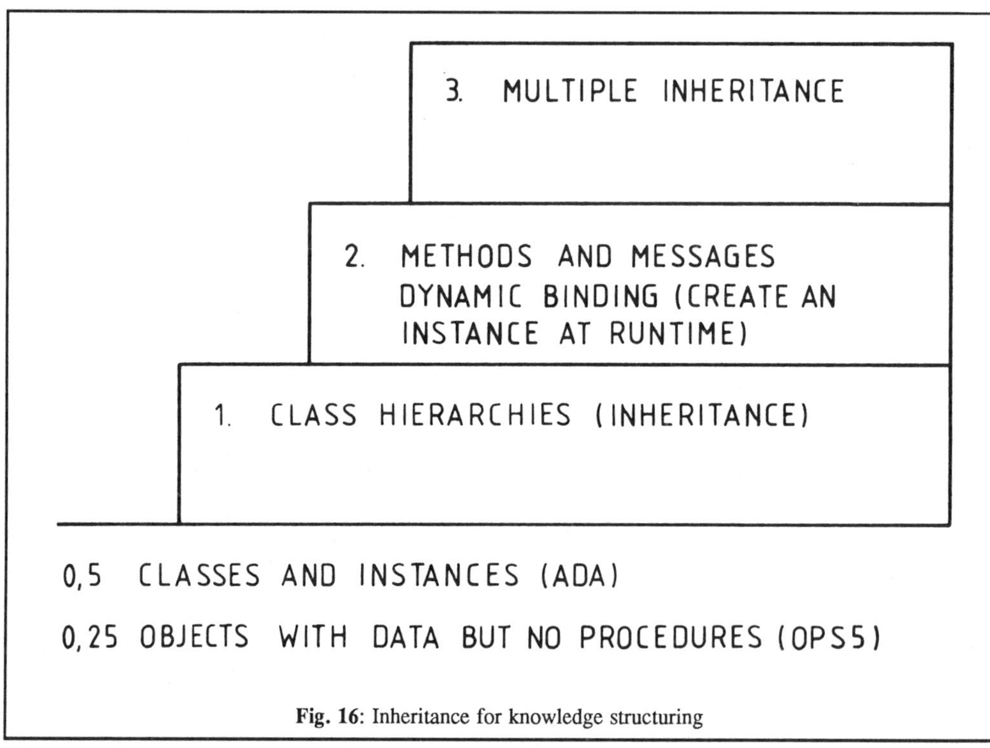

Fig. 16: Inheritance for knowledge structuring

Example 60: Inheritance

From the higher class "Trading strategy", the object "Bond balance" might inherit trading trigger rules. ■

Moreover, inheritance eases modification of the system; for example, if the method to select investments for liquid assets is changed, all subclasses inherit the changed method.

v. Object-oriented software design

Object-oriented software design is radically different from procedural or declarative designs, and it takes time to get accustomed to it, although the productivity gains are remarkably high. The usual steps are:

- identify the objects, e.g. "share balance"
- classify the objects into classes, including predefined classes; e.g. "client's portfolio" would be a subclass of "Network" (predefined), with instance variables "Asset/Loan Types", and with a dictionary of all the asset/loan types; in turn, "Asset/loan type" would be a subclass of the predefined "Network Node", "Trade" would be a subclass of e.g. Prolog methods implemented in an object-oriented environment, with instance variables "Quantity", "Term"

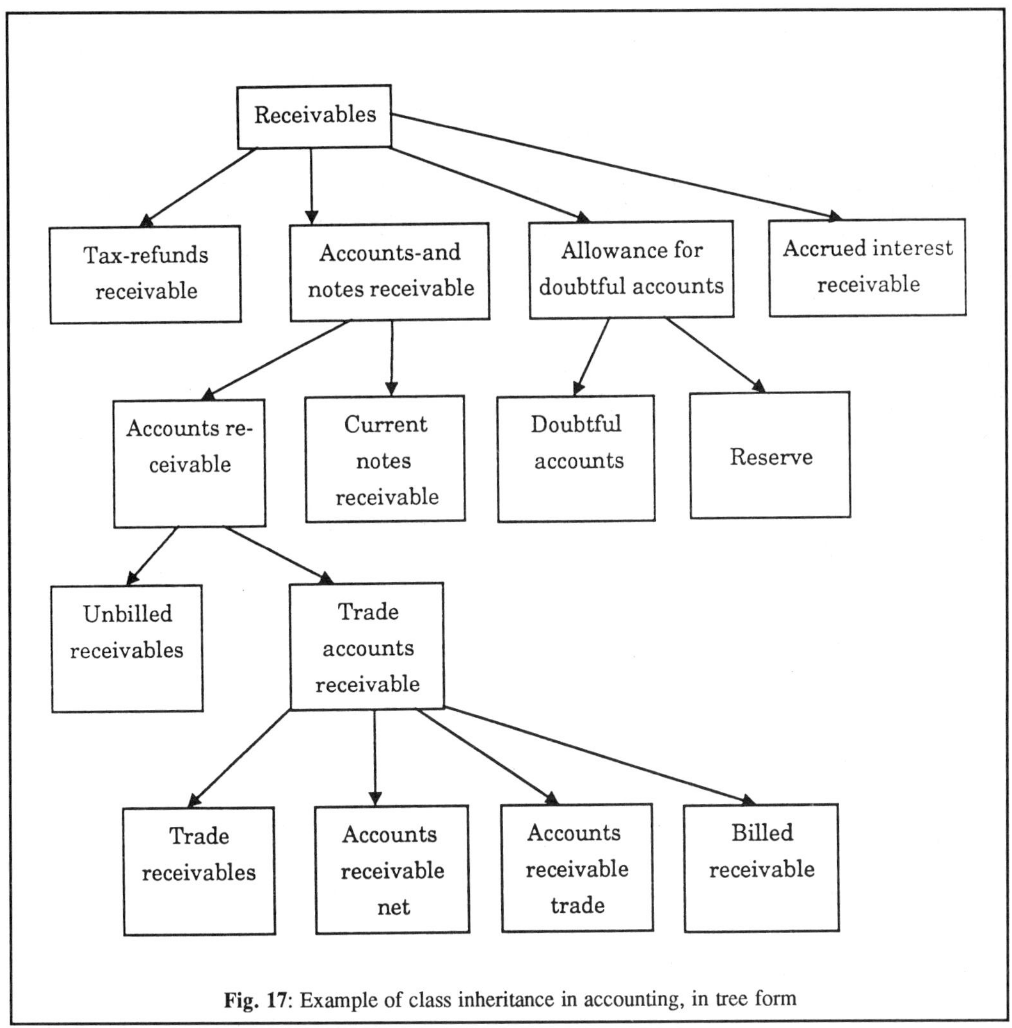

Fig. 17: Example of class inheritance in accounting, in tree form

"Buy/Sell", "Term", "Market", and "Avoid" which could be a list of all the securities to be avoided

- define messages and the corresponding methods

Example 61: Trading methods

. trading"Trading strategy" methods can be enabled via the messages:

ShareTrade :	MarginBuy:	Share
LimitLosses :	Hedge :	Share Option

. "Trade"logic methods also involve messages sent to predicates:

find(Share, PriceEarning) less (PriceEarning, 6)

■

Example 62: Class inheritance in accounting software

Fig. 17 illustrates general class inheritance helping in structuring software development and code. This Figure shows the actual classes and instances in this field. ■

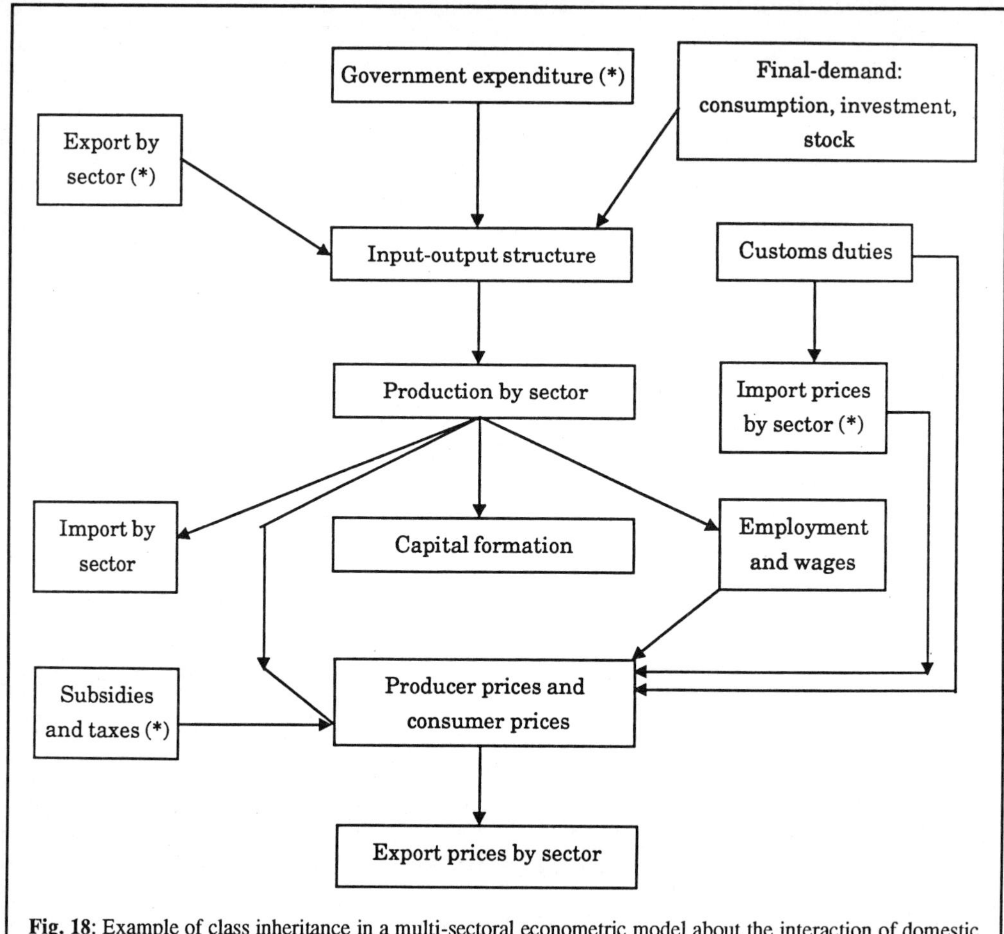

Fig. 18: Example of class inheritance in a multi-sectoral econometric model about the interaction of domestic and international trade; this inheritance involves multiple parents. (*) designates exogenous variable; all other are endogenous

Example 63: Class inheritance in a multi-sectorial econometric model

Fig. 18 illustrates class inheritance as well but this time in an econometric model. The main differences with Example 62 are first that some inheritance relations concern either endogenous or exogenous data structures and methods, and next that feedback is allowed thus breaking the tree structure. ■

5 Search and causal analysis

5.1 Motivation

In Chapter 3 the idea was introduced of representing knowledge as symbolic structures, and knowledge manipulation (i.e.reasoning) as formal symbolic manipulation. We also stressed how each knowledge representation formalism limits the set of allowable symbolic structures and manipulations, thus enforcing a consistent abstraction of the real world and/or achieving useful properties. In this chapter we deal with *search*, i.e. the general problem of finding a sequence of allowable symbolic manipulations transforming a set of given structures into another target set. Examples of target sets are:

- goals to be fulfilled
- hypotheses or pre-conditions to be found
- hypotheses to be evaluated
- explanations

Chapter 1.1 already introduced some basic motivations behind the need for search. In fact, uncertainty/incompleteness in the knowledge translates into the following limitations:

- there are several alternative candidate manipulations for each symbolic structure
- it is impossible to tell *a priori* which manipulation is the most convenient to reach the target set

To clarify this point consider the two following cases.

In linear programming, the problem description consists in a set of equations and inequalities; the process of solving a linear programming problem is well-known (e.g.the Simplex algorithm); the sequence of manipulations is therefore codified a priori (e.g. the steps of the Simplex algorithm); there is no need for search.

In investment planning, there is no a priori established method for optimal investment decision making; the planner needs to explore different alternative courses of decisions, check them against economic expectations/expected returns and finally select a plan, which is in turn subject to revisions as new data become available; thus the process of planning involves search. AI problems are closer to "investment planning" than to "linear programming", and therefore do involve search.

5.2 State-based representation of problems

To understand search, it is convenient to introduce the notion of *state* and of *state space* [Newell and Simon, 1975]. In a system theoretical sense, a state is the information set characterizing completely a system. Similarly, in a knowledge-based system, the state is the collection of available knowledge, in the form of symbolic structures. The state space can be defined as the set of all allowable states. Then, in its simplest and more general sense, search means scanning through all allowable states, until a state satisfying some Boolean test (called a *goal state* or goal) is found, the only prerequisite for this search being the availability of a function orderly generating all allowable states.

Example 1: Unstructured state space search

Assume a portfolio selection process, in which the state of a security (or commodity) is defined according to the triple:

- (price schedule, short-term moving average schedule, 14-day RSI schedule)

where RSI is the Relative Strength Index, an oscillator first defined in [Wilder, 1978].

The state of a portfolio is a collection of securities, with quantities (or percentages) specified for each. The state space of the portfolio selection problem is then the set of all possible portfolios. Note that combinatorial enumeration is restricted by portfolio constraints, due to trading regulations, institutional policies, risk hedging purposes or client-oriented investment guidelines. In our approach, it is the responsibility of the state generation function to take the above limitations into account.

The search procedure then selects each state, and applies to it an evaluation test. The test may consist in some global measure of merit, e.g. combining distance from the short term-moving average (seen as a stop-loss for long positions), oversold index, etc. The first state satisfying the evaluation test is returned as a (possibly non-optimal) solution. ■

In many cases, it is possible to exploit with advantage the *structure* of the state space. By structure is meant a set of relations among the states in the state space, e.g. dependency of one collection of states on another state. In the case of knowledge-based systems, knowledge manipulation procedures can be seen as specifying allowable state transitions, transforming a state into a different one. More generally, we will call *operator* any manipulation procedure (mathematical, knowledge-based, logical) defining an allowable transition from one state to another. Operators define a "reachability" relation over the state space as follows:

Let s_A and s_B be states. s_B is reachable from s_A if and only if there is an operator O1 transforming s_A into s_B. The key properties of the relation "reachability" are *asymmetry* and *transitivity*. The relation is asymmetric because "s_B is reachable from s_A through O1", does not imply that there exist an operator O1' such that "s_A is reachable from s_B through O1' ". Transitivity means that if s_B is reachable from s_A through O1, and s_C is reachable from s_B through O2, then s_C must be reachable from s_A (which obviously holds: O1 followed by O2 performs the task). In particular, let s_A be the *initial state* of the problem (often shorted S for "Start"), and s_G any state satisfying the goal test: then the sequence of operators to be applied to transform s_A into s_G is called the *solution* of the problem. Transitivity makes it possible to solve problems through repeated considerations about "local reachability" involving just one operator: i.e. s_G is reachable from s_A if and only if s_G is reachable from one of the states locally reachable from s_A. This is the basis for all algorithms *searching* for solutions to problems (see Section 5.1). In the following example, the search method sketched in Example 1 is improved by exploiting the structure of the portfolio selection task.

Example 2: Structured state space search in portfolio selection

Given an initial portfolio, the portfolio selection process can be seen as a set of transactions, transforming one portfolio into a different one.

Then a search procedure can be designed as follows: one transaction is selected, which replaces a lower merit security in the portfolio with a better security on the market; allowable transactions are again limited by regulations and costs. The resulting portfolio, obviously, has a higher merit than the previous one. By iteratively applying this method, increasingly attractive portfolios can be built. Furthermore, many lower merit portfolios are never taken into account, so that the total number of states examined by the search procedure is smaller than in Example 1. ■

5.3 Problem graphs

Graphs and trees are useful tools for understanding the state space representation of a problem and the related concept of search. Graphs and trees were first introduced in Chapter 3.3. Definitions mentioned there will be extensively used throughout this Chapter.

Let a *unique* node in a graph be associated to each state in a problem state space. Furthermore, let two nodes n_A, n_B be connected by a directed arc (n_A, n_B) only if there is a knowledge manipulation procedure transforming s_A into s_B, i.e. if s_B "is reachable" from s_A. The graph (or tree) G(P) thus obtained is an alternative, pictorial representation of a problem P, in which the structure of P (defined as reachability between states) is made explicit as the *topology* of G(P) (pattern of connections). So, the children of a given node in G(P) are the states reachable from the associated state in P by applying just one operator. Their number is called the *outdegree* (or *branching factor* , see Chapter 3.3.3) of the node, and is equal to the number of operators applicable to the state. Since the problem-solver must decide which operator to apply as a further step in an hopefully successful path, the outdegree is a measure of the uncertainty in knowledge. As a further example, if in P a state is not derivable through the allowable manipulations (e.g. a logical axiom in a theorem prover), the corresponding node in G(P) has no arcs (links) incident to it (i.e. is a source). Finally, s_N is derivable from s_A in P if and only if there is at least one *directed path* from n_A to n_N in G(P): this is because the relation "is reachable" defined over the state space of P (see Section 1 above) is mapped to the relation "there is a directed path" defined over G(P). It is easy to check that both relations have exactly the same properties.

Problem graphs have already shown up in previous chapters (most notably, production systems, see Chapter 3.6.6, Figs. 8, 9 and 10). In Sections 6 and 10, for instance, graphs will be introduced as an alternative to matrices for representing economic models.

Assuming that:

- the graph representation of a problem is known
- there is a node belonging to the graph labelled as the initial node (namely, the node corresponding to the initial state)
- there are one or more nodes labelled as goal nodes (namely, the nodes corresponding to states satisfying the goal test),

then, from what was said above, problem-solving amounts to the process of *finding a path* in the corresponding graph between the start node and one of the goal nodes. Such a path, if found, is sometimes called a *successful path* and represents one problem solution. Path-finding is an interesting way of thinking about problem-solving, because it is a well-defined concept, whose computer implementation is straightforward, although expensive in terms of computational resources (i.e. memory consumption and/or computation time).

However, given a directed graph, the interpretation of a path critically depends on the intended interpretation of arcs: e.g. if arcs stand for an intransitive relation (see Example 9, Chapter 3.4.3), paths have no clear meaning in the problem domain, and search procedures should not be used. Sometimes, the interpretation of a path, although meaningful, is different from the interpretation associated to the arcs (see Section 6): in such cases, the result of a search should be interpreted with care. In Section 5.1, some terminology about search procedures is introduced, and a template search algorithm is sketched out.

5.3.1 Implicit representation of graphs and trees

Usually, the topology of graphs associated to knowledge-based problems is not completely known as search is started. In fact, knowledge-based problems are generally given in implicit form (an initial state, and a set of operators defined on the states). Their graphs could be built by applying all allowable operators to existing states, and then recursively applying the operators again to all the newly generated states, until only states with no applicable operators remain. In some specific cases, such a graph may be effectively built, at least in part. For instance, in the case of a rule-based system (see Chapter 3.6), the subgraph of the problem graph may be used to avoid repeated pattern-matching over the knowledge base at each inference cycle, thus improving the response time of the system. Then search could start processing the graph over again. This process is inefficient, and sometimes impossible.

However, explicit graph representation before a one-shot search is a nonsense. The recursive algorithm for graph generation is at the same time a search algorithm, provided a goal test is added to stop it as soon as a goal node is found. Furthermore, there are some problems with infinite state space. Graph explicitation would therefore never terminate, while some search methods are guaranteed to terminate if a finite solution path exists (see Section 9). For these reasons, search methods always assume an **implicit** representation of the problem graph, and recursively generate it, stopping as soon as either a goal node is found, or the whole space has been scanned, or preset limits in the computational resources are exceeded.

Please note that if a problem is represented as a systems of equations (see Section 10 below), the topology of the associated graph is on the contrary completely specified from the beginning, at no additional cost. However, none of the search methods introduced in the rest of this Chapter depends on this feature. Therefore, they can be used for both implicit and explicit state spaces.

5.4 Search and knowledge

There is a clear *trade-off* between search and knowledge: namely, search can be reduced by providing more knowledge; conversely, less knowledge is required with more extensive search. Usually, there is some discretion in operational problem-solving about the relative amount of search and knowledge.

Among several other considerations, one strong point in favour of more knowledge is the increase in efficiency of the problem-solver: if an investor has a clear knowledge of the effects of a high inflation rate on the return of different assets, he can use said knowledge to drastically reduce the investment alternatives in periods of high inflation. Furthermore, search can only better exploit the knowledge available, not create new one (see, however, learning in Chapter 6). So there is a lower bound on knowledge, below which the performance of the problem-solver degrades.

One strong point in favour of more search is cost saving in finding and extracting additional knowledge from human experts: the cost of acquiring more precise information about the expected performances of an industry could be higher than the expected return generated by that information; in that case it is more convenient to live with uncertain knowledge and explore different assumptions. Furthermore, taking into account all available knowledge may make the problem-solver less efficient than allowing for a little search.

The optimal trade-off depends of course on the specific application: in some fields of finance first hand knowledge may be quite expensive; in other fields knowledge may simply not be available or may not exist. In such cases it is reasonable to emphasize the role of search. In other cases, knowledge may be very cheep or even free (think about regulations of the stock exchange markets), and it is therefore reasonable to emphasize knowledge.

5.5 Search procedures

5.5.1 A generic search procedure

A search method (or procedure) is a *plan* for performing search; it is important to have a plan when exploring alternatives, because otherwise there is the risk of exploring more than once the same alternative, which is a waste of computational resources (lack of efficiency); or of forgetting to explore some alternatives, thus missing potential solutions (lack of completeness). A complete search method is also called *exhaustive* . Finally, it should be designed in such a way that, if the graph to be searched is finite, it *terminates* .

Such a plan is readily implemented for instance by the following template of an algorithm:

1.	A node N is *selected* among a set of alternative nodes, and removed from that set. If the set of candidates is empty, the search fails.
2.	N is *explored,* i.e. tested for goal satisfaction.
3.	If N is a goal, then the search result is returned.
3'.	Else N is *expanded,* i.e. all or part of its children are generated.
4.	The result of expanding N is added to the set of alternatives.
5.	Search resumes from Step 1.

Steps 3 and 5 implement repeated generation of locally "reachable" states (see Section 2 above), until the goal test in Step 2 is satisfied. Hence search procedures are essentially recursive. If all states have been examined (Step 1) without finding the goal, search fails.

Note the alternating role of *exploration* , *expansion* and *selection* steps. Most of them need further specification: how is N to be selected from the candidate set (Step 1) ? What is exactly the search result returned (Step 3) ? How many children are generated, and how is this knowledge maintained, so that children are not generated twice ? The exact answers to the above questions may vary, reflecting the consideration that different people, given the same problem represented by the same causal graph, may come to a solution in different ways, depending on their psychological attitudes and on the scope of their interests. In problem-solving terminology, this amounts to say that there are several methods for searching for a solution in a causal graph, each method being adequate for different kinds of reasoning (see Sections 8 and 9 below for an example).

The requirements of efficiency, completeness and termination mentioned above are really minimal; in general, search procedures should be able to exploit knowledge about how to solve a problem (i.e. control knowledge, see Chapter 3.1.7), as well as information gathered from the search conducted so far. The purpose is to select the next candidate manipulation in such a way as to maximize the likelihood that it is part of a solution. However, search must still explore and maintain alternatives with little initially sustaining evidence or structure.

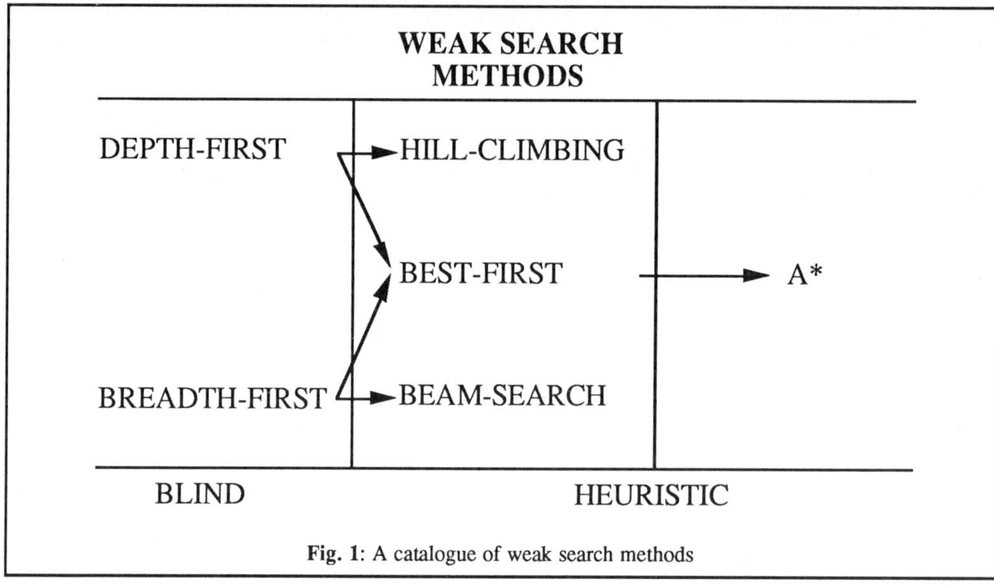

Fig. 1: A catalogue of weak search methods

5.5.2 Classification of search methods

Fig. 1 is an ordered catalogue of the most popular *weak search methods* , i.e. search methods formulated independently of the problem domain: they trade effectiveness for generality. Moving from the left of the table to the right, methods get more sophisticated, their efficiency is increased, but deeper knowledge about the problem is assumed as well. However, such knowledge still fits a generic paradigm, so that methods are still formulated in a domain-independent style. The arrows between methods in Fig. 1 show how more advanced methods depend on simpler ones; in other words, methods on the left side of the arrow are special cases of the methods on the right side.

Depth-first and breadth-first algorithms orderly explore all alternatives, until they run into a solution. For this reason they are called *blind methods* . Selection steps (refer to the generic search algorithm, Section 5.1 above), do not evaluate the relative goodness of the alternatives, but are designed in such a way that all alternatives sooner or later get selected once, and just once.

The other methods in the middle and right columns exploit on the contrary the assumption that a rating, called *evaluation function* , is made available to assess the relative merit of alternatives, thus directing the search procedure toward the most promising ones; such methods are called *heuristic methods*. Sections up to 10 are only concerned with blind search methods, while Section 11 introduces heuristic methods.

5.5.3 Application-specific search and mixed procedures

Often problem-specific knowledge is available, constraining the number of alternatives to be considered. For instance, a program for portfolio selection may constrain a priori the investment alternatives to be explored in a situation where increasing interest rates are expected, by exploiting the knowledge about the consequences of variations in the interest rates on different assets, such as bonds. Such knowledge should be included whenever possible, because it results in search procedures much more efficient (and focused toward the goal of the search) than general methods: e.g. just one rule relating the price of bonds to the interest rate may be used to discard investment alternatives based on bonds from the focus of attention of the problem-solver.

A generic search method can then be used to solve the remaining ambiguity; the overall search method is then a *mixed procedure* , relying on knowledge for coarse alternatives selection, and on application-independent search for the final selection of a specific choice.

5.5.4 Optimization criteria

There are different optimization criteria for search methods, such as:

i. *minimize* the cost of finding a solution, i.e. avoid the exploration of wrong alternatives, without concern for the quality of the solution found

ii. find the *best* solution, without concern for the time spent searching for an optimal solution

iii. become easily *adaptable* to external context-dependent updates or controls.

The first criterion may be seen as emphasizing the efficiency of search; the second addresses effectiveness; the third, flexibility and ease of specialization. The relevant optimization criterion depends on the requirements of the problem.

For many applications, the second criterion can be given a stronger, more specific formulation. If there is a cost associated to each operator, it may be possible to define the optimality of a solution as a function (usually the sum) of the costs of the operators composing the solution path. Thus an algorithm finds the optimal solution if it returns the least-cost path connecting the initial state to a goal state. Some search procedures assume that optimality can be expressed as a least-cost constraint on the solution path. In some other applications, however, the quality of a solution can be evaluated based on the quality of the final state found, rather than on the cost of the solution path.

5.6 Application: a simple economic model in graph form

Fig. 2 shows the graph representation of the structure of an elementary economic model (see Section 10 below for a precise definition of structure), equivalent to Fig. 5 in Chapter 3.4.3. Depth-first (this Section) and breadth-first (Section 9 below) search algorithms will be demonstrated based on this example. The interpretation of nodes and links (Chapter 3.4.3) is repeated here for convenience:

- nodes represent states
- links stay for the relation "has a direct influence on"

The above interpretation is true for networks capturing causal structures in general. A directed influence link (see Section 10 below for a more precise definition of causality) exists between two states only if a change in the state at the initial end-point of the influence link causes a change in the state at the terminal end-point of the causal link, *all other states being kept constant* . Such an influence is called a *direct influence* .

Direct influence is not an "ontological" property of a model, but depends on the level of detail of the representation. So, in Fig. 2 there is a direct influence between "salary index" and "orders". However, in a more detailed model, a change in the salary index would influence orders either through income and consumption (from the demand side) or through a shift in the optimal

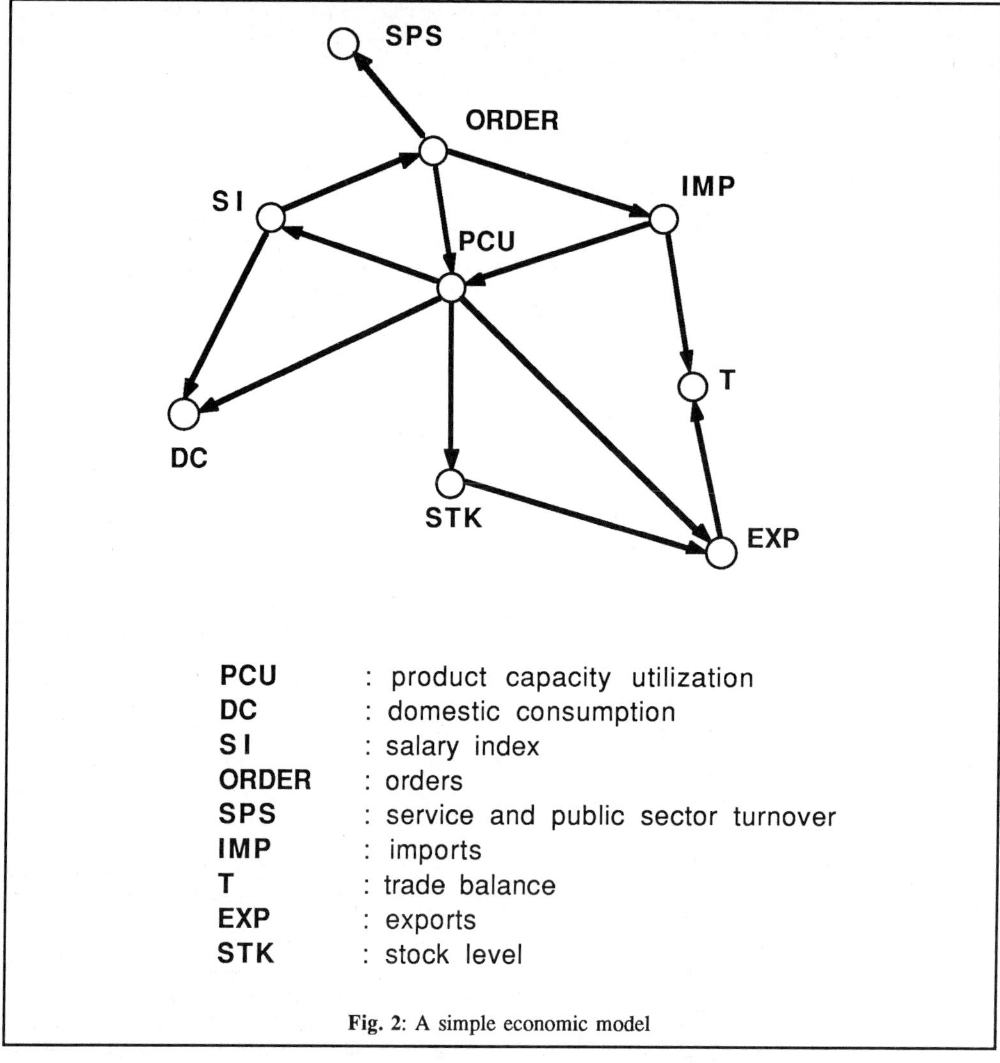

Fig. 2: A simple economic model

production level (from the output side). A change in the salary index, assuming constant both consumption and the marginal product of labour, would not affect orders.

It is clear that if "salary index has a **direct** influence on orders", and "orders have a **direct** influence on imports", then the correct conclusion is that "salary index has an **indirect** influence on imports". Hence, the meaning of chaining together relations of the kind "has a direct influence on" is different from the primitive relation itself. This difference is not irrelevant. Assume one state (e.g. an exogenous, stochastic phenomenon) indirectly influences a different state: a policymaker could legitimately ask whcther any instrument is available in the model for minimizing such influence at some intermediate state. Of course, this question cannot be answered by a coarsc model in which the above influence is direct. Therefore, one should specify if the solution searched for, is:

- direct influence: there must be a path of length one between the initial and the goal state, i.e. if the goal state is a child of the initial state (see Chapter 3.3.2 for a definition of length)

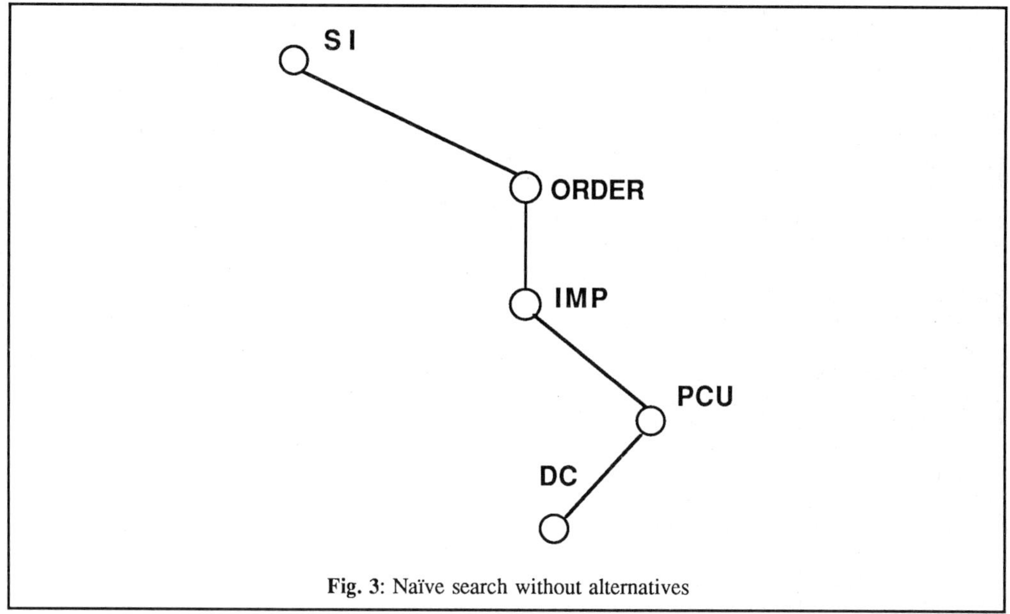

Fig. 3: Naïve search without alternatives

- indirect influence: the length of the shortest path between the initial and the goal state must be greater than one
- direct or indirect influence: there must be a path of any length between the initial and final state

In discussing depth-first, we always assume that the last interpretation holds. The second interpretation motivates breadth-first search (Section 9 below).

5.7 Simple propagation

The most primitive use of structural models one can imagine is shown in Fig. 3: it consists of just one path between two states, say "salary index" and "domestic consumption".

Psychologically, this corresponds to a problem-solver taking into account just one single effect of any event (hence assuming everything else is constant), and never reconsidering its assumptions. In other words, only one direct influence is considered at each step. For instance, variations in the level of the orders also cause variations in the service and public sector spending and in capacity utilization (secondary effects); however, such variations are not taken into account. Avoiding criticizing past assumptions, saves mental (and computational) resources; however, the exploitation of the available knowledge and hence the problem-solving performances are bad in most cases. In fact, unless infallible selection criteria are available to the problem-solver at each decision point to univocally commit to one specific decision (in which case the problem-solver is called deterministic), disregarding alternatives may lead to wrong (or no) solutions. From Section 1, we know that infallible selection criteria are simply not available in most of the cases. Therefore, Sections 8 and 9 below introduce non-determinism in problem-solvers.

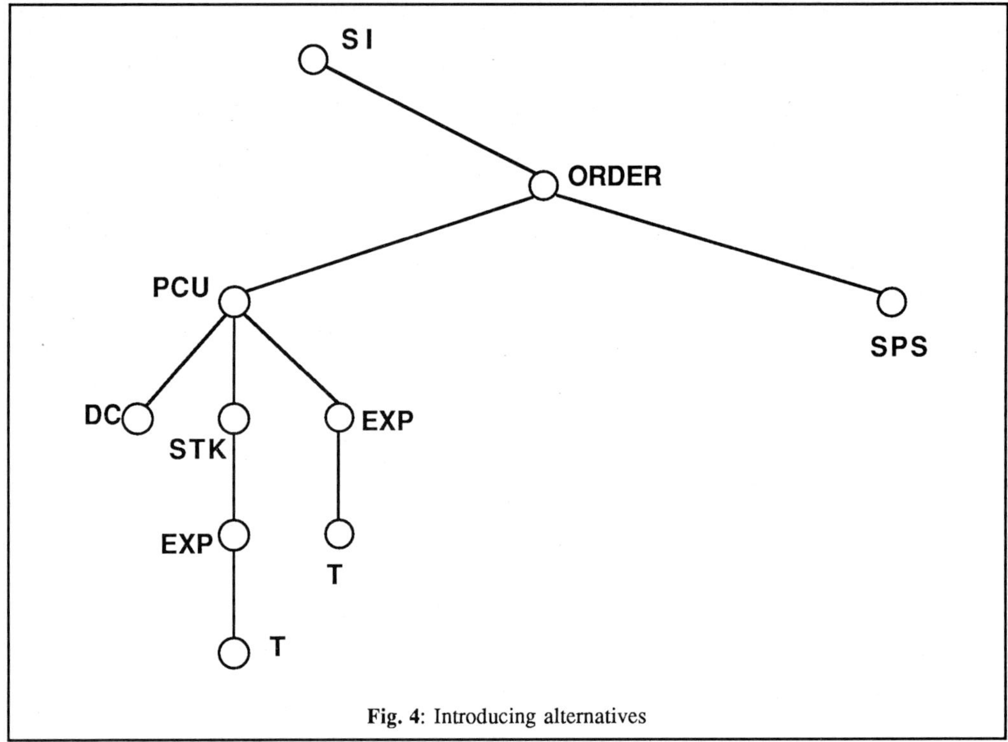

Fig. 4: Introducing alternatives

5.8 Propagation with alternatives: depth-first

Consider now the slightly more complex representation in Fig. 4, where the influences of a variation in the production capacity utilization over stock level and exports are considered in the reasoning, together with the influence of a variation of the orders over the service and public sector. The important *qualitative* difference of Fig. 3 with respect to Fig. 4 is that the latter has *alternatives* , to be explored through search. Search in turn implies more advanced computational capabilities, whose exact extent depends on the search method adopted, along the template in Section 5.1. Most notably, there is a need for storage, to be used to record past actions (already explored states). Depth-first, introduced in Section 8.2 below, is the simplest exhaustive search method.

5.8.1 Representation of directed graphs

Several techniques have been proposed for representing graphs as the input to computer programs (such techniques are especially relevant when the graph to be searched is large).

On one side, starting from the adjacency matrix associated to a graph (see Section 10), is it possible to exploit sparse matrix representation techniques (see for example [McCalla, 1988]). The same is true of other matrices associated to the graph (incidence matrix, reachability matrix, see [Deo, 1974] for a survey). However, recall from Section 3.1 that the problem graph is mostly implicit, i.e. its topology becomes clear during search: therefore, it cannot be passed as an argument to the search methods. Hence the above representations are not directly applicable in general, although some of them readily accommodate dynamic extensions of the graph.

Furthermore, even the elementary operation of successor generation is a problem-dependent, often difficult task, involving algorithms such as pattern-matching and conflict resolution (see Chapter 3.6.7). Understanding, more than efficiency, being the key concern of this work, the chosen representations and algorithms are simple enough to be easily readable, while not hopelessly inefficient. In the two following paragraphs, directed graph representations in LISP resp. Prolog are introduced.

1. LISP

Graph nodes are represented as LISP atoms. This is only adequate for focusing attention about search; however, in more realistic applications, states are usually complex collections of assertions/data.

Links are not directly represented. Instead, the children of a node are stored as a property of the node, under the property CHILDREN. When needed, parents of a node can be stored under a property called PARENTS.

The above representation makes it easy to recover the topology of the graph, but not to change it. For instance, the deletion of a node is costly, since each node is stored in several places. In order to make this representation easy to change, children generation is always hidden in a separate procedure, called "get-children".

Example 3: LISP representation of the economic model in Fig. 2

Evaluate the following functions to get the graph of the model in Fig. 2:

```
;; global variable containing all nodes
(SETQ allnodes '(ORDER SPS IMP TB PCU SI DC STK EXP))

;; initializing CHILDREN property
(SETF (GET 'ORDER 'CHILDREN) '(SPS IMP PCU))
(SETF (GET 'SPS 'CHILDREN) '())
(SETF (GET 'IMP 'CHILDREN) '(T PCU))
(SETF (GET 'T 'CHILDREN) '())
(SETF (GET 'PCU 'CHILDREN) '(SI DC STK EXP))
(SETF (GET 'SI 'CHILDREN) '(ORDER DC))
(SETF (GET 'DC 'CHILDREN) '())
(SETF (GET 'STK 'CHILDREN) '(EXP))
(SETF (GET 'EXP 'CHILDREN) '(T))

;; initializing PARENTS property
(SETF (GET 'SPS 'PARENTS) '(ORDER))
(SETF (GET 'ORDER 'PARENTS) '(SI))
(SETF (GET 'IMP 'PARENTS) '(ORDER))
(SETF (GET 'T 'PARENTS) '(IMP EXP))
(SETF (GET 'PCU 'PARENTS) '(ORDER IMP))
(SETF (GET 'SI 'PARENTS) '(PCU))
(SETF (GET 'DC 'PARENTS) '(SI PCU))
(SETF (GET 'STK 'PARENTS) '(PCU))
(SETF (GET 'EXP 'PARENTS) '(STK PCU))
```

The following example shows how properties values can be recovered, and gives the implementation of the function "get-children"

```
>(GET 'PCU 'CHILDREN) ;; recovers value stored under property CHILDREN in node 'PCU
(SI DC STK EXP)

(DEFUN get-chidren (Node) ;; definition of the function returning the successors of a node
        (GET Node 'CHILDREN))
```

■

2. Prolog

A graph is a predicate with two arguments. The predicate is true, if the node in the first argument is a father of the node in the second argument. Nodes can in principle be terms of any kind (in the following implementations: atoms). The direction of the link is captured by the order of the arguments. The Prolog inference engine automatically returns one successor at a time and backtracking ensures that a new successor is returned each time the predicate is resatisfied.

Example 4: Prolog representation of the economic model in Fig. 2

Let the predicate "arc" be associated to the graph in Fig. 2. The graph can then be represented as follows:

```
arc(si, order).     arc(si, dc).         arc(order, sps).
arc(order, pcu).    arc(order, imp).     arc(imp, pcu).
arc(pcu, si).       arc(pcu, dc).        arc(pcu, stk).
arc(pcu, exp).      arc(stk, exp).       arc(exp, t).
arc(imp, x).
```

■

5.8.2 A description of the depth-first algorithm

Let the problem-solver consider (see Section 7 above) just one path in the graph, again disregarding secondary effects during propagation. However, should the considered path fail, give the problem-solver the capability to switch to a different path, until either a solution is found or all paths have been considered without success. A path is said to fail when its terminal endpoint has no children (hence cannot be continued), and at the same time no state along the path is a goal. This is the essence of depth-first.

The rest of the method is concerned with a strategy for switching to a new path preserving the requirements of efficiency and completeness mentioned in Section 5.1. Such a strategy is called *backtracking* , and it simply consists in reconsidering the latest decision point upon failure. A decision point is a node with alternatives. Therefore, upon failure, depth-first resumes the search from the latest decision point: the previously selected alternative (leading to failure) is discarded, and a new alternative is selected instead. Backtracking is a simple error-recovery strategy with some practical applications: as an example, it is the search mechanism embedded in Prolog interpreters (see Chapter 4.4.10).

Fig. 5 graphically displays the process, by marking step-by-step the way depth-first searches a tree. Labels to nodes are as in Fig. 2. The following color codes apply:

- nodes on the path under consideration are filled in gray
- nodes irrelevant for the rest of the search are discarded (e.g. terminal nodes in a failed path; nodes whose all children have already been discarded)
- white nodes are unknown to the search procedure.

Practically, searching a structural network depth-first means considering just the direct effects of a change in a state over an economic variable (by assuming no secondary effects), i.e. just one causal chain at time. Upon failure, the alternatives are used to generate different causal chains, to be orderly examined, until a causal chain demonstrating the desired dependency is found. This way of searching is typical of fields (like *finance*) in which the short-term, limited analysis (i.e. the analysis of direct-effects) is relevant, while secondary effects most of the time are not important.
Finally, note that often the expression "depth-first search with backtracking" is simply shortened as "backtracking" or as "chronological backtracking", to stress the fact that decisions are retracted based on the order in which they were made (the last decision is retracted first). An obvious

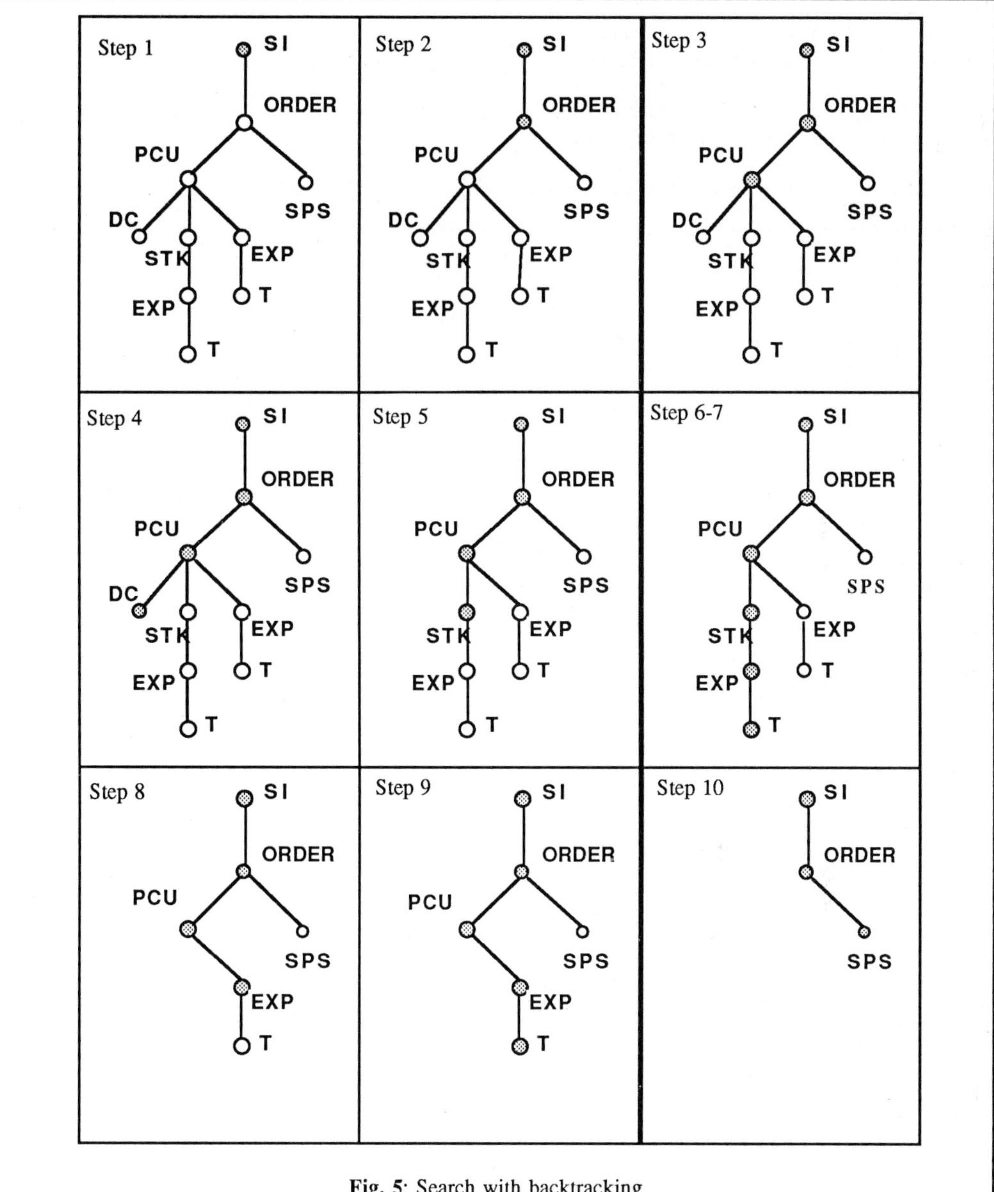

Fig. 5: Search with backtracking

improvement to the search is obtained through an analysis of the reasons for failure, and of which decisions to retract in order to overcome it ("dependency directed backtracking").

5.8.3 An implementation of depth-first algorithm

This section may be skipped by readers not interested in technical details. Please note that this, as well as all other implementations in this Chapter, are purposely restricted to the language primitives introduced in Chapters 4.3 (LISP) and 4.4 (Prolog), with a few exceptions, in order to keep the reader's understanding effort reasonable. Pre-defined primitives appear in Appendix 2.

Better and more robust implementations need to be generated if such code is to be used on a routine basis. For other implementations of search methods, see [Bahrami, 1988], [Winston, 1989] for LISP, [Bratko, 1986], [Rowe, 1988], [Sterling and Shapiro, 1986].

This section, and likewise Section 9.2 below, are organized into three parts: procedural style pseudo-code, LISP code and Prolog code.

a. Step-by-step pseudo-code description of depth-first in procedural style:

1	Put the start node S on Path.
2	If Path is empty, return a failure message and STOP.
3	Select the first node from Path and call it n.
4	If n is a goal, return the found Path, issue a message of successful search completion and STOP.
5	If n has no successors, remove it from Path and go to 2.
6	Expand n, generating all its successors S.
7	Select a node from S, call it s and remove it from S.
8	If s is a member of Path, go to 7.
9	Put s in front of Path.
10	Go to step 2.
END	

Note the index numbers left of each step in the description above. In LISP resp. Prolog code, numbers left of expressions resp. predicates point to steps in the pseudo-code description implementing a corresponding functionality. Numbers are used for documentation purposes (they can be used to retrieve a rough explanation in English for each expression resp. predicate) as well as for appreciating how the algorithms are reorganized to fit the different paradigms.

b. LISP code

All external functions have been defined previously. To locate the definitions, please look up the function names (in capital letters) in Appendix 2.1.

```
        (DEFUN depth-first (Start Goal-node)

6        (DEFUN get-children (N)
           (GET N 'CHILDREN))

         (DEFUN recursive-search (Candidates Solution)
2, 5       (IF (NULL Candidates) NIL
7           (LET ((N (CAR Candidates)))
8            (COND ((MEMBER N Solution) (recursive-search (CDR Candidates) Solution))
4                  ((EQUAL N Goal-node) (REVERSE (CONS N Solution)))
                   (T
9, 10              (LET ((result (recursive-search (get-children N) (CONS N Solution))))
5                   (IF (NULL result) (recursive-search (CDR Candidates) Solution)
                        result)))))))

1        (recursive-search (LIST Start) NIL))
```

c. Prolog code

One new predefined Prolog predicate is introduced in this code, the infix predicate "univ", noted =.. :

Pred =.. List

succeeds if Pred is the predicate whose functor is the first element of the list, and whose arguments are remaining elements of the list. All other predicates have been previously defined; to locate their definitions, please look up the predicates in Appendix 2.2. As in the following code, "=.." is used to switch from predicate to list representation and vice-versa:

Step	Code
1	depth_first(Start, Goal_node, Graph, Path) :- recursive_search(Start, Goal_node, Graph, [Start], Path), !.
8	loop(Next, History) :- not single_member(Next, History).

6, 7	get_child(X, Next, Graph) :-
	    Pred =.. [Graph, X, Next],
	    Pred.

4	recursive_search(Goal_node, Goal_node, _, _, [Goal_node]).

2 - 10	recursive_search(X, Goal_node, Graph, History, [X|Path]) :-
	    get_child(X, Next, Graph),
	    loop(Next, History),
	    recursive_search(Next, Goal_node, Graph, [Next|History], Path).

	/* UTILITIES */ single_member(H, [H|T]) :- !. single_member(A, [H|T]) :- single_member(A, T).

Remarks:

- To start the search, query the predicate "depth_first". For an explanation of the predicate arguments, see Section 8.1
- History contains the current path, only in reverse order. Path is used in order to avoid the reverse operation
- Step 6 generates only one successor at time, as opposed to the corresponding Step in the pseudo-code implementation and in LISP. This is due to the fact that the Prolog inference engine marks already explored children, so the search program does not need to perform explicit bookkeeping. Similarly, bactracking is not explicitily implemented

d. Time and memory requirements

Depth-first searches a graph in linear time; in fact, it explores any node at most once. Combinatorial explosion is not a feature of search algorithms, rather of the problem graph.

In principle, depth-first is the most memory economic search method. The memory space needed by the most economic implementations increases linearly with the depth of the search, but independently of the branching factor.

An important limitation of depth-first is that it is not guaranteed to terminate, if it starts diving deep into a search path of infinite length with no solution (here infinite can be understood either as mathematically infinite, or as very large compared to the computational resources available).

5.8.4 Examples

This Section shows how depth-first search can be used to obtain interesting information about the structure of a model.

Example 5: Problem decomposition

Section 5.1 above introduced the view of search as a recursive process. Assume that the goal of a problem-solver is to find a set of states in the state space satisfying given conditions P_0. Call such a set S_0. Sometimes, conditions P_0 are difficult to check. However, assume it is possible to find a set of subproblems P_1', P_1'', etc. such that the solutions to each of them S_1', S_1'', etc. are easier to find, and are in a known relationship to the solutions of P_0. By solving one of these subproblems, at least one solution to the initial problem can be found. If all of the problems P_1', P_1'', etc. are too difficult, problem simplification can be applied again, until the solution to one subproblem is trivial. The following depth-first pseudo algorithm defines a template for problem-solving through simplification:

```
(DEFUN solve (p)
  (IF (trivial? p) (return-solution p)
          (LET ((p-list (problem-decomposition p)))
            (construct-solution p (solve-list p-list)))))

(DEFUN solve-list (p-list)
  (LET ((solved (solve (CAR p-list)))
     (IF solved solved
           (solve-list (CDR p-list)))))
```

For instance, in the case of path finding:
(trivial? p) <=> (EQUAL p goal)
problem-decomposition <=> get-children
construct-solution <=> CONS ■

Example 6: Propagation of disturbances

Suppose a state s_N in a structural model undergoes a change. One important information is which other states in the model will be affected, i.e. which is the set of nodes directly or indirectly influenced by s_N. In graph theory, such a set is called the *accessible set* of s_N, and by definition it includes s_N (see for instance [Carré, 1979]). Some changes are possible to this algorithm with respect to the one in Section 8.3 above: no path must be returned, the goal test is useless (search must continue until failure). Here we present a more traditional implementation with two data structures, OPEN and CLOSED. A node is CLOSED if its children have already been generated, while it is OPEN if its children have not been considered yet.

```
(DEFUN accessible+ (Node)

 (DEFUN loop? (Children Open Closed)
  (REMOVE-IF #'(LAMBDA (N) (OR (MEMBER N Open) (MEMBER N Closed))) Children))

 (DEFUN get-children (N)
  (GET N 'CHILDREN))

 (DEFUN recursive-search (Open Closed)
  (IF (NULL Open) Closed
     (LET ((children (get-children (CAR Open)) ))
       (IF (NULL children)
        (recursive-search (CDR Open) (CONS (CAR Open) Closed))
        (recursive-search
         (APPEND (loop? children (CDR Open) Closed)
                (CDR Open))
         (CONS (CAR Open) Closed)))))

(recursive-search (LIST Start) '()))
```

Using the above algorithm, it is possible to show that a change in the product capacity utilization in the model in Fig. 2, will cause a change on every other state in the model. If such a change is not empirically demonstrated, and there is evidence that the model is correct, then cancellation due to opposite influences of equal magnitude must have occurred. ■

Example 7: The role of instruments

Another interesting question is how an endogenous state s_N is affected by the other states in the models. This question involves finding the set of variables influencing s_N directly or indirectly. The following program, along the guidelines of the program in the above Example 6, does the job:

```
(DEFUN related-exogenous (Node)

 (DEFUN loop? (Children Open Closed)
  (REMOVE-IF #'(LAMBDA (N) (OR (MEMBER N Open) (MEMBER N Closed))) Children))

 (DEFUN get-parents (N)
  (GET N 'PARENTS))

 (DEFUN recursive-search (Open Closed Result)
  (IF (NULL Open) Result
    (LET ((parents (get-parents (CAR Open)) ))
      (IF (NULL parents)
       (recursive-search (CDR Open) (CONS (CAR Open) Closed) (CONS (CAR Open) Result))
       (recursive-search
        (APPEND (loop? parents (CDR Open) Closed)
               (CDR Open))
        (CONS (CAR Open) Closed)
       Result)))))

(recursive-search (LIST Start) '() '()))
```

To the policymaker, it might be of interest to know which instruments do affect and which instruments do not affect an endogenous state. Of course, an algorithm along the pattern of the preceding one could be easily developed, for instance selectively cumulating root nodes into the Result list, instead of cumulating everything.

Less efficiently, the LISP built-in functions INTERSECTION and SET-DIFFERENCE together with functional composition provide the answers in just two lines of code; the arguments are two lists, interpreted as sets; the result is according to the well-known set theoretic operations:

```
(INTERSECTION list-of-instruments (related-exogenous 'sN))
(SET-DIFFERENCE list-of-instruments (related-exogenous 'sN))
```

■

Example 8: Computation of strong components

A strong component is the maximum subgraph of a given graph showing the property of strong connectivity, i.e. for every pair of nodes s_A, s_B in a strong component, there is a path from s_A to s_B as well as a path from s_B to s_A. That means that any state in a strong component has an influence on any other state in the same strong component and vice-versa. Structurally, strong components are the consequences of feedbacks in the model. Causally, within a strong component it does not make sense to ask which variable influences which other variable, because all of them influence each other, without possibility establishing a sound ordering among them. Computationally, a strong component corresponds to a set of interdependent equations. Finally, qualitative propagation of disturbances along strong components produces ambiguous results. For all of the above reasons, it is interesting to know the strong components in a model. First of all, note that from the above definition the function:

```
(INTERSECTION (accessible+ 'sA) (accessible- 'sA))
```

returns the strong component containing s_A. Therefore, by repeating the process for all nodes not belonging to previously found strong components, one finds all strong components in a given model. The following (awfully inefficient!) algorithm performs this task:

```
(DEFUN strong-components (Node-list)

 (DEFUN recursive-search (Nodes Result)
  (IF (NULL Nodes) Result
   (LET ((component
        (intersection (accessible+ (CAR Nodes))
                              (accessible- (CAR Nodes)))))
    (recursive-search (set-difference Nodes component)
                   (CONS component Result)))))
```

```
(recursive-search Node-list NIL))
```

Applied to the model in Fig. 2, it would correctly recognize the following strong components:

{PCU ORDER IMP SI} {SPS} {DC} {STK} {EXP} {T}

■

Example 9: Finding all paths between two nodes

The following algorithm retrieves all elementary paths between two nodes, i.e. the complete (direct or indirect) effects of a change in one node on another node. Therefore, in feedback-free systems, such propagation computes the multiplier between the initial and the terminal states (the initial state being assumed as exogenous). Since by definition depth-first disregards side-effects, the algorithm consists of a repeated application of depth-first, whereby each repetition computes a path which is by construction different from all others by at least one node. Each path found is cumulated in a result list. When no further path exists, the cumulated result, a list of paths, is returned.

LISP makes possible a very elegant approach to this and similar problems, by providing primitive functions whose effect is to modify the behavior of other functions, for instance by repeatedly applying them to all elements of a list (see Chapter 4.3.9). The newly introduced primitive MAPCAN is one of these:

(MAPCAN Function List)

where Function must have a functional definition. Roughly, it applies Function to each element of the list, and APPENDs the results.

```
(DEFUN all-paths (Start Goal-node)

 (DEFUN get-children (N)
   (GET N 'CHILDREN))

 (DEFUN recursive-search (Path)
  (IF (NULL Path) NIL
    (IF (EQUAL (CAR Path) Goal) (REVERSE Path)
          (MAPCAN
            #'(LAMBDA (X) (recursive-search (CONS X Path)))
            (REMOVE-IF
              #'(LAMBDA (X) (MEMBER X Path))
                 (get-children (CAR Path)))))))

(recursive-search (LIST Start)))
```

Note the effect of functional composition on the ordering of the Steps. First the function "get-children" is called, then its result, the children of that node, is fed as an argument to REMOVE-IF, whose result, the list of children without feedback nodes, is fed as an argument to MAPCAN, whose result is finally returned. It is often convenient, in LISP, to reason in terms of streams of data, "flowing" through filter and mapping functions transforming and combining them. Of course, a similar concept could have been used in defining depth-first as well, the only difference being that the first non-NIL path found should be returned, instead of cumulating all paths. This could have been achieved by replacing MAPCAN in the previous code with SOME, another built-in function. There would be some inefficiency though, as all children are tested for circuits, while some of such tests may be useless, if a solution is found before. Such inefficiency can be overcome by using a technique called "delayed evaluation", which is outside the scope of this book (see [Abelson et al., 1985]). ■

5.9 Introducing side effects: breadth-first

Depth-first is search without side effects; namely, just one path is under consideration until a failure occurs. All the rest is bookkeeping to avoid getting trapped in circuits and repeated examination of the same states.

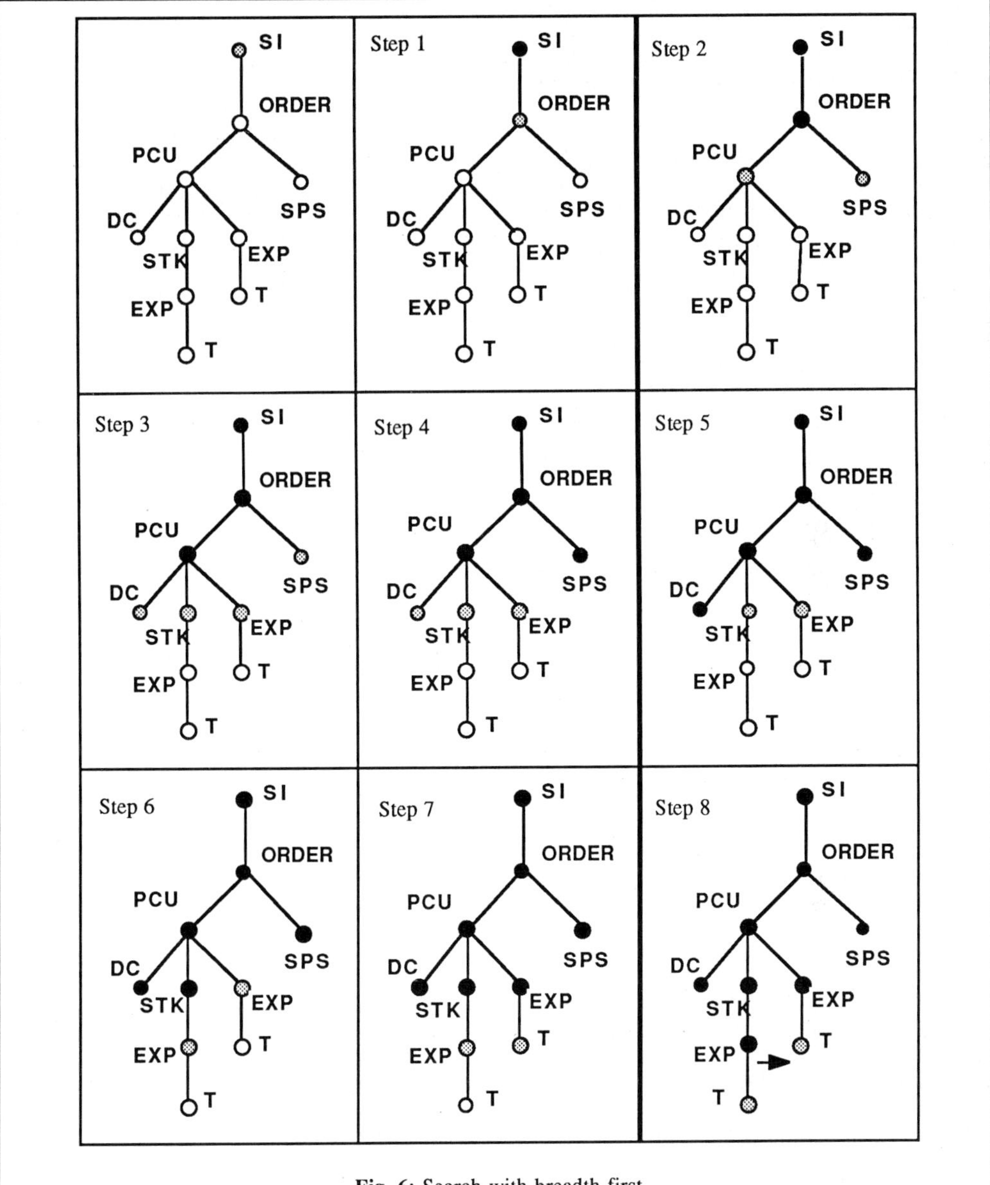

Fig. 6: Search with breadth-first

Breadth-first is search without backtracking. No decision is made about which alternative to explore first among a set of alternatives; every alternative is considered and extended in parallel. Therefore there can be no error in selecting the wrong alternative, hence the lack of motivation for backtracking.

5.9.1 A description of the breadth-first algorithm

The plan adopted in breadth-first search is to first examine all direct consequences of a change in a state (the initial state), then all dependencies at the second level (i.e. direct influences from the children of the initial state), and so on until there are no more levels to explore, or the desired effect has been derived. Hence, breadth-first will never expand a node if there is a comparatively higher level node still to be expanded. This is just the opposite to depth-first, where no node was expanded if a deeper unexplored alternative existed.

In breadth-first, the problem-solver does not track a specific path until success or failure, but maintains several search lines at the same time, and expands them in parallel. For this reason, breadth-first is a very difficult way of approaching problems. It requires a lot of memory (to store the complete influence tree) and a lot of flexibility, since the lines of reasoning (search paths) are intermixed, and the problem-solver continuously jumps from one path to the other (this repeated shift of attention is very critical for humans, much less for computers). However, as suggested above, it is the only method which takes completely into account the causalities in the model.

Fig. 6 graphically displays the process, by marking step-by-step the way depth-first searches a tree. The labels to nodes are as in Fig. 2.

The following color codes apply (same as in Section 8.2 above):

- nodes on the path under consideration are filled in gray
- nodes irrelevant for the rest of the search are discarded (e.g. terminal nodes in a failed path; nodes whose all children have already been discarded)
- white nodes are unknown to the search procedure

When doing long-term economic analysis, one is interested in all possible consequences of a change in each variable over the economy (this applies to exogenous or instrumental variables); therefore the depth-first approach is inappropriate for, say, a macroeconomist, because it limits the analysis to direct effects only. Breadth-first is a method for orderly exploring *all effects* of the variation of one state over all other states in the model. Of course, as a by-product, the causal chain(s) between two specified variables is (are) obtained; if a problem-solver is only interested in a single causal chain, it can stop the search as soon as one is found.

A nice feature of breadth-first is that it always returns a solution if a solution exists and if the graph is locally finite (i.e., the branching factor is finite); as opposed to depth-first, it does not "sink" more and more in wrong, perhaps infinite paths. In addition, it finds the shortest solution path, if the length is measured as the number of links in the path. The major drawback of breadth-first is its high memory consumption. Because of this, it is seldom used in its blind form, or on the full graph, but possibly on restricted and decomposed domains.

5.9.2 An implementation of the breadth-first algorithm

This section may be skipped by readers not interested in technical details.

a. Step-by-step pseudo-code description of breadth-first in procedural style:

1	Put the start node S on OPEN; CLOSED is empty.
2	If OPEN is empty, return a failure message and STOP.
3	Select the first node from OPEN and call it n.
4	Remove n from OPEN and put it on CLOSED.
5	If n is a goal, follow the pointers back to s. Return this path, issue a message of successful search completion and STOP.
6	Expand n, generating all its successors.
7	If there are successors of n already on OPEN, discard the newly generated successors.
8	If there are successors of n already on CLOSED, discard the newly generated successors.
9	Direct pointers from the remaining successors to their father n.
10	Put the remaining successors *at the end* of OPEN.
11	Go to step 2.
END	

<u>Remarks:</u>

- OPEN is a list containing alternatives generated by the search algorithm, but not yet explored. For exploration, the method selects always the first alternative in OPEN (Step 3)
- CLOSED is a list containing all nodes already explored (and failed)
- The principles of efficiency and termination, when applied to directed OR-graphs, imply avoiding getting lost in circuits and loosing search effort in cycles. Hence, before n is accepted as a new candidate, it is tested if it is already in OPEN or CLOSED. If one of the tests succeeds, then either the "new" n or the n already in the list must be discarded. If the candidate is at the same time in CLOSED, then it should be discarded (otherwise, paths would be reconsidered). In the above implementation, a candidate is discarded also if it is already a member of OPEN
- If you replace the words in italic in Step 10 with "at the beginning", a new implementation of the depth-first search algorithm (Section 8.3 above) is obtained. This highlights only one difference between the two methods, namely the order in which nodes are considered. The other major difference is in storage requirements

<u>b.</u> LISP code

All external functions have been defined previously. To locate their definitions, please look up the function names (in capital letters) in Appendix 2.1.

```
          (DEFUN breadth-first (Start Goal-node)

5          (DEFUN return-solution (Pair Path Closed)
            (LET ((Father (CADR Pair)))
              (IF (EQUAL Father Start) (CONS Start Path)
                (return-solution (ASSOC Father Closed) (CONS Father Path) Closed))))

7, 8       (DEFUN loop? (Children Open Closed)
            (REMOVE-IF #'(LAMBDA (N) (OR (ASSOC N Open) (ASSOC N Closed))) Children))

6          (DEFUN get-children (N)
            (GET N 'CHILDREN))

9          (DEFUN update-pointers (Father Children)
            (IF Children (MAPCAR #'(LAMBDA (X) (LIST X Father)) Children)))

           (DEFUN recursive-search (Open Closed)
2           (IF (NULL Open) NIL
3             (LET ((N (CAAR Open)))
5              (COND ((EQUAL N Goal-node) (return-solution (CAR Open) (LIST N) Closed))
                     (T
6                    (LET ((children (get-children N) ))
                        (IF (NULL children)
11                       (recursive-search
4                          (CDR Open) (CONS (CAR Open) Closed))
11                       (recursive-search
10                         (APPEND
4                                  (CDR Open))
7, 8, 9                           (update-pointers N (loop? children (CDR Open) Closed))
4                        (CONS (CAR Open) Closed))))))))))

1         (recursive-search (LIST (LIST Start)) '()))
```

<u>c.</u> Prolog code

The primitive "setof" is introduced in the following code for the first time:

setof(<expression with variable(s)>, <predicate with variable(s)>, <list>).

The predicate in the second argument is instantiated in all allowable ways. For each instantiation, the returned bindings are substituted for the variables in the expression in the first argument. Expressions for all instantiations are cumulated in the list in the third argument. "setof" is very similar to the previously described predicate "findall" (see Appendix 2.2), except that "setof" discards equal instantiations of the variables in <expression>.

All other external predicates have been previously defined; to locate their definitions, please look up the predicates in Appendix 2.2.

```
        breadth_first(Start, Goal_node, Graph, Path) :-
9           make_state(Start, no_father, State),
1           recursive_search([State], [], Goal_node, Graph, Path), !.

        get_node(has_father(X, _), X).
        get_father(has_father(_, F), F).
        make_state(Node, F, has_father(Node, F)).

6       get_child(Node, Next, Graph) :- Pred =.. [Graph, Node, Next], Pred.

        child_and_father(F, State, Graph) :-
            get_node(F, Node),
6           get_child(Node, Next, Graph),
9           make_state(Next, Node, State).

5       return_solution(X, Father_list, Path, L) :-
            get_node(State, X),
            single_member(State, Father_list),
            get_father(State, Y),
            test_father(X, Y, Father_list, Path, L).
        test_father(Start, no_father, _, Path, [Start| Path]) :- !.
        test_father(X, Y, Father_list, Path, L) :- return_solution(Y, Father_list, [X|Path], L).

7,8     loop([], _, _, []).
        loop([H|T], Open, Closed, Good_children):-
            get_node(H, X),
            get_node(State, X),
            (single_member(State, Closed); single_member(State, Open)),
            loop(T, Open, Closed, Good_children).
        loop([H|T], Open, Closed, [H|Good_children]) :-
            loop(T, Open, Closed, Good_children).

5       recursive_search([H|T], Closed, Goal_node, _, Path) :-
            get_node(H, Goal_node),
            return_solution(Goal_node, [H|Closed], [], Path).
11,2    recursive_search([X|T], Closed, Goal_node, Graph, Path) :-
6,9         (setof(Z, child_and_father(X, Z, Graph), Children); Children = []),
7,8         loop(Children, T, [X|Closed], Good_children),
10          append(T, Good_children, Open),
11          recursive_search(Open, [X|Closed], Goal_node, Graph, Path).

        /* "single_member": same definition as in Section 8.3 c.*/
```

5.9.3 Examples

First note that all examples in Section 8.4 above could be rewritten using breadth-first instead, by simply changing the order in which newly generated nodes are added to the argument Open.

Example 10: Minimal path between two nodes

As mentioned in Section 9.1 above, breadth-first automatically returns the shortest path between two nodes in a graph, if the path length is measured as the number of arcs in the path (or of operators applied). This is a nice feature if in the problem domain some *fixed* cost is associated to each path (e.g. transaction cost, time delay, etc.). In such case, breadth-first returns the cheapest solution. ■

Example 11: Paths of length k from a node

Sometimes it is useful to know which states located at a distance equal or less than k from s_N will be affected by a change in state s_N. One reason for this could be that in a certain model influences are damped proportionally to the length of the connection path, or again that delays are associated to state transitions (no effects propagate instantaneously). This problem, a generalization of the problem in Example 6 above, can be easily solved by adding to the standard breadth-first algorithm, a counter (sometimes called depth-bound) which causes the algorithm to stop when a predefined length of the solution path(s) is reached. The following algorithm returns a list of the reachable nodes, each associated with a number, corresponding to the length of the shortest path to it from the Start node.

The following implementation does the job (note that depth-bounds can be associated to depth-first methods as well, and usually are, in order to avoid getting lost in long paths):

```
(DEFUN accessible-k (Start Depth-bound)

 (DEFUN loop? (Children Open Closed)
  (REMOVE-IF #'(LAMBDA (N) (OR (ASSOC N Open) (ASSOC N Closed))) Children))

 (DEFUN get-children (N)
  (GET N 'CHILDREN))

 (DEFUN recursive-search (Open Closed)
  (IF (NULL Open) Closed
    (LET ((N (CAAR Open))
          (level (CADR Open)))
      (IF (> level k) Closed          ;; this test is enough, because of the strategy of breadth-first
       (LET ((children (get-children N)))
         (IF (NULL children)
           (recursive-search (CDR Open) (CONS (CAR Open) Closed))
           (recursive-search
              (APPEND (CDR Open)
                      (MAPCAR #'(LAMBDA (X) (LIST X (1+ level)))
                           (loop? children (CDR Open) Closed))))
           (CONS (CAR Open) Closed))))))))

(recursive-search (LIST (LIST Start 0) '()))
```

■

5.10 Case study: causal analysis in linear economic models

5.10.1 Causality representation in economic models

It is customary in macroeconomics, and also quite often in microeconomics, to formalize a numerical model in terms of the following quantities:

i. a set of *state variables* X, where each state has properties attached to it; a state variable is normally an identified quantity in terms of economic concepts and official statistics or accounts

ii. a set of *instrumental variables* U, which are a subset of X, restricted to those variables under the control of a decision-maker which may set their values

iii. a set of *endogenous variables* , which are a subset of X, restricted to those variables in (X - U) which are not under the control of the decision-maker

iv. a set of *exogenous quantities* E, which are describing the economic context and its parameters, and thus impacting the state variables

The relations between state, instrumental , exogenous variables, their time distributed values, and time itself, then build the model, with a set of constants t, functions, constraints, attached to it.

Causality in a model is an asymmetric relation between two entities, such that a change in one entity causes a change in the other, but not vice-versa. In case of uncertainty, more subtle definitions apply, however. For example, in a company, an increase in the labor force normally produces an increase in the output; the converse would normally be an unusual reasoning. Other important asymmetric relations of the same type were already met earlier: e.g. logical implication (see Chapter 3.5) clearly distinguishes among premises and conclusions, with premises and conclusions belonging to different sets.

Models consisting only of a set of simultaneous equations between state variables, do not capture causality. Equations are namely non-directional constraints, and as such symmetric with respect to the variables involved. Variables can be moved freely between the left and right sides of the equation without altering its mathematical content. However, given a model, the causal structure underlying it can be explicited by e.g."causal ordering" [Simon, 1977]. The most striking feature of this method is that it is purely syntactical, i.e. it only needs knowledge of which variables appear in which constraints: it is fully independent of the model parameters.

Implicit to each application domain and its model, is a decision structure, a management organization, and possibly legal conditions, which dictate a significant part of the causality relations between elements of U and X. This fact is very often overlooked in many qualitative economic AI models, although it must be emphasized to be of overriding importance: the same set (X,U,E) can be governed in entirely different ways, not because causalities are free, but because the decision and legal structures are most diverse (see Chapter 12.5, 12.7).

Further to this complexity of the actual causal relations, is the fact that models are in general difficult to understand by users, especially when they get large.This is because the organization of the domain knowledge crystallized into equations or predicates does not reflect aforementioned knowledge about the social and management organizations. Especially, the justification for the exogenous parameters E is most difficult, even if justified by statistical estimation criteria. This raises the basic issues of how to uncover the causal impacts and choices of state variables X and U meeting a decision structure, how to identify those which are specified, and how to check on their consistency with the decision goals.

5.10.2 Causal analysis of a simple economic model

To illustrate the concerns in previous Section 10.1, we select a simple model involving an asset sector and a physical "real" sector. The asset equations of the model state monetary equilibrium (1), an interest parity condition (2), and an expectation scheme for the expected currency depreciation rate (3).Furthermore, an equation (4) defines the domestic price index:

ASSET SECTOR:

$$M-Q=-aI+bY \qquad (1)$$

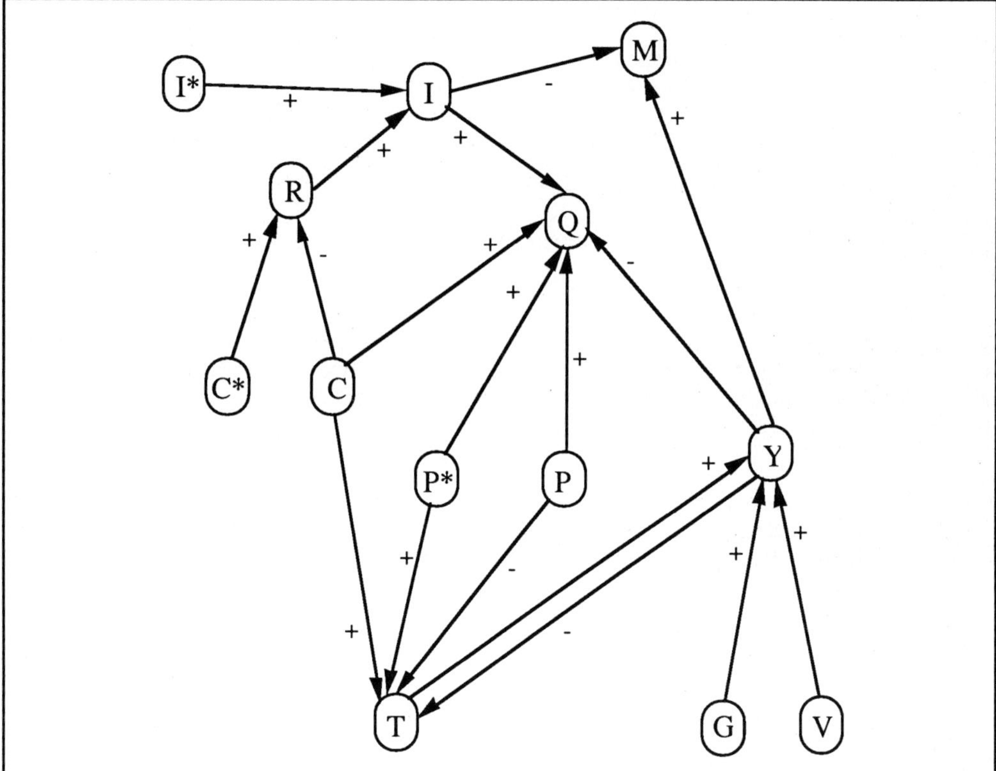

Fig. 7: Causality graph: price and exchange rate model; the sign + designates a positive partial derivative of the downstream node with respect to the upstream node, and the sign - otherwise

$$I=I^* + R \qquad (2)$$

$$R=-c(C-C^*) \qquad (3)$$

$$Q=dP+(1-d)(C+P^*) \qquad (4)$$

In the "real" sector, (5) assumes full employment to express aggregate demand, while the long-run full-adjusted values of the trade balance is given by (6):

REAL SECTOR

$$Y=V+eG+gT \qquad (5)$$

$$T=h(C+P^*-P)-iY \qquad (6)$$

where:

- all lower case symbols a,.., i are constants (in set E)
- all starred upper case symbols are exogenous: P*, I*, etc.. (in set E)
- all upper case symbols are state variables (in set X):

C:	exchange rate
G:	government expenditure
I:	domestic interest rate

M:	domestic money supply
P:	price level
Q:	domestic price index
R:	expected rate of currency depreciation
S:	tax rate
T:	trade balance
V:	private expenditure
Y:	domestic output

All above equations (1) to (6) can be rewritten implicitely as:

$$g_i(X,E) = 0$$

Please note that the state and exogenous variables are generally assumed to be expressed in relative value to express changes w.r.t. a nominal path, and that furthermore the logarithmic form is used, although in some equations (e.g. (2)) it is not so. Also, the constants a, ..., i are assumed to be non-negative.

The causal analysis deals with finding which, and by how much, some state variables are affected by an instrumental change in one state variable, and whether these effects are consistent with the hypotheses or goals attached to these states. For example, consider the implications of a one-time increase in government spending G; it can be shown that the signs of the derivatives are:

$$dC/dG < 0$$
$$dP/dG > 0$$
$$d(C-P)/dG < 0$$

which proves that the increase in G has an impact, and that those changes are in the negative, resp. positive, direction for some other state variables around the nominal path.

It is customary to visualize the causalities by a graph having as many nodes the states and endogenous variables, with an arc going between variables appearing in the same equation of the model. The arc will be directed, going from the variable closest to the decision making (i.e. closest to the instrument variables), to the one closest to the endogenous outputs. The arcs will be labeled, either with the sign of the partial derivative of the downstream node w.r.t. changes in the upstream node, or/and by the qualitative assessment of the impact. See Fig. 7 for an example related to the model above. However, assume now that the decision making process imposes an increase in the exchange rate C, due to that measure on G, although the model tells that a decrease is to be expected. Then, a trend inconsistency has been detected.

Next, assume that model dynamics are introduced on state variables such as C, P, leading to overshoots on e.g. C w.r.t. to its long term values. If the increase on government spending induces temporarily too high a value on the exchange rate in contradiction with policy goals on C, then there is an amplitude inconsistency.

Also, instrumental inconsistency occurs if, when selected instrument variables are added or retracted from U, the amplitude change constraints on some goals are not met. This is the case if a tax rate instrument S is added to the model, whereby G should throughout be replaced by (G + S.V), and V elsewhere by (1-S)V.Then an activist fiscal rule designed to achieve price and exchange rate stability over time, may conflict with a stable monetary mass evolution M.

Finally, model parametric inconsistency corresponds to the case where the values of some state or instrumental variables exceed limits on them for the model itself correctly to be defined structurally, or to be estimated correctly from the econometric viewpoint. E.g. if the price evolution P is characteristic of hyper-inflation, several equations will no longer be valid structurally and numerically.

There is one more basic principle in causality analysis, that is that the causality is the strongest if the length of the decision path is the shortest. This means that if a given state variable is causally influenced by two others belonging to two different consistent causal paths, then in case of a tie in their effects, the shortest path will dominate.

5.10.3 Causal ordering

The method can be described as follows (see [Iwasaki and Simon, 1986]). Let S be a system of n equations in n unknown (such as in Section 10.2). Let S_0 be the union of all subsets of S, $S_{0(i)}$, such that:

- for each i, there are so many equations as variables in $S_{0(i)}$
- for each i, no subset of $S_{0(i)}$ has this property

Then each $S_{0(i)}$ is called a minimal complete subset, and S_0 the set of all minimal subsets of zero order. Obviously, given the above definitions, each $S_{0(i)}$ must either consist of just one equation in one unknown, or of a set of interdependent equations. Then each $S_{0(i)}$ can be solved independently of the rest of S and of the other $S_{0(i)}$'s. All variables in $S_{0(i)}$ (and in S_0 as well, of course), become exogenous in the system S' obtained by removing the already solved equations $S_{0(i)}$. So, a change in any variable belonging to one of the $S_{0(i)}$ will affect at least one variable in S' (if not, the system is trivially decomposable into two different systems, which can be analyzed separately). On the contrary, no change in any variable in S' can ever affect any variable in one of the $S_{0(i)}$. State variables in $S_{0(i)}$ can be seen as being the causes for the state variables in S', with equations being responsible for causal propagation. The process is then repeated with S', thus leading to the determination of the minimal subsets of order 1 and of the residual set S", and so on. The process stops when the decomposition in causal components has completely covered the set S. The result is a partially ordered partition of the variables.

Let every causal component be represented by a node, and two components $S_{w(l)}$ and $S_{i(k)}$ be linked by an arc directed from $S_{i(k)}$ to $S_{w(k)}$ if some variables in $S_{w(l)}$ are determined by variables in $S_{i(k)}$. Then, by construction, i < w. We will call the resulting graph the *causal graph* of the system S. Such a graph is unique, since causal ordering is deterministic. Causal relations can be read out as topological relations in the causal graph. So two variables are causally unrelated if there is no path between the associated components in the graph. Similarly, two variables are related if there exist a path between the corresponding component, the direction of the path determining the direction of the causality. Finally, there is a direct causality among two variables if there is an arc between the two corresponding components.

Causal ordering goes beyond, by finding all strong components in a graph, e.g. by the algorithm in Section 8.3, Example 8. A strong component is a set of nodes, with the property that there is a path in both directions between any nodes in it. Within a strong component, there is circular causality related to sets of interdependent equations in the model.

Causal ordering requires a set of structural equations as its input (such as Section 10.2). A model is structural, if each equation corresponds to just one mechanism/interaction process among variables in the described domain: in economics, such mechanisms are behavior (how do economic agents react to given inputs), technology (production equations), and equilibrium conditions. Furthermore, identities define new concepts. Structural equations insure that the causal graph being built has an obvious interpretation. Furthermore, it makes it possible to maintain justifications for each equation, and to retract equations, should the underlying reasons be no longer satisfied (many hidden assumptions below a model are of this kind). Note that most allowable mathematical operations on a system of equations do not conserve structure. For instance, if two equations are combined into a new one, the resulting equation is no longer structural. Hence, it must be the responsibility of the modeler to provide the causal analysis algorithm with a structural model. Principles to do this are explored in [Iwasaki, 1987], while some common heuristics are mentioned in [Iwasaki and Simon, 1986].

The following Section 10.4, introduces algorithms deriving a causal order among the states if any, as well as sets of causally equivalent states. The approach can be seen as a further application of the graph representation of problems, and of depth-first search over the graph.

5.10.4 Algorithm for causal assignment

The following causal ordering algorithm is divided into two steps [Gilli, 1978]: first, a normalization algorithm is given for normalizing a system of equations (i.e. associating to each equation one and only one endogenous variable). Second, the normalized system is used as the starting point for the causal ordering process (see Section 8.3).

Assume the following simple set of equations is given, where the only condition imposed is that the number of equations matches the number of (endogenous) variables. This is a theoretical model; refer to Section 10.2 above for a real one.

$$g_1(x_1, x_2) = 0$$

$$g_2(x_1, x_2) = 0$$

$$g_3(x_1, x_3, x_4) = 0$$

$$g_4(x_4, x_5) = 0$$

$$g_5(x_5, x_3, x_2) = 0$$

$$g_6(x_1, x_2, x_3, x_4, x_5, x_6) = 0$$

Such a model can be represented as shown in Fig. 8, where there are only links between variables and equations, and each variable is linked to all equations it is involved in. The normalization problem is then topologically equivalent to finding a pairing between variables and equations such that each variable belongs to one and only one pair, and the same for each equation. In graph theory, such a problem is known as the assignment problem. The algorithm below can be seen as either using the augmenting chains method, or as a limit case of the algorithm broadly used in operations research for the maximum flow in networks (see [Berge, 1962]). It is essentially a repeated application of depth-first search,whereby each time a path is found the graph is modified, and search is resumed on the modified graph. The structure of the graph is again implemented as a set of property lists. Nodes representing equation have a PARENTS property list containing all variables occurring in that equation. The associated variable is stored in the property CHILD. Nodes representing states store the equations they are part of, under the property CHILDREN. The selected associated equation node is stored under the property FATHER. The properties names hint at the causal relationship. If normalization fails, the algorithm returns NIL, otherwise it returns T. There is no need to return the graph itself as a value, since the topology is stored in the property lists. However, should normalization fail (NIL), then it can be shown that the system is qualitatively singular, and inconsistent in one of the four ways described in Section 10.2 [Gilli, 1978]. If normalization succeeds, then it is not unique, as the non determinism of depth-first implies. However, some simple relation exists among different normalizations.

First, here is the representation of the above example:

```
(SETF (GET 'x1 'CHILDREN) '(g1 g2 g3 g6))
(SETF (GET 'x2 'CHILDREN) '(g1 g2 g5 g6))
(SETF (GET 'x3 'CHILDREN) '(g3 g5 g6))
(SETF (GET 'x4 'CHILDREN) '(g3 g4 g6))
(SETF (GET 'x5 'CHILDREN) '(g4 g5 g6))
(SETF (GET 'x6 'CHILDREN) '(g6))

(SETF (GET 'g1 'FATHER) '(x1 x2))
(SETF (GET 'g2 'FATHER) '(x1 x2))
(SETF (GET 'g3 'FATHER) '(x1 x3 x4))
(SETF (GET 'g4 'FATHER) '(x4 x5))
```

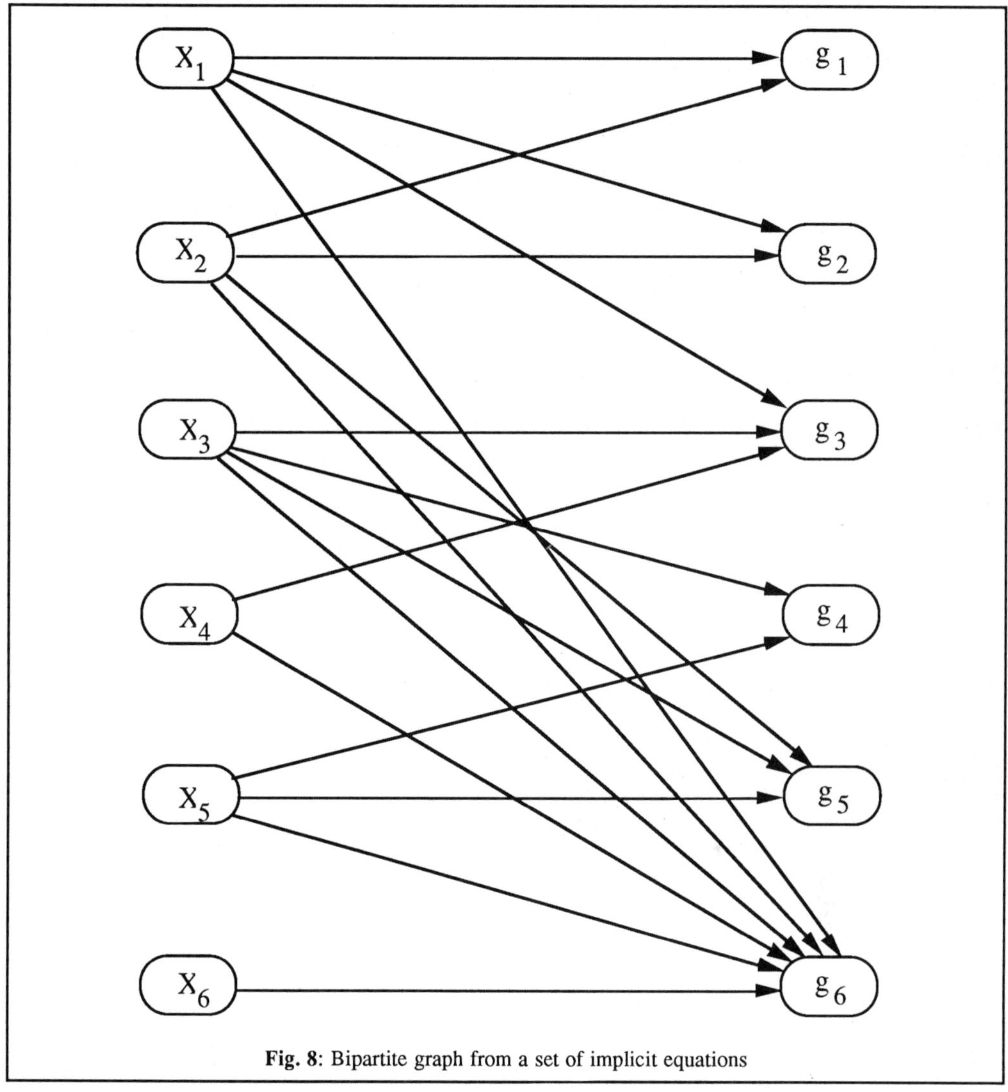

Fig. 8: Bipartite graph from a set of implicit equations

```
(SETF (GET 'g5 'FATHER) '(x5 x3 x2))
(SETF (GET 'g6 'FATHER) '(x1 x2 x3 x4 x5 x6))
```

The causal assignment (or normalization) LISP code is:

```
(DEFUN assignment (Endogenous)

  (DOLIST (endo-variable Endogenous T)
    (IF (NULL (find-path (LIST endo-variable) 0)) (RETURN NIL))))

(DEFUN good-children (Node)
  (REMOVE-IF #'(LAMBDA (X) (EQUAL X (GET Node 'FATHER))) (GET Node 'CHILDREN)))

(DEFUN find-path (Path Counter)
  (IF (ODDP Counter)
    (IF (NULL (GET (CAR Path) 'CHILD))
      (modify-graph Path)
```

```
    (find-path (CONS (GET (CAR Path) 'CHILD) path) (1+ Counter)))
  (DOLIST (child (good-children (CAR Path)) NIL)
    (IF (find-path (CONS child path) (1+ Counter)) (RETURN T)))))

(DEFUN modify-graph (Path)
 (IF (NULL Path) T
 (PROGN (SETF (GET (CAR Path) 'CHILD) (CADR Path)
                 (GET (CADR Path) 'FATHER) (CAR Path))
   (modify-graph (CDDR Path)))))

 (DOLIST (endo-variable Endogenous T)
  (IF (NULL (find-path (LIST endo-variable) 0)) (RETURN NIL))))
```

5.10.5 An algorithm for causal analysis and consistency

Let us return for a moment to Section 10.2, assuming the algorithms of Section 10.3 and 10.4 to have given us, after normalization, the strong components, and also the causal links. It is here fundamental to stress that so far, we have only exploited the arc directions in the causal graphs to represent the causal influences between nodes representing each states in the economic model.

This has not yet given us the means of assessing said economic model for the purpose of carrying out any qualitative reasoning on it. Checking for model parametric inconsistencies and instrumental inconsistencies is the first level for this reasoning, as the model should be considered invalid if structurally inconsistent.

The next level is to go beyond just separating the strong components from the rest of the model, and to enter the world of qualitative economic scenarios. We mean hereby the fact that all decision makers are eager at getting some rough indications (and even explanations) about the quantitative effects of changes due to the manipulation of some instrument or exogenous variables.This we call causal propagation, and it is designed to check that decisions generate direct and indirect state changes which are consistent with quantitative constraints on each state due to the decision structure.Trend and amplitude inconsistencies reflect these concerns.

The solution proposed is a causal propagation algorithm which will feature a qualitative interval coding of each direct causal link: the + or - labels introduced in Section 10.2 will be replaced by the following grammar of labels attached to each arc between nodes in the directed causal graph:

Label := (Sign)(Level)

where:

- Sign stands for POS, NEG, or NIL, representing the sign of the partial derivative of the value of the down-stream node w.r.t. the value of the up-stream node, or nil if such a trend cannot be stated; we assume that nil multiplied by + or - is nil; see Fig. 7 for an example
- Level can have the values H, M, S which stand for high, medium or small, and which are assigned qualitatively to represent the strength of the direct causal link. They can be viewed as qualitative elasticities; see Chapter 4.3.6

The algorithm will use an algebra operating on these Labels to allow for the evaluation of any causal path, by propagating the label values along any causality path (direct as well as indirect). This algebra is purposively non-associative, but aims at deriving levels of causal influence by propagating the Labels through the arcs in the causal paths. The tricky part is the trade-off between, say, a large positive impact (+H) and a medium negative one (-M); other algebras can be designed, but the following one obeys sociological preference relations [Case, 1979]:

- *add* , which is the addition applicable to the Label pairs. Pred(Level) stands for the Level immediately below Level (e.g. Pred(H) = M), or Pred(S) = S. Sup($Level_1$, $Level_2$) stands for the higher of the two levels (e.g. Sup(M, H) = H). Please note that one formula involves a branching, inducing the same path segment to have two Labels until filtered out by the causal propagation described below:

  add(Label, Label) = Label

  add((Sign, $Level_1$), (Sign, $Level_2$)) = (Sign, Sup($Level_1$, $Level_2$))

  add(($Sign_1$, Level), ($Sign_2$, Level)) =
  ($Sign_1$, Pred(Level)) AND ($Sign_2$, Pred(Level))

  add(($Sign_1$, $Level_1$), ($Sign_2$, $Level_2$)) =
  (Sign(Sup($Level_1$, $Level_2$)), Max($Level_1$, $Level_2$))

- *mult* , which is the multiplication applicable to Label pairs. Inf($Level_1$, $Level_2$) stands for the lower of the two levels (e.g. Inf(M, H) = M). One important feature of mult is that the result sign (resp. level) only depends on the input signs (resp. levels), but not on the input levels (resp. signs), as clearly shown by the following definitions:

  mult($Label_1$, $Label_2$) = (Sign, Level), where:

  Level = Inf($Level_1$, $Level_2$)

  Sign = NIL, if $Sign_1$ = $Sign_2$ = NIL
  $Sign_i$, if $Sign_k$ = NIL, i = 1 or 2, k = 3 - i
  POS, if $Sign_1$ = $Sign_2$ ≠ NIL
  NEG, if $Sign_1$ ≠ $Sign_2$, $Sign_1$ and $Sign_2$ ≠ NIL

LISP code implementing the above algebra is shown in Appendix 1.2.1. The code is designed to work properly with any number of levels, not just three. If more than three levels are used, operation results are defined as a straightforward generalization of the above rules. As a consequence of non-associativity, operations are not designed to accept more than two operands.

Next, the causal propagation algorithm will rely on sociological principles of causal impact, and of decidability: a breadth-first search algorithm applies at any node of the causality graph to select causality paths; the Labels are calculated along all these paths by the algebra above; to select the best causality path for further propagation, only two down-stream paths are considered, namely those with the highest Level value in the Label calculation; selecting more would make the problem undecidable; in case of a tie in the causality path selection, because they yield the same Level, then the two shortest paths of minimal length are considered (for reasons mentioned in Section 10.2).

The inconsistencies with the decision structure are detected all along, assuming that the decision maker has himself labelled some of the state nodes with a Level (i.e. a policy target Level) or with constraints on the same Level at the time of a tentative activation of a change in one or several instrument variables. This change will be positive (POS), negative (NEG) or there will be none (NIL). Trend or amplitude inconsistencies, if any, can be spotted immediately if the Levels induced by this/these changes violate the bounds assigned by the decision maker on some nodes.

The motivation for expanding in this way simpler causal economic models, is that the causal propagation very rapidly becomes meaningless as it is impossible to balance off influences along a causality path if only the directions and Signs are known.

Finally, an explanation facility has now been constructed implicitly, in that the causal paths can be related directly to those economic state variables for which the policy objectives are violated in qualitative terms; these causal paths can also be ordered, all this taking place without ever having to run a quantitative simulation or the like. By the way, as all labels are syntactic, this explanation can be produced in a natural language framework. This facility can consequently be exploited in order to achieve model simplification by distinguishing important from irrelevant instruments and causal chains.

A skeleton LISP code for the propagation algorithm is shown in Appendix 1.2.2. This is working code designed for small models, showing how primitive consistency checks and explanations can be performed, as a result of qualitative propagation. Depending on the application, more advanced implementations of such facilities may be needed.

5.11 Heuristic search methods

Both depth-first and breadth-first can be improved by finding a way for ranking alternatives; the most promising are then chosen first. By *heuristic knowledge* it is meant generic or, most often, problem-specific knowledge useful for guiding the selection among alternatives. One could equivalently say that an heuristic is information on how to perform search.

Whenever heuristic knowledge is available, it is a good idea to embed it in the search procedure for focusing the search toward the goal, for consequently reducing the number of useless nodes explored and/or achieving an higher-quality or even optimal solution; a search procedure using heuristic information (or application specific knowledge) is called an *heuristic search method*. As already mentioned in Chapter 1.1, heuristic information is not always assured to direct search in the proper direction; but it is known to do so most of the time. It will be explained later, however, that if the heuristic used enjoys certain properties, it will make search more efficient without indulging in errors or degrading the quality of the solution.

Example 12: Heuristics for macroeconomic reasoning

In an economic causal network similar to the graph in Fig. 2 or 7, information which could be used to define a heuristic includes:

- the gap between targeted endogenous values (so called: target values) and measured values: if the gap between the current state and the state is large, presumably there are better ways to reach the solution. Usually, a preference function is defined to assess the policymaker's satisfaction as a function of the values of the instruments/policy targets. If such a function (or its gradient) is available, it can be used to direct the search in the value space of the instruments
- the estimated delays of the effects of different policy instruments over the economy: if the path currently under consideration has high delays, and the gap to the goal state is large, it is perhaps better to switch to another path
- a measure of the uncertainty of the causal links (expected vs. unknown exogenous states, uncertainty in the causality, sensitivity to exogenous events, regressive forecasts etc.)

This information could be used to direct the search, using for instance the following criteria:

- discard the causal paths with delays beyond the planning schedule
- if there are several paths achieving the same effects with different social costs, choose the one minimizing the social cost
- choose the policy minimizing the difference between observed and target values

■

In the most general case, the only requirement on the heuristic information is that it should be able to establish a partial ordering (a preference ranking) among alternatives. Comparison criteria for ranking alternatives may depend on the features of the alternatives under considerations, on the goal of the search, on past search activity, or on external knowledge. If heuristic information is available as qualitative knowledge, the usual techniques of Knowledge-based Systems (see Chapters 3 and 4) can be applied for coding it in a knowledge representation language and use it to direct the search (e.g. metarules, see Section 3.6.8). The search procedures can then be simple blind search algorithms or can incorporate further heuristic principles, as explained below.

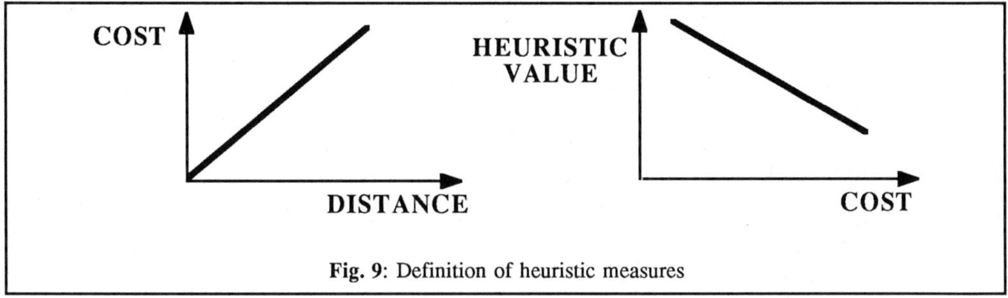

Fig. 9: Definition of heuristic measures

For the purposes of abstraction, it is assumed that the overall result of heuristic information is an estimation of the "*distance* " between each of the current alternatives to the (closest) goal state, in that the "distance" can be measured along several dimensions/properties and need not coincide with the number of operators to be applied. In some special cases, the "distance" can be given a numeric value or *cost* . The heuristic preference for an alternative is then *monotonically decreasing* with its cost (see Fig. 9). Costs associated with the various nodes are compared, and the node with the lowest cost is selected for expansion.

For heuristics expressible as numeric values, it is customary to distinguish between the evaluation function and the heuristic function. The *evaluation function* returns the estimated cost of reaching a goal node from the alternative under examination. It is generally a function of the node, as well as possibly of other parameters external to the search.

The following implementations of heuristic search methods assume that an evaluation function exists, returning a number representing the cost of a solution related to the alternative under examination. Selection among alternatives can be based on one of the following selection criteria:

- expand first the node which is most similar to one of the final states, i.e. which has the largest heuristic preference
- choose first the operator which reduces most the difference between the current state and the closest final state

The heuristic search methods described below include *hill-climbing* (Section 11.1), *beam-search* (Section 11.2), *best-first* (Section 11.3) and *A** (Section 11.4). The presentation follows the guidelines for blind search methods.

A new predicate called "Evaluate" is needed by the LISP search functions, to be bound to an application-specific function for the computation of the heuristic values. Arguments to such function are left unspecified in all but the most simple algorithm (hill-climbing, Section 11.1). Prolog algorithms are designed according to a slightly different implementation choice, i.e. it is assumed that a predicate named "evaluate" be available in the knowledge base. A minimal form for it is assumed, although of course a more complex implementation may be needed in real-world applications.

As a final remark, note that the amount of information upon which to base useful heuristic functions is often quite large; this in turn implies potentially expensive computations at each cycle of the search procedure, and therefore loss of efficiency. It is well possible that the search time saved by avoiding the expansion of unpromising nodes is spent in computing the heuristic function; hence exploiting all available knowledge for selection of alternatives may be a bad idea, even though, in the best case, no useless nodes are expanded. Good heuristics must be simple to compute, while providing a discrimination sufficient to search significantly better than with a blind (or random) strategy.

5.11.1 Hill-climbing algorithm

Hill-climbing searches in a depth-first style, however without backtracking. Search procedures with no provisions for reconsidering a past choice are called irrevocable; hill-climbing is the most important irrevocable strategy.

When depth-first chooses the node to expand next, it does so randomly among all the nodes of maximum depth available so far. Hill-climbing orders the available nodes according to a preference function, and irrevocably selects the most promising one for further expansion. This is implemented by associating a score to each node. The score must be an estimate of the cost of a solution passing through the associated node, as returned by the heuristic function f(n) (see the pseudo-code description below, steps 7 and 8). Nodes with higher preference have a lower cost (i.e. lower heuristic scoring, see Fig. 9) and are expanded first.

If the heuristic is good (the estimation is close to reality) then hill-climbing may be very efficient. However, if the heuristic is not reliable, hill-climbing may get lost on a wrong path and return a failure, even though a solution exists in the graph.

a. Step-by-step pseudo-code description of hill-climbing in procedural style:

1	Put the start node s on PATH.
2	If PATH is empty, return a failure message and STOP.
3	Select the topmost node n in PATH.
4	If n is a goal node, return PATH, issue a message of successful search completion and STOP.
5	If n should not be expanded, return a failure message and STOP.
6	Expand n, generating all its successors.
7	For each successor n_i of n compute $f(n_i)$.
8	Choose the n_i with the *smallest* heuristic value $f(n_i)$ and put it on the top of PATH.
9	Go to step 2.
END	

b. LISP code

All external functions have been defined previously; to locate their definition, please look up the function names (in capital letters) in Appendix 2.1.

```
      (DEFUN Hill-climbing (Start Goal-node Evaluate)

4       (DEFUN return-solution (List)
            (REVERSE List))

        (DEFUN loop? (Children Path)
           (REMOVE-IF (FUNCTION (LAMBDA (X) (MEMBER X Path))) Children))

6       (DEFUN get-children (Node)
         (GET Node 'CHILDREN))

        (DEFUN recursive-search (Path)

8         (DEFUN best-element (Evaluated-list)
           (ASSOC (APPLY 'MIN (MAPCAR 'CAR Evaluated-list)) Evaluated-list))

2         (IF (NULL Path) NIL
3          (LET ( (N (CAR Path)) )
4           (IF (EQUAL Goal-node N) (return-solution Path)
6            (LET ((Children (loop? (get-children N) Path)))
              (IF (NULL Children) NIL
7               (LET ((Eval-list (MAPCAR
7                                  #'(LAMBDA (X) (LIST (FUNCALL Evaluate X Path) X))
```

```
           Children)))
8,9        (recursive-search (CONS (CADR (best-element Eval-list)) Path))))))))

1      (recursive-search (LIST Start)))
```

Remarks:

- "Evaluate" depends on both the state of the search and the current node; therefore Path must be passed as a parameter as well
- An element in Eval-list has the form (value node)

c. Prolog code

All external predicates have been previously defined; to locate their definition, please look up the predicates in Appendix 2.2.

```
1      hill_climbing(Start, Goal_node, Graph, Path) :-
7          evaluate(Start, Val, State),
           recursive_search(State, Goal_node, Graph, Path), !.

7      evaluate(Node, Val, value(Val, Node)) :-

6      get_child(X, Next, Graph) :-
           Pred =.. [Graph, X, Next],
           Pred.
7      evaluate(Node, Val, value(Val, Node)) :- has_value(Node, Val).

       get_node(value(_, Node), Node).
       get_value(value(Val, _), Val).

6,7    child_and_value(F, State, Graph):-
           get_child(F, Next, Graph),
           evaluate(Next, Val, State).

8      best_child(H, [K|Rest], Best) :-
           get_value(H, Val1),
           get_value(K, Val2),
           Val2 < Val1,
           best_child(K, Rest, Best).
       best_child(H, [_|Rest], Best):- best_child(H, Rest, Best).
       best_child(Best, [], Best).

4      recursive_search(State, Goal_node, _, [Goal_node]) :-
           get_node(State, Goal_node).
       recursive_search(State, Goal_node, Graph, [Node|Path]) :-
           get_node(State, Node),
6,7        setof(Z, child_and_value(Node, Z, Graph), [H|T]),
8          best_child(H, T, Child), !,
       recursive_search(Child, Goal_node, Graph, Path).
```

d. Memory requirements:

They are the same as for depth-first (see Section 8.3).

5.11.2 Beam-search algorithm

Breadth-first can be improved in several ways through a heuristic function. One possibility is to select at any level only a fixed (predefined) number of nodes, namely those with the best heuristic ranking: that is beam-search. This strategy is attractive because it keeps the amount of memory bounded (and known in advance). Like hill-climbing, however, beam-search is not exhaustive, and hence it is possible that existing solution paths be missed, if the heuristic function is not precise enough.

From the point of view of economics, searching according to beam-search can be justified as follows: consider again the causal graph in Fig. 2. Suppose that only the k most important causal chains are followed, when appreciating the consequences of a change in a state. This way of reasoning about a problem is exactly a case of beam-search.

Human reasoning is in general different from beam-search in that the number of causal chains to be followed is not defined in advance, but rather dynamically adjusted depending on the interest in the current situations. It is relatively simple to modify beam-search to retain at each level either k nodes (cognitive limitation), or all nodes below a certain threshold of the heuristic function (interest in the current situation), whichever is smaller.

In the pseudo-code description below, f(n) represents as usual the heuristic function computed at the node n. f(n) is assumed to follow the convention in Fig. 9, i.e. to be monotonically decreasing with preference.

a. Step-by-step pseudo-code description of beam-search in procedural style:

1	Put the start node s on OPEN; CLOSED is empty.
2	If OPEN is empty, return a failure message and STOP.
	For each node n_i on OPEN, starting from the topmost:
3	Remove it from OPEN and put it on CLOSED.
4	If n_i is a goal node, follow the pointers back to s.
	Return the solution path, issue a message of successful search completion and STOP.
5	If n_i is not expandable, remove it from CLOSED and go to step 2.
6	Expand n_i, generating all its successors.
7	For each successor m_i of n_i:
7a	Calculate f(m_i).
7b	If m_i is neither on OPEN nor on CLOSED, direct its pointer to n_i and put it on OPEN.
7c	If m_i is already on OPEN or CLOSED, compare it to the newly calculated one;
	if the former value is smaller, redirect the pointer to n_i and assign the new value of f(m_i).
7d	If m_i was on CLOSED, put it on OPEN.
8	Sort the nodes on OPEN for descending order of their evaluation functions (the node with the smallest evaluation function on top). Retain only a number "breadth" of nodes choosing them among those with smallest evaluation function; discard the other.
9	Go to step 2.
END	

b. LISP code

The primitive "SORT" is introduced in the following code for the first time:

(SORT <List> <Predicate> :key <key>)

"SORT" sorts the List according to Predicate, which must be a two-argument predicate defining an ordering relation. The last argument in SORT (the one preceded by the keyword ":key") should be a one-argument function extracting the key of a list element. The key is a field in a structure to be used as the ordering criterion.

Similarly, the function MEMBER:

(MEMBER <Element> <List> :key <key>)

tests whether Element occurs in List, the key being the membership criterion.

All other external functions have been defined previously; to locate their definition, please look up the function names (in capital letters) in Appendix 2.1.

```
     (DEFUN beam-search (Start Goal Evaluate Breadth)

          (DEFUN state (Node) (CAAR Node))
          (DEFUN cost (Node) (CDAR Node))
          (DEFUN get-father (Node) (CDR Node))
          (DEFUN make-node (Node Value) (CONS Node Value))
          (DEFUN add-father (Node Father) (CONS Node Father))

          (DEFUN test-if-member (Node Father-list) (CAR (MEMBER Node Father-list :key #'state)))

4      (DEFUN return-solution (Node Path Father-list)
          (LET ((Father (get-father (test-if-member Node Father-list))))
            (IF (EQUAL Father Start) (CONS Start Path) (return-solution Father (CONS Node Path)
     Father-list))))

       (DEFUN prevent-loop (Children New-open Father-list K)
8       (IF (OR (NULL Children) (= K 0))
         (recursive-search New-open Father-list)
         (LET ( (N (CAR Children)) )
7c        (LET ((m-c (test-if-member (state N) Father-list)))
             (IF (AND m-c (<= (cost m-c) (cost N)))
7c,d           (prevent-loop (CDR Children) New-open Father-list k)
               (prevent-loop (CDR Children) (CONS N New-open) (CONS N Father-list) (- k 1)))))))

6       (DEFUN get-children (Node) (GET Node 'CHILDREN))

        (DEFUN recursive-search (Open Father-list)
2        (IF (NULL Open) NIL
4         (IF (test-if-member Goal Open) (return-solution Goal NIL Father-list)
           (LET ((Children
                 (MAPCAN #'(LAMBDA (X)
                                 (MAPCAR #'(LAMBDA (Y)
7a                               (add-father (make-node Y (FUNCALL Evaluate Y <arguments>))
                                               (state X)))
6                               (get-children (state X))))
                              Open)) )
             (IF Children
8             (prevent-loop (SORT Children '< :key #'cost) NIL Father-list Breadth))))))

      (recursive-search (LIST (add-father (make-node Start (FUNCALL Evaluate Start <arguments>)) NIL))
           (LIST (add-father (make-node Start (FUNCALL Evaluate Start <arguments>)) NIL))))
```

Remarks:

- The above implementation is quite different from the previous procedural description: "recursive-search" is written for processing all children at a given level at the same time, instead of considering children sequentially (step 7 in the procedure under a.). Therefore the top level loop (step 2 of the procedural description) is not implemented directly
- A generic specification of the arguments needed by the evaluation function "Evaluate" is impossible. Appropriate arguments must be substituted for the place-taker <arguments> according to the definition of "Evaluate"

c. Prolog code

All external predicates have been previously defined; to locate their definition, please look up the predicates in Appendix 2.2.

```
     beam_search(Start, Goal_node, Graph, Width, Path) :-
        evaluate(Start,Val,Y),
```

```
                    make_state(Y, no_father, State),
                    recursive_search([State], [State], Goal_node, Graph, Width, Path), !.

                evaluate(Node, Val, value(Val, Node)) :- has_value(Node, Val).

                get_node(has_father(value(_, X),_), X).
                get_value(has_father(value(V, _), _), V).
                get_father(has_father(_, F), F).
                make_state(Value, F, has_father(Value, F)).

6,7a            get_child(X, Next, Graph) :- Pred =.. [Graph, X, Next], Pred.
                child_and_father(F, State, Graph) :-
                    get_node(F, Node),
                    get_child(Node, Next, Graph),
                    evaluate(Next, Val, Y),
                    make_state(Y, Node, State).

4               /* "return_solution": same definition as in Section 9.2 c. */

4,6,7a,7b       all_children([], [], _).
                all_children([H|T], L, Graph) :-
                    (setof(Z, child_and_father(X, Z, Graph), Children); Children = [] ),
                    all_children(T, Rest_children, Graph),
                    append(Children, Rest_children, L).

8               sort_test(A, B) :-
                    get_value(A, V1),
                    get_value(B, V2),
                    V1 =< V2.

                loop([], New_father_list, [], New_father_list, _):- !.
                loop(_, New_father_list,[], New_father_list, 0):- !.
7c,d            loop([H|T], Father_list, New_children, New_father_list, K) :-
                    get_node(H, Node),
                    get_node(Y, Node),
                    single_member(Y, Father_list),
                    sort_test(Y, H),
                    loop(T, Father_list, New_children, New_father_list, K).
7b              loop([H|T], Father_list, [H|New_children], New_father_list, K) :-
                    K1 is K - 1,
                    loop(T, [H|Father_list], New_children, New_father_list, K1).

4               recursive_search(Open, Father_list, Goal_node, _, _, Path) :-
                    get_node(X, Goal_node),
                    single_member(X, Open),
                    return_solution(Goal_node, Father_list, [], Path).
                recursive_search([H|T], Father_list, Goal_node, Graph, Width, Path) :-
6                   all_children([H|T], Children, Graph),
8                   insort(Children, S_children, sort_test),
7                   loop(S_children, Father_list, Open, New_father_list, Width),
9                   recursive_search(Open, New_father_list, Goal_node, Graph, Width, Path).

                /* "single_member": same definition as in Section 8.3 c. */

                /* sorting algorithm */
8               insort([], [], _).
                insort([H|T], M, Test) :-
                    insort(T, L, Test),
                    insortx(H, M, L, Test).
                insortx(X, [H|T1], [H|T], Test) :-
                    Pred =.. [Test, H, X],
                    Pred,
                    !,
```

```
        insortx(X, T1, T, Test).
        insortx(H, [H|T], T, _).
```

Remarks

- Prolog has no built-in sort predicate similar to the LISP function "SORT". "insort" implements a simple and well-known sorting method.

d. Memory requirements:

Let M be some measure of the memory consumption, d the depth of the tree being searched, and width the number of nodes retained at each depth. Then:

$$M \approx width * d$$

i.e. the memory consumption increases linearly with the depth of the search.

5.11.3 Best-first algorithm

Best-first is in a certain sense a generalization of hill-climbing and beam-search. While hill-climbing chooses the most attractive among the deepest nodes and beam-search the k most attractive nodes at the same level, best-first expands the most attractive node, no matter where it is in the search space. Depending on the nature of the problem, best-first may move around like hill-climbing, beam-search or something in the middle; in any case, for the same evaluation function, it will be at least as efficient as the other methods.

An interesting special case arises if the evaluation function is chosen to be simply a measure of the cost from the starting node to the node currently evaluated. Best-first will then expand at each step the end node of the *cheapest path* currently discovered from the initial node. As a consequence, it will also find the cheapest path to a goal node, that is the cheapest solution. If, moreover, the cost associated is simply the depth of the node, then best-first becomes the same as breadth-first.

Note that in the cases above no heuristic is used, since no estimation is made about the future evolution of the search; what is used is only historical information. Of course, in the most general case, heuristic as well as historical information are combined in the evaluation function; more details about this point are given in the description of the A* search method (Section 11.4).

As opposed to hill-climbing and beam-search, best-first is exhaustive, therefore one is guaranteed to find a solution, if one exists. In the pseudo-code description below, f(n) indicates the heuristic function, with n being the node to which the function is applied. As before, it is assumed that the function behaves qualitatively as in Fig. 9, i.e. the most preferable nodes are assigned a lower score.

a. Step-by-step pseudo-code description of best-first in procedural style:

1	Put the start node s on OPEN; CLOSED is empty.
2	If OPEN is empty, return a failure message and STOP.
3	Select from OPEN *the node with smallest evaluation function value*, and call it n.
4	Remove n from OPEN and put it on CLOSED.
5	If n is a goal node, follow the pointers back to s. Return the found path, issue a message of successful search completion and STOP.
6	Expand n, generating all its successors.
7	For each successor m_i of n:
7a	Calculate $f(m_i)$.
7b	If m_i is neither on OPEN nor on CLOSED, direct its pointer to n and put it on OPEN.
7c	If m_i is already on OPEN or CLOSED, compare the newly calculated value of $f(m_i)$ with the previous one; if the former is smaller, redirect the pointer to n and assign the new value of $f(m_i)$.

7d	If m_i was on CLOSED, and its pointer was redirected, move it to OPEN.
8	Go to step 2.
END	

b. LISP code:

All external functions have been defined previously; to locate their definition, please look up the function names (in capital letters) in Appendix 2.1.

```
          (DEFUN best-first (Start Goal Evaluate)

            (DEFUN state (Node) <same definition as in Section 11.2 b.>)
            (DEFUN cost (Node) <same definition as in Section 11.2 b.>)
            (DEFUN make-node (Node Value) <same definition as in Section 11.2 b.>)
            (DEFUN test-if-member (Node Father-list) <same definition as in Section 11.2 b.>)

            (DEFUN state-value (Node) (cost Node))

5         (DEFUN return-solution (Node Path Father-list) <same definition as in Section 11.2 b.>)

          (DEFUN prevent-loop (Children Open Father Father-list)
3,8        (IF (NULL Children) (recursive-search (SORT Open '< :key #'state-value) Father-list)
            (LET ( (N (CAR Children)) )
             (LET ((m-o (ASSOC (state N) Open))
                   (m-c (test-if-member (state N) Father-list)))
7c            (COND ((AND m-o (< (cost N) (cost m-o)))
                     (prevent-loop (CDR Children) (CONS N (REMOVE m-o Open :test #'EQUAL))
                                   Father (CONS (CONS N Father) Father-list)))
7c,d                ((AND m-c (< (cost N) (cost (CAR m-c))))
                     (prevent-loop (CDR Children) (CONS N Open)
                                   Father (CONS (CONS N Father) Father-list)))
7b                  ((NOT (OR m-o m-c))
                     (prevent-loop (CDR Children) (CONS N Open)
                                   Father (CONS (CONS N Father) Father-list)))
7c,d                (T (prevent-loop (CDR Children) Open Father Father-list))))))

6           (DEFUN get-children (Node) (GET Node 'CHILDREN))

            (DEFUN recursive-search (Open Father-list)
              (IF (NULL Open) NIL
3              (LET ( (N (CAR Open)) )
5               (IF (EQUAL Goal (state N)) (return-solution (state N) NIL Father-list)
                  (prevent-loop
7a                 (MAPCAR #'(LAMBDA (X) (make-node X (FUNCALL Evaluate X <arguments>)))
6                          (get-children (state N)))
4                  (CDR Open) (state N) Father-list)))))

           (recursive-search (LIST (make-node Start (FUNCALL Evaluate Start <arguments>)))
             (LIST (CONS (make-node Start (FUNCALL Evaluate Start <arguments>)) NIL))))
```

c. Prolog code:

All external predicates have been previously defined; to locate their definition, please look up the predicates in Appendix 2.2.

```
best_first(Start, Goal_node, Graph, Path) :-
    evaluate(Start,Val,Y),
    make_state(Y, no_father, State),
    recursive_search([State], [], Goal_node, Graph, Path), !.
```

```
            evaluate(Start, Val, value(Val, Start)) :- has_value(Start, Val).
            get_node(has_father(value(_, X),_), X).
            get_value(has_father(value(V, _), _), V).
            get_father(has_father(_, F), F).
            make_state(Value, F, has_father(Value, F).

        get_child(X, Next, Graph) :- Pred =.. [Graph, X, Next], Pred.

6       /* "child_and_father": same definition as in Section 11.2 c. */

5       /* "return_solution": same definition as in Section 9.2 c. */

6,7a    all_children(H, Children, Graph) :-
            (setof(Z, child_and_father(X, Z, Graph), Children); Children = []).

        /* "sort_test": same definition as in Section 11.2 c. */

7c,d    loop([], Father_list, []).
        loop([H|T], Father_list, New_children) :-
            get_node(H, Node),
            get_node(Y, Node),
            single_member(Y, Father_list),
7c          sort_test(Y, H),
            loop(T, Father_list, New_children).
        loop([H|T], Father_list, [H|New_children]) :-
            loop(T, [H|Father_list], New_children).

5       recursive_search([H|T], Father_list, Goal_node, _, Path) :-
            get_node(H, Goal_node),
            return_solution(Goal_node, [H|Father_list], [], Path).
2,3     recursive_search([H|T], Father_list, Goal_node, Graph, Path) :-
            all_children(H, Children, Graph),
            insort(Children, S_children, sort_test),
            loop(S_children, [H|Father_list], Good_children),
            merge_check(Good_children, T, [], Open, sort_test),
            recursive_search(Open, [H|Father_list], Goal_node, Graph, Path).

        /* "insort": same definition as in Section 11.2 c. */

        /* utility */
        merge_check([], [], _, [], _):- !.
        merge_check([], [A|B], Previous, Result, _):-
            merge_check_x(A, [], B, Previous, Result, _).
        merge_check([H|T], [], Previous, Result, _):-
            merge_check_x(H, T, [], Previous, Result, _).
7c      merge_check([H|T], [A|B], Previous, Result, Test) :-
            Pred =.. [Test, A, H],
            Pred,
            !,
        merge_check_x(A, [H|T], B, Previous, Result, Test).
        merge_check([H|T], [A|B], Previous, Result, Test) :-
            merge_check_x(H, T, [A|B], Previous, Result, Test).
        merge_check_x(A, Rest1, Rest2, Previous, Result, Test) :-
            get_node(A, Node),
            get_node(Elm, Node),
            single_member(Elm, Previous),
            merge_check(Rest1, Rest2, Previous, Result, Test).
7b      merge_check_x(A, Rest1, Rest2, Previous, [A|Next], Test) :-
            merge_check(Rest1, Rest2,[A|Previous], Next, Test).
```

Remarks:

• "merge_check" merges two sorted input lists into one result list, which is again sorted. In the merging process, duplicated elements within each input list are filtered, as are elements common to both input lists. The filtering process retains only one element, i.e. the one with lowest heuristic value, and discards all other matching elements.

5.11.4 A* algorithm

Up to now no restrictions were made on the evaluation function. Important results, both from a theoretical and practical viewpoint, can be obtained with some stronger assumptions.

The search procedure A* assumes that f(n) be the sum of two terms:

$$f(n) = g(n) + h(n),$$

where:

- g(n) is a cost term, representing the cost of the path from the start node to the node under evaluation; g(n) is known at the time the evaluation function is computed
- h(n) is an estimation term, also called the heuristic term of the evaluation function, representing a heuristic estimation of the cost of the path from the node under evaluation to the nearest goal.

f(n) can be thought of as an estimation of the cost of a solution bounded to pass through the considered node n. The term g(n) is usually computed by *adding* the costs associated to the operators making up the path from the start node to n (these costs must be positive). h(n) is estimated from problem-specific information. A* requires that h(n) be an *underestimation* of the minimum cost from n to any goal. Denoting by h*(n) the actual cost, it must satisfy:

$$h(n) \leq h^* (n).$$

Under the above assumptions it can be shown that A* always returns the *optimal* (least cost) solution path, if a solution path exists and if the branching factor is not unbounded. Intuitively, assuming the estimation along a given path as optimistic, it will be corrected automatically by the search methods as the operators along that path are applied and its real cost becomes known (added to g(n)). Possibly, corrections will cause a different path to show a better scoring.

It can be further shown that the closer the heuristic estimation is to the actual cost h*(n), the smaller is the number of wrong nodes examined; in the ideal case of perfect estimate, a solution would be produced directly.

Example 13: Some heuristics decomposable into a cost and an estimation term

In Example 12, Section 11, a list of possible heuristics for economic reasoning was introduced. The decomposition of such heuristics into a cost and an estimation term follows:

- for a gap heuristic, assign to each state a score proportional to the difference between that state and the goal state. Let the cost of an operator be defined as a positive measure of the difference between its initial and its goal node. Then, g(n) is positive and monotonically increasing with the depth of the search, as required. Care must be taken that h(n) underestimates the distance to the goal node
- in the search for an economic policy with minimal delays, delays can be seen as costs. It is easy to verify that delays associated with a policy decision are always positive. Also, delays are additive, although maybe not independent. Again, h(n) must underestimate future delays, in order to guarantee that the shortest-term policy is selected
- an heuristic not fulfilling the requirements for A* would consist in assuming as cost of a path the cost of the mostly undesired (past or expected) side-effect in the decision process

■

Just to put the A* method into perspective note that if:

- h(n) is 0 for all nodes
- g(n) is equal to the depth of each node n (i.e. each operator is assumed to contribute with the same cost to the global cost of the solution), then the evaluation function imposes a breadth-first strategy. As it was mentioned above, we are still guaranteed to find the least-cost solution, even if the number of nodes explored becomes large

In the pseudo-code implementation below, let f(n) be as usual the evaluation function at the node n. The value returned by f(n) is then, according to the above restrictions:

$$f(n) = g(n) + h(n)$$

Now, let m be the father node of n. The evaluation function at the node n can be rewritten:

$$f(n) = g(m) + g(m, n) + h(n)$$

where g(m,n) is the cost associated to the operator transforming m into n

a. Step-by-step pseudo-code description of A* in procedural style:

1	Put the start node s on OPEN; CLOSED is empty.
2	If OPEN is empty, return a failure message and STOP.
3	Select from OPEN the node with smallest evaluation function, and call it n.
4	Remove n from OPEN and put it on CLOSED.
5	If n is a goal node, follow the pointers back to s. Return this path, issue a message of successful search completion and STOP.
6	Expand n, generating all its successors.
7	For each successor m_i of n:
7a	Calculate $f(m_i)$; $f(m_i) = g(n) + g(n, m_i) + h(m_i)$
7b	If m_i is neither on OPEN nor on CLOSED, direct its pointer to n and put it on OPEN.
7c	If m_i is already on OPEN or CLOSED, compare the newly calculated value of $f(m_i)$ with the previous one; if the former is smaller, redirect the pointer to n and assign the new value of $f(m_i)$.
7d	If m_i was on CLOSED, and its pointer was redirected, move it to OPEN.
8	Go to step 2
END	

b. LISP code:

The implementation is basically the same as in best-first search, Section 11.3. In the following, only the functions affected by he following modifications are reimplemented:

- since two numbers (corresponding to g(n) and h(n)) must be maintained, a node is a list of three elements, instead of just two, that is:

  (n   g(n)   h(n))

- the child generation process must return a new child together with the cost of reaching it from its father
- nodes are stored on Closed together with their heuristic values, which are then used in "prevent-loop"

All external predicates have been previously defined; to locate their definition, please look up the predicates in Appendix 2.1.

```
(DEFUN A* (Start Goal Evaluate)

  (DEFUN state (Node) (CAR Triple))
```

```
        (DEFUN evaluation (Node) (CADR Triple))
        (DEFUN cost (Node) (CADDR Triple))
        (DEFUN make-node (state-name e-value cost) (LIST state-name e-value cost))
6       (DEFUN get-children-and-cost (Node) (GET Node 'CHILDREN-AND-COST))
        (DEFUN test-if-member (Node Father-list) <same definition as in Section 11.2 b.>)
7a      (DEFUN state-value (X) (APPLY '+ (CDR X)))

5     (DEFUN return-solution (Node Path Father-list) <same definition as in Section 11.2 b.>)

7,8   (DEFUN prevent-loop (Children Open Father Father-list) <same definition as in Section 11.3 b.>)

      (DEFUN recursive-search (Open Father-list)
2       (IF (NULL Open) NIL
3         (LET ( (N (CAR Open)) )
5           (IF (EQUAL Goal (state N)) (return-solution (state N) NIL Father-list)
              (prevent-loop
              (MAPCAR #'(LAMBDA (X) (make-node (CAR X)
                                                 (FUNCALL Evaluate (CAR X) <arguments>)
7a                                               (+ (CDR X) (cost N))))
6                       (get-children-and-cost (state N)))
4             (CDR Open) (state N) Father-list)))))

      (recursive-search (LIST (make-node Start (FUNCALL Evaluate Start <arguments>) 0))
         (LIST (CONS (make-node Start (FUNCALL Evaluate Start <arguments>) 0) NIL))))
```

c. Prolog code

All external predicates have been previously defined; to locate their definition, please look up the predicates in Appendix 2.2.

```
      astar(Start, Goal_node, Graph, Path) :-
          evaluate(Start, Val, 0, Y),
          make_state(Y, no_father, State),
          recursive_search([has_father(Y, no_father)], [], Goal_node, Graph, Path), !.

          evaluate(Node, Val, Cost, value([Val, Cost], Node)) :- has_value(Node, Val).
          get_node(has_father(value(_, X),_), X).
          get_value(has_father(value(V, _), _), V).
          get_father(has_father(_, F), F).
          get_cost(has_father(value([_, C], _),_), C).
          make_state(Value, F, has_father(Value, F).

7a    get_child(H, Next, Cost, Graph) :-
          get_node(H, X),
          Pred =.. [Graph, X, Next, Op_cost],
          Pred,
          get_cost(H, C),
          Cost is Op_cost + C.

      /* "child_and_father": same definition as in Section 11.2 c. */
      /* "return_solution": same definition as in Section 9.2 c. */
      /* "all_children": same definition as in Section 11.3 c. */

      sort_test(A, B) :-
          get_value(A, [E1, C1]),
          get_value(B, [E2, C2]),
          V1 is E1 + C1,
          V2 is E2 + C2,
          V1 =< V2.

      /* "loop" and "recursive_search": same definition as in Section 11.3 c. */
```

6 Neural processing and inductive learning

6.1 Introduction

As most economic and financial analysis and decision making problems are characterized by frequently changing conditions, such as economic climate, regulatory framework, competitive situation, it is crucial for most knowledge-based applications to be supplemented by some knowledge acquisition capabilities (see Chapter 1.1 and 1.4.7). Unfortunately, this knowledge acquisition is almost invariably still carried out today by a combination of interviewing, data analysis [Pau and Valstorp, 1977], and data base retrieval techniques (see Chapter 8.5). The numerical model parameters can be re-estimated based on recent past observations by statistical parameter estimation techniques, econometrics, or by model identification algorithms, including adaptive control. In some instances, search may be added to said estimation or parameter fitting, as in Chapter 7. However, in some limited instances, and awaiting further progress in the machine learning area, some current recent techniques from these fields can in their own merit serve useful purposes for specific applications in economics and finance, but are still often disconnected from the larger knowledge acquisition requirements. It is the purpose of this Chapter to present two such techniques and related applications of:

- neural processing for learning and classification
- induction for knowledge acquisition and classification

The presentations below give by no means complete coverage of these fast growing areas, but point at important directions, and provide references for further reading.

All supervised learning problems rely on a decomposition of all information into three sets, and are ultimately dependent upon the way in which these are constituted:

i. Supervised learning or training set L= (x(n),c(x(n))):
this is a set of related data x(n), n=1, ..., to which known labels c(x) are attached describing their nature as taught by whoever tells

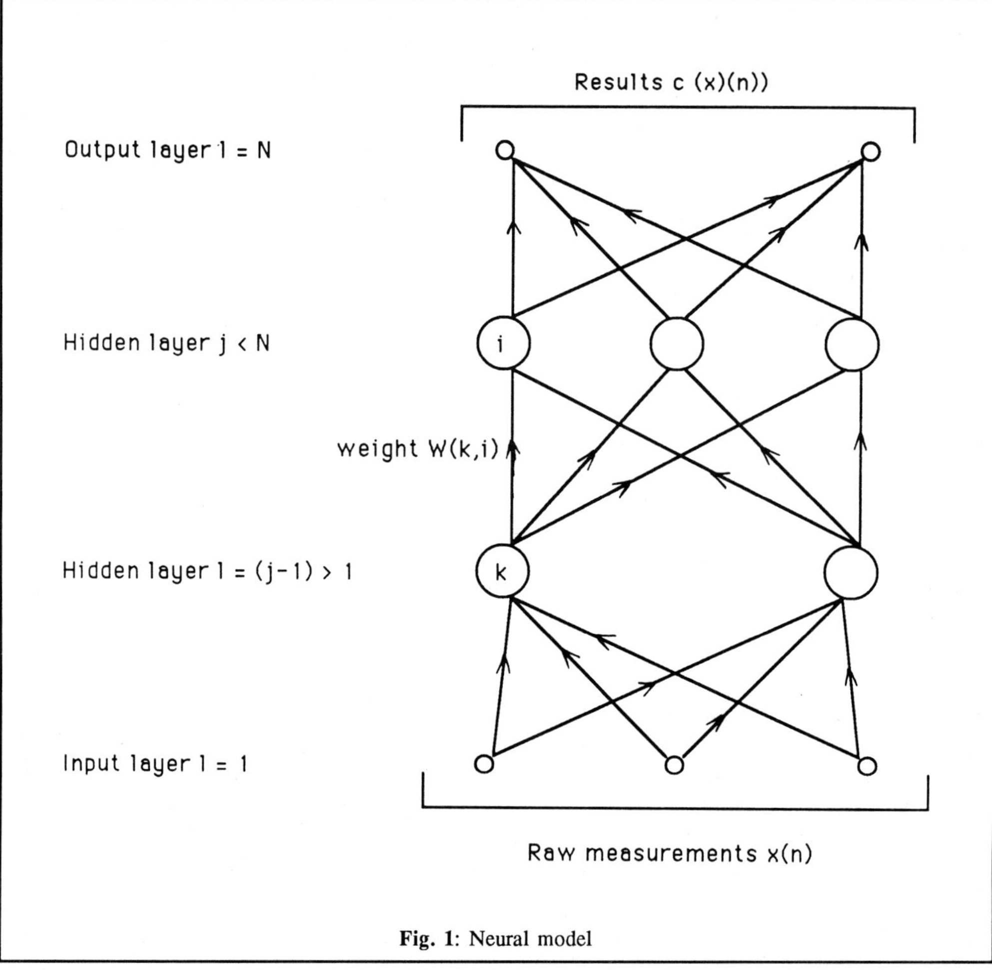

Fig. 1: Neural model

the "truth" (sometimes called the "teacher"). All characteristics of the machine learning procedure will be determined from L alone

ii. Test set T=(y(n),m(y(n))):
this is a set of data y, of same nature than x, to which known labels m(y) are attached describing their nature as taught by the same or a consistent "teacher" to the one used for L. The performances of the machine learning procedure will be determined by executing this procedure on the data y(n) alone, and comparing the labels c(y) generated by this procedure with the true ones m(y(n)). It is highly recommended that L and T be independent, but this may be difficult to achieve. The leave-one-out method consists then in selecting T identical with L, except one element in L used as a test sample y

iii. Working set W=(z(n)):
this is a set of data z, of same nature than x, for which labels c(z) will be assigned by the results of the learning procedure, although no "true" label is known.

In the above, the labels c(x) and m(y) may be either class assignments, such as those available when the data are to be categorized, or forecasted values, when prediction is the goal of learning, or causal inputs explaining the source of x and y as in behavioral analysis.The term unsupervised learning is used when no learning set L can be found which contains labels for all its elements.

6.2 Neural processing for learning and classification

6.2.1 Neural models

Neural models involve a network of individual processing cells, the behavior of which approximate that of neurons, linking inputs to outputs ([Caudill, 1987-1988], [Hopfield and Tank, 1985], [Pao, 1989]). All these elemental processing units, also called neurons, are massively interconnected among themselves. Typically (see Fig. 1), the cells are organized in several layers l = 1, ..., N, including the input layer l = 1 receiving all raw measurements, the output layer l = N providing all results, and a number of intermediate "hidden" layers. Of course, several neural networks can in turn be interconnected by letting the output layer of some become part of the input layer of others. Each neuron i in layer j > 1, also called node in the neural network, is itself typically characterized by (see Fig. 2):

i. weights w(k,i) applied to any link between neuron k in layer l=(j-1) and neuron i in layer l=(j)

ii. an adder which cumulates all inputs to that node:

$$\text{net}(i, j) = \sum_{k} w(k, i)\, \text{out}(k, j\text{-}1) \qquad (1)$$

iii. a threshold t(i) which is applied to net(i,j) before the neuron processes inputs to it:

$$\text{input}(i, j) = \begin{cases} \text{net}(i, j) \text{ iff } \text{net}(i, j) > t(i) \\ 0 \text{ iff } \text{net}(i, j) < t(i) \end{cases} \qquad (2)$$

This is also called a "hard limiter"

iv. a continuous transfer function f(i, .) which gives the transform performed by that neuron :

$$\text{out}(i, j) = f(i, \text{input}(i, j)) \qquad (3)$$

Equations (2) and (3) together define the transfer function of each processing element or neuron.The output vector from layer j will be noted out(., j)= out(i, j), i in j.

The above architecture is called a feed-forward network, due to Eq. (1) [Rummelhart and McClelland, 1986]; of course other architectures are possible, e.g. (see [Hopfield and Tank, 1985], [Pao, 1989], [Lipmann, 1987]):

- mapping nets: backpropagation (BPN), counterpropagation (CPN)
- spatiotemporal nets: avalanche (SPE)

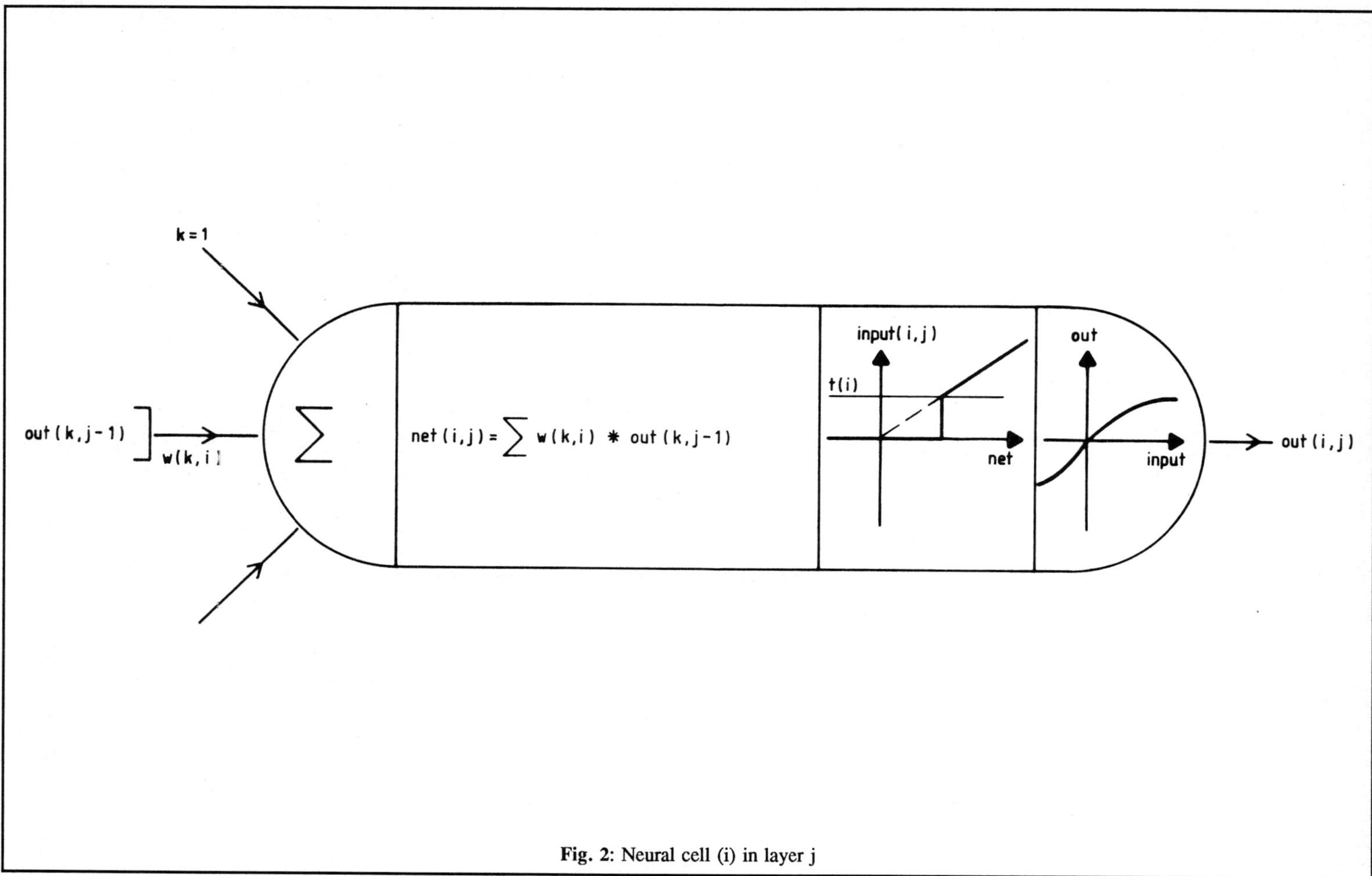

Fig. 2: Neural cell (i) in layer j

- annealing: Boltzman machines, ...
- self-organizing systems: Carpenter-Grossberg classifier, Kohonen self-organization feature map
- associative memories: Anderson, Hopfield neural net (BAM)
- others: adaptive resonance theory (ART), Hamming net, perceptron, ...

Example 1: Biological neuron functions

The following transfer functions are used frequently because of their similarity to the behavior of biological neurons:

- Linear: out= slope*input
  where slope is a constant
- Sigmoid:

$$out = \frac{slope}{1 + e^{-input}} \tag{4}$$

The sigmoid has the important property that its derivative can be expressed in terms of the function itself. ■

As it can be seen from the above definitions, the neural network architecture provides a way to map the inputs in layer l=1 to the outputs out(i,N) in layer l=N. It is moreover an intrinsically non-linear mapping because of the thresholds iii. and node transfer functions iv. The neural network architecture is determined by its topology (i.e. number of layers and assignment of neurons to each layer), thresholds, transfer functions and weights.

6.2.2 Neural learning

The whole purpose of neural learning, is to turn it into a "teacher", by finding an architecture such that when the input layer l=1 is exposed successively to all training data x(n) in L, the output layer l=N indeed produces exactly the values in the corresponding labels c(x(n)) which the teacher might have selected.

Example 2: Investment ratings

Let us consider the classification problem of how to grade some stocks into one of the following rating classes telling about their suitability for investments :

c:A : Investment grade

c:B : Good quality

c:C : Speculative

The stocks are in the example regional banks, described only by the following vector data of dimension 3 :

x(n)=(Price-earnings ratio, Yield(in %), Ratio of loans to assets (in %))

The learning data L are given in Table 1.A, and contain the investment ratings of a number of regional banks, for the same accounting period.

The neural network corresponding to this problem is presented in Fig. 3, and displays the three components of x(n) as the three nodes i = 1, 2, 3 of the input layer l = 1, and the three possible grades c = A, B, C as the outputs of the three output nodes i=1, 2, 3 to the output layer l = 3. This neural network has only one hidden layer l = 2. ■

The neural learning consists in generating a specific architecture of the neural network in Fig. 3, such that the inputs and outputs of it match exactly the contents of Table 1.A. The testing is discussed in Example 10.

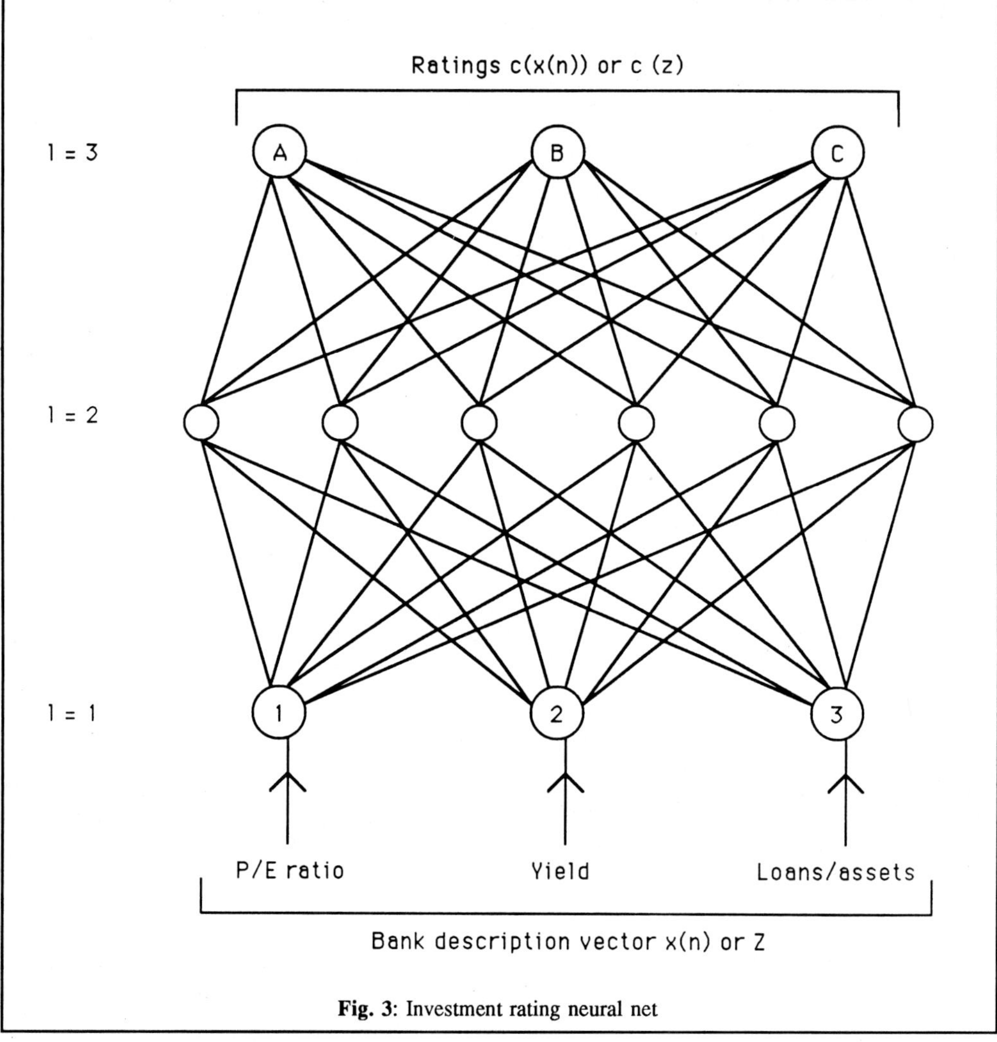

Fig. 3: Investment rating neural net

6.2.3 Neural learning algorithms

There is a wide diversity of neural learning algorithms, and many more are being researched as this has been recently a very active field; these are being discussed e.g. in [Hopfield and Tank, 1985], [Pao, 1989].

Example 3: Back-propagation algorithm

The gradient descent algorithm will try to minimize the total error experienced when training the network on the learning set L. The thresholds and weights are modified recursively by back-propagation of the errors ||c(x(n))-out(.,N)||, where ||.|| is the norm of a vector, by a formula such as:

$$||w(k, i)(n+1) - w(k, i)(n)|| = LR * D(i) * out(k,j-1) + A * ||w(k, i)(n) - w(k, i)(n-1)||$$

where:

n: is the learning set data sample x(n)

Price / Earnings ratio	Yield (%)	Loan / Assets ratio (%)	Ratings of security
12	3	12	B
11	4	10	B
12	4	32	B
11	2	22	A
11	4	30	B
10	3	43	B
10	3	33	B
12	3	21	A
11	2	13	B
8	3	19	B
22	5	95	B
9	4	32	B
16	2	76	C
6	6	95	C
8	4	29	B
11	3	23	A
10	2	55	B
8	2	98	C
95	0	23	C
9	4	94	B
10	3	97	C
10	2	17	B

Table 1.A: Learning data for Example 2

w(k,i)(n): is the trained weight between neurons k and i after n learning samples

LR: is the learning rate parameter

A: is a smoothing factor to prevent oscillations, called momentum

D(i): is the error signal at node i, calculated by:

- if i belongs to output layer l=N corresponding to target value c(x(n,i)) in learning set L:

$$D(i) = (c(x(n, i)) - out(i,N)) * f'(i, input(i, N))$$

$$D(i) = (c(x(n, i)) - out(i, N)) * f(i, input(i, N)) * (1 - f(i, input(i, N)))$$

where the second formula only applies for f: sigmoid

- if i belongs to a hidden layer 1<l<N, the values of D(i) can be inferred from similar values at an upper layer (l+1) with neurons k, and the estimated value is a linear combination of the higher layer D's:

$$D(i) = \sum_k D(k)\, w(i, k) \text{ , k in layer (l+1)}$$

At each presentation of a training element n from L, the corrections on the weights are calculated, and averaged over L; the corrections are carried on until the value of the total error norm is acceptably small. The network is then considered to have learned a representation of all associations from L presented to it. ■

Example 4: Non-linear clustering

This is a particular set of learning algorithms, of which a number have become commercial patents, usually not described in the open literature. They involve grouping together in a multi-dimensional space all learning samples from L having the same label c(x), and sub-dividing those clusters with same c(x) successively until all subclusters satisfy some shape property enforced by a standard encoding element. This encoding element can be looked upon as a neuron, but with multidimensional input. Moreover, the analysis can be repeated at interrelated levels if the encoding unit geometry is appropriate. Such an algorithm is used in the popular neural processing shell NESTOR [Nestor, 1989], which was employed in Example 2. ■

Example 5: Unsupervised learning [Pao, 1989]

The clustering of Example 4 can be enabled as well when the samples are unlabelled, that is without c(n). The strategy is to group them by proximity based e.g. on some multi-dimensional distance measure: the first sample is automatically a cluster center; the next is assigned to the same cluster unless its distance to it is too large; if it joins the first cluster, the center hereof (e.g. centroid) is affected; otherwise, it builds a second cluster, etc. ■

There is no guarantee that an arbitrary neural network architecture will actually converge to a global minimum of the errors. Determining the neural net architecture for training a particular data set L, will especially involve selecting the number of layers, assigning the neurons to the layers, and selecting the learning algorithm parameters (here the learning rate LR and momentum A). Please note that the number of these parameters is independent of the size of the learning set L.

Unless specific processor architectures or powerful processors are used, the learning time required for a possible convergence of an algorithm on a significant learning data set L, can be considerable. It is quite usual to spend 24 hours and more when training a network on a personal computer. This, by itself, poses severe restrictions upon the nature of the applications which can be tackled: on one hand, learning should help cope with changing environments, on the other hand said learning may require time which is longer than the speed at which the underlying process is changing.

In practice, the selection of the network topology is delicate and involves mostly trial-and-error. The number of nodes in the intermediate layers $1<l<N$ should be less than the product of the number of input nodes in layer $l=1$ by the number of output nodes in layer $l=N$. For many applications, a configuration of N= 4-6 layers is sufficient, each composed of no more than 15 neurons. A bad configuration can be detected early, either by enormous final errors, no convergence, too slow convergence, or bad results on the test data T.

Neural learning suffers from the disadvantage, compared with expert systems (see Chapters 1 and 2), not to give the user the capability to request an explanation about the chain of reasoning followed to reach a specific goal, or the consequences of some set of hypotheses. This is because the learning algorithms above involve no causal reasoning whatsoever. Explanation facilities can, however, be developed after convergence, in terms of relations between grammars describing the input nodes and/or output nodes [Pau and Götsche, 1989].

6.2.4 Consultation

This is the process whereby data z from the working set W are presented to a network trained as indicated in the previous Section 2.3, and which must also have been found to behave satisfactory when tested with data from the test data set T.

Example 6: Investment ratings (continued from Example 2)

Here, the financial analyst will present to the input layer of the trained network, the data:

z = (Price-earnings ratio, Yield, Ratio of loans to assets)

of new regional banks for the same period, or for the same regional banks used in the learning set L. In this way, he/she can achieve faster consistent ratings, or spot changes in these ratings on a consistent basis. As a matter of fact, were the contents of the input data extensive enough, e.g. by distributing out to several analysts the task to derive their own inputs, the ratings can be produced automatically. ■

Example 7: Bond investment ratings

In the area of bond ratings, a rating service must be consistent, and preclude ratings on all offerings, which is a huge task where neural processing can help a lot off-loading the effort from the production of the ratings, for the benefit of more thorough quality assurance of the input data z. An early attempt is reported in [Dutta and Shekhar, 1989]. ■

In a feed-forward network, forward propagation (from input to output) in a layerwise fully connected net of N layers with M neurons in each layer, involves (N-1)*M*M additions and M*N sigmoid function evaluations if Eq. (4) is used. Consequently, a very acceptable computational effort is required by neural consultation, as opposed especially to the training. Moreover, the neural consultation time is not dependent upon the size of the training set.

Example 8: Currency trading

The high speed of neural processing, and the ability to cope essentially with very long input vectors with scalar products (Eq. (1)) is crucial to fast response in e.g. currency trading. In this instance, the input nodes in layer l=1 are split into:

- instantaneous variations (in points or %) of e.g. 30 currency contract prices (spot and futures), w.r.t. to the previous rates and a base currency
- interest rates (spot and term) on the same 30 currencies

The thresholds t(i) on all input nodes, as well eventually on the output nodes, can accommodate the specific increments practised on each contract or market, but may also allow to trigger the neural processing higher or lower according to some strategy. As a matter of fact, in the case of hedging or currency portfolio trading, the current holdings on each contract (since the last market close) can be reflected directly into these thresholds, so that the output (net(i, j) - t(i)) becomes a net gain.

The 30 nodes of the output layer l=N are to produce the numbers c(i) of contracts to be placed instantaneously to maximize the total gain, with buys positive and sales negative. This involves either scaling the weights w going into the output layer, or scaling of the sigmoidal functions (4). ■

Example 9: Portfolio balancing

It is a classical problem, in a portfolio e.g. decomposed into the following groups of shares (or commodities):

Dow Jones "upside " rating

Dow Jones "downside" rating

Volume accumulation

Volume distribution

to select the shares going into each group as to achieve a portfolio mix with specified risks (see also Chapter 11). This involves first identifying some indicators all related to strength, volume, and volatility relative to the market; next, all candidate shares or contracts must be screened, assuming that the market trend has been accounted for to some extent.

This can be achieved by neural learning, on a combination of said indicators, and next by the presence or absence of features provided by technical analysis (such as those extracted and interpreted in Chapter 7). ■

6.2.5 Performance evaluation

There are many ways to estimate the validity of a specific neural learning and processing; some deal with the classification errors observed when running the trained network on the test data set T, others with the training time, and some also with the risks involved in the automatic neural processing. To serve as guidelines for other applications, we give here the results corresponding to Example 6.

Example 10: Investment ratings (continued from Examples 2 and 6)

We used an implementation of the neural backpropagation learning algorithm of Example 3 on the training data of Table 1.A, with the following network architecture and paramaters:

Input layer l=1 : 3 nodes (1-3) Learning rate :LR= 0.9

Hidden layer l=2 : 9 nodes (4-12) Momentum: A= 0.75

Output layer l=3 : 3 nodes (13-15) Sigmoid slope: slope= 0.35

Then, after 600 iterations in the supervised learning mode, the following weights were learned:

w(1,4): -0.111 w(1,5): 0.356 w(1,6): -0.695 w(1,7): 0.414
w(1,8): 0.405 w(1,9): -0.445 w(1,10): -0.625 w(1,11): 0.057 w(1,12): -0.258

w(1,4-12)= -1.214 * w(1,4-12)
w(2,4-12)= -0.601 * w(1,4-12) where w(1,*) are the values above
w(3,4-12)= -1.103 * w(1,4-12)

w(4,13): -0.248 w(5,13): 0.293 w(6,13): -0.453 w(7,13): 0.645
w(8,13): 0.375 w(9,13): 0.345 w(10,13):-0.715 w(11,13): -1.03 w(12,13): -0.38

w(4-12,13)= -1.398 * w(4-12,13)
w(4-12,14)= -0.535 * w(4-12,13), where w(*,13) are the values above
w(4-12,15)= -1.895 * w(4-12,13)

These weights should be displayed on Fig. 3, but to avoid jamming, are given here only in compact form.■

Example 11: Investment ratings (continued from Examples 2, 6 and 10)

We used here the neural learning algorithm of Example 4 on the training and test data of Table 1.A and Table 1.B respectively, with the following network architecture and parameters (see [Nestor, 1989] for details beyond the scope of this book):

- Encoding unit: ONE_THR with feature resolution (8) and minimum influence field (5 %)
- Liberal classification procedure, with consensus threshold (3) and consensus difference (2)
- Exclusive prototype weight (3), overlapping weight (1), nearest neighbour (on), and maximum influence field (14 %)

The test results on test data from Table 1.B (18 banks) are:

- Identified correctly: 61.1 % (A: 66.6 %, B: 63,6%, C: 50 %)
- Identified incorrectly: 33.3 %
- Unidentified: 5.5 % (one bank of grade B)
- Prototypes exclusive: 43.7 % (7)

Price / Earnings ratio	Yield (%)	Loan / Assets ratio (%)	Ratings of security
9	3	31	B
11	2	27	A
10	4	94	B
7	5	94	C
9	3	10	C
12	4	94	B
13	2	18	B
10	3	86	C
22	5	37	B
28	3	23	B
10	4	94	B
13	2	25	B
11	3	30	A
10	3	10	A
9	4	93	B
7	5	94	B
9	3	65	C
12	3	48	B

Table 1.B: Test data for Example 11

- Prototypes overlapping: 56.2 % (9)

The analysis also reveals the existence of 6 sub-clusters, thereby confirming that the 3 training classes A, B, C were not compact! ■

6.3 Inductive learning

6.3.1 Introduction

Inductive learning methods can be viewed as "learning from examples", in view of acquiring or accumulating knowledge as required by knowledge-based tasks (see Chapter 1). Such methods are essential in all cases where the user or expert, or both, are not exactly aware of which decision or evaluation rules they apply [Shaw, 1987].

By mapping examples into rules, and in association especially with predicate logic (Chapter 3.5) and causal analysis (Chapter 5.10), one can exactly map out the inconsistencies between decision or evaluation rules used by different people or organizations, and point at the authors of said inconsistencies.

6.3.2 Concept learning

In inductive learning, the labels c can be inferred from the description of individual instances x having that label c (Table 2). Each label c can be viewed as a concept which is described by a production rule having as the hypothesis part, called pattern, a logic combination of conditions on the components of x. More precisely, the concept is a symbol which is true when applied to a learning set describing that concept correctly, and false otherwise. An example x(n) which satisfies the concept definition is called a positive example of that concept, and negative otherwise.

Example 12: Patterns in loan granting

If we take as example small business loans (see also Chapter 1.4 for a more extensive approach), the learning set L contains positive examples about n loan applications, with their attributes, and labels about loan risk group designations, e.g. I-A, I-B, II-A, II-B, III, etc. From L, one derived pattern could be, expressed in predicate logic form:

(Assets > 0.5 M$) and (Debt < 0.3 M$) --> Class(1) c=I-A

whereas the examples x(.) from L are in tabular form:

(1)	(2)	(3)	(4)	(5)	Class
Application	Assets	Debt	Staff	Export	c(x)
3	0.1	0.15	7	45	III
5	0.9	0.3	23	12	I-A

■

A generalization of an example x, is a concept definition which describes a set containing that example, e.g. L. Thus the inductive learning can be viewed as a process of repetitively generalizing the descriptions observed from examples x in L until the inductive concept definitions are found and are consistent with all the examples in L.

The generalization process itself, or inductive learning algorithm, will produce a set of M patterns, resulting in concepts c(1), .., c(M) covering all those encountered in the learning set L of positive and negative examples.

6.3.3 Induction algorithms

The input to an induction algorithm consists of three parts:

i. a set L of positive and negative examples

ii. the generalization rules of the induction algorithm

iii. criteria for successful learning

Induction algorithms fall into similarity (also called preference) based methods [Michalski, 1983], [Rendell, 1986], [Quinlan, 1979], [Quinlan, 1986] and explanation based methods [Mitchell and

TRAINING EXAMPLES FROM L		DECISION RULES
Case x(1) : decision c(1)		Pattern (I) : decision c(I)
Case x(2) : decision c(2)		Pattern(II) : decision c(II)
....	INDUCTIVE	....
....	LEARNING	....
Case x(n) : decision c(n)		Pattern (M) : decision c(M)

Table 2: Inductive learning from examples

Keller, 1986] (see Section 3.5). All suffer from combinatorial explosion, especially in those steps involved in finding possible patterns which confirm a positive example, and which do not cover any of the negative examples. To achieve realistic results, beam searching (see Chapter 5.11.2) is used to limit the number of pattern descriptions to a predetermined number.

We will below describe one such algorithm, and refer to the literature for others.

6.3.4 ID3 induction of decision trees

The ID3 algorithm [Quinlan, 1979], [Quinlan, 1986], produces a decision tree [Breiman, 1984] that partitions the examples with respect to combinations of attribute values of the examples in L, such that it classifies correctly the given cases. The decision tree algorithm builds the tree so that all training samples on a leaf of the tree belong to the same class. It takes an information theoretic approach, by generating splits in the tree each time there is information gained from it about some specific attribute.

Define :

i: the attribute number i of the examples x, also noted (i)

Q(i): is the number of values of (i) ,where (i) is a nominal variable; if the range of values of (i) is split into two sub-ranges (+) and (-),then Q=2

Pos: a set of p positive examples of a label (+)

Dif: a set of n positive examples of a label (-)

log: the logarithm of base 2

Inf(Pos/Dif) = - (p/(p+n))log(p/(p+n)) - (n/(p+n))log(n/(p+n)) (bits)

the information amount needed to produce the message Pos or Dif from all samples in the union set of positive examples of (+) or (-)

Inf((i)) = Sum ((p(q)+n(q))*Inf(Pos(q)/Dif(q)) / (p+n)) (bits)

q=1,..,Q(i)

is the expected information required for the subtree with (i) as the root.

The basic ID3 algorithm then involves the following steps:

Algorithm ID3:

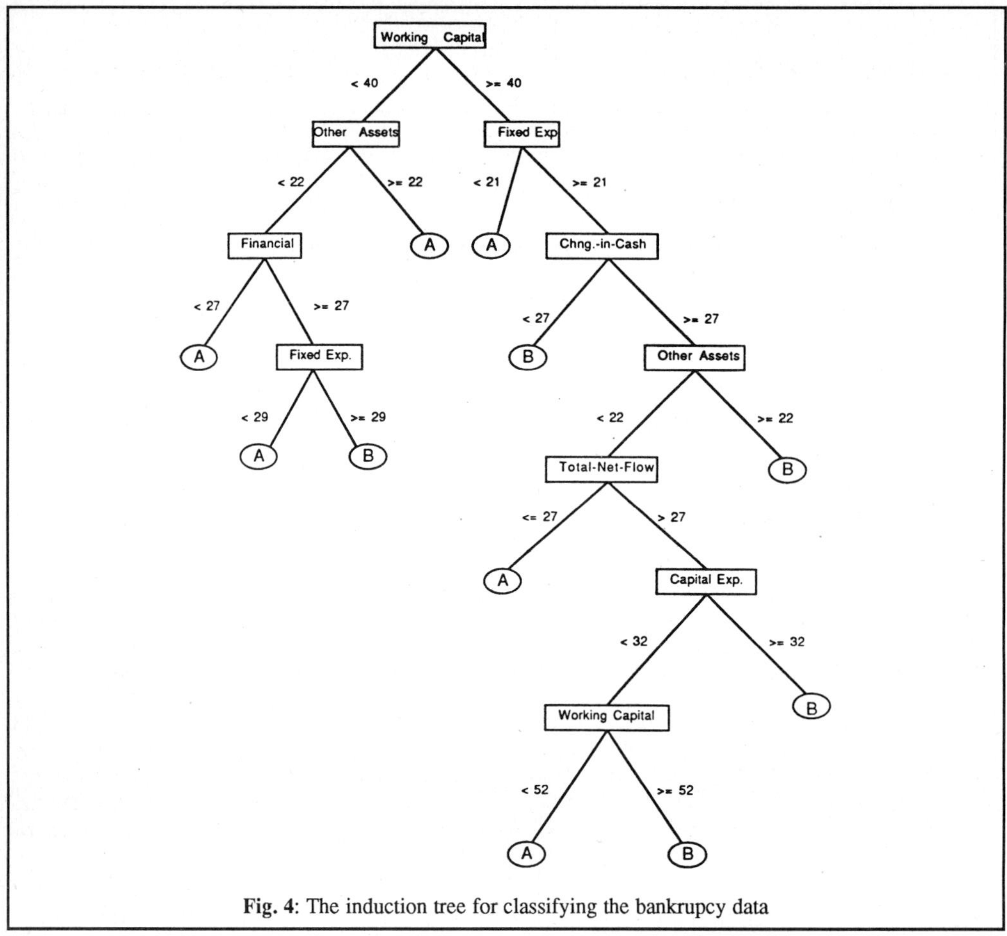

Fig. 4: The induction tree for classifying the bankrupcy data

Step 1. Create the root node of the decision tree, by selecting e.g. the Pattern (I) as identical with the single attribute (1); thereafter, try selectively to find other attributes, such as (2), (3), etc. to expand Pattern(I) and branch the tree;

Step 2. If all positive examples of the prevailing Pattern at the current node have the same label c, then Stop. If there are positive and negative examples, but Gain((i)) is always zero for all partitions, then Stop.

Step 3. For each attribute (i), make a partition, decomposing all samples classified by the tree according to that attribute, into subsets of samples where attribute (i) has the same value for all samples in each subset. Only one subset is allowed for each attribute value. Find the partition giving the largest information gain Gain ((i)) derived from partitioning that (i):
Gain ((i))= Inf(Pos/Dif) - Inf((i)) (bits)
The attribute which gives the largest gain is chosen as a node of the tree, and as a leaf to the prior attribute nodes. The quantity Gain((i)) can be interpreted as follows. Assuming a Q=2 two-class case first, a given sample may belong to class (+) with probability p/(p+n) and to class (-) with the probability n/(p+n); Inf(Pos/Dif) is then the amount of information needed to partition the set of samples from (+) or (-), into a binary split. More generally, the i-th subtree relating to attribute (i) (and with counts n,p) will partition into Q(i) subtrees, and each of those will have p(q) cases (+) in Pos(q) sustaining that split and n(q) cases (-) in Dif(q).

Step 4. For each branch node, repeat Step 2.

When the training sets L are large, the procedure above can be speeded up by a windowing scheme that reduces the samples to a subset at the time in Steps 2 and 3, and produces a partial decision tree for such subsets only; the exceptions to the current partial tree are pooled with samples not yet processed. The procedure is repeated until there are no more such exceptions.

6.3.5 Examples

In economics and finance, a few experiments have been carried out, some with success, others with less than traditional knowledge acquisition methods. The major disadvantages have been huge data amounts necessary for the induction of non-trivial rules, and the computation time. Advantages have been to help with an early knowledge structuring, through the rule patterns (Fig. 4), from source [Shaw et al., 1990], in contexts where nothing solid was known, and to identify the most important attributes occurring high up in the tree :

- bankruptcy prediction from cash flow changes [Gentry and Newbold, 1985], [Shaw et al., 1990], [Messier and Hansen, 1989] (see Fig. 4)
- stock market trading [Lee, to appear], [Breiman, 1984], using as attributes a price-volume composite indicator estimated on several time horizons
- business loan risk classification [Shaw et al., 1990]
- credit card loan applications, using ID3 [Carter and Catlett, 1987a]

Similarity-based induction and neural networks are adequate for data intensive domains with noisy data, to infer cycles, patterns, or regularities, besides classification. These regularities help the algorithm compress large data amounts into a few induced rules, and where there is "no theory", i.e. where correlation dominates as opposed to causality.

Explanation-based induction requires a causal model to be built a priori, and involves knowledge transformation rather than acquisition. Based on the analysis of a few training examples, and guided by the causal or explanatory model, new operational rules can be deduced. They typically have a higher innovation content and usefulness, by generating more focussed concepts.

6.4 Extensions to neural processing

6.4.1 Neural decision logic

As suggested in Section 2.1, several neural networks can be interconnected, by letting the output layers of some serve in the inputs of some other networks.

Furthermore, these additional networks (called subnets) may be trained separately, or may express in neural network form some standard decision functions.

Example 13: Hamming distance classifier

This specialized network serves the purpose of classifying the input vector x as belonging to a class c on the basis of the Hamming distance between that sample (assumed to have binary components) and the output node label c representing that class [Pao, 1989]. It can be shown that the network which achieves this property the most efficiently has a special Hamming feed-forward topology different from the one in Section 2.1, which augments the largest node outputs while suppressing others. The threshold t(i) is furthermore non-linear, being defined as:

0, if net (i,j)<0

t(i) = net(i,j) if 0<net(i,j)<1

1 if net(i,j)>1

and called a threshold logic. ■

Example 14: XOR decision

This network has 2 nodes (1, 2) in the input layer l=1, one node (3) in the hidden layer l=2, and one node (4) in the output layer l=N=3. The output c(x) for the input x=(x1, x2) must be the logical exclusive-OR value of the binary components x1 and x2; that is c(x) is 1 if x1 and x2 are equal, and -1 otherwise.This corresponds to a network which can be analyzed to be the following, or which can be trained by the algorithm of Example 3 to be:

w(1, 4) = w(2, 4) = 1
w(1, 3) = w(2, 3) = 1
w(3, 4) = - 2
t(4) = 0.5

This can be further extended to other logic operations [Clocksin and Mellish, 1987] by neural logic networks [Teh, 1989] which are essentially neural networks as defined in Section 2.1, but with two scalar weights (usually different) w(i, j) = (w1(k, i), w2(k, i)) for each link between a node i and a node j , separate summations by Equation (1) for w1 and w2 weights resp., and a final majority decision between the two outputs in the output layer l=N. ■

6.4.2 Learning how to forecast

Let us extend the definition of the training samples x(n) in L by a time argument: we let the coordinates of the vector x(n): (x(n, t)) be time-indexed over a time horizon t = 1, ..., T. Furthermore, let the label c(x(n)) be the observed value of x(n,t) for some t beyond the training horizon T, e.g. c(x(n))=x(n, T+1).

If the training data L, test data T, and working data W, are defined in this way, then any learning procedure should yield forecasts for x(n, T+1); neural learning and inductive learning are therefore forecasting techniques:

- neural learning will produce weights w(t,i) to the inputs x(n,t) of the input layer l=1, reminiscent of signal filtering, but add all the other non-linear processing elements of the neural architecture to produce minimum forecasting error forecasts [Pau and Johansen, 1990]

- inductive learning will select time-dependent Patterns(.) combining time-dependent attributes, to produce a forecast such that the generalization process is true within the training set; in this sense inductive learning generalizes knowledge based technical analysis (Chapter 7)

Few experiments have been carried out so far based on the forecasting techniques proposed here. The results of [Pau and Johansen, 1990] tend to indicate, however, that neural forecasting alone is less powerful than knowledge based forecasting, which in turn assumes a knowledge acquisition of the type inductive forecasting offers.

6.4.3 Other applications

Besides the Examples above, there is a large diversity of potential applications in economics and finance of neural networks and learning. Most are still untested, such as:

- foreign currency trading from information services data feeds (about 25 different input items)
- credit scoring on consumer loans,with about 100 input data on each application
- mortgage screening
- selection of target audiences after a market survey

7 Technical analysis for securities trading

7.1 Introduction

Technical analysis consists in studying the curves representing price, index, ratio, and volume fluctuations over time, in order to infer some investment decisions from the local and/or global shape of such curves [Cootner, 1964], [Kaufman, 1978], [Kaufman, 1978a]. It is therefore essentially a two stage process, with:

i. visual segmentation of the curve(s) into primitive shapes of some portions hereof, such as valleys, peaks, rebound, steep rise or fall, etc.

ii. a knowledge-based correspondence established between the time sequence of such primitive shapes found in the curve, and specific investment decisions, including forecasts or trend assessments (long term growth, cyclical, sell, sell on recovery, etc.)

Here is examined how syntactic curve pattern recognition [Fu, 1979] can be applied to the technical analysis of financial data (process i.), combined with a knowledge-based user-specific interpretation hereof reflecting an investment policy (process ii.).

A system based on this work was already developed over 1987-1988 as part of a government sponsored product development [Pau, 1988] involving a mixed object-oriented and logic programming environment (Smalltalk/V and Prolog/V, [Digitalk, 1986]). More recently, a similar product emphasizing portfolio management as part of Process ii. above has been launched [Wyatt Software, 1989]. Very recently also, the idea of using a syntactic grammar has been presented again in [Miller, 1990].

Whereas it is not the purpose here to provide theoretical nor empirical justification for the use of technical analysis in Process ii. (see Sections 6 and 7 below, and [Kaufman, 1978], [Kaufman, 1978a]), it is important to show that curve interpretation in economics and finance are today technically feasible by theory and tools presented below in Sections 2-4.

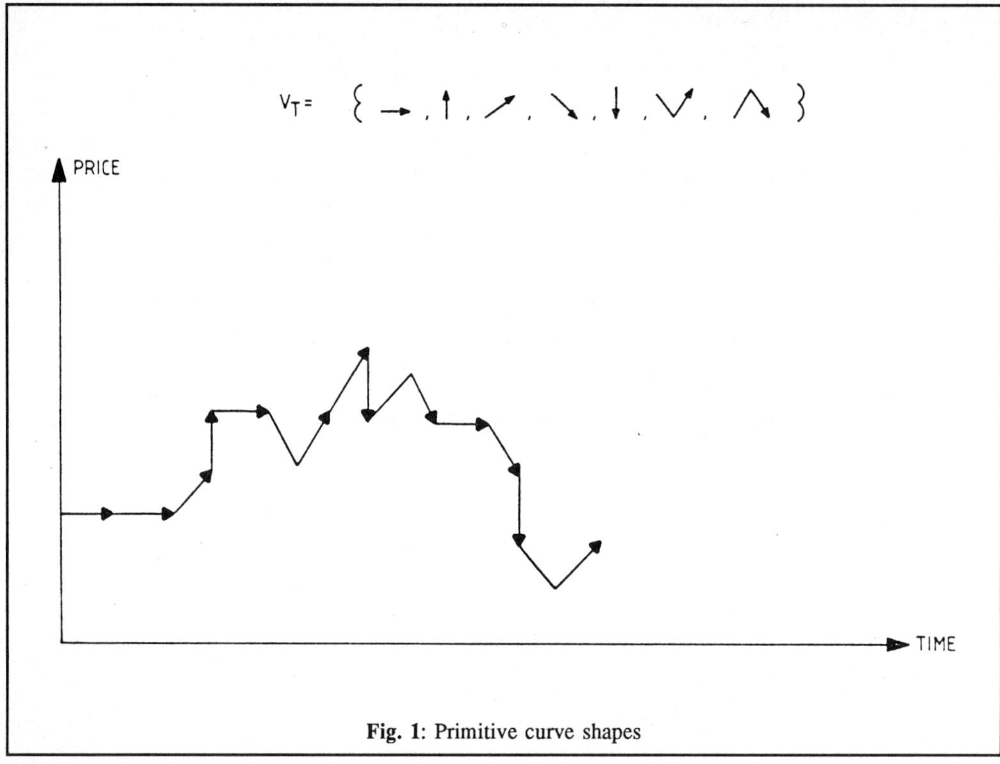

Fig. 1: Primitive curve shapes

The application-specific customization of generic interpretation rules, such as those in Section 5 below can now be implemented with all the ease of knowledge-based processing techniques. Short examples hereof are given, both for analysis (see Sections 8, 9, 10) as well as for investment decisions or trading (Sections 8, 11). These examples are given purely for illustration purposes, and do not in anyway represent complete "real" detailed examples as offered on a regular basis by tools such as [Pau, 1988] and [Wyatt Software, 1989]. Other interpretation principles and domains can be considered instead of technical analysis [Pring, 1985] such as fundamental analysis, relative strength, etc. or applications to commodity, trading, bonds, currencies, etc.

7.2 Curve generation by a syntactic grammar

To describe the possible curve shapes, a grammar $G = (V_T, V_N, \{p\}, S)$ is defined through the following constituents [Fu, 1979]. These possible curve shapes are called the language L(G) generated by G.

i. Terminal vocabulary: V_T: For technical analysis, V_T is the set of primitive elementary shapes which can be encountered, such as:

V_T = {→, ↑, ↗, ↘, ↓, ↘↗, ↗↘, A, B, C, TRANSITION, ELBOW}

Terminal symbols are capital letters, or figures, or words. Other typical meaningful basic price curve shapes, include: head and shoulders, flags, pennants, double tops (See also Fig. 1)

ii. <u>Initial symbol: { s} $\in$ V_N</u>

This is the symbol used to initiate the sequence of rewriting rules below, or the symbol needed to generate all curve shapes L(G)

iii. <u>Auxiliary (or non-terminal)vocabulary V_N:</u>
This is a set of non-meaningful symbols or words, usually referred to via lower case letters, which serve purely to manipulate the rewriting rules and the sequence hereof:

V_N = { a,b,c,d... ,downtrend, uptrend}

iv. <u>Rewriting rules {p}:</u> The derivation process is governed by rules, called rewriting rules, whereby a sentence, represented by a string of terminal and non-terminal symbols, can be replaced by another similar sentence. An example of such a sentence can be, in list notation:

α = ↗ . ↠ . uptrend.TRANSITION. ↗↘ . downtrend

which is a mixture of symbols from V_T and V_N

The first rewriting rules transform the initial symbol s into such sequences. At the end of the derivation process, the generated sentences must only contain terminal symbols from V_T; such a sentence is then nothing else than a price curve.

Example of rewriting rules p_i from {p} are:

p1: <uptrend> → ↗

p2: <downtrend> → ↘

p3: <uptrend> <downtrend> → <peak>

p4: <downtrend> < uptrend> → <valley>

p5: <valley> → ↘↗

p6: <peak> → ↗↘

p7: <down> → < down> < downtrend> | <downtrend>

p8: <up> → <up > < uptrend > | < uptrend >

For the notation used here, see Chapter 4.2.1. Please remark that peak/valley are context-sensitive rules, as opposed to context-free rules uptrend/downtrend.

In general, if $(V_T \cup V_N)^*$ denotes the set of all sequences of symbols in V_T or V_N, such as α above, then a rewriting rule takes the form:

$$p: \quad \alpha \in (V_T \cup V_N)^* \rightarrow \beta \in (V_T \cup V_N)^*$$

Prolog

append (p, nil, π)	—>	rule (p, s, w)
append (p, π, π1)	—>	rule (p, x, g) member (q, w) rule (p, y, alpha · x · beta)
append (p, π, π1)	—>	rule (q, x, alpha · y · beta) member (q, w) rule (p, y, gamma)

Table 1: Earley top-down segmentation of the curve represented by the curve sentence: $w = A_0 \cdot A_1 \ldots \cdot A_n$ into the sequence $\pi = (p_0, p_1, \ldots, p_m)$ of production rules

where α must contain at least one symbol from V_N.

When dealing with price curves, some further considerations apply:

- the time durations attached to each primitive shape in V_T must be known, so that the symbol analysis procedure can be made sensitive to short term fluctuations
- the set of primitive shapes in V_T can be more or less exhaustive and complex to allow for the description of complex curve shapes, global trends, and alike

7.3 Curve segmentation

This is the reverse problem to the curve generation: the segmentation (also called parsing) will test whether the given curve $W = A_0 \cdot A_1 . \ldots . \cdot A_n \in V_T{}^*$ can be derived by a grammar G. In other words, the segmentation will look at the primitive shapes found in the curve, to test whether or not that curve could itself have been generated by the grammar G. In the simpler case of so-called context-free grammars G, the rewriting rules {p} must be of the form:

$$p : \quad a \in V_N \rightarrow \beta \in (V_T \cup V_N)^*$$

which means that the non-terminal a is replaced by the string β independently of the context in which a appears, see also Chapter 4.2.3.

For context-free grammars, simple parsers can be derived (see Table 1) [Earley, 1970], where the initial symbol s is expanded by successively substituting non-terminals to try to fit the sentence to be parsed $W = A_0 \cdot A_1 . \ldots . \cdot A_n$. (Fig. 1) (see [Giannesini et al., 1986] for further explanation of the parser in Table 1). The ordered sequence $\pi = (p_0, p_1, \ldots, p_q)$ of substitutions will then be the signature which characterizes the input price curve W.

7.4 Segmentation of noisy curves

However, more complex types of grammars are frequent, e.g. context sensitive ones (see also Chapter 4.2.2, 4.2.3), and moreover the price curve patterns are often noisy because of very short term volume-related fluctuations. A measure of likelihood or similarity is then required to make comparisons, in that the parser must then look for sentences from the language L(G) which are the most similar to the given noisy pattern W.

One such similarity measure is the Levenshtein distance d(x,y) [Levenshtein, 1966] between two sentences from $(V_T \cup V_N)^*$:

$$d(x,y) = \text{Min}\ (n_s, n_d, n_i)$$

which is the smallest number of transformations required to derive β from α, following:

i n_s substitutions in V_T:

$$p\ \text{substitution}: \begin{bmatrix} A,B \in V_T: & \alpha A \beta \rightarrow \alpha B \beta, \\ A \neq B & \end{bmatrix}$$

ii n_d deletions:

$$p\ \text{deletion}:\ A \in V_T\ :\ \alpha A\ \beta \rightarrow \alpha \cdot \beta$$

iii n_i insertions:

$$p\ \text{insertion}:\ A \in V_T:\ \alpha b \rightarrow \alpha A \beta$$

Error-correcting parsing ([Aho and Peterson, 1972], [Tanaka and Fu, 1978]) or segmentation searches for a sentence W from the language L(G) such that, given a sentence Y:

$$d(W,Y) = \underset{Z}{\text{Min}} \{d(Z,Y) \mid Z \in L(G)\}$$

which means that the segmentation finds a price pattern $\pi = (p_o, p_1, ..., p_q)$ associated with a non-noisy curve W which is the closest to the noisy curve Y [Aho and Peterson, 1972]. References [Aho and Peterson, 1972], [Tanaka and Fu, 1978] give calculation algorithms for d(W,Y). The resulting error-correcting parser will again work from top to bottom, but with provisions for operating on sentences derivable from the observed curve by substitution, deletion, and insertion error grammar rules, and for accumulating the similarity values.

7.5 Analysis evaluation rules

After parsing of the price curve $W = A_0 \cdot A_1 .... \cdot A_n$, as a result of the sequence $\pi = (p_0, p_1, ..., p_q)$ of rewriting rules {p} of the grammar G, the question remains how to perform specific investment decisions, including forecasts or trend assessments. This is easily carried out using the three following notions:

i. shape-filters are predicates operating on W, determining its length n, counting the number of terminal symbols in W of each type, and weighing these counts with the positions to produce a list D_1, $D_2 ... D_m$ of alternative hypotheses or decisions in that case by:

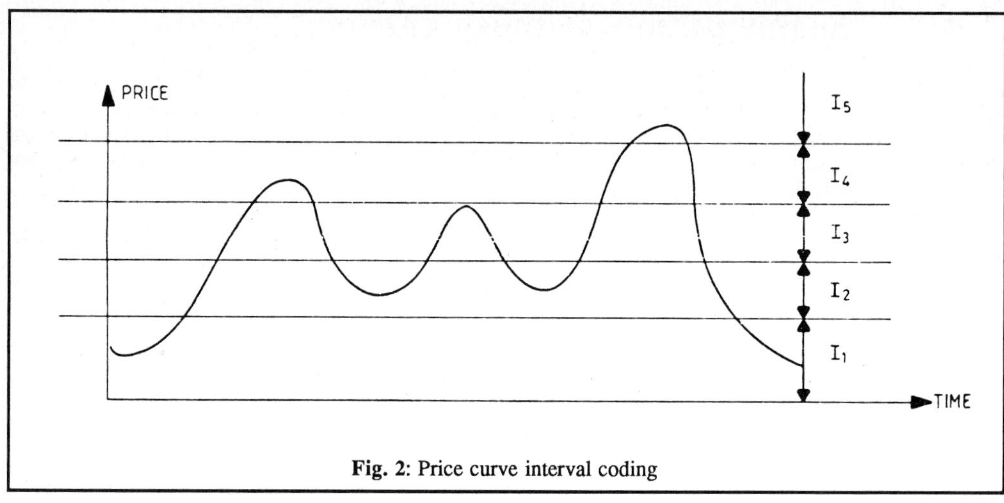

Fig. 2: Price curve interval coding

shape-filter (i, W, n, D_1. D_2...D_n)

ii. level-crossing-filters, which are predicates operating on the price levels attained at the end of each primitive curve shape A_l, to tell in which price interval I_i the price can now be positioned (Fig. 2) ; we denote it:

level-crossing-filter (j, A_l, I_i)

iii. decision-filters, who essentially combine the two previous filters, to further refine the alternative decisions or hypotheses (by substitution, deletion, insertion rules) which can be considered in view of both price curve shape and levels:

decision-filter (k,n,j,W,D'_1....D'_r) $\rightarrow$
shape-filter (i,W, n, D_1.D_2...D_n)
level-crossing-filter (j, A_l, I_i)
member (A_l, W).

Because the decision-filter depends on the price intervals I_j, through the level-crossing filter, the later generated trading decisions (Section 8) will be directly related to the price intervals and thus price levels.

7.6 Technical analysis on several curves and software implementation

Frequently, it is necessary to track several curves at the same time, such as price, earnings, volume, sales, etc., some of which, by the way, are not continuous but represented by step functions or staircase functions. Section 7 will also define a number of derived feature curves. Two approaches are then possible:

i. when one curve is dominant, let us say price, over the other curves in significance for the evaluation, then the procedures of Sections 3, 4 are still applied to the price curve; however, the level-crossing-filters of Section 5 may then be derived from the other curves as well

ii. when really more than one curve is significant in terms of shapes and trends, the approach is to define symbols in the terminal vocabulary V_T, which are t-uples or combinations of primitive shape elements. For example if the terminal vocabulary is:

$$V_T = \{➻, ♠, ➶, ➴, ❣\}$$

for any curve separately, then (Fig. 3):

$$V_T^N = \otimes V_T = \{(A_1, ..., A_N) \mid A_i \in V_T\}$$

is the terminal vocabulary for N curves jointly. The procedures of Sections 3, 4, 5 still hold thereafter. However, "new" basic symbols and curve patterns not described adequately and uniquely by V_T^N, may occur in practice. The final sentence generated by V_T^N will be correct, but highly subject to noise (Section 4).

The software implementations of the techniques described above can be carried out in different ways [Pau et al., 1988], [Wyatt Software, 1989] which, however, all rely on:

i. an interpreted numerical processing language, eventually compiled to allow for grammar specification in BNF (Backus-Naur) form (Section 2), and curve segmentation (Sections 3, 4); this can be further enhanced by object-oriented facilities, thus the choice of Smalltalk [Digitalk, 1986] in the systems [Pau et al., 1988], [Wyatt Software, 1989]

ii. a declarative symbolic processing language, and/or IF_THEN_ rule editor, for the interpretation or action rules of Section 5; here Prolog was chosen [Pau et al., 1988], as it allows both for efficient grammar parsing, for declarative rules, as well as for search

iii. when the host processor is a personal computer, multiprocessing extensions are necessary for simultaneous acquisition of raw financial data via information services, and for interpretation; both [Pau et al., 1988] and [Wyatt Software, 1989] have used the Communications extension kit to [Digitalk, 1986], with [Pau et al., 1988] recently upgraded to the more performant kit [Computas Expert Systems, 1988]

7.7 Time series analysis

The previous Sections 2 - 6 were dealing with the use of syntactic pattern recognition, to describe and analyze sequences of basic patterns as encountered in price, volume, earnings, charts. We will now define the types of curves analyzed in portfolio technical analysis, in terms of the preprocessing carried out on raw price, volume, etc. data. Sections 8, 9, 10, 11 will give examples of knowledge-based processing applicable to such curves, once they have been analyzed by the procedures of Sections 1- 6.

Technical analysis involves two basic approaches [Kaufman, 1980]: concurrent analysis and predictive analysis. The predictive method attempts to forecast the extent of price movements over a future time period. The concurrent analysis, also called autoregressive, is a determination of the direction of the price at the moment of decision, and may be one of only three states: up, down, sideways. The present chapter deals primarily with concurrent approaches.

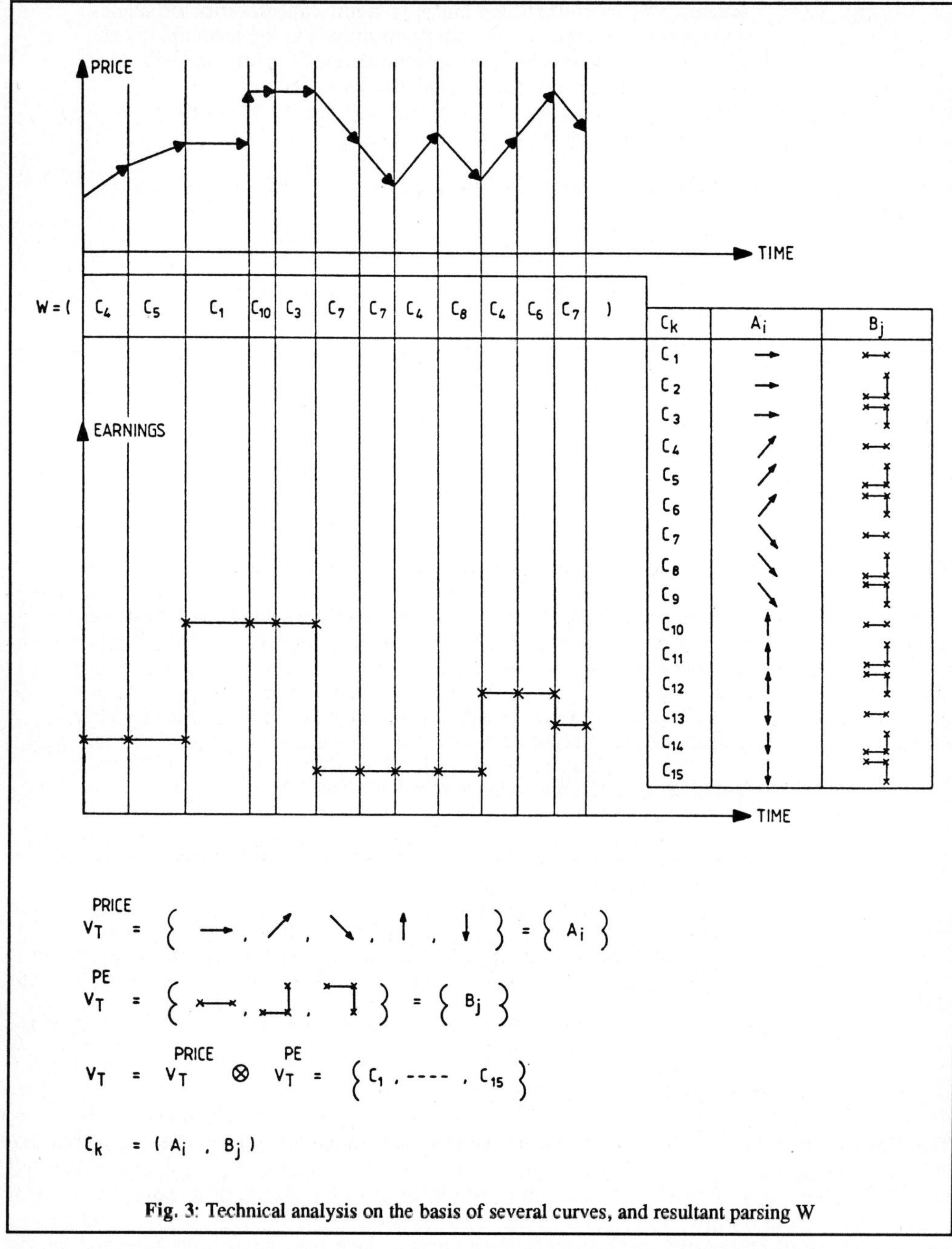

Fig. 3: Technical analysis on the basis of several curves, and resultant parsing W

The most well known concurrent approach is the moving average, and its direction of movement. The simple average (M.A.) of N days closes are calculated including today's close:

$$M.A(N) = [Close (M) + Close (M-1) +..+ Close (M-N+1)] /N$$

where:

M: date of close
N: number of days

M.A.(N) can be replaced with linearly weighted or exponentially smoothed sums, to emphasize the most recent prices. Frequently, two or more M.A. models are used with different values of N, to reflect short-term or long-term averages.

A variant of the M.A. is the average directional movement index rating, which expresses price volatility:

$$ADMR(M) = \frac{|Close(M) - Close(M-1)| - |Close(M) - Close(M+1)|}{|Close(M) - Close(M-1)| + |Close(M) - Close(M+1)|}$$

and must itself be replaced by its moving average over N days:

$$ADX(N) = [AD\ MR\ (M) + \text{--} + AD\ MR\ (M-N+1)]\ /N$$

For generality, we will later at times denote the moving average M.A. of a time-series X(.) with parameters P, as M.A. (X,P); for example:

$$M.A.\ (Close, [N]) = M.A.\ (N)$$

This corresponds in Prolog to extending the arity of the M.A. predicate

To take a simple interpretation rule, when prices cross the average M.A. or ADX moving up, we may consider it a signal of a new upward trend; the trend remains upward until prices penetrate the moving average going down. Breakout systems such as point-and-figure and swing techniques also qualify as autoregressive; they define the current trends and assume a continuation of a trend until a contrary signal occurs. Other features, which can be calculated and charted separately, with knowledge-based analysis applying to each, are:

- momentum, which is the rate of change x(t)/x(t-1) in the series x(.), e.g. price
- acceleration, which is the rate of change of momentum
- extension, which is the distance of a series x(.) at time T from a particular moving average of the same at time (T-U).

Predictive methods include the use of price objectives in any form, most commonly those based on seasonality or cycles. A simple chart analysis of price objectives may not require a time interval; such a support line is a M.A. (N) trend over many days (N large), whereas a resistance line R(N) is defined by:

$$R(N) = M.A.\ (Close\ (M)\ |\ M \text{ is minimum over the interval } N)$$

Reaching a support or resistance line may occur either quickly or over a long interval. The use of seasons or cycles emphasizes time and not price. Cycles may happen either as fluctuations about a normal value, or as long-term effects.

7.8 Examples of concurrent trading rules

Note that rules may inhibit the firing of certain others, through appropriate meta-rules implementing a conflict resolution strategy.

Rule 1 M.A. stop rule: If today's close Close (M) penetrates the moving average M.A. (N) on the upside, a Buy is placed on the opening tomorrow

Rule 2 M.A. stop rule: If today's close Close (M) penetrates the moving average M.A. (N) on the downside, a Sell is placed on the opening tomorrow

Rule 3 If the high and low of the next day are equal, then the assumption is made that the market is locked the limit, and a trade cannot be made on that day. The trade will be done on the first day the market is not locked the limit

Rule 4 When a new Buy or Sell signal is generated, the old position is liquidated simultaneously

Rule 5 Cross over rule: If M.A. (P) > M.A. (N), with P < N, a Buy is placed on the opening tomorrow

Rule 6 Cross over rule: If M.A. (P) < M.A. (N), with P < N, a Sell is placed on the opening tomorrow

Rule 7 Intraday closing price rule: a Buy signal is generated if the price Close (M+1) exceeds the highest close of the last N days; a Sell signal is generated if the price Close (M+1) is lower than the lowest close of the last N days

Rule 8 Contrarian rule: take a contrarian position when a bullish extreme is reached, with a 90% or greater bullish consensus, or a 20% or less bullish consensus

Rule 9 Contrarian stop rule: take a contrarian stop order (Rules 1,2) to Sell or Buy resp. when the bullish consensus exceeds 80% or is less than 30%

Rule 10 Reversal rule: when over 80% or under 30% bullish consensus is reached (the respective borders of the overbought and oversold areas), a sudden reversal in the price trend could occur at any time, and switch to the contrarian Rules 8,9. The closer the bullish consensus approaches 100% or 0%, the greater the contrarian price move

Rule 11 Open contracts: if the M.A. (N) of the number of open contracts is increasing steadily, do not take a contrarian position (Rules 8,9), regardless of the bullish consensus. The consensus is likely to remain high until the number of contracts stabilizes. The price trend is also likely to continue as the open interest is increasing, new speculators entering the market

The theory of Elliott Waves [Neely, 1988] gives further rules:

Rule 12 (Elliott):
If a peak peak-1 is followed by a valley, and the bottom of the valley-1 is above 62% of the top of the peak; AND, if a subsequent peak-2 following valley-1, exceeds the peak-1, peak-1 is impulsive (5), and "Buy"

Rule 13 (Elliott):
If a peak peak-1 is followed by a valley valley-1, and the bottom hereof is 100% below the top of peak-1, several observations need to be made before a decision on peak-1

7.9 Off-line analysis for learning

This consists in applying the same knowledge-based analysis techniques as in Sections 5, 6, 7 above but to past actual data over some period, and in recording the actual performances achieved if the decisions generated had been executed; the performance evaluations would apply to accumulated profitability during the selected period, percentage of profitable trades, and number of trades.

More specifically, assume that we have recorded, on one hand a set of financial data curves over the same past interval $[T_1, T_2]$, next the parameters Z of the present procedure, and finally the cumulated actual performances according to some performance goal $g([T_1, T_2])(Z)$. These parameters Z are e.g. (see notations in Sections 4, 5, 7 above):

$$Z \triangleq [n_S, n_d, n_i, j, n, k, N, P,]$$

Using the fact that in Prolog, all parameters in Z can be declared as unbound variables, and that PROLOG related unification on Z can then be enabled, this inference will e.g. search for all allowable values of Z, such that, over the training period $[T_1, T_2]$, the cumulated profit g $([T_1, T_2])$ (Z) using the series M.A. (X,P) exceeds a% (percent) AND b% (percent) of the trades generated were profitable, AND there were at most c trades, where a, b, c, are given constants.

The unification will proceed from the learning goal (in pseudo_PROLOG):

```
learning_goal(Z)   →   gt(g([T1, T2])(Z), a);
                       gt(profitable_trade_% (Z), b);
                       lt( trade_count, c).
```

where gt(·, a) stands for $\geq$, and lt(·, a) for $\leq$

A similar use of search applies to the selection of features, e.g. of the proper moving average signals M.A. (X,P) (type of M.A., length N, nature X of the series), to satisfy a joint selection screen on the selected training period. For example, one may search for the (T,U)_tuples of the extension feature, satisfying on this decision basis alone, cumulated profits $g([T_1, T_2)](Z)$ of a % at least, when T,U are defined as in Section 7.

The unification on Z has been carried out in the tool [Pau et al., 1988] on a selective testing basis, especially after major market events. Whereas the potential of this approach could be high, it is still felt delicate to evaluate its results, except in detecting past changes from short-term to medium-term decision horizons in the market. This is by itself no small accomplishment! What is still lacking is a causal analysis for these learned parameter shifts; in other words, there is not yet an objective and less exhaustive way to analyze the reasoning path uncovered from the terminal symbols in V_T to the different trades generated, and vice-versa. The backward alternative paths are still too numerous to be compared, as experience shows, especially when several financial data series are used as in Section 6. Whereas numerical simulations would be adequate to explain the forward paths from symbols to decisions, they just cannot help finding the backward paths.

7.10 Forecasting

Forecasting first requires to fix the series, features, and moving average parameters, to be rolled out into the future.

Next the forecasting horizon must be selected.

Third, the last estimated moving averages and features are mechanistically extrapolated until the end of that forecasting horizon.

Finally, the knowledge base is queried sequentially over time, by using the hypothetical price / volume values instead of the current ones, and the extrapolated moving averages and features.

On this basis, the trade generated, or other types of processing, can be made by selecting hypothetical prices /volumes at selected points in the future.

7.11 Trade generation

This part of the knowledge-based technical analysis consists in generating a trade plan, that is a sequence of trades organized over time, on the basis of current assets and of a trading horizon.

If no forecasting is used, the trading horizon is reduced to the current instant. In that case, the various rules may generate conflicting trades applicable to the same class of assets or liabilities. One approach is to relate the type of trade (Buy / Sell) and its amount, to respectively the sign and value, of the cumulated number of rules, when all single rules recommending a Buy are generating the value +1, and -1 for a sale. The principle can be extended by weighing the rules differently.

If forecasting is used, then the underlying assets and liabilities must be sequentially updated on the basis of executed trades generated by the system according to the procedure above; of course, bounds on the balances of assets and liabilities must then be added, and the planner must minimize transaction costs.

8 Intelligent information screens

8.1 Introduction

Information screens essentially consist in:

i. monitoring a continuous stream of formatted data arriving on asynchronous lines

ii. detecting in this stream specific items of information, specified by information filters, implementing string matching

iii. retrieving said filtered data, and logging them into a user-defined database (running in either the foreground or the background)

iv. making said filtered data available to other user-defined applications, such as spreadsheet, graphic utilities, etc.

v. enabling knowledge-based processing on the filtered data.

Example 1: Tick-by-tick streams

Tick-by-tick streams of share or bond data (prices, year high-low, dividend, yield, earnings, price/earnings, etc.) related to each symbol representing a traded security; the user may want to watch out for e.g.either a specific share, or for high-yield securities [Rizzo et al.,1989]. ■

Example 2: Screens on current accounts

Screens on current accounts in a deposit bank, to watch the flow of transactions; the user may here want to watch out for e.g.account balances falling below a secured credit amount (or zero), or for high transaction counts. ■

Intelligent information screens for financial data thus constitute an especially important class of practical applications of knowledge-based systems; such applications are surveyed in [Pau, 1986] and [Pau et al., 1989].

8.2 Selective object-oriented data acquisition

On operating systems offering multitasking, the data acquisition involves three low-level (assembler) procedures:

- a "*read* " process reading data from the serial port that is awaiting requests from the host; when the port gets a request, the operating system forwards it to the filter, via an operating system message queue
- a "*filter* " process then, if the match condition is met, requests information updates from the network for that selected item, and transmits each message to a "write" process over another message queue
- a "*write* " process puts the selected data into packets in a format compatible with other host based applications, and transmits it to the host or terminals or non-multitasking processors attached to it.

The selective information- selection and retrieval is best defined, together with the user display windowing layout, by an object-oriented language or environment. This language will allow to build (see Chapter 4.5);

- objects which process streams of data that communicate with each other through the object based message system;
- a collection of modular methods,which are messages sent to those objects, and are thus relayed from object to object.

Furthermore, the object-oriented nature is necessary so that each instance of a function or method call can remember the state of its calculations for faster recalculations.

Example 3: The "Chart" object

In most user interface, one frequently used object is "Chart", which draws a window on the display, its axes, and sets scales on each of them. It takes arguments: the first being the data stream object from which it receives its data; the second thru the fifth are the names of the two axes and the corresponding units; the remaining two, which are optional, are names for the chart, one used for display to the user, and the other a unique object name that other objects can use to reference to the data of the "Chart".

The formula used to create a chart of the last or closing price of share XYZ versus the last or closing price of its mother company TUV, would be:

Chart (Close ("XYZ"/"TUV"), "Last price XYZ", 1 , "Last price TUV", 1/4 , "XYZ-TUV price relation", "428").

The syntax in each argument, e.g.Close, is the standard Backus-Naur notation (Chapter 4.2.1). The arguments are those for each function or method.

If the intelligent information screen was to show data from that chart, or allow the user to use the values contained in it as input to another procedure, it could refer to it by the name "XYZ-TUV price relation". ■

Example 4: Simple moving average

Another commonly used object is called M.A. (n) (Simple moving average), which computes the sum of the last n prices and divides that by n (see Chapter 7.7). Often, a technical analyst will overlay moving averages on a chart. If, for example, you wanted to overlay a chart of the n = 14 simple moving average of the last price of "XYZ" on the same chart as Example 3 above, one would add the following formula:

Chart (M.A. (Close (" XYZ"), 14), "Last price XYZ" , 1 , "Day" , 1 , "Moving average (14) XYZ", "429").

■

Typical methods implemented are those of Chapter 7.7, including Gann angles, volume histograms, ratio, spread, moving average convergence/divergence, high/low/close bar charts, time-interval slicing, zoom, etc. An advantage of the object-oriented approach, is that much code is shared between similar methods; for example, a weighted moving average, and a moving average convergence/divergence are subclasses of the moving average class objects. And M.A. is also a subclass of the "sum" object which computes the sum of the last n data elements. The fact that many objects share code, means writing less code, and when you need to add new functionality to a class of objects, you only have to do it in the superclass.

8.3 Knowledge-based information screens

The knowledge-based processing applicable to the results of Section 2 above, depends on the requirements:

- ad hoc queries, for example any open problems for a given client, or what's the status of the specific problem report; this only requires the set-up of appropriate filters;
- timely information, for example staff cannot wait for someone to look up for information; filters are then activated temporarily by a rule of the type:

  IF (time = xxx) THEN (enable filter)

- unstructured queries, if staff cannot access information without assistance; a sequence of rules are then assembled to formulate the queries, the dialogue, and collect user selections for search control;
- detailed analysis, if e.g. management is interested in statistics while support staff requires detailed reports; this is best implemented by a hierarchy of methods linked together (see Section 2 above).

8.4 Knowledge-based filters for financial information screens

Specific examples, related to trading in financial instruments [Pau, 1989a], were already given in Chapter 7.8 for the screening rules mentioned in Sections 1 and 3.

8.5 Information retrieval aspects

In Section 1, it was assumed that the filters implemented an exact string match between templates specified in the information filters, and strings encountered in the stream of incoming data. This exact string match applies e.g. when data are indexed. However, this is not always so, in which case other information retrieval techniques must be used.

One such technique is partial match retrieval, which essentially consists in producing document rankings in the stream of incoming data, to reflect the uncertainty of retrieval. These rankings between document fields operate on similarity measure calculations S, between the goal value specified in the information filter, and each data field in the incoming field; thereafter these fields are ranked by decreasing values of similarity S, and the field with the highest is selected.

In the probabilistic partial match model, the terms in each document field are assumed independent, and no account is made of their within-document frequency counts. The similarity S_d is:

$$S_d = \sum_{\text{All terms (i) in d}} w_i \log \frac{P_1(i)(1-P_2(i)}{P_2(i)(1-P_1(i))}$$

where:

P_1 $\stackrel{\Delta}{=}$ probability that term i occurs in the relevant set of document fields

P_2 $\stackrel{\Delta}{=}$ probability that term i occurs in the non-relevant set of document fields

w_i $\stackrel{\Delta}{=}$ weight (see below)

d $\stackrel{\Delta}{=}$ document field to be ranked

initialized as follows:

$P_1(i)$: equal value for all terms i found in the information filter query, and zero otherwise
$P_2(i)$: can be estimated using the total collection of documents fields

Relevance feedback provides information for more accurate estimation of P_1, as the user may have to adjust his information filter query.

The formula for S_d can be used with all weights w_i =1, or these can be set equal to the so-called tf.idf weights (within-document frequency plus inverse document frequency over all document fields) ([Belkin and Croft, 1987], [Biswas et al., 1987], [Davies, 1986]).

Other techniques usable both for exact or partial match techniques are:

- stopward removal in the incoming data fields
- synonym thesaurus establishing a correspondence between the information filter query string(s), and other equivalent ones.
- neural networks (see Chapter 6)

Many other techniques exist, such as cluster network based matches, structure-based retrieval, knowledge-based retrieval [Biswas et al., 1987], but these require full access to all document fields first, and do not easily meet the operational requirements of intelligent screens.

8.6 Data fusion

Very frequently, the intelligent information screen will have to scan a range of alternative asynchronous lines, each tied up to heterogeneous or physically distributed information servers (or databases) (see Fig. 1).

In such instances, one must add to the "read" process (Section 2), a "scan" process. This "scan" process (above "read") will embody :

- a plan giving a sequence for reading specific lines by the "read" process

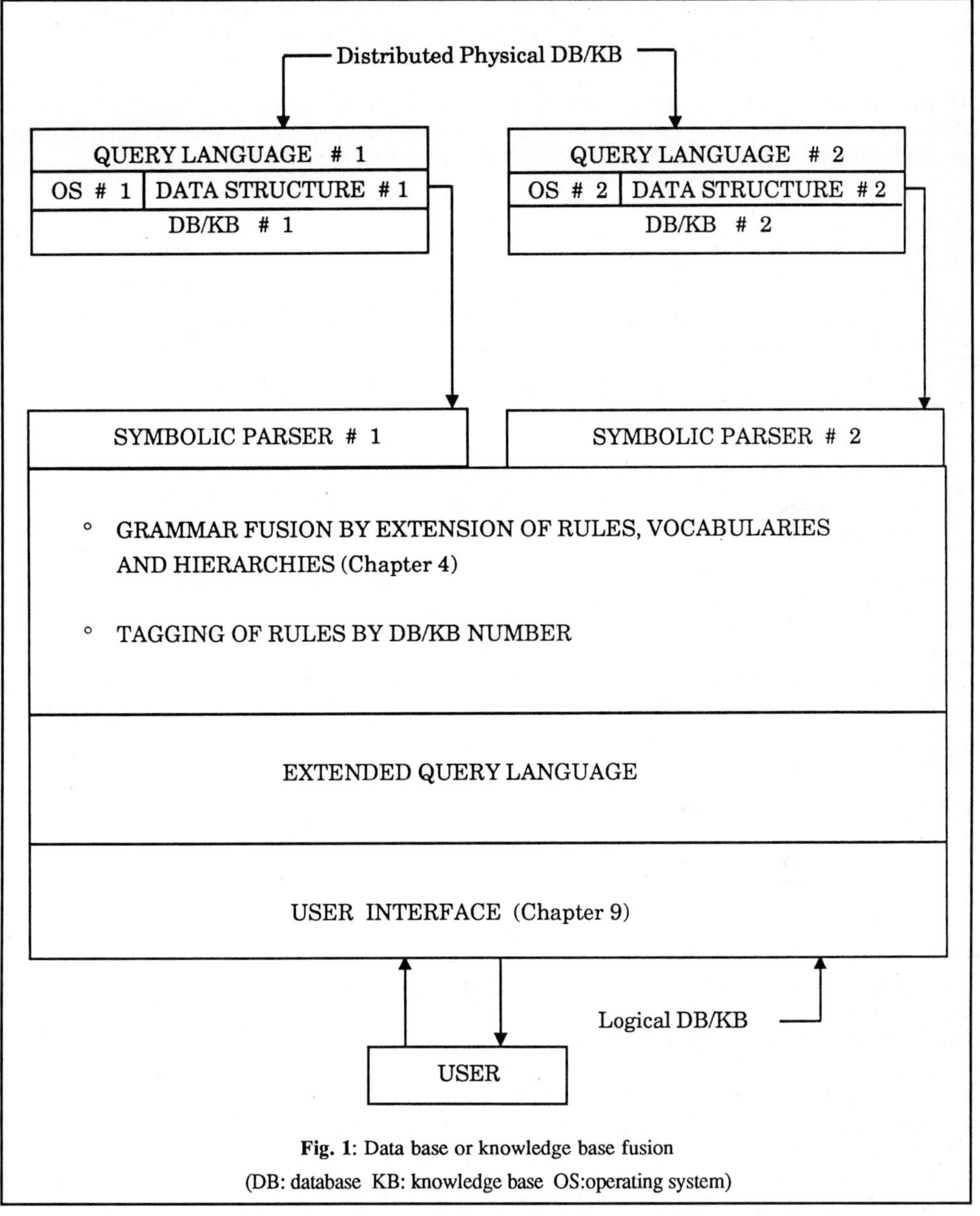

Fig. 1: Data base or knowledge base fusion
(DB: database KB: knowledge base OS:operating system)

- a table of symbolic parsers, which will parse the output of "read", and rewrite it into a common format

- a tagging facility to label each output from "read" by the number or name of the information source

- a pointer specifying whether the symbolic grammars (see Chapters 4.2.2, 9) are used to parse the outputs of the "read" processes, or, on the contrary, to generate the filter query in a data format compatible with that information channel; this enables the filter match to be carried out either on the common data format (by the process "filter") or upfront within the read of each line.

If data fusion is performed, then at the knowledge-based processing level (Section 3), rules must be added to list all attributes known about a given object, and to detect conflicts between different information sources delivering incompatible or contradictory data on the same objects.

8.7 Correlation

When scanning alternative information channels for financial data, it is sometimes relevant to take into account correlation or correlation coefficients between them. This serves a triple purpose:

- adapt the scanning frequency, to avoid to scan too often two highly positive correlated channels, while giving a higher priority to the others

- carry out approximate forecasts on a correlated channel #2, given a reading of the first channel #1 and knowledge of the average correlation amongst #1 and #2

	USA	Japan	UK	FRG	Switzer-land	Swe-den	Den-mark
USA	1	0,94	0,92	-0,45	-0,50	0,26	-0,38
Japan		1	0,90	-0,60	-0,29	0,45	-0,58
UK			1	-0,41	-0,16	0,24	-0,18
FRG				1	0,34	-0,41	0,29
Switzer-land					1	-0,31	0,06
Sweden						1	-0,20
Den-mark							1

Fig. 2: Correlation coefficients between major stock market indices, estimated over 1986--1988

- detect major changes when there is a shift between the continuously updated correlation and its historical value

Example 5: Correlation coefficients between stock markets

Fig. 2 gives the table of correlation coefficients between major national stock market indices. Such values are typically used for portfolio balancing, like in Chapter 11. But it can also serve the three purposes above dealing with intelligent information acquisition at minimum cost or risk. It appears that data most negatively correlated are: USA, Japan, Denmark, Germany and possibly Sweden; these data are the ones requiring the highest scanning frequency. ■

9 Natural language front-ends to economic models

9.1 Introduction

Many users in the business, financial and economic worlds are not trained computer scientists; at best they can handle choice menus, but this limitation excludes to a large extent the flexibility in the selection of goals, of knowledge or of input data which is generally assumed in most knowledge-based systems. For example, none of the 7 sentences from Table 1 could be handled, neither in terms of a form editor, nor for their understanding, by any menu, window or graphical interface.

The most important response to these issues is natural language analysis (NL): within a syntactic and semantic world corresponding to a given language subset, natural languages analysis will analyze an input string of text, assign a meaning to each word, and feed the user dialogue, a knowledge base, or another procedure as a result. One simple NL program listed in Appendix 1.3 can e.g. handle all 7 sentences from Table 1.

In some applications, the same NL techniques will help generate a text, e.g. an explanation for a search, based on the query results. Furthermore, for simple semantic and syntactic structures, a NL system can be set-up as to handle input in several languages, provided the dictionaries or cross-referencing of all words have been established, and the formal languages be included.

Natural language analysis is a highly developed field on its own [Bara, 1984], [Bobrow and Collins, 1975], [Bolc, 1987], [Cercone, 1983]. This short Chapter only serves the purpose through examples to give a simple introduction to the use and design of NL in front-ends to economic or business knowledge-based systems or models.

9.2 Prolog parser for NL front-ends

A simple NL front-end will be built of the following parts:

Test Sequences

1. the monetary mass increases 8 percent with low inflation
2. Fed implements a restrictive monetary policy for lower consumption in households
3. the policy requires more investment after a tight credit
4. a 6 % unemployment with decreasing tendency seen in private sector with a high capacity
5. households work less
6. growth with tight salaries helps government income up 20 billion
7. industry with high growth wishes more savings from households

Table 1: Sentences accepted by a natural language front end

i. a vocabulary for the restricted language which the NL interface should be able to accept; all terms in this vocabulary must be grouped into grammatical classes as defined in ii.; see Appendix 1.3.1 for an example

ii. a formal grammar, expressed e.g.in Backus-Naur form (BNF) (see Chapter 4.2.1); see Appendix 1.3.2 for an example which is here a definite clause grammar (DCG) (see Section 3); such a grammar should, within the context of a limited application, describe all allowed sentences involving the vocabulary defined in i

iii. a procedure rewriting the grammar ii. into e.g. Prolog clauses, for processing by the parser iv. (see Section 4)

iv. a parser, which inputs and decomposes any sentence or text from the language, into a parsing tree with each term labeled by its grammatical class, and the sentence structure characterized by tree relations between the later; see Appendix 1.3.3 for an example written in Prolog, besides Section 5 and Chapter 4.2.2 for details

v. a configuration manager, which will trigger, activate or configure the back-end system (knowledge-based system, economic model), according to the results of iv. (see Section 6)

Because Prolog provides a convenient notation for ii. and iv., only NL environments in that language are considered here, although of course similar or better systems can be implemented in LISP etc.

9.3 Definite clause grammar in Prolog

Definite clause grammars (DCG) are an extension of the well-known context-free grammars (see Chapter 4.2.3). A grammar rule in Prolog takes the general form:

head --> body.

meaning "a possible form for head is body" (about Prolog see Chapter 4.4). Both body and head are sequences of one or more atoms linked by the standard Prolog conjunction operator ',' (comma).

Definite clause grammars extend context -free grammars in the following ways:

- a non-terminal symbol may be any Prolog term (other than a variable or integer)
- a terminal symbol may be any Prolog term. To distinguish terminals from non-terminals, a sequence of one or more terminal symbols is written within a grammar rule as a Prolog list. An empty sequence is written as the empty list ' [] '. If the terminal symbols are ASCII character codes, such lists can be written (as elsewhere) as strings. An empty sequence is written as the empty list ('[] ' or ' "" ')
- extra conditions, in the form of Prolog procedure calls, may be included in the right-hand side of a grammar rule. Such procedure calls are written enclosed in curly brackets '{ ' and ' } '
- the left-hand side of a grammar rule consists of a non-terminal, optionally followed by a sequence of terminals (again written as a Prolog list)
- alternatives may be stated explicitly in the right-hand side of a grammar rule, using the disjunction operator ' ; ' (semi-colon) as in Prolog; the disjunction operator can also be written as ' | ' (vertical-bar)
- the cut symbol ' ! ' (exclamation point, see Chapter 4.4.11) may be included in the right-hand side of a grammar rule, as in a Prolog clause. The cut symbol does not need to be enclosed in curly brackets. The conditional arrow '-->' can also be used in grammar rules without the curly brackets

9.4 Translation of DCG grammar rules into Prolog clauses

Each DCG grammar rule must be translated into a Prolog clause for parsing; the principle here is that the grammar rule takes an input list of symbols for preliminary analysis, while producing the remaining or enlarged list as output for further analysis. The translation, therefore, adds input and output lists.

For example, the DCG grammar rule:

```
p (X) --> q (X)
```

is translated into:

```
p (X,SO,S) : - q (X,SO,S).
```

Here, X, S, SO must be interpreted as follows:

- SO is the complete input string
- X is the left-hand string to be matched, and which is variable , in SO
- S is the remaining string to the right of X in SO.

If there is more than one non-terminal symbol from the DCG on the right-hand side of the grammar rule, as in:

```
p (X,Y) --> q (X), r (X,Y), s (Y).
```

the corresponding input and output arguments are identified in Prolog:

[industry, with, high, growth, wishes, more, savings, from, households]

```
sentence
          noun_phrase
                    noun
                              industry
          rest_phrase
                    prep_phrase
                              relate
                                        with
                              noun_phrase
                                        adjective
                                                  high
                                        noun
                                                  growth
                    verb_phrase
                              verbg
                                        verb
                                                  wishes
                              prep_phrase
                                        preposition
                                                  more
                                        noun_phrase
                                                  noun
                                                            savings
                              relate
                                        from
                              noun_phrase
                                        noun
                                                  households
```

Table 2: Parsing tree to sentence 7 in Table 1

```
p (X,Y,SO,S): -
        q  (X,SO,S1),
        r  (X,Y,S1,S2),
        s  (Y,S2,S).
```

where:

- SO is the full input string
- S1 is the full string in the right clause, aligned with the right end of SO

DCG terminals are translated by built-in predicates, and explicit procedure calls, the cut, and disjunction translate into themselves; e.g.:

```
p (X) --> {integer (X), X > O}, q (X).
```

translates to:

```
p (X,SO,S): - integer (X), X > O, q (X,S1,S), SO = [ X I S1].
```

9.5 DCG parser

Parsers will operate by unification, resulting in a top-down, bottom-up, or mixed inference analysis and generation of the parsing tree (see Chapter 4.2.2). Appendix 1.3.3 gives a very simple top-down parser which instantiates the top grammar predicate "sentence" of the variable input sentence (X) to prove if it meets or not that goal. A parsing tree corresponding to Table 1 is shown in Table 2.

Much more sophisticated parsers are described in [Bolc, 1987].

9.6 Reasoning from NL analysis

Several utilizations can be made of the output of a NL analysis.

9.6.1 Form input

The terms identified as terminals in the original grammar (e.g. nouns, numerical values, adjectives...) can feed attribute slots or data input to knowledge-based or modeling systems.

9.6.2 Validation of the input

Because the parser essentially verifies the hypothesis of whether the input sentence conforms or not with the original grammar and vocabulary, NL analysis can serve validate form or text inputs for compliance. One such example is the NL analysis of SWIFT money transfer wires, to check for completeness and validate the individual non-terminals for coherence and authorizations (see Chapter 2.6).

9.6.3 Modeling from NL analysis

The idea is to enhance the DCG grammar as to distinguish causal relations expressed by verbs (e.g. "causes", "implies", "induces", "gives", "have") or suitable grammatical expressions rendering causality ("is the result of", "is due to"). The output of the parser is then, for each sentence or grammatical group with a causal kernel (verb, grammatical expression), a list of objects which are causal factors and a list of objects which are causal endogenous results.

The causal factors can be further split between exogenous variables, if they have themselves no causal factors, or instrument variables.

The result of this general and highly powerful approach, is to allow to infer the structure of any causal model (e.g.input-output or control model) from the NL processing of verbal/descriptive texts describing the underlying economic/business reasoning (policy statements, verbal economic analyses, press articles, speeches, position papers [Marcus, 1980]).

The result of this process is a semantic net (see Chapter 3.4) showing causal relations between factors, all of which are terminal symbols of the original grammar. One specific economic reasoning can then be displayed as a path in the graph, and it shows very clearly distributed feedback effects.

Furthermore, based on a policy expressed verbally or in text form, one can then retrieve time series of regression variables (causality factors) and endogenous variables, as selected by the NL analysis, to produce a customized regression equation for forecasting or integration purposes (see Fig. 1).

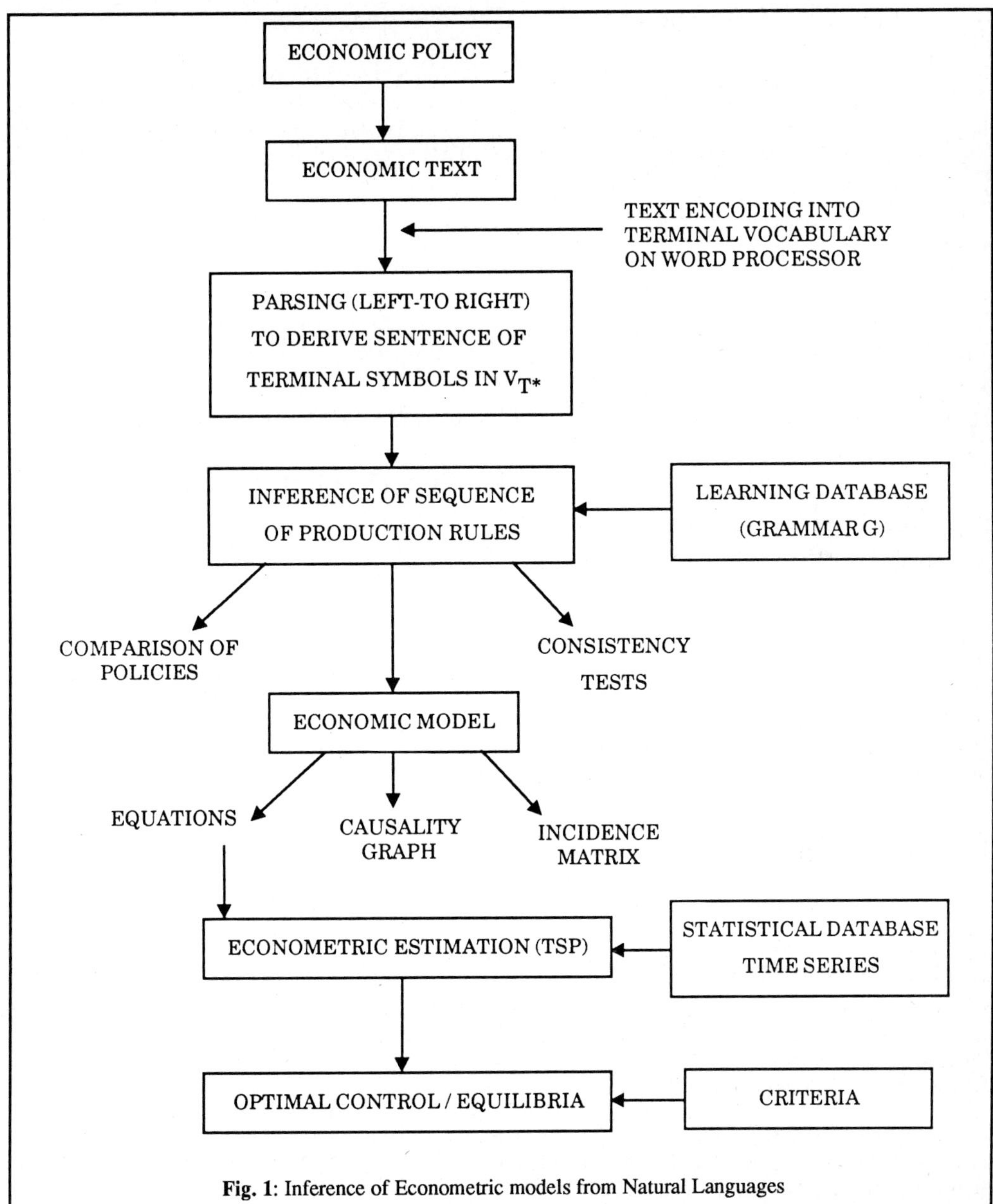

Fig. 1: Inference of Econometric models from Natural Languages

9.6.4. Generation of temporal reasoning from NL analysis

As highlighted in Chapter 3.8.3, time-interval reasoning involves selecting actions and properties, with a scheduler. Whereas temporal logic by itself will generally be satisfied, text descriptions of the temporal reasoning may help reduce the combinatorial search complexity hereof, and also to refine the way in which temporal relations are defined.

10 Trade selection with uncertain reasoning on technical indicators

10.1 Introduction

Up to this point in this volume, it has always been assumed that knowledge can be expressed as a collection of symbolic structures in a formal language, with formal mechanisms for deriving new knowledge from the available one. This Chapter provides one important extension to this view, by highlighting that said structures may have *attributes* , qualifying the validity resp. applicability of a given structure in given situations. More precisely, uncertainty is one such important attribute especially in reasoning systems coping with economic, financial and business problems.

In general, problem-solvers designed for real world tasks will face uncertainty at various levels in the solution process, and will therefore need several uncertainty management criteria and methods.

In Chapters 1.1, 3 and 5, attention was focussed to problem-solving uncertainty: its source was identified in the simultaneous availability of different symbolic structures apparently relevant to the current problem-solving state, without a priori sufficient selection criteria to discard all alternative structures but one, i.e. the most useful for the task at hand. Such uncertainty surfaces in different ways, depending on the representation formalism (or mix-up of formalisms) used. In modular representation languages (rules, see Chapter 3.6, logic, see Chapter 3.5), in which each symbolic structure captures a piece of domain knowledge, problem-solving uncertainty arises as an insufficiency in control knowledge, whereby a list of candidates cannot be sufficiently pruned, but must be dealt with by delaying commitment and search (see Chapter 5). Depending on the structure of the domain, the uncertainty problem can be relieved by including further knowledge (e.g. metarules, modularization in the knowledge base), by exploiting the domain dependency structures showing how some knowledge depends on other knowledge (see Chapter 5.10), by supporting search with heuristic measures for hinting at the most promising search direction (heuristic search, Chapter 5.11), or in the worst case by simply relying on blind search over all possible candidates (see Chapter 5.8 and 5.9). Problem-solving uncertainty is a sort of *global* uncertainty about the problem to be solved, and the most suited problem-solving strategies.

A different kind of uncertainty reflects the uncertainty in the problem environment "per se", and is basically related to a lack of definite knowledge about the truth value of a symbolic structure, in that different knowledge structures support one or the other truth value with varying strength. In knowledge-based problem-solving, such uncertainty arises in roughly the following three broad classes, whereby appropriate knowledge representation languages must be devised (and partly have been) to deal with each class [Bonissone and Tong, 1985], [Halim, 1986]:

i. random and/or statistic phenomena, with probability theory as the dominating representation formalism. This uncertainty is intrinsic in the environment, i.e. it has the property that further knowledge is not helpful in reducing it. In many cases, assumptions about the laws governing these phenomena are made, in order to make the problem computationally tractable

ii. subjective belief judgements, assessing the confidence in a piece of knowledge, not based on repeated experiments, but mostly based on an informal account of past experiences. Observed causalities in expert behavior have often this form, whereby the expert does not develop a complete formal model accounting for its reasoning, but a guess for weak causalities (i.e. causalities in which the consequence does not always follow from the premises). Such a situation arises because of the complexity of the problem domain, of bounded rationality, or of insufficient modeling effort and theoretical background

iii. imprecise assessment of the value of any measurable property, whereby uncertainty arises when such assessment must be translated into a more precise language for the purposes of further computation and fusion with other knowledge, causing uncertainty to compensate for increase in granularity (imprecision - uncertainty trade-off). Think of the assertion "a period of high inflation is expected" (as excerpted from a news item or speeches of economic authorities) to be matched with a rule premise "if expected inflation is 10% or higher then ..."

Uncertainty of type i. above is represented according to the axioms of probability theory; for uncertainty of type ii. several formalisms are available, most notably Bayesian inference [Duda et al., 1981], certainty factors [Shortliffe, 1976], fuzzy reasoning [Klir and Folger, 1988], [Zadeh, 1978], and the Dempster-Shafer theory [Shafer, 1976], which is the subject of this Chapter; finally, uncertainty of type iii. is mostly dealt with using formalisms associating "distributions" of scale values to linguistic labels, together with switching mechanisms among these two representations, thus ensuring internal computability and a coherent, purely linguistic external user interface.

Common to all uncertainties of type i to iii is that they affect specific pieces of knowledge, as well as knowledge derivable directly or indirectly from them. Uncertainty is thus measured *locally* to each affected proposition, and is independent of problem-solving uncertainty recalled at the beginning of this Section. Although no one representation of local uncertainty is suited to all types i.-iii. (hence the number of formalisms mentioned), common features are desirable to all candidate representation formalisms, such as rules for assessing the uncertainty of the knowledge derived from uncertain premises (propagation), for fusing uncertainty from different sources pertaining the same structure, for detecting or dealing with contradictory uncertainty assignments. Note, finally, that purely qualitative methods of uncertainty, not relying on a uniform explicit or implicit numeric translation have been proposed [Cohen, 1985]. Propagation, fusion and contradiction recovery in such methods are handled according to problem specific rules.

This Chapter is narrowly focussed on one formalism, Dempster-Shafer theory (see Sections 2 and 3 below), and on one application of it, fusion of evidence from different sources, which is of great importance to many economic and financial knowledge-based systems. The discussed application is trade selection in the short term, and more specifically the translation of disparate market evidence about a restricted set of securities into a measure of credibility of trade success. Key features of Dempster-Shafer theory application to this domain are its capabilities of accounting for partly contradictory evidence, of smooth transition from low-level numeric estimates to high-level logic statements, and of interval-based representation of uncertainty, which makes this theory more readily usable by domain experts.

10.2 The theory of Dempster-Shafer

In this section we present the basic concepts of the theory of Dempster, as extended by Shafer [Shafer, 1976] to the representation of uncertain beliefs. In this context, a belief is a proposition about the problem domain. Dempster-Shafer approach has triggered a wide development of related methods for the representation of uncertainty, mostly in rule-based expert systems [Quinlan, 1983], [Garvey et al., 1981].

10.2.1 Basic probability assignment

Let Θ represent the set of all elementary propositions in the domain. Θ is then called the *frame of discernment* (it corresponds to the universe set in classical probability theory). In the following sections, we assume that elements in the frame of discernment be mutually exclusive and exhaustive, i.e. they should form a partition of the domain of discourse (it is up to the designer to select the appropriate level of granularity). Any proposition about the problem domain can then be expressed as a subset of the frame of discernment, while union, intersection, inclusion and complementation operations on propositions generate other propositions.

Dempster's theory enables *sources of evidence* to express confidence about one proposition (a subset), without committing to support other propositions. Such support is defined as a function conventionally denoted with m, associating to each element of the power set of Θ, a number m(.), satisfying the following constraints:

i. $m(\varnothing) = 0$

ii. $m(A_i) \geq 0 \ \forall A_i$

iii. $\sum_{\Theta \supseteq A_i} m(A_i) = 1$

where the first axiom means that no confidence can be attributed to the empty set, and the last that the whole of one's confidence (normalized to 1) must go to propositions in the power set of the frame of discernment. Any so defined function is called a *basic probability assignment* over the frame of discernment. Form the above conditions, it immediately follows:

$$m(A_i) \in [0, 1]$$

for each A_i (but the empty set). $m(A_i)$ represents the degree of confidence in propositions, as resulting from one piece of evidence. If A_i is not an elementary proposition, then the confidence $m(A_i)$ is to be understood as being attributed to the propositions in the set as a whole, with no specification of how it should affect subsets or elements of A_i. One can imagine $m(A_i)$ as a mass free to move inside A_i, but constrained not to get out of it [Shafer, 1976].

A basic probability assignment on a frame of discernment may *not* be a probability over the same set, since from axioms i.-iii. above it does *not* necessarily follow that:

$$m(Aj),\ A_j = A_i \cup A_k,\ A_i \cap A_k = \emptyset, \text{ is equal to } m(A_i) + m(A_k)$$

although any probability is obviously an allowable basic probability assignment. Therefore, Dempster's theory is more general than probability theory, in that the union axiom is dropped.

An important consequence of this generalization is the capability of expressing ignorance, which is the lack of belief in one proposition, and hence lack of commitment. In the Bayesian approach, there is no clean way to express ignorance (knowledge that every event is equiprobable is even a valuable piece of knowledge, quite distant from ignorance). Assume a frame of discernment consisting of just proposition A and its negation ¬A. If a probability P(A) is assigned to A, then from the union axiom it follows that P(¬A) + P(A) = 1, i.e. one's commitment is automatically assigned to ¬A as well. In Dempster's framework, the assignment m(¬A) is independent from the assignment m(A), the only constraint being:

$$m(A) + m(\neg A) + m(\Theta) = 1$$

where m(Θ) can be readily interpreted as the confidence which cannot be attributed to A or to ¬A, i.e. non committed confidence. This would corresponds in the probability language to [Halim, 1986]:

$$P(A) + P(\neg A) + P(\text{don't know whether A or } \neg A) = 1$$

which is unfortunately not consistent with the definition of probability. On the contrary, conventional probability can be recovered from the Dempster's framework in this example by imposing $m(\Theta) = 0$.

10.2.2 Credibility belief and plausibility

In the previous section it was explained how a source of evidence assigns confidence to the set of relevant domain propositions. From the basic probability assignment two subjectively justified measures of belief in propositions can be derived, called credibility belief (Bel, or credibility, Cr) and plausibility (Pl):

$$Bel(A_i) = \sum_{A_i \supseteq A_j} m(A_j)$$

$$Pl(A_i) = \sum_{A_i \cap A_j \neq \emptyset} m(A_j)$$

As it is readily seen from the definitions, Bel is the sum of all confidence values attributed either to A_i or to its subsets, and therefore directly supporting A_i. Pl is the sum over all confidence values which are not in conflict with A_i, i.e. which must not, but could support A_i. Since the definition of plausibility includes, but is not limited to, all elements in Bel's definition, it follows:

$$Bel(A) \leq Pl(A)$$

It is further easily seen from the definitions that:

$$Pl(A) = 1 - Bel(\neg A)$$

$$Bel(A) = 1 - Pl(\neg A)$$

i.e. the plausibility Pl of a proposition is directly related to the credibility Bel of its negation. The following limit cases give a feeling for the meaning of Bel and Pl associated to a proposition:

- $Bel(A) = 0$ $Pl(A) = 0$ proposition is false (i.e. $\neg A$ is true)
- $Bel(A) = 0$ $Pl(A) = 1$ ignorance (no belief commitment to A or $\neg A$)
- $Bel(A) = 1$ $Pl(A) = 1$ proposition is true (i.e. $\neg A$ is false)
- $Bel(A) > 0$ $Pl(A) = 1$ some support for A, no support for $\neg A$
- $Bel(A) > 0$ $Pl(A) < 1$ support for A and $\neg A$ (partly conflicting evidence)
- $Bel(A) = Pl(A)$ equiprobability of A and $\neg A$

Finally, it can be shown that:

$$Bel(A) \leq P(A) \leq Pl(A)$$

i.e. Bel and Pl resp. lower- and upper-bound the probability for that event, and therefore define an interval-based probability representation. For those cases in which enough information is available, Dempster's theory reduces to conventional probability. The difference:

$$U = Pl(A) - Bel(A) = Pl(\neg A) - Bel(\neg A)$$

is a measure of *ignorance* , or lack of resolution in the evidence, in the sense that it is the amount of confidence for which it cannot be decided whether is affects A or $\neg A$. As it is to be expected, if no ignorance affects the domain, the method simplifies to Bayesian uncertainty. A special case in which no ignorance can affect a proposition A is whenever A is a single element of the frame of discernment, rather than a subset of it. Then plausibility and belief have the same value, and U is zero.

10.3 Pooling evidence

Sections 2.1 and 2.2 showed how evidence is translated into credibility beliefs and plausibilities. However, uncertain reasoning would be impossible without a method for combining uncertainty from different sources. Dempster's rule of combination is a formula whereby probability assignments from *independent* sources of evidence affecting the same frame of discernment Θ can be combined (pooled). Let m_1 and m_2 be two such probability assignments to Θ. Then the result of combining these assignments is:

$$m_1 \oplus m_2(C_i) = \frac{1}{1-k} \sum_{A_j \cap B_k = C_i} m(A_j)m(B_k)$$

where A_j and B_k are subsets of Θ for which the first resp. second assignments have a non-zero confidence value. k is a measure of conflict among the pooled evidences, i.e. the confidence assigned to the empty set by disjunct A_j, B_k:

$$k = \sum_{A_j \cap B_k = \emptyset} m(A_j)m(B_k)$$

Such contradicting evidence is redistributed in proportion to the other evidence; should this not be the case, then the assignment resulting from Dempster's rule of combination would not satisfy axiom i. in Section 2.1 above.

For the following application, a slight modification to the above formula is needed. In fact, in many applications, not all evidence can be considered of the same quality, and therefore one wants to control the weight of each evidence source in the result of the combination. This can be easily achieved, in that part of the confidence in the lower quality evidence is proportionally shifted from propositions with confidence assigned to them, to the frame of discernment Θ itself:

$$m_1'(A_i) = \partial\, m_1(A_i)$$
$$m_1'(A_j) = \partial\, m_1(A_j)$$
$$\vdots$$
$$m_1'(\Theta) = 1 - \partial(1 - m(\Theta))$$

Since confidence assigned to Θ is neutral with respect to the composition rule, the overall effect is a reduction in the weight for the less reliable evidence ($\partial < 1$), or an increase for the comparatively more reliable inference ($\partial > 1$).

10.4 Application: pooling evidence about trading

Consider a generic trading system. In the present section we restrict our attention to trading decisions over the short/medium term using a restricted set of financial instruments and commodities, as usually done by professional traders.

Let's first define the frame of discernment Θ, including, for each security types in the trader's portfolio, two elementary propositions, of which one is bullish (e.g. "increment long position in security s"), and the other bearish (e.g. "increment short position in s"). To simplify the problem, we do not include in the frame of discernment propositions supporting more complex financial operations, such as hedging, options and futures strategies, etc., although this could in principle be done.

Consider the sources of information required for the trading decisions as a pool of computerized experts (technically: demons), each one watching for some relevant technical, macroeconomic or political event. Hereinafter, we'll call one such expert E_i. A possible list of events to be watched for investment decisions includes:

Technical indicators (see Chapter 7):

- stock (or portfolio) index
- blue chips index
- short term moving average of the stock (portfolio) index
- medium term moving average (weighted or not)
- one short term oscillator
- one medium term oscillator
- etc.

Timing of actions:

- special trading days
- major events (public elections, etc.)
- beginning of a trend
- inversion of a trend

Macroeconomics:

- trade balance
- interest rate
- currency rate
- employment
- industrial production
- capacity utilization

Policy

- elections and elections results
- international meetings
- international instabilities
- trade restrictions

As soon as one such event is noticed, each involved expert E_i inputs to the procedure a basic probability assignment mi(.) on the frame of discernment, i.e. probabilities to each of the trading positions. Dempster's framework enables E_i to commit confidence to just the relevant trading positions, assigning the remaining confidence to the frame of discernment itself.

As an example of pooling evidence about trading, assume the data inputs taken into account by the trading program to involve two experts:

- a price curve parser (Chapter 7), called E_1
- a natural language understanding system, called E_2, to be viewed as an intelligent data channel about natural language information sources (Chapter 9)

Dempster's rule of combination being commutative and associative, extension of the following reasoning to more than two knowledge sources is straightforward, since any number of evidence bodies can be pooled iteratively, provided they are (nearly) independent for the purposes at hand.

Let the frame of discernment Θ be defined as specified at the beginning of this Section, i.e. a collection of proposition of the kind "increment long position on s", "increment short position on s", one pair for each security, whereby it is assumed that these propositions are incompatible the one with the other, i.e. that just one trade is allowed. This could be justified by observing that in the short term, intraday trading, it is important to select the next operation which affects the most critical position in the portfolio.

Assume that the first expert, attached to a price schedule, detects in the market the completion of a reversal head and shoulders, leading to the following basic probability assignment on Θ:

m_1("increment short position in s") = 0.70
m_1($\neg$"increment long position in s") = 0.20
$m_1(\Theta)$ = 0.10

The proposition $\neg$"increment long position in s" is not elementary, but can be represented as the set complementation of "increment long position in s". The above value 0.20 is assigned to that set, without commitment about which specific element in it should receive the weight. The following structure of beliefs/plausibilities results from the above assignment:

Bel("increment short position in s") = 0.70
Pl("increment short position in s") = 1.00

Bel("increment long position in s") = 0

Pl("increment long position in s") = 0.10

Such an assignment can typically be estimated by simulation over past data, or interviews with trading experts, as well as through an assessment of the technical conditions under which the observed pattern took place, such as volume, time duration of the pattern, etc. Note the low plausibility of the proposition "increment long position in s", which makes that decision a very "risky" one.

Assume further that the parsed language sentence from a wire service monitored by E_2 is a statement about an increase in the interest rate. Let the resulting probability assignment on the investor's portfolio be:

m_2("increment short position in REIT") = 0.6
m_2("increment short position in all securities") = 0.3
$m_2(\Theta)$ = 0.1

where "increment short position in REIT (REIT: real estate investment trust)", as well as "increment short position in all securities" are defined in the obvious fashion, as a disjunction of elementary propositions about the individual securities x. As opposed to the previous indicator, such a probability assignment can be dynamically determined as the result of an upstream application of Dempster-Shafer theory, analyzing evidences supporting the hypothesis of an upturn in the interest rates, and pooling them into one final assessment about the credibility of the reported news item. Thereafter, a propagation rule, also affected with uncertainty, will capture the effects of an actual increase in the interest rates upon the specific classes of securities in the client's portfolio. Rule propagation under Dempster-Shafer theory is discussed for example by [Lowrance and Garvey, 1986], [Chatalic et al., 1987], [Provan, 1989].

Now the Dempster's rule can be used to pool the evidence available from the two sources (Section 3). The result of this pooling obviously depends on whether security s is a REIT, or not. If security s is a REIT, it is easy to see that the two evidences are perfectly compatible. The weight 0 is assigned to the empty set (noted by k in Section 3 above, and representing a conflict between two evidences). As a result of such a compatibility, the credibility belief and plausibility of the proposition "increment short position in s" are not changed.

In the case where s is not a REIT, the new basic probability assignment is computed as follows:

k = m_1("increment short position in s") *
m_2("increment short position in REIT") = 0.42
m("increment short position in s") =
m_1("increment short position is s") *
(m_2("increment short position in all securities") +
$m_2(\Theta)$) $(1 - k)^{-1}$ = 0.483
m(¬"increment long position in s") =
m_1(¬"increment long position in s") * $m_2(\Theta)$ $(1 - k)^{-1}$ = 0.03
m("increment short position in REIT") =
m_2("increment short position in REIT") *
(m_1(¬"increment long position in s") +
$m_1(\Theta)$) $(1 - k)^{-1}$ = 0.310
m("increment short position in all securities") =
m_2("increment short position in all securities") *
(m_1(¬"increment long position in s") +
$m_1(\Theta)$) $(1 - k)^{-1}$ = 0.155

with the following resulting belief and plausibility values of the proposition "increment short position in s":

Bel("increment short position in s") = 0.483
Pl("increment short position in s") = 0.685

Both the belief and credibility are reduced in the pooled assignment m(.), because the evidence represented by m_2 tends to support the view that other securities should be sold, specifically the REITs, thus partly contradicting m_1.

Finally, consider the new basic probability assignment:

m_1'("increment long position in s") = 0.7
m_1'(¬"increment long position in s") = 0.2
$m_1'(\Theta)$ = 0.1

replacing the previous m_1. m_1' and m_2 are highly conflicting evidences, as the confidence assigned to the empty set is about 60%, as the reader may easily check. While in most AI applications such conflicting evidence would be discarded, this should not in general be the case in financial applications. In the above example, conflict results from rating a security on the long side during a period of bearish market evidence. Although to many investors such conflicting evidence could be sufficient to motivate a conservative attitude, there are still cases in which such "risky" investments are carried out.

Near independence can be assumed for short term trading among most of the evidences listed above, such as short term vs. medium term indicators, trend indicators vs. oscillators, time evidence vs. other indicators, and therefore they can all be added as further knowledge sources to the above analysis. Corrections must however be provided for some dependencies (e.g. short term exchange rates and official disclosure of inflation/employment data).

At each time instant, trading propositions with assigned beliefs can be queued. Dempster' framework makes it possible to use at least three queuing criteria:

- by credibility: trades with the highest credibility (success) belief are scheduled highest
- by plausibility: trades with the lowest failure belief are scheduled highest
- by risk: trades whose ignorance measure U is lowest are scheduled highest

11 Currency risk management

11.1 Introduction: risk planning over time

We have seen in Chapter 10 methodologies whereby to represent uncertainty and manipulate uncertainty-affected propositions. One particular class of uncertainty is the likelihood of the loss (or gain) of an asset or of return on it, which in a generic way can be one definition of "risk". In general terms, insurance of property and financial assets is the most common way whereby this risk can be limited, and possible losses recouped. However, in most cases, such insurance will have a cost whereby the risk can be protected over a time span; the notion of "premium" corresponds to the payment of the cost of this insurance over a specified time interval.

One basic approach to risk management is to analyse the factors and the probabilities involved. The mortgage loan credit granting system introduced in Chapter 1.4 exemplifies this approach. After that, meaning after the risk has been taken, the remaining approach is to allocate available resources in view of minimizing the likelihood for loss. This corresponds to the role assumed by insurance companies, credit rating agencies, but also commercial enterprises committed to deliver a good/service at a fixed price in the future. To exemplify this last risk allocation approach, we will in this Chapter 11 present a knowledge-based technique addressing this last type of risk management. Of course, this methodology could be extended to the other two main classes of such activity.

Specifically, this Chapter deals with the issue of how to combine, in a knowledge-based way, the currency exposure of an investor or of a company, in view of a portfolio of N assets and liabilities in two currencies. The largest risk are a devaluation, and currency rate fluctuations. This technique consists in several steps:

- i. a single period model, which does not take into account the time profile of the exposure to the two currencies
- ii. a multi-period model, extending i.
- iii. a risk management procedure, or allocation procedure, for the N assets and liabilities, which will refine ii., and thus update i.

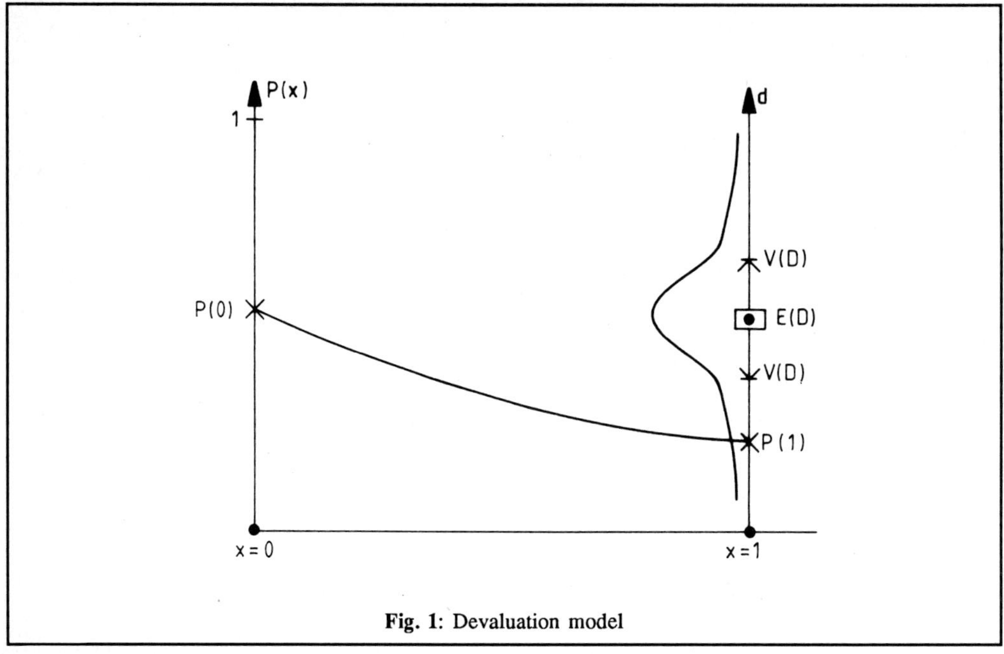

Fig. 1: Devaluation model

In Steps i. and ii. the exposure for each asset or liability i = 1, ..., N is the sum of commercial, financial and currency futures transactions, represented by their flows of payments over time.

11.2 Single period model

The assumed quantities are (Fig. 1):

x:	stochastic variable for a devaluation happening, equal to 0 or 1
P(x):	probability for a devaluation of the reference currency [0] versus currency [1]
d:	size of the devaluation, as a fraction of the unit of reference currency [0]
E(D):	expected size of d
V(D):	variance of d
I(0), I(1):	market interest rates in currencies [0], [1]
F:	futures premium in currency [0], as a fraction of the normal exchange rate of [1] vs [0]
p_t:	currency rate for [1] in currency [0] at time t

For the assets and liabilities i = 1, ..., N (Fig. 2):

R_i:	total net profit (or expense) from exposure i, expressed in currency [0]

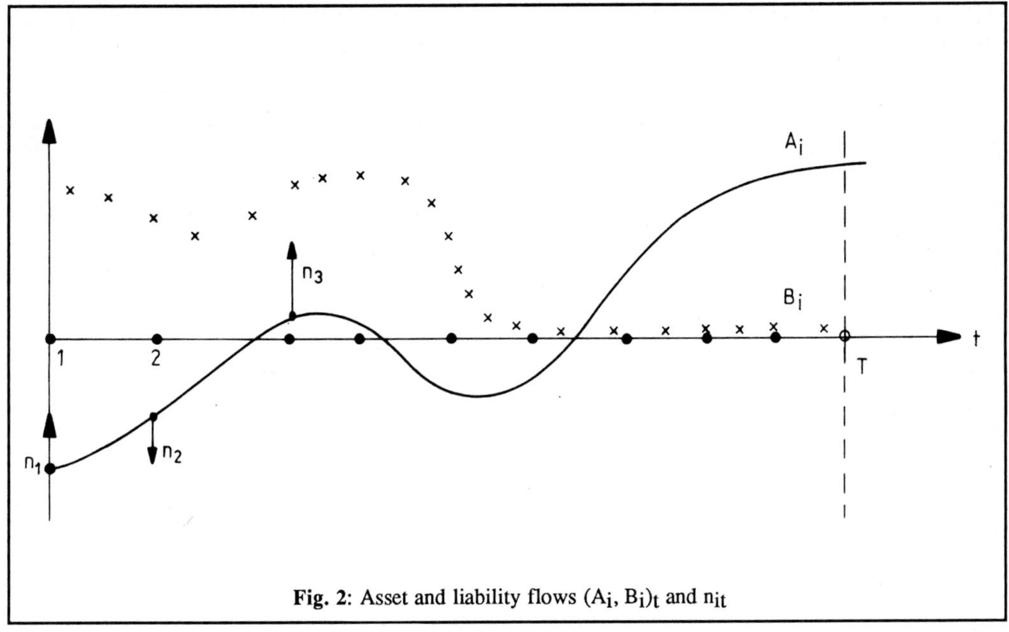

Fig. 2: Asset and liability flows $(A_i, B_i)_t$ and n_{it}

A_i: expected net profit (or expense) from exposure i, without devaluation

n_i: random deviation of A_i, with mean zero, and variance V_i, without devaluation, as related to the investment itself

B_i: net exposure i subject to devaluation, and counted as a devaluation profit,

which are then related as follows:

$$R_i = A_i + n_i + B_i \cdot x \cdot d$$

If n_i, d are independent random variables, the expected value of R_i becomes:

$$E(R_i) = A_i + B_i \cdot [\, P(1) \cdot E(D) \,]$$

and its variance:

$$V(R_i) = V_i + B_i^2 \cdot P(1) \, [\, (E(D))^2 \, (1 - P(1)) + V(D) \,]$$

The currency futures premium between currencies can be estimated by:

$$F_{1/0} = \frac{I(1) - I(0)}{1 + I(0)} = \frac{p_{(1)}}{p_{(0)}} - 1$$

according to classical interest rate equilibrium theory, which equates in currency [0] the currency [0] amount after one period [1 + I(0)], with the equivalent amount [1 + I(1)] invested in currency

[1] (following currency conversions to and from it). The formula above of course applies to each time period.

11.3 Multi-period model

First, we replace (A_i, B_i) and R_i by the corresponding flows of income over time, by adding the time index t. Over a planning horizon T, the cumulated net profit, expressed in currency [0] becomes:

$$R = \sum_{t=1,T} \sum_{i=1,N} R_{it}$$

resulting in a cumulated profit having an expected value of:

$$E(R) = \left(\sum_{t=1,T} \sum_{i=1,N} A_{it} \right) + \left(\sum_{t=1,T} \sum_{i=1,N} \left[P(1)_t \, E(D)_t \right] B_{it} \right)$$

The variance V(R) is, however, quite complicated to calculate, and even worse to estimate, as it will depend on the covariances between n_i at different periods of time. The covariances cannot be estimated.

11.4 Knowledge-based risk management

Carrying out an allocation procedure for the N assets over the time horizon T, will involve a search amongst all possible values of the flows (A_{it}, B_{it}) to determine an efficient portfolio, which will essentially maximize E(R) while minimizing V(R), or maximize a linear combination hereof such as:

$$H = a - E\,(R) - V\,(R)$$

The most efficient tools to this end are:

i. to manipulate the relative contract, settlement and payment dates

ii. to generate futures trades, to hedge the variances $V(R_i)$ when they get too large in some periods for some assets i.

Such dispositions must use additional explicit facts about them, especially the dates:

$0(A_i/B_i)$: decision date

$S(A_i/B_i)$: settlement date

$D(A_i/B_i)$: delivery date

(where 0, S, D are the dates where the flows A_{it} or B_{it} are decided), and explicit knowledge about legal or other dispositions governing such transactions or futures trades. Such knowledge can be formulated as production rules:

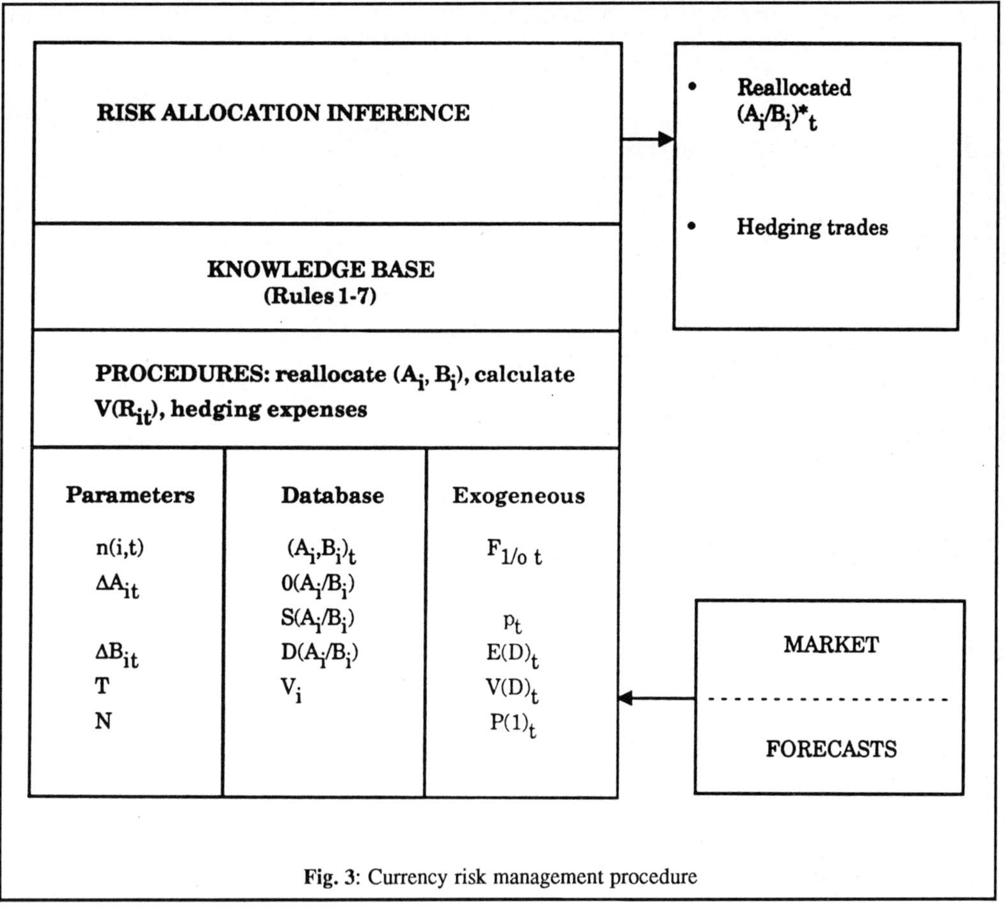

Fig. 3: Currency risk management procedure

Rule 1	Postponement of decision
IF	(i,t) changed to [i,t + n (i,t)] at $0(A_i/B_i)$
THEN	time-warp the flows (A_{it}, B_{it}) with unchanged supplier credit between dates $S(A_i/B_i)$ and $D(A_i/B_i)$

Rule 2	Early settlement and delivery
IF	(i,t) changed to [i, t - n (i,t)] in $D(A_i/B_i)$
THEN	time-warp the flows (A_{it},B_{it}) with reduced exposure and supplier credit between $0(A_i/B_i)$ and $S(A_i/B_i)$

Rule 3	Early settlement and delivery
IF	(i,t) changed to [i,t - n(i,t)] in $D(A_i/B_i)$ and $S(A_i/B_i)$
THEN	time-warp the flows (A_{it}, B_{it}) with reduced exposure between $0(A_i/B_i)$ and $D(A_i/B_i)$

Rule 4	Aggregate assets or liabilities
IF	$(V(R_{kt}) \leq [V(R_{it}) + V(R_{jt})]$ for some period t, by combining i and j into one asset/liability k
THEN	combine these assets i and j into k for the longest period [t_1, t_2] which includes t

Rule 5 Selection of assets/liabilities
IF $V(R_{it})$ largest for all $i = 1,N$ $t = 1,T$ for (i^*,t^*)
THEN enable Rules 1 - 5 for i^*

Rule 6 Generate hedged assets or liabilities by futures
IF $E(R)$ is increased by changing (B_{it}) into $(B_{it} + \Delta B_{it})$ and (A_{it}) into $(A_{it} + \Delta A_{it})$, with ΔA_{it}, ΔB_{it} selected from futures prices F_t
THEN update A_i, B_i, $0(B_i)$, $S(B_i)$, $D(B_i)$ accordingly

Rule 7 Link futures premium to devaluation probability
IF $(F_{1/o\ t} \cdot p_t > d_t)$, which means that the futures market anticipates a devaluation at t
THEN reset $E(D)_t = F_{1/o\ t} \cdot p_t$;
AND reset all $B_{it} = 0$

11.5 Risk allocation inference

As it appears, the risk management procedure above involves altogether (Fig. 3):

- risk allocation by portfolio theory
- risk allocation by heuristics such as Rules 4, 5
- structural changes in the exposed assets and liabilities by procedures such as in Rules 1 - 4
- risk prediction by the use of exogenous predictions and financial instruments, such as in Rules 6 - 7.

12 Reasoning procedures in knowledge-based systems for economics and management

12.1 Introduction

Applications of AI, and especially knowledge-based systems (KBS), in economics, finance and management, result from the convergence of several streams of research, especially of decision support systems, of economic theories, and of knowledge representation and search (Fig. 1) [Pau, 1986], [Apté, 1987], [Cohen, 1981]. The first discipline offers a conceptual framework whereby to carry out structural analysis of the decision processes; the second discipline contributes by the mapping of causality relations between instruments and observables; the third discipline allows for knowledge-based or procedural search, and for information consolidation.

In the area of econometrics, testing economic theories and coping with imperfect data (e.g. overfitting lags), requires a well structured sequence of test procedures (goodness of fit, well behaved errors, estimators), which must be built into the search methods involved in the decision process (e.g. [David Hendry, Oxford Univ., personal communication], [Boyer, 1984], [Dhrymes, 1981], [Judge, 1986], [Hanssens, 1987]); see also [Economist, 1987], [Pau, 1979] for strengths and deficiencies in quantitative economic modeling and control techniques.

In the area of business management, the allocation, evaluation and optimization procedures incorporate substantial amounts of judgmental knowledge, which, along with data, must be converted into actions or analysis after search for alternatives [Naylor, 1984], [Worcester, 1986], [Zeelenberg, 1986].

Altogether, there is an essential duality between knowledge (quantitative as well as qualitative) and search (see also Chapter 5.4):

- search compensates for lack of knowledge
- knowledge reduces uncertainty, thus also search

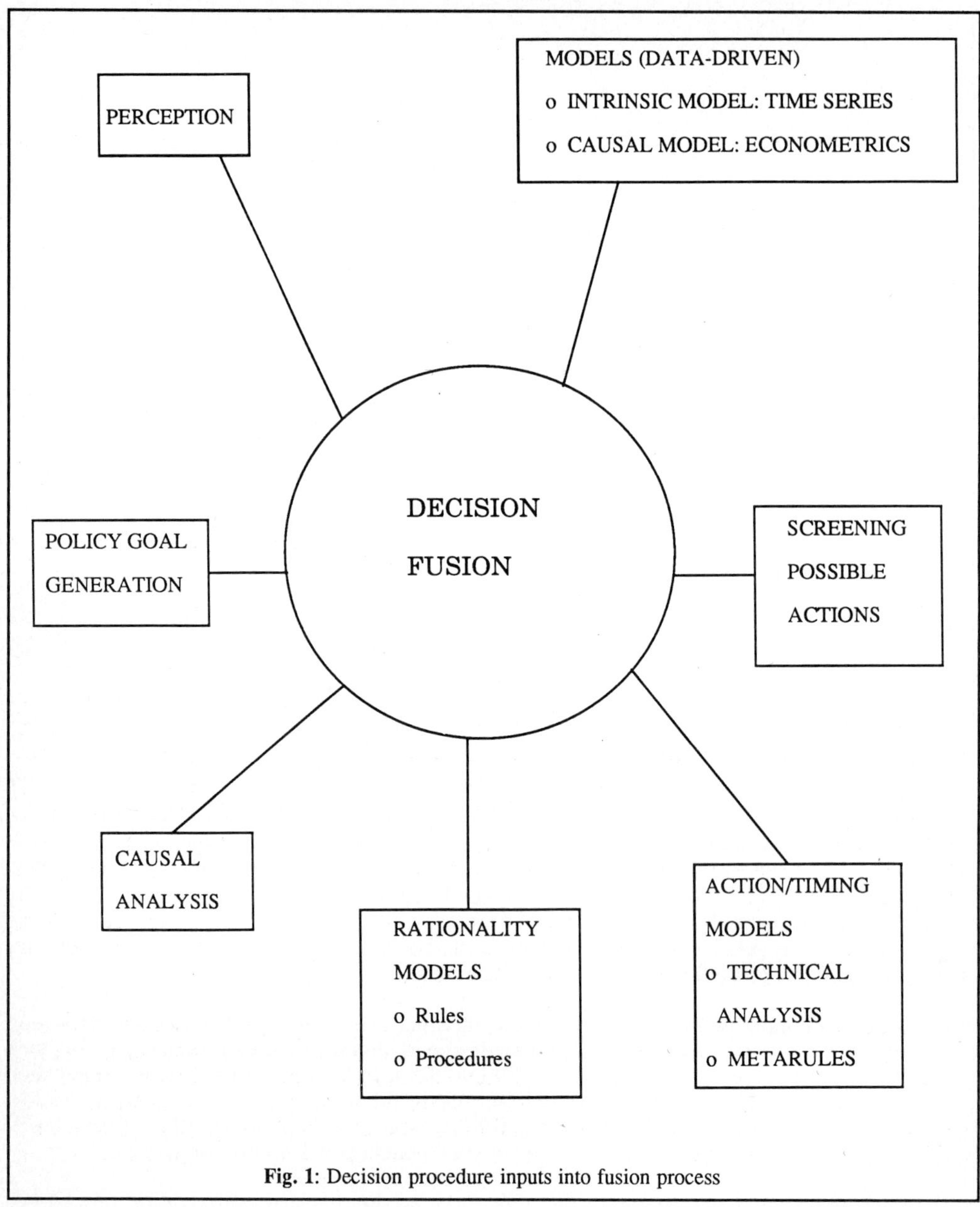

Fig. 1: Decision procedure inputs into fusion process

Artificial intelligence [Kanal, 1986] [Nilsson, 1976] has contributed many general purpose search strategies, such as depth-first, breadth-first, backward chaining, AND/OR graphs, A* etc. (see Chapter 5 and Section 8).

However, this Chapter will emphasize the fact that the duality between knowledge and search in economics and management, brings in the requirement for other search strategies in these application areas, which often incorporate to some extent their own proven search concepts. It appears that the many knowledge based systems have stressed knowledge and its (difficult) elicitation, rather than search. Most KBS's have poor search concepts, whereas the areas of economic management have much to contribute there.

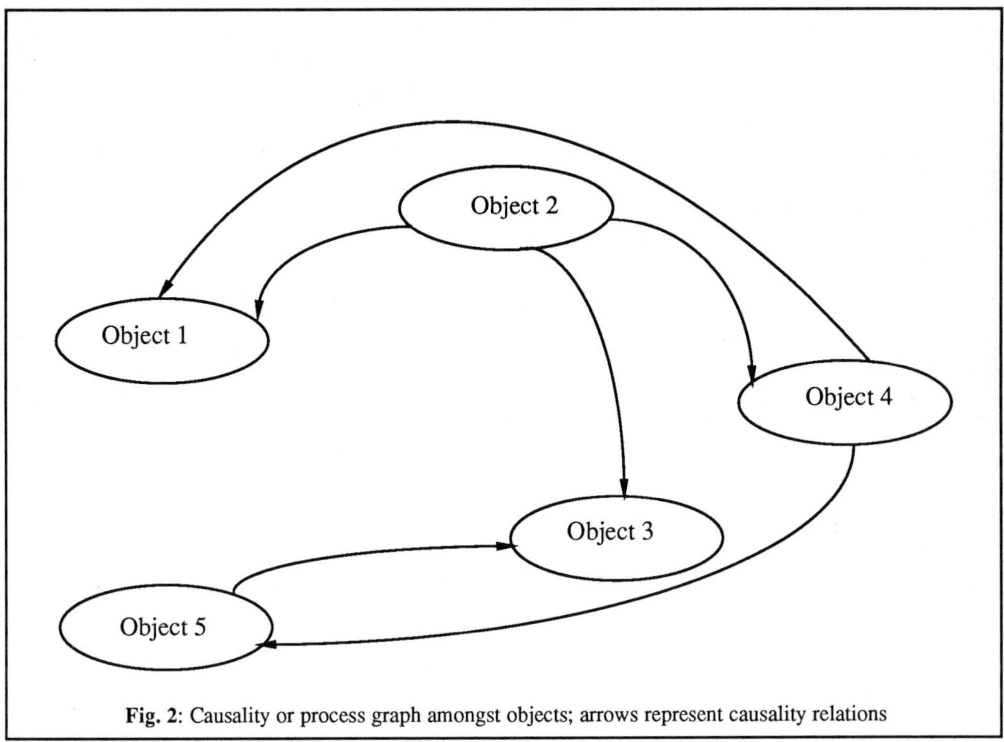

Fig. 2: Causality or process graph amongst objects; arrows represent causality relations

The goal of this Chapter is thus to review, and propose, a number of mostly search and concept manipulation techniques which would greatly enhance the foundations and performances of KBS in economics, finance and management. The required search involves heuristic procedures to guide towards alternative solutions to a problem. The concept manipulation is stressing object representation, and the fusion of different knowledge sources (Chapter 8.6 and Fig. 1).

12.2 Objects in decision analysis

A decision or analysis process, is fundamentally a process whereby information is transformed into actions or evaluations. Software engineering offers an interesting parallel hereto, the object-oriented approach (Chapter 4.5): here, each concept evoked in the said decision or analysis process, is called an object. Its essential features include hierarchy, encapsulation and inheritance of properties. "Methods", organized into libraries are "sent" to objects organized into trees or graphs; each object is characterized by its properties, independently of the data values hereof, and the properties revised by the methods get inherited in the tree or graph.

The parallel in decision analysis involves "objets" which are states of the economy or business, or concepts related to the later. The decision-maker or analyst, assesses the situation by applying to each alternative decision some analysis processes, which are "methods" from object-oriented programming. To be carried out, each method may invoke knowledge, in the form of a fixed body of cognitive or calculation procedures.
In an object-oriented framework, evaluations are carried out by sending methods to the objects, represented as nodes in a causality or process graph. An object can be either a hypothesis or a goal, in that each method sent to it must be tagged by the query label hypothesis or goal, thus differentiating the two types of objects. In the causality or process graph (Fig. 2), labels are attached

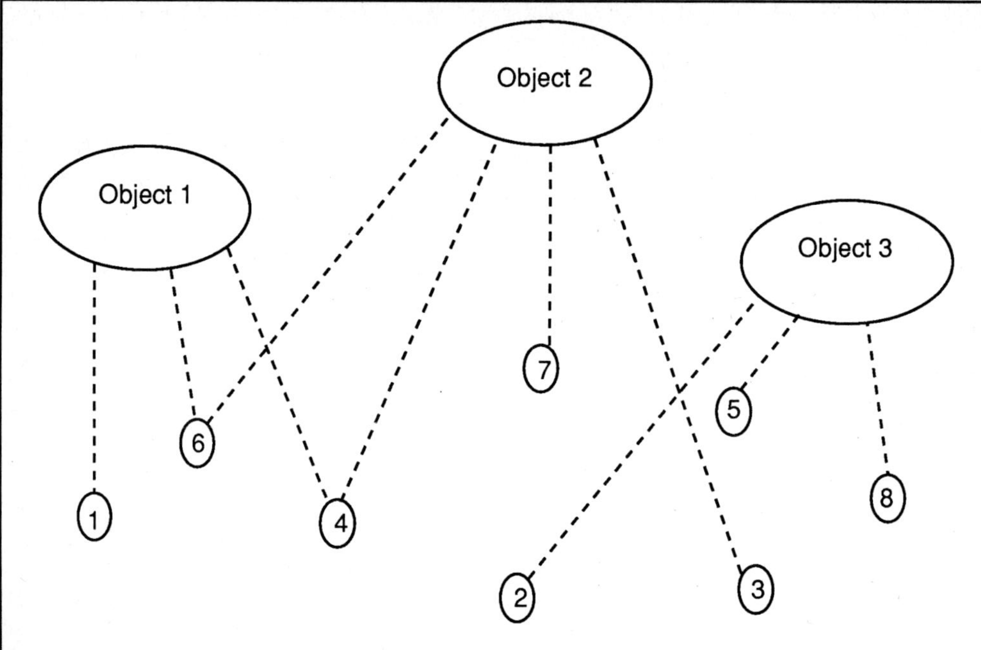

Fig. 3: Circled numbers represent attributes of objects; arrows correspond to attribute relations

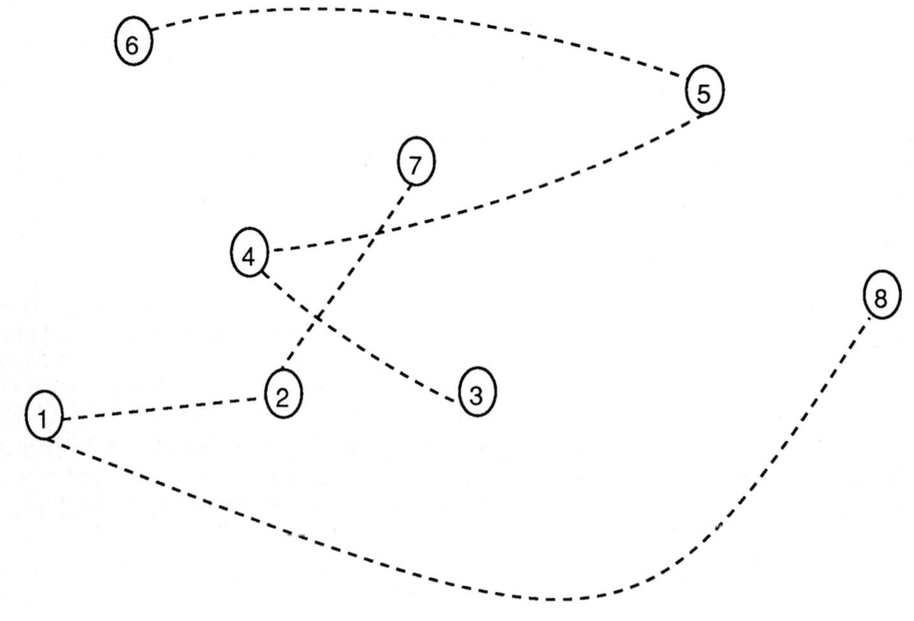

Fig. 4: Attribute graph in the case of a search initiated at object-1; the arrows illustrate the search path, or pruning taking place

	FIELDS OR PREDICATE	PRIMITIVE OR RELATION
0	INHERITANCE	FATHER(R)
1	PRIORITY	SOLVE_BEFORE (R_1, R_2)
2	RESTRICTION	FREEZE_RELATION(R_1, R_2), FREEZE_ATTRIBUTE(R,x)
3	NEED/SOLVABILITY	NEED (R)
4	CONTROL	SOLVE_FIRST(R), BRANCH(R_1, R_2)
5	DECISION THEORY	ECONOMIC_THEORY_SELECTION (ORDER_H, ORDER_C)
6	HYPOTHESIS (WITH PRIORITY RANKING, AND ATTRIBUTES)	ORDER_H (R,H_i), PRIOR_H (H_i, H_J), ATTRIBUTE_H (H_i, x_i)
7	CONCLUSIONS (WITH PRIORITY RANKING, AND ATTRIBUTES)	ORDER_C (R, C_l), PRIOR_C (C_l, C_M), ATTRIBUTE_C (C_l, x_P)
8	ATTRIBUTE CONSTRAINTS	$Ax \leq b$
9	EQUILIBRIUM	EQUILIBRIUM_CONDITION (R,x)

Table 1: Knowledge representation for economic/management problems: typical attributes of objects

to each arc to describe either the causality influence (-->, <--, +, -), or the time ordering, or some information about the context. At the same time, the attributes of each object (Fig. 3 and 4) are a set of measurements (data, strings, lists, trees) or instances, sometimes shared in an attribute graph. It is further possible to formalize in a frame based way the attribute fields (or slots) appropriate for most such economic objects. These are specified in Table 1 for economic and management problems, where the left column describes in the form of relations or logic predicates the methods applicable to these fields (again assuming an object-oriented concept). Fig. 5 offers one example related to the Yen/USD exchange rate determination; it displays a tree of objects which are economic properties, each having some attributes, and the later having attribute ranges.

12.3 Classification of decision methods

If decisions are methods sent to objects in an object-oriented paradigm, then it is interesting to categorize decision methods according to some three basic criteria, namely: perception, rationality, and action (Table 2).

Others, e.g. Scott Morton, have found five axioms for organizational goal formation. However, we found our three basic criteria easier to use in practice by reducing overlap between axioms in specific cases.

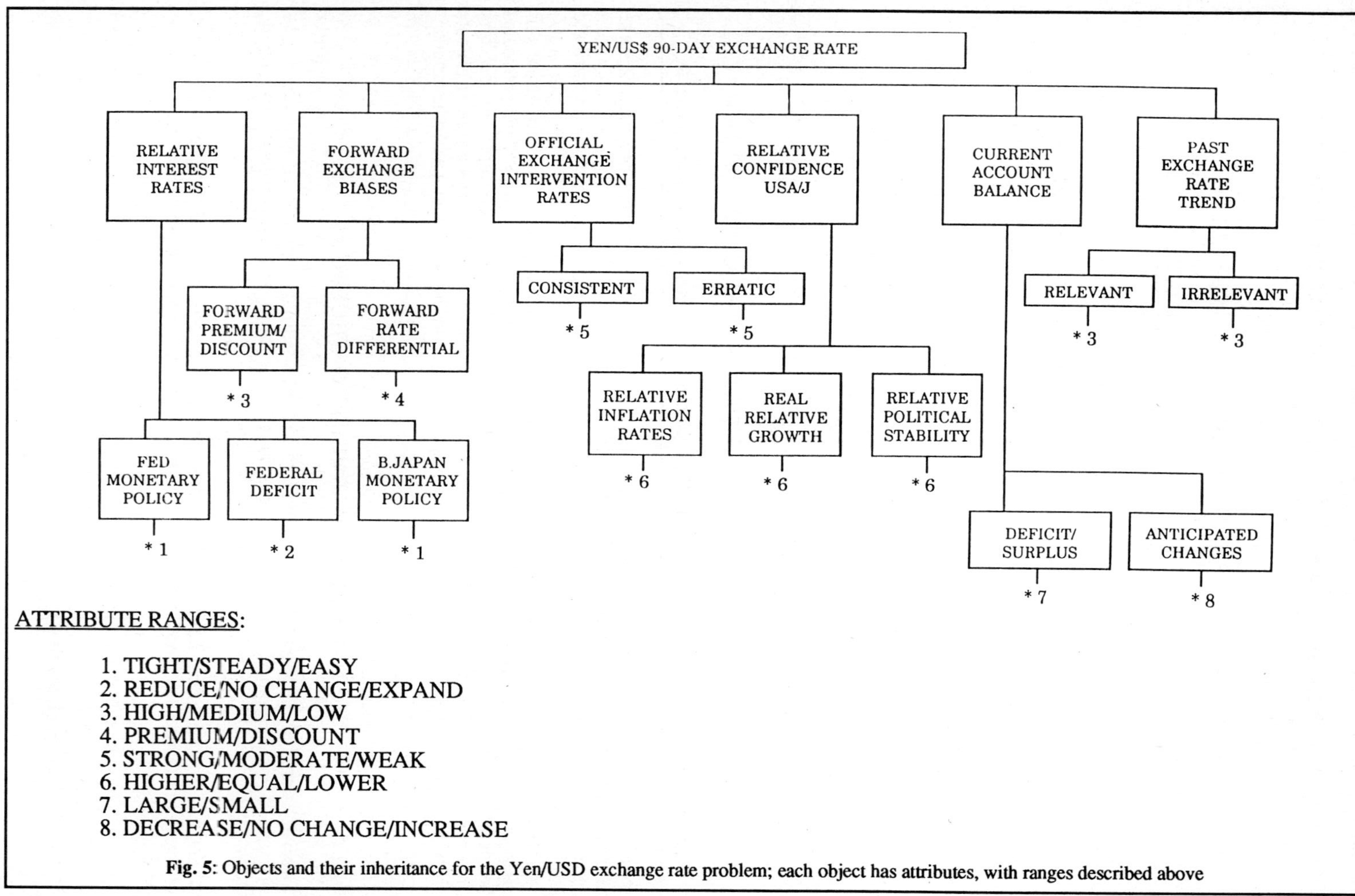

Fig. 5: Objects and their inheritance for the Yen/USD exchange rate problem; each object has attributes, with ranges described above

DIFFERENTIATION OF DECISION PROCESSES	BEHAVIORAL KNOWLEDGE BASE OF DECISION MAKER	TYPE OF KNOWLEDGE BASED SYSTEM
PERCEPTION ("GUT-FEEL")	LARGE INFORMATION BASES ("FACTS")	KNOWLEDGE REPRESENTATION + SEARCH / INFERENCE
RATIONALITY ("MUST OBEY RULES")	SUBJECTIVE RULES OR PROCEDURES ("WHAT TO DO")	TRUTH MAINTENANCE OR CONSTRAINT PROPAGATION + KNOWLEDGE SEGMENTATION + ACCUMULATION OF EVIDENCE AND APPROXIMATE REASONING
ACTION	METAKNOWLEDGE ("KNOW-HOW")	DECISION AID LANGUAGES + SITUATION LOGIC

Table 2: Framework for economic and management control in knowledge based systems

12.3.1 Perception criterion

As already mentioned, a decision process basically is a transformation process of information into actions, and likewise for evaluations resulting in analyses. The task of the decision-maker is to understand the problem he encounters by referring to the image he perceives of the cognitive environment, which is imaged through the information set he operates on.

A first major criterion is thus the extent to which the action/evaluation processes apply to larger information sets, this size being often but not always related to the responsibility level. Three action/decision levels can be identified:

- strategic level, involving a general policy of the organization and goals hereof
- management level, involving the best use of the available resources in view of the assigned goals, which is an allocation problem; allocation procedures involve heavy enumeration and search
- operational level, involving the execution of specific tasks

This highlights the knowledge representation issues involved in acquiring and manipulating the cognitive information, especially about the context in which decisions/evaluations are made. The knowledge bases involved can become large, raising concerns about their consistency, validation and testing [Pau, 1987].

12.3.2 Rationality criterion

[Simon, 1960] has highlighted the "limited rationality" principle, according to which there are bounds to the decision-maker's efficiency if he only refers to the dominant rationality in the organization.

In situations where the assessment of the decision-maker bears dominant weight, he expects better results by referring to a subjective rationality, based in value judgments which are his own, rather to a behavioral rationality related by the goals and structures of the organization.

The differentiation of decision/evaluation processes according to the rationality used as a reference by the decision-makers, implies for knowledge-based systems widely different reasoning/search processes. Such processes will be quite apart, according to whether management/policy rules or procedures are highly structured (with little search) [Dremick, 1986], or whether they rely heavily on subjective criteria related to a problem context (with typically extensive search).

In other words, search and reasoning are mostly tied to subjective rationality, which requires approximate reasoning, that is search/reasoning strategies which take into account, both:

- the inaccuracy of the goals and decision criteria
- the inaccuracy about the applicability of knowledge according to the conditions in which a problem may occur.

12.3.3 Action criterion

In the theory of organizations, it is customary to focus on the factors which determine an action selected within a space of opportunities. Such actions or opportunities belong to either of three classes:

- organization actions, dealing with the allocation of human, material, financial resources to action units according to the goals hereof
- coordination actions (Fig. 6), which should preserve the coherence of decisions made by several agents involved in solving the same problem or reaching the same goal; approaches are the prediction of interactions, or the decoupling of interactions [Mesarovic, 1970], resulting in hierarchical coordination (if no subjectivity), or auto-coordination (if full or subjective rationality, and information distribution)
- control actions, which validate action procedures, including correcting observed deviations between goals and performances of action units

All those three classes of actions have as effect to modify the knowledge base describing the environment in which decisions/evaluations are made. They also require, besides management techniques, a know-how which is unique to each decision-maker.

The reasoning involved in actions is thus relying on a situation logic, possibly implemented partly through event driven constraints. The reasoning process will differ a priori according to the context and according to the space of opportunities. Thus, that process is really an interaction between event driven constraints (corresponding to the cognitive perception of the environment), and metaknowledge (corresponding to processes tied to the decision-maker's know-how, and needed to act upon the environment).

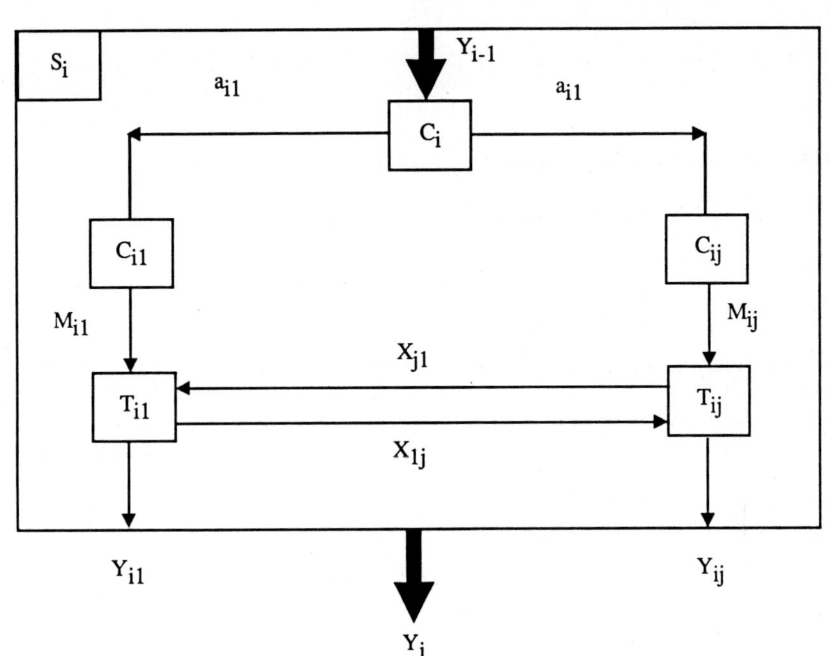

PROCEDURES	PRINCIPLE	INFERENCE TYPE
COORDINATION BY PREDICTION	Coordination efficiency for S_i depends on the speed and accuracy whereby C_i predicts X_{ij}'s by adjusting a_{ij}.	Forward chaining amidst constraints relating to the decision environment Y_{i-1}, and the behavioral knowledge bases for T_{ij}'s.
COORDINATION BY DECOMPOSING INTERACTIONS	C_i sends to C_{ij}'s coordination parameters such that Y_i meets goals, but each T_{ij} selects X_{ij}'s.	Backward chaining from goals on Y_i, and generate plan for parameters a_{ij}.
COORDINATION BY PLANS	Coordinate resource allocations M_{ij}, assuming objective rationality of all agents T_{ij}	Fixed point algorithm, and selection of criteria and feasibility constraints
HIERARCHICAL COORDINATION	Coordination by prediction with shared access to same fact base from units C_i, C_{ij} at all levels	Forward chaining with flavours and central blackboard
SELF COORDINATION	All units C_{ij} at the same level coordinate their actions in open loop	Cooperative equilibria corresponding to balanced truth compromise search, with subjective rationality, see Section 12

Fig. 6: Coordination procedures

12.4 Logics and constraints

Most procedures applied to decision problems involve resource constraints, or activity constraints, of the equality or inequality type. This is bound to remain so in general, simply because these bounds are themselves the outcome of another allocation decision process.

The above constraints should hopefully have the following alternative realizations:

i. (condition numerical) ≤ a

ii. (condition logical _ proposition) = true/false

iii. (condition text) ≤ a

where, in object-oriented notation, the method "condition" is sent to either "text" or "numerical", with a number as a result for comparison with "a". Constraints of type i. are typically accounted for in mathematical programming, with linear constraints being the simplest case (for which Lagrange multipliers are constants). Constraints of type ii. are logical predicates, which can be formulated in logic programming languages by Horn clauses to facilitate the proof of assertions by resolution (see e.g. [Kowalsky, 1979]). In economic and management applications, such logical constraints are predicates of the type:

action (agent, type_action, conditions) --->;
allocate (benefits, agents, conditions) --->;
interaction (agent-1, agent-2, benefits) ---> action-1 action-2;

Auctions, trades, plans and evaluations can be formulated in this way (see [Miller, 1986] for a case).

Constraints of type iii. are difficult to treat, in that they involve a parser of the text string "text", a syntactic analysis, a morphological analysis, a semantic analysis, and a valuation of the semantic relations [Fu, 1975], [Pau, 1985]. The first few levels can be treated by finite or infinite trees, using relations, lists and trees with identifiers (also called t - uples < , >) [Colmerauer, 1984] (see Chapters 4.2 and 9). The last few levels are much more delicate, especially as the valuation must be mapped into the same space as "a"; see [Pau, 1986] for a related attempt.

A common formulation of constraints of all three types is being researched [Colmerauer, 1987], together with related unification and search procedures, by predicates of the type (1) and (2) below:

(constraint ii)$_0$ ----> {(constraint ii)$_1$ {constraint i)$_2$} (1)

This means that during the unification of logical predicates of type ii, the range on the variables involved is tested against linear numerical constraints of type i.; this is called constrained logic programming. This can be extended to the case of tree representations of text, but not to the semantic nor valuation levels, by the selection of the proper data structures:

(constraint ii (tree iii) 0 ----->
{ (constraint ii)$_1$ }
{ (constraint ii (tree iii))$_2$)
{ (constraint i)$_3$ }

This gives already now the opportunity e.g. to combine simplex algorithms from linear programming, with text analysis, within a logic programming framework.

12.5 Truth maintenance as rational decision-making

Although variants of rationality, especially partial or subjective rationality, are more appropriate in economics and management, it is essential to relate that approach to some better known search or resolution strategies in AI (see Chapter 5).

It has been shown that the basic axioms of logic (identity in the terminology, excluded-middle, and non-contradiction) are not satisfied in many of the most current econometric models involving rationality [Swamy, 1984]; such cases are: approximate demand systems [Theil, 1975], causality tests [Boland, 1982], rational expectations (in the sense of [Wallis,1980]).

The reason for this is often a failure to meet the non-contradiction axiom. If this is the case, then if two contradictory statements are admitted, any statement whatsoever could be admitted [Popper,1962].

Bayesian inference imposes the condition of coherence, i.e. that a collection of probability/values is free from contradictions [Heath and Sudderth, 1978]. Rational expectations models will fail the condition of coherence if their equations constitute an inconsistent sampling model.

It follows from the above that the structural knowledge on which a model is based must be logically consistent if it is to provide a true explanation of anything. Although the logical consistency of any explanation does not necessarily imply its truth, it is a necessary prior condition to any explanation of the real world. [Boland, 1982] argues that the only objective and non arbitrary test to be applied to theories or models is that of logical consistency and validity. That consistency is related to the structural inconsistency discussed in Chapter 5.10.

Thus, truth maintenance procedures must be used if any kind of rationality is to be maintained in an inference or reasoning process. Such truth maintenance metapredicate can be stated as:

truth (x, {truth_conditions}, model) ?

where:

- x is the new hypothesis to be tested as belonging or not to the theory "model"
- {truth_conditions} is the set of truth maintenance conditions, such as:

i. statistical test of hypothesis on data x for the statistical model validity

ii. non-contradiction test of hypothesis on text x for the regulatory "model" (laws, regulations)

iii. non-violation by the vector x of the feasibility constraint set of "model"

iv. non-violation of a preference ranking or coalition by decision x w.r.t. the social preference "model"

v. conditions related to causal inconsistency (see Chapter 5.10.2)

Global coherence and truth maintenance among all possible competing models is not possible. Fortunately, the perception level and action levels offer reasoning procedures, (respectively model switching through search, and context related evaluation), which allow for model selection. At the same time, due to events and uncertainty, the performance of the selected truth maintenance may change. One must therefore be prepared continually to check the performances of a rational model against those of its competitors, as long as each is logically consistent.

12.6 Search over time and disequilibrium

It is generally acknowledged that artificial intelligence offers no significant improvements in the way temporal phenomena are described, over the classic approaches from operations research. Time is accounted in KBS by either of the following:

- time interval logic (see Chapter 3.8)
- agendas and blackboard knowledge representation
- state transition graphs (see Chapter 3.4 and 3.8, Fig. 15)

This would induce the belief that KBS's have no contribution to planning and economic equilibria.

Not so! But, it is the other way around, as disequilibrium theory in economics offers highly relevant approaches to time-dependent aspects in KBS.

While time is irrelevant as such in e.g. Walras-Arrow-Debreu logical economics, it naturally plays the fundamental role in any sequential economic model. As the central features, for which time is crucial, are processes of accumulation and information (e.g.: predictions, investments, money, uncertainty), typical of disequilibrium models [Leijonhufvud, 1968], [Clover, 1965]. The implementation architecture for such disequilibrium economic models , is to consider micro-founded macro-models [Weintraub, 1977], with search procedures; amongst these search procedures are the separable signal algorithm (SSA), or the Scarf algorithm [Scarf, 1973], which segments compact and convex sets.

Most such disequilibrium models use divide-and-conquer algorithms of the type:

$$M(0) = 0$$

$$M(n+1) = f(n+1) + \min_{i+j=n} (M(i) + M(j))$$

where f is the cost of merging micro subproblems, whereas M (i), M (j) are the costs of solving each subproblem; f is monotonic non decreasing. When f is strictly convex, then the solution fulfils:

$$M(n+1) = f(n+1) + M(n)$$

When f is concave:

$$M(n) = f(n) + M(2k - 1) + M(n-2k)$$

where $3 \times 2\,K\text{-}1 \leq (n+1) \leq 3 \times 2\,k$. Thus exact balancing amongst subproblems is not always good, and search is required. See best-first search as a special case (Chapter 5.11.2).

12.7 Conflict resolution

Goals are usually conflicting, and require criteria for evaluation, or other social choice procedures [Arrow, 1963].

Current knowledge-based systems architectures provide rather giving poor conflict resolution procedures, such as logic filters (AND / OR / NOT conditions) or weighting by likelihoods (Chapter 1.4). Conflict resolution must, however, be a set of selectable methods, yielding a subset upon which voting or selection may be carried out (see Section 9).

We suggest below, for inclusion in economic and financial KBS's, a set of conflict resolution approaches which can readily be implemented in AI environments:

1. Identify mutually exclusive goals, by logical exclusion, social exclusion, or pure competition
2. Identify preservation goals, which are undesirable goals coming into existence because of a precondition state
3. Goal abandonment
4. Conflict resolution by introducing a new agent or object
5. Calculation of core equilibrium amongst goals, in order to achieve as many goals as possible, and reselect goals
6. Calculation of Pareto equilibrium amongst goals, in order to maximize the value of the goals achieved
7. Calculation of Nash equilibrium amongst goals, in order to exclude unilateral gains [Pau,1979], [Pau, 1980]
8. Change the reference context
9. Conceal actions, give false incentives, or focus attention elsewhere

12.8 Search over AND/OR graphs

Many games and conflict resolution do not require equilibrium determination and rely instead on heuristic search involving a sequence of decision points. If these elementary decisions can be narrowed to either AND or OR choices, specific search algorithms apply operating over so-called AND/OR graphs representing the decision tree.

Example 1: Option strategies

The choice of an option strategy can be represented as an AND/OR tree (or graph). AND nodes represent:

- uncontrollable events, such as the evolution of the market; the representation is simplified in that the market can behave in three different ways (bullish, bearish, stable) without consideration for the strength of the trend. Since market behavior is outside the trader's control, appropriate trading strategies must be found for *each* possible behavior. In other words, each child of an AND node is a sub-problem to be solved.
- investor's actions

OR nodes represent alternative strategies. Consider the tree in Fig. 7. AND nodes are pictured with an arc crossing the outcoming links, in order to distinguish them from OR nodes. It is assumed that the investor owns the underlying securities or a covered write (for instance, as a part of an hedging strategy); depending upon the evolution of the market, the different follow-up actions are shown (possible alternative actions have been reduced by assuming that the covered write is far from expiration).

Candidate heuristics for search methods over option strategy trees are:

- the investor's risk attitude (in-the-money, out-of-the-money calls and puts)
- the expected return or loss (based upon the volatility of the underlying asset)
- the amount of down-side coverage
- transaction costs

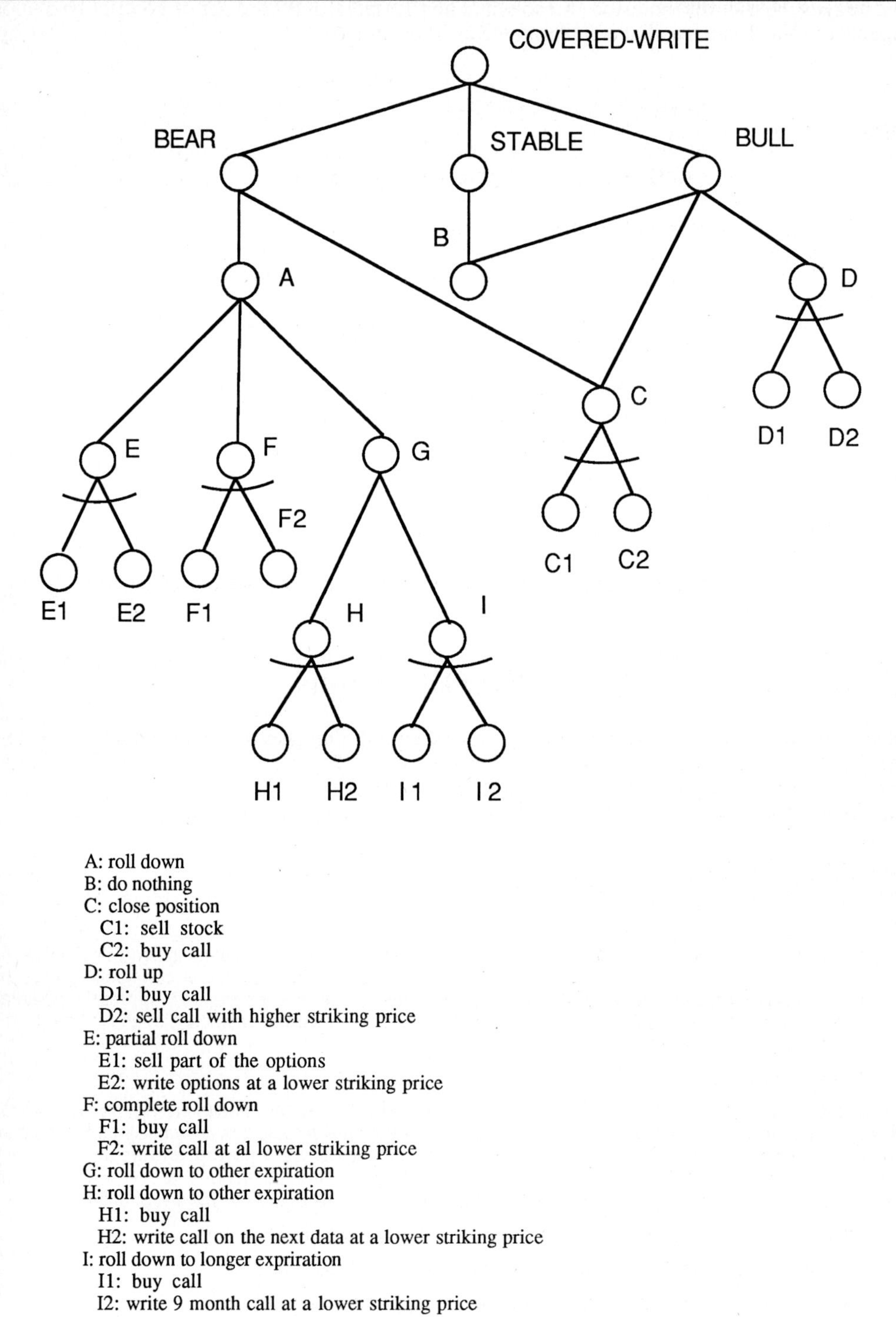
COVERED-WRITE
BEAR
STABLE
BULL
B
A
D
C
E
F
G
F2
D1
D2
C1
C2
E1
E2
F1
H
I
H1
H2
I1
I2
A: roll down
B: do nothing
C: close position
C1: sell stock
C2: buy call
D: roll up
D1: buy call
D2: sell call with higher striking price
E: partial roll down
E1: sell part of the options
E2: write options at a lower striking price
F: complete roll down
F1: buy call
F2: write call at al lower striking price
G: roll down to other expiration
H: roll down to other expiration
H1: buy call
H2: write call on the next data at a lower striking price
I: roll down to longer exprimation
I1: buy call
I2: write 9 month call at a lower striking price

Fig. 7: Option strategies

- margins requirements

etc. ■

A solution by an AND/OR graph takes the form of a tree instead of that of a path. The solution tree consists of just one successor for each OR node in it, and of all successors for each AND node. All leaf nodes must be satisfied at the same time for the tree to be a solution tree.

Some implementations of search procedures for AND/OR graphs do indeed store and maintain a tree. The structure of the search is the same; for instance, just as paths are compared through an heuristic function and the most promising is selected, AND/OR algorithms compare alternative trees and select the best scoring one. We will in the following present a simpler implementation, the equivalent to depth-first over OR trees; just one tree is maintained, and backtracking is used when needed.

a. Step-by-step pseudo-code description of AND/OR graph search in procedural style:

1	Make start the current node
2	If the current node n is an OR node, then goto 4.
3	If the node to be searched is an AND node, then goto ...
	-- OR NODE --
4	Select one child of n, discard it from the children of n, make it the current node, and goto 2.
5	If N has no children, return NIL
6	If no solution is found in step 4, goto 4
7	If a solution is found, add n to the solution and return the solution
	-- AND NODE --
8	Select one child of n, discard it from the children of n, make it the current node, and goto 2.
9	If N has no children, return the solution found (if any)
10	If no solution is found in step 4, return NIL
11	If a solution is found, goto 8

b. LISP code:

Node children, node type (and/or) and goal attribute (T: node is a goal; NIL: node is not a goal), are all stored in properties.

All external functions have been defined previously. To locate their definitions, please look up the function names (in capital letters) in Appendix 2.1.

```
     (DEFUN and-or-tree-search (Node)

       (DEFUN get-children (Node)
         (GET Node 'CHILDREN))

       (DEFUN get-type (Node)
         (GET Node 'TYPE))

       (DEFUN solvable? (Node)
         (GET Node 'GOAL))

       (DEFUN dispatch (Node)
         (IF (solvable? Node) (LIST Node)
           (LET ((children (get-children Node)))
             (IF (NULL children) NIL
               (IF (EQUAL (get-type Node) 'AND)
3                (recursive-and-search Node Children NIL)
2                (recursive-or-search Node Children))))))

       (DEFUN recursive-and-search (Node Children Solution)
9        (IF (NULL Children) (CONS Node Solution)
8         (LET ((result (dispatch (CAR Children))))
10          (IF (NULL result) NIL
```

```
11          (recursive-and-search Node (CDR Children) (CONS Result Solution))))))

        (DEFUN recursive-or-search (Node Children)
5         (IF (NULL Children) NIL
4          (LET ((result (dispatch (CAR Children))))
7           (IF result (CONS Node (LIST result))
6              (recursive-or-search Node (CDR Children))))))

1       (dispatch Node))
```

c. PROLOG code:

Although AND/OR search could be designed in PROLOG along the same guidelines as LISP, it can be done in a much easier way by referring to the metainterpreter in Example 55, Chapter 4.4.12. In the following, it it supposed that a predicate "type_of_node" is available for each node, specifying if it is an AND-node or an OR-node:

```
type_of_node(Node, and).
type_of_node(Node, or).
```

Furthermore, the usual predicate "arc" must be present in the database, defining the topology of the graph (or a different definition for "get_child" must be provided). Note that all solutions are returned, one after the other, through backtracking.

All external functions have been defined previously. To locate their definitions, please look up the function names (in capital letters) in Appendix 2.2.

```
and_or_tree_search(Node, Is_goal, Solution):-
        recursive_search(Node, Is_goal, Solution).

recursive_search(Node, Is_goal, [Node]) :-
        Pred =.. [Is_goal, Node],
        call(Pred).
recursive_search(Node, Is_goal, [Node|[Next]]) :-
        type_of_node(Node, or),
        get_child(Node, Child),
        recursive_search(Child, Is_goal, Next).
recursive_search(Node, Is_goal, [Node|Next]) :-
        type_of_node(Node, and),
        findall(X, get_child(Node, X), Children),
        list_search(Children, Is_goal, Next).

list_search([], Is_goal, []).
list_search([H|T], Is_goal, [Next|Rest]) :-
        !,
        recursive_search(H, Is_goal, Next),
        list_search(T, Is_goal, Rest).

get_child(Node, Child) :- arc(Node, Child).
```

12.9 Power relations and gaming for the selection of solutions

12.9.1 Game theory and AI

It turns out that long neglected cooperative game theory is ideally suited for implementation in symbolic languages with search capabilities, and moreover that it is highly needed for selecting between alternative candidates after search. This section describes a procedure, and related definitions, to evaluate search results in a multiple criteria/goal or multiple agent framework. A coalition involves, either criteria, or agents called players.

12.9.2 Definitions

In cooperative game theory [Shubik, 1983], [Owen, 1971], [Brams, 1975] a winning coalition is one that can achieve anything that the grand coalition of all the players could achieve. A losing coalition, cannot achieve anything that its members could not achieve individually. A game, or compromise search, in which all coalitions are either winning or losing, is called simple.

Simple games help explain, and implement compromise search, by stressing the combinatorial search procedures involved themselves in the voting rules amongst players, rather than the conflicts of interest that the voting rules might be called upon to resolve.

Let:

$D = 2^N$	denote the set of all subsets of the list $N = \{1,..,n\}$ of goals or players, corresponding to all possible coalitions
$C < D$	a coalition
C^+	the set of supersets of members of C
C^m	the set of minimal members of C, i.e. those that have no proper subset in C; members of C^m are called minimal winning coalitions
C^n	intersection of all elements of C
C^u	union of all elements of C

A simple game $G = (N, \Sigma)$ is specified by its player set N and its set of winning coalitions $\Sigma < D$, satisfying:

i	$N \in \Sigma$
ii	$\varnothing \notin \Sigma$
iii	$\Sigma = \Sigma^+$

Player (or goal) $i \in N$ is a dictator if $(i) \in \Sigma$, a veto player if $(i) \in C^n$ and a "dummy" if $i \notin C^{mu}$. The symmetric n-player game in which $S \in C^m \Leftrightarrow |S| = k$ is denoted $M_{n,k}$. The product of two games $G_1 = (N_1, \Sigma_1)$ and $G_2 = (N_2, \Sigma_2)$, denoted $G_1 \otimes G_2$, is the game where $S < N_1 \cup N_2$ wins if and only if $(S \cap N_1) \in \Sigma_1$ and $(S \cap N_2) \in \Sigma_2$. Similarly, in the sum $G_1 \oplus G_2$, the coalition ($S < N_1 \cup N_2$) wins if and only if ($S \cap N_1) \in \Sigma_1$ or ($S \cap N_2) \in \Sigma_2$. A two step decision process (e.g. bicameral legislature) is an example of a product.

Proper structures of the form $H \otimes (G_1 \oplus G_2)$ are often found in practice, where H may be a single goal or individual playing the role of tie-breaker or arbiter.

The power of a goal or individual in a compromise/voting system comes down ultimately to the question of his being essential to a marginal coalition. If Y is a set of predicates or properties who hold true on a compromise issue, then we call goal/agent i a "swinger" for Y if:

either: $i \in Y, Y \in C, Y \{i\} \in$ (losing coalition)

or : $i \in Y, Y \in$ (losing coalition), $Y_u\{i\} \in C$

We call solution/goal/agent i a "pivot", if:

- for all permutations π such that $i \notin \pi$: $\pi \in$ (losing coalition)
- for all permutations π such that $i \in Y, Y \in$ (losing coalition), $Y_u\{i\} \in C$

12.9.3 Relations to search strategies

In a decision-making/evaluation process, the fact that a goal is satisfied or not, means that the corresponding logic predicate is true or not.

When counting the number of goals which are satisfied to reach a compromise decision for action purposes, one really carries out a vote amongst conflicting goals, with coalitions winning or losing in terms of tipping the balance in favour or not of such an action.

It is highly important to compare the goals or alternative solutions, in view of their relative power index, and to highlight those who are pivots or swingers. Irresolution can be detected.

Likewise, it is convenient to decompose the search algorithms by factoring them out by $\oplus$ or $\otimes$, to reduce the combinatorial complexity.

Appendix 1 Software codes

1.1 Prolog code for the tax adviser

Program developed using Prolog 2 from Expert Systems Ltd. on a PC/XT. For an overview of the program see Chapter 4.4.13.

1.1.1 Starter

The predicate starter looks for tax databases in the disk directory and loads the one selected by the user. Databases are named according to the sections in the tax form, and contain the knowledge relevant to their filling.

The following predicates are introduced for the first time in the code below, mostly consisting of input/output primitives for interfacing with the user or the file system:

file(File_name, Full_name)
: searches for a file matching File_name (which may use wildcard characters), and returns the match with all wildcard characters instantiated, in the second argument. Succeeds if a file is found, fails otherwise. This predicate may not be compatible with other Prolog systems

nl
: a no argument predicate outputting an empty line to the current output stream (e.g. the screen); it always succeeds

read(Term)
: "Term" is read from the current input stream (e.g. the keyboard); "Term" must be a syntactically correct Prolog term

reconsult(File)

loads the content of "File" into the Prolog database. "File" must be a Prolog database. Definitions in "File" override definitions for the same predicates already in the database, if any

repeat

a predicate with no arguments which always succeeds and can always be resatisfied. Used to implement iteration

retractall(Predicate)

removes all clauses for "Predicate" from the database. "retractall" always succeeds, even if no clauses were removed.

write(Term)

writes "Term" to the current output stream (e.g. the screen); it always succeeds; "Term" must be a syntactically correct Prolog term

All other predicates have been previously defined; to locate their definitions, please look up in Appendix 2.2.

```
/* note:        IRPEF: national tax on personal income; ILOR: local tax on personal income. */

starter:-
        tab(24),write('EXSYS740 Compilation of tax form.740'),nl,nl,
        write('Available sections are:'),nl,
        (not file(a, _); write('Section A - land income;'),nl),
        (not file(b, _); write('Section B - real estates income;'),nl),
        (not file(c, _); write('Section C - dependent work and similar income;'),nl),
        (not file(d, _); write('Section D - dependent work income subject to separate taxation;'),nl),
        (not file(r, _); write('Section R - reimbursed taxes and expenses;'),nl),
        (not file(p, _); write('Section P - deductible expenses;'),nl),
        (not file(n, _); write('Section N - IRPEF calculation;'),nl),
        (not file(o, _); write('Section O - ILOR calculation;'),nl),
        (not file(a1, _); write('Section A1 - income deriving from breeding cattles;'),nl),
        (not file(e, _); write('Section E - independent work income;'),nl),
        (not file(f, _); write('Section F - firm income (only firms with simplified accounting);'),nl),
        (not file(g, _); write('Section G - firm (firms with normal accounting);'),nl),
        (not file(h, _); write('Section H - income from participations;'),nl),
        (not file(i, _); write('Section I - capital income;'),nl),
        (not file(l, _); write('Section L - sundry income;'),nl),
        (not file(m, _); write('Section M - independent work income subject to separate taxation;'),nl),
        write('Input the letter relevant to the Section to be compiled'),nl,
        repeat,
        read(Section_requested),nl,
        exists_file(Section_requested),
        (database_resident(Section_requested);load(Section_requested)).

load(Section_requested):-
        (clause(#(Name_fact,_,_,_),_), Question=..[Name_fact,_,_,bw], retractall(Question), fail);
        (retractall(database_resident(_)), assert(database_resident(Section_requested)), reconsult(Section_requested)).
```

1.1.2 Control Rules

This section of the program contains the rules defining the inference engine, a skeleton of user interface, as well as utility packages, such as those for pretty-printing terms and numbers. See comments within the code for more information.

The following predefined predicates are used for the first time in the code below:

consult(File)

loads the clauses in "File" into the Prolog database

var(Term)
succeeds if "Term" is an unbound variable

nonvar(Term)
fails if "Term" is an unbound variable, succeeds otherwise

functor(Term, Functor, Arity)
succeeds if "Term" has functor "Functor" and arity "Arity". Either Term, or both "Functor" and "Arity", must be instantiated

Term1 \= Term2
succeeds if Term1 and Term2 cannot be matched

Term1 == Term2
compares "Term1" and "Term2", with the current instantiation for the two terms, and succeeds if the two terms are equal. No variable is instantiated in the comparison

integer(Term)
succeeds if "Term" is an integer number

numeric(Term)
succeeds if "Term" is either a real or an integer number

real(Term)
succeeds if "Term" is a real number

fix(Real_number)
this is a function converting a real number "Real_number" into an integer, by rounding "Real_number" to the closest integer smaller than or equal to "Real_number" (in absolute value)

real_round(Real_number)
this is a function rounding "Real_number" to the closest integer, and then converting it back to a real number

restart
a zero argument predicate aborting the current execution

Expression1 > Expression2
succeeds if the result of the arithmetic expression Expression1 is greater than the result of the arithmetic expression Expression2

Expression1 >= Expression2
succeeds if the result of the arithmetic expression Expression1 is greater than or equal to the result of the arithmetic expression Expression2

print(Term)
tries to print "Term" using a user-supplied predicate "portray(Term)" (which must be present in the database). If no such predicate is found, the built-in predicate "write" is used instead

All other predicates have been previously defined; to locate their definitions, please look up the predicates in Appendix 2.2.

```
start:- (starter;(consult(starter),starter)), !, volunteering.
```

```
volunteering:-
        write('Input desired fact name (or "?" for a listing)'), nl,
        read(Fact_name), nl, requested_fact(Fact_name),
        volunteering.

/* user can volunteer information, or let the system drive the dialogue */

/* list of allowable facts */
requested_fact(?):-
        tab(20),write('- List of valid names -'),nl,
        clause(#(Fact_name,_,_),_),
        Question =.. [Fact_name,_],
        clause(Question,_),
        not(already_written(Fact_name)),
        write(Fact_name),nl,
        retractall(already_written(_)),
        assert(already_written(Fact_name)),
        fail; retractall(already_written(_)).

/* requested fact is already asserted. Explains how it was derived */
requested_fact(Fact_name):-
        Fact=..[Fact_name,_],
        clause(Fact,true), !,
        write_fact(Fact,_), write(' because ...'),nl,nl,
        how(Fact_name).

/* requested fact is not in the database. The system asks an appropriate question, or tries to prove it */
requested_fact(Fact_name):- Fact=..[Fact_name,_], clause(Fact,_), prove(Fact), forward_true.

/* invalid name */
requested_fact(Fact_name):- write(Fact_name),write(' invalid name'),nl.


/* HOW EXPLANATION */

/* retrieves the clause used to derive the fact, and outputs the clause right-hand side */
how(Fact_name):-
        clause(#(Fact_name,_,_,N),Queue),
        member(N,list_true), !,
        ((queuemember(Fact,Queue), not(functor(Fact,is,_)), write_fact(Fact,Queue), fail);
         (Fact=..[is,_,Exp], queuemember(Fact,Queue), write(Fact_name), write(' = '),
                        pretty_print(Exp,Queue),write('.'),nl,nl);
         nl).

/* fact was volunteered by the user */
how(Fact_name):-
        clause(#(Fact_name,_,_,N),_), member(N,list_useless), !, write('inputted directly by the user.'),nl,nl.

/* retrieves cause for failure, by listing non-satisfiable clauses and their subgoals */
how(Fact_name):-
        clause(#(Fact_name,_,_,_),Queue),
        queuemember(Fact,Queue),
        ((write_fact(Fact,Queue),fail);
         (Fact=..[Name,Status], write(Name), write(' expected value, '),
                ((var(Status),write('known'));(nonvar(Status),print(Status))),
                write(', has not been satisfied.'),nl);
         (pretty_print(Fact,Queue),write(' has not been satisfied.'),nl)),
        write('Again ? (y/n)'),nl, read(n),nl.

/* no further motivation possible */
how(Fact_name):- write('There are no other reasons.'),nl,nl.
```

```
/* USER INTERFACE: asks and reads values */

/* asks question, unless question is a consequence of a forward rule */
ask(T,Fact_name,Status,List, History):-
        template(T,Fact_name), read(Answer),nl,
        process_answer(Answer,Fact_name,Status,List, T, History).

/* templates for queries. Exploits high regularity of requested items (e.g. numeric values, yes/no questions, etc.) */
template(1,Fact_name):- write('Input the amount of '),write(Fact_name),write(' (n/why/?)'),nl.
template(2,Fact_name):- write('Input '),write(Fact_name),write(' (n/why/?)'),nl.
template(3,Fact_name):- write('Are you '),write(Fact_name),write(' ? (y/n/why/?)'),nl.
template(4,Fact_name):- write('Is it '),write(Fact_name),write(' ? (y/n/why/?)'),nl.
template(5,Fact_name):- write('Does it hold '),write(Fact_name),write(' ? (y/n/why/?)'),nl.
template(6,Fact_name):- write('Do you want '),write(Fact_name),write(' ? (y/n/why/?)'),nl.


/* INFERENCE RULES */

/* implementation of the basic backward inference engine */
prove(#(Rule_name, Info, X, N), Body, History) :-
        prove_rhs(H, Body, [#(Rule_name, Info, X, N)|History]), !.

/* prove (with two arguments) tries to prove facts */
prove(Pred, History) :-                              /* built-in predicates */
        functor(Pred, Pred_name, _),
        syspred(Pred_name),
        !,
        call(Pred).
prove(Pred, History) :-                              /* fact asserted previously*/
        Pred =.. [Fact_name, X],
        Pred1 =.. [Fact_name, Y],
        clause(Pred1, true),
        !,
        Y=X.
prove(Pred, History) :-                              /* the user is queried */
        Pred =.. [Fact_name, X],
        History \= [#(_, _, fw, _)|_],
        clause(Pred, Ask), !,
        Ask =.. Ask_list,
        append(Ask_list, [History], New_ask_list),
        New_ask =.. New_ask_list,
        call(New_ask), !,
        History = [#(_, _, _, N)],
        not(member(N, list_fail)).
prove(Pred, _) :- call(Pred).                        /* other predicates */

prove_rhs(A, A, History) :- A\=(_, _), !, prove(A, History).   /* proof of a conjunction of goals */
prove_rhs(Goal, (Goal, Rest), History) :-
        prove(Goal, History), !,
        prove_rhs(H, Rest, History).

/* process_answer processes the user's answer and triggers the backward or forward_fail inferences as appropriate */

process_answer(y,Fact_name,Status,[], _, _):-        /* answer is yes */
        !,
        add_database(Fact_name,true), add_useless(Fact_name),
        forward_fail(Fact_name,true), Status=true.
process_answer(n,Fact_name,Status,_, _, _):-         /* answer is no */
        !,
        add_database(Fact_name,false), add_useless(Fact_name),
        forward_fail(Fact_name,false), Status=false.
process_answer(why,Fact_name,Status, List, T, History):-   /* answer is why */
        History = [#(Rule_name, _, bw, N)|Rest],
```

```
        write('You are asked '),write(Fact_name),nl,
        write('because, during the derivation of '),write(Rule_name),
        write(' ...'),nl,nl,
        clause(#(Rule_name,_,bw,N),Queue),
        queuemember(Fact,Queue),
        ((Fact=..[Fact_name, Status], write(Fact_name),write(' must be '),
         ((var(Status),write('known'));(nonvar(Status),print(Status))),
          write('.'),nl,nl, !,
          ask(T, Fact_name, Status, List, History));
         (write_fact(Fact,Queue), fail)).
process_answer('?',Fact_name,Status,_, _, History):-          /* answer is unknown */
        Pred =.. [#, Fact_name, Info, bw, N],
        clause(Pred, Body),
        not(member(N, list_fail)),
        (prove(Pred, Body);(add(N,list_fail), fail)),          /* backward chaining derivation is started */
        !,
        add_database(Fact_name,Info),
        add(N,list_true),
        add_useless(Fact_name),
        forward_fail(Fact_name,true),
        Status=Info.
process_answer('?',Fact_name,Status,_):-                      /* catch all for answer unknown*/
        !,
        add_database(Fact_name,false),
        forward_fail(Fact_name,false),
        Status=false.
process_answer(Answer,Fact_name,Datum,List, T, History):-     /* answer is a Datum; checks if allowable */
        List\==[],
        convert(Answer,Datum),
        try(Datum,List),
        !,
        add_database(Fact_name,Datum),
        add_useless(Fact_name),
        forward_fail(Fact_name,true).
process_answer(_,Fact_name,Status,List):-                     /* catch-all */
        write('Answer not acceptable: retry'),nl,
        read(Answer),nl,
        process_answer(Answer,Fact_name,Status,List).


/* FORWARD REASONING */

/*
All rules usable in forward chaining are retrieved and fired, unless already fired previously. Full retrieval of all rules
is quite inefficient, and inadequate for most applications. It is, however, acceptable for the present tax adviser, since
the knowledge base (quite large) is highly modular, the modularity being a consequence of the decomposition of a
taxform into sections. A better algorithm should be used in different application areas.
*/
forward_true:-
        clause(#(Fact_name,Info,fw,N), Body),
        not(member(N,list_useless)), not(member(N,list_fail)), not(member(N,list_true)),
        prove(#(Fact_name,Info,fw,N), Body, []),
        add_database(Fact_name,Info),
        add(N,list_true),
        add_useless(Fact_name),
        forward_fail(Fact_name,true),
        forward_true.
forward_true.                                                 /* catch-all */

/* forward_fail reasoning */
```

```
/*
Retrieves all compatible rules, and searches for a different value of an asserted fact in their right-hand side. If found, the rule being examined is discarded because it can never fire. For remarks about efficiency, see the comment to the predicate "forward_true" above.
*/
forward_fail(Fact_name, Status):-
        clause(#(Rule_name,_,bw,N),Queue),
        not(member(N,list_useless)), not(member(N,list_fail)), not(member(N,list_true)),
        Fact=..[Fact_name,Request],
        queuemember(Fact,Queue),
        ((Status=true,Request==false);(Status=false,Request=true)),
        add(N,list_fail),
        not((clause(#(Rule_name,_,bw,M),_), not(member(M,list_fail)))),
        add_database(Rule_name,false),
        forward_fail(Rule_name,false),
        fail.
forward_fail(_,_).                          /* catch-all: forward_fail always succeeds */


/* UTILITIES */

append([], List, List).                     /* standard append */
append([A|Rest], List, [A|Result]) :- append(Rest, List, Result).

/* representation and output of numbers */

convert(X,Datum):-
        real(X), Datum is X*1E3.

convert((A,B),Datum):-
        integer(A), numeric(B),
        Datum is A+B/10.

convert([A|B],Datum):-
        real(A),
        integer(B),
        Datum is A*1E6+B.
convert([A|B],Datum):-
        real(A), real(B),
        Datum is A*1E9+B*1E3.
        convert(Datum,Datum).

try(_,[]).
try(Datum,[H|T]):- call(H), try(Datum,T).

add_database(Fact_name,Info):-                  /* add a fact to the database */
        Fact=..[Fact_name,Info],
        clause(Fact, true),
        !.
add_database(Fact_name,Info):-
        Fact=..[Fact_name, Info],
        assert(Fact),
        write(Fact_name),write(' is '),print(Info),write('.'),nl,nl.

queuemember(Y,(Y,_)).                           /* searches conjunction of goals */
queuemember(Y,(_,C)):- queuemember(Y,C).
queuemember(Y,Y):- Y\=(_,_).

/* predicates for accessing/modifying the bookkeeping lists */

member(N,List_name):- L=..[List_name,List], call(L), belongs(N,List).

belongs(X,[X|_]).                               /* this is the standard Prolog member */
```

```
belongs(X,[_|Y]):- belongs(X,Y).

add(N,List_name):- member(N,List_name), !.                /* updates a list */
add(N,List_name):-
        L=..[List_name,List],
        call(L),
        retractall(L),
        New_list=..[List_name,[N|List]],
        assert(New_list).

/*
"add_useless" retrieves all rules whose conclusion matches a given predicate name, and adds them to the list "useless", unless they are already members of some other list
*/
add_useless(Rule_name):-
        clause(#(Rule_name,_,_,N),_),
        not(member(N,list_true)), not(member(N,list_fail)),
        add(N,list_useless),
        fail.
add_useless(_).

terminate:-                                               /* the session is terminated */
        write('Session is terminated...'),nl,nl,
        additional_information,
        write('Do you want save data in memory ? (y/n)'),nl,
        read(y),nl,
        save_data,
        fail.
terminate:- clear_memory, write('Type "start" to start again'),nl, restart.

save_data:-                                               /* data saving utility */
        database_resident(Database),
        (progressive_number(Database,N);N is 0),
        retractall(progressive_number(Database,_)),
        M is N+1,
        assert(progressive_number(Database,M)),
        ((clause(#(Fact_name,_,_,_),_),
         Fact=..[Fact_name,Status],
         clause(Fact,Queue), Queue=(!,_),
         New_fact=..[Fact_name,Status,M],
         assert(New_fact:-Queue),
         fail);
         true).

cancel:-
        write('Session is annulled ...'),nl,nl,
        additional_information,
        clear_memory, write('Type "start" to start again'),nl,restart.

additional_information:-
        write('Do you need additional information ? (y/n)'),nl, read(y),nl,
        write('Input desired fact (or "?" for a listing)'),nl, read(Fact_name),nl,
        ((Fact_name\='?', Fact=..[Fact_name,_], not(clause(Fact,(!,_))),
                write(Fact_name),write(' was not asserted'),nl);
         requested_fact(Fact_name)),
         additional_information.
additional_information:-nl.

clear_memory:-                                            /* retracts all facts proved in the session */
        (clause(#(Fact_name,_,_,_),_), Fact=..[Fact_name,_], clause(Fact, (!, Y)), retract((Fact :- (!, Y))), fail);
        cancel_lists.

cancel_lists:-                                            /* resets the bookkeeping lists */
```

```
        retractall(list_true(_)),assert(list_true([])),
        retractall(list_fail(_)),assert(list_fail([])),
        retractall(list_useless(_)),assert(list_useless([])).

/* OUTPUT predicates */

write_fact(Fact,_):-
        Fact=..[Fact_name,Status], call(Fact), write(Fact_name),write(' is '),print(Status),nl,!.
write_fact(Exp,Queue):-
        functor(Exp,_,2), instantiate(Exp,Queue), call(Exp), pretty_print(Exp,Queue),write('proved'),nl.

instantiate(Exp,Queue):- nonvar(Queue), instantiate(Exp,Queue,true).
instantiate(Elem2,(Elem1,Elem2,_),True):- call((True,Elem1)),!.
instantiate(Exp,(Elem1,Elem2,Rest),True):- instantiate(Exp,(Elem2,Rest),(True,Elem1)).
instantiate(Elem2,(Elem1,Elem2),True):- call((True,Elem1)), !.

pretty_print(Exp,Queue):-
        nonvar(Exp), not(numeric(Exp)), Exp=..[Functor,Term1,Term2],
        pretty_print(Term1,Queue), write(Functor), pretty_print(Term2,Queue), !.
pretty_print(Term,Queue):-
        (var(Term), queuemember(Fact,Queue), Fact=..[Fact_name,Datum], Term==Datum, write(Fact_name),!);
        (numeric(Term), print(Term)).

/* portray: see the built-in predicate "print" */

portray(X):- var(X), write('true').
portray(Datum):-                                              /* output of numbers */
        real(Datum), Datum>=1000, !,
        E9 is fix(Datum/1E9), E6 is fix((Datum-E9*1E9)/1E6), E3 is fix((Datum-E9*1E9-E6*1E6)/1E3),
        E0 is Datum-E9*1E9-E6*1E6-E3*1E3,
        ((E9>0,write(E9),write('.'),write0(E6),write('.'),write0(E3));
        (E6>0,write(E6),write('.'),write0(E3));
         write(E3)),
        write('.'),write0(E0).
portray(Datum):-
        real(Datum), Int is fix(Datum), Dec is fix(real_round((Datum-Int)*10)), write(Int), write(','), write(Dec).

write0(X):- X<100, write('0'), fail.
write0(X):- X<10, write('0'), fail.
write0(X):- ((real(X), Y is fix(X)) ; Y=X), write(Y).

database_resident('?').                                       /* initializations */
list_true([]).
list_fail([]).
list_useless([]).
```

1.1.3 A knowledge base about fiscal regulations

This example section deals with the part of the tax form involving income from land ownership and farming activities. It also contains section-specific completeness and consistency rules, checking if the section has been correctly filled.

The following predefined predicate is used for the first time in the code below:

Expression1 =< Expression2
: succeeds if the result of the arithmetic expression Expression1 is less than or equal to the result of the arithmetic expression Expression2

```
/* note:     "predial" is income from land ownership, "agrarian" is income from land cultivation */
```

```
#(section_A_column_1,Amount,X,1) :- income_predial_total(Amount).

#(section_A_column_2,Amount,X,2) :- quota_IRPEF_predial(Amount).

#(section_A_column_3,Amount,X,3) :- quota_ILOR_predial(Amount).

#(section_A_column_4,Amount,X,4) :- income_agrarian_total(Amount).

#(section_A_column_5,Amount,X,5) :- quota_IRPEF_agrarian(Amount).

#(section_A_column_6,Amount,X,6) :- quota_ILOR_agrarian(Amount).

#(section_A_column_7,Amount,X,7) :- deduction_ILOR(Amount).

#(income_predial_total,Income_predial_total,X,8) :-
        land_owner(true), income_exempt(false), income_predial(Amount),
        land_rented_for_farming(true), annual_rental_fee(Fee),
        Fee<Amount*4/5, Income_predial_total is Fee.
#(income_predial_total,Income_predial_total,X,9):-
        land_owner(true), income_exempt(false),
        income_predial(Amount), land_rented_for_farming(false),
        failed_land_cultivation(true), Income_predial_total is Amount*0.3.
#(income_predial_total,Income_predial_total,X,10):-
        land_owner(true), income_exempt(false),
        income_predial(Amount), Income_predial_total is Amount.

#(quota_IRPEF_agrarian,Quota_IRPEF_predial,X,11):-
        income_predial_total(Income_predial_total), share_of_possession(Percentage),
        period_of_possession(Days),
        Quota_IRPEF_predial is Income_predial_total*Percentage/100*Days/365.

#(quota_ILOR_agrarian,Quota_ILOR_predial,X,12):-
        quota_IRPEF_agrarian(Quota_IRPEF_predial), mountain_lands(true),
        Quota_ILOR_predial is Quota_IRPEF_predial*0.5.
#(quota_ILOR_agrarian,Quota_ILOR_predial,X,13):-
        quota_IRPEF_agrarian(Quota_IRPEF_predial), Quota_ILOR_predial is Quota_IRPEF_predial.

#(income_agrarian_total,Income_agrarian_total,X,14):-
        greenhouse_and_mushroom_cultivations(true),
        cultivated_area(Area), max_cadastral_rate(Rate),
        Income_agrarian_total is Area*Rate.
#(income_agrarian_total,Income_agrarian_total,X,15):-
        land_owner(true), income_exempt(false),
        failed_land_cultivation(false), share_of_tenancy(Percentage),
        Percentage>0, income_agrarian(Amount),
        Income_agrarian_total is Amount*Percentage/100.
#(income_agrarian_total,Income_agrarian_total,X,16):-
        tenant_for_farming(true), income_exempt(false),
        failed_land_cultivation(false), income_agrarian(Amount),
        Income_agrarian_total is Amount.

#(quota_IRPEF_agrarian,Quota_IRPEF_agrarian,X,17):-
        income_agrarian_total(Income_agrarian_total), share_of_tenancy(Percentage),
        period_of_tenancy(Days),
        Quota_IRPEF_agrarian is Income_agrarian_total*Percentage/100*Days/365.

#(quota_ILOR_agrarian,Quota_ILOR_agrarian,X,18):-
        quota_IRPEF_agrarian(Quota_IRPEF_agrarian), mountain_lands(true),
        Quota_ILOR_agrarian is Quota_IRPEF_agrarian*0.5.
#(quota_ILOR_agrarian,Quota_ILOR_agrarian,X,19):-
        quota_IRPEF_agrarian(Quota_IRPEF_agrarian), Quota_ILOR_agrarian is Quota_IRPEF_agrarian.

#(deduction_ILOR,Deduction_ILOR,X,20):-
```

```
        income_agrarian_total(Income_agrarian_total), labourer(true),
        Income_agrarian_total>=14E6, Income_agrarian_total=<28E6,
        period_of_tenancy(Days), share_of_tenancy(Percentage),
        Deduction_ILOR is Income_agrarian_total*Days/365*Percentage/100*0.5.
#(deduction_ILOR,Deduction_ILOR,X,21):-
        income_agrarian_total(Income_agrarian_total), labourer(true),
        Income_agrarian_total>28E6,
        period_of_tenancy(Days), share_of_tenancy(Percentage),
        Deduction_ILOR is 14E6*Days/365*Percentage/100.

#(income_exempt,true,X,22):- losses_in_normal_production_due_to_natural_events(true).
#(income_exempt,true,X,23):- public_parks(true).

#(land_owner,true,fw,24):- income_agrarian(Amount), numeric(Amount), tenant_for_farming(false).
#(land_owner,true,fw,25):- income_predial(Amount), numeric(Amount).

#(income_predial,false,fw,26):- land_owner(false).

#(share_of_possession,false,fw,27):- land_owner(false).

#(period_of_possession,false,fw,28):- land_owner(false).

#(share_of_tenancy,0,fw,29):- land_rented_for_farming(true), income_agrarian(false).
#(share_of_tenancy,Percentage,fw,30):-
        land_rented_for_farming(false), share_of_possession(Quota),
        numeric(Quota), Percentage is Quota.

#(period_of_tenancy,Days,fw,31):-
        land_rented_for_farming(false), period_of_possession(Period),
        numeric(Period), Days is Period.

#(land_rented_for_farming,true,fw,32):-
        land_owner(true), income_agrarian(false).

#(tenant_for_farming,true,X,33):-
        income_agrarian(Amount), numeric(Amount), land_owner(false).

#(losses_in_normal_production_due_to_natural_events,false,fw,34):- income_exempt(false).

#(public_parks,false,fw,35):- income_exempt(false).

#(income_agrarian,_,bw,36).

#(annual_rental_fee,false,fw,37):- land_owner(false).

#(failed_land_cultivation,_,bw,38).

#(mountain_lands,_,bw,39).

#(greenhouse_and_mushroom_cultivations,_,bw,40).

#(cultivated_area,false,fw,41):- greenhouse_and_mushroom_cultivations(false).

#(max_cadastral_rate,false,fw,42):- greenhouse_and_mushroom_cultivations(false).

#(labourer,false,fw,43):- income_agrarian(false).

#(abandon_session,_,bw,44).

#(automatic_filling,_,bw,45).

/* rules defining complete and correct filling of a section */
#(section_A_filled,true,X,46):-
```

```
        section_A_column_1(Imp1), numeric(Imp1),
        section_A_column_2(Imp2), numeric(Imp2),
        section_A_column_3(Imp3), numeric(Imp3),
        section_A_column_4(Imp4), numeric(Imp4),
        section_A_column_5(Imp5), numeric(Imp5),
        section_A_column_6(Imp6), numeric(Imp6),
        section_A_column_7(_).
#(section_A_filled,true,X,47):-
        section_A_column_1(Imp1), numeric(Imp1),
        section_A_column_2(Imp2), numeric(Imp2),
        section_A_column_3(Imp3), numeric(Imp3),
        failed_land_cultivation(true).
#(section_A_filled,true,X,48):-
        section_A_column_1(Imp1), numeric(Imp1),
        section_A_column_2(Imp2), numeric(Imp2),
        section_A_column_3(Imp3), numeric(Imp3),
        land_rented_for_farming(true),
        share_of_tenancy(0).
#(section_A_filled,true,X,49):-
        section_A_column_4(Imp4), numeric(Imp4),
        section_A_column_5(Imp5), numeric(Imp5),
        section_A_column_6(Imp6), numeric(Imp6),
        section_A_column_7(_),
        tenant_for_farming(true).

#(terminate,true,fw,50):- section_A_filled(true), terminate.

/* rules checking consistency over the section */
#(cancel,true,fw,51):- income_exempt(true), cancel.
#(cancel,true,fw,52):- land_owner(false), tenant_for_farming(false), cancel.
#(cancel,true,fw,53):-
        income_predial_total(Income_predial_total), numeric(Income_predial_total),
        quota_IRPEF_agrarian(Quota_IRPEF_predial), numeric(Quota_IRPEF_predial),
        Quota_IRPEF_predial>Income_predial_total,
        cancel.
#(cancel,true,fw,54):-
        income_predial_total(Income_predial_total), numeric(Income_predial_total),
        quota_ILOR_agrarian(Quota_ILOR_predial), numeric(Quota_ILOR_predial),
        Quota_ILOR_predial>Income_predial_total,
        cancel.
#(cancel,true,fw,55):-
        income_agrarian_total(Income_agrarian_total), numeric(Income_agrarian_total),
        quota_IRPEF_agrarian(Quota_IRPEF_agrarian), numeric(Quota_IRPEF_agrarian),
        Quota_IRPEF_agrarian>Income_agrarian_total,
        cancel.
#(cancel,true,fw,56):-
        income_agrarian_total(Income_agrarian_total), numeric(Income_agrarian_total),
        quota_ILOR_agrarian(Quota_ILOR_agrarian), numeric(Quota_ILOR_agrarian),
        Quota_ILOR_agrarian>Income_agrarian_total,
        cancel.
#(cancel,true,fw,57):-
        income_agrarian_total(Income_agrarian_total), numeric(Income_agrarian_total),
        deduction_ILOR(Deduction_ILOR), numeric(Deduction_ILOR),
        Deduction_ILOR>Income_agrarian_total/2,
        cancel.
#(cancel,true,fw,58):- section_A_filled(false), cancel.
#(cancel,true,fw,59):- abandon_session(true), cancel.

/* automatic filling of the section: the system drives the dialogues */
#(automatic,true,fw,60):- automatic_filling(true), #(section_A_filled,true,bw,_), terminate.
```

1.1.4 Queries to the user about unknown facts

The following rules, one for each fact to be asserted above, define ad hoc user queries. Queries are issued in intermediate steps, in the case the user can provide an early answer and thus avoid a useless derivation (see Section 1.3 above). Furthermore, they are used to gather knowledge about basic facts, which the user must know, otherwise the program would fail. Note that queries are not directly associated to facts. Rather, the first argument in the predicate "ask" (Section 1.3 above) acts as a reference to a template with a suitable question for groups of related facts.

```
section_A_column_1(Income_predial_total):-
        ask(1,section_A_column_1,Income_predial_total,[real(Income_predial_total)]).
section_A_column_2(Quota_IRPEF_predial):-
        ask(1,section_A_column_2,Quota_IRPEF_predial,[real(Quota_IRPEF_predial)]).
section_A_column_3(Quota_ILOR_predial):-
        ask(1,section_A_column_3,Quota_ILOR_predial,[real(Quota_ILOR_predial)]).
section_A_column_4(Income_agrarian_total):-
        ask(1,section_A_column_4,Income_agrarian_total,[real(Income_agrarian_total)]).
section_A_column_5(Quota_IRPEF_agrarian):-
        ask(1,section_A_column_5,Quota_IRPEF_agrarian,[real(Quota_IRPEF_agrarian)]).
section_A_column_6(Quota_ILOR_agrarian):-
        ask(1,section_A_column_6,Quota_ILOR_agrarian,[real(Quota_ILOR_agrarian)]).
section_A_column_7(Deduction_ILOR):-
        ask(1,section_A_column_7,Deduction_ILOR,[real(Deduction_ILOR),Deduction_ILOR<14E6]).
income_predial_total(Amount):-
        ask(1,income_predial_total,Amount,[real(Amount)]).
quota_IRPEF_predial(Amount):-
        ask(quota_IRPEF_predial,Amount,[real(Amount)]).
quota_ILOR_predial(Amount):-
        ask(quota_ILOR_predial,Amount,[real(Amount)]).
income_agrarian_total(Amount):-
        ask(1,income_agrarian_total,Amount,[real(Amount)]).
quota_IRPEF_agrarian(Amount):-
        ask(1,quota_IRPEF_agrarian,Amount,[real(Amount)]).
quota_ILOR_agrarian(Amount):-
        ask(1,quota_ILOR_agrarian,Amount,[real(Amount)]).
deduction_ILOR(Amount):-
        ask(1,deduction_ILOR,Amount,[real(Amount)]).
income_exempt(Status):-
        ask(4,income_exempt,Status,[]).
land_owner(Status):-
        ask(3,land_owner,Status,[]).
income_predial(Amount):-
        ask(1,income_predial,Amount,[real(Amount)]).
annual_rental_fee(Fee):-
        ask(1,annual_rental_fee,Fee,[real(Fee)]).
failed_land_cultivation(Status):-
        ask(5,failed_land_cultivation,Status,[]).
losses_in_normal_production_due_to_natural_events(Status):-
        ask(5,losses_in_normal_production_due_to_natural_events,Status,[]).
public_parks(Status):-
        ask(4,public_parks,Status,[]).
share_of_possession(Percentage):-
        ask(2,share_of_possession,Percentage,[numeric(Percentage),Percentage>0,Percentage=<100]).
period_of_possession(Days):-
        ask(2,period_of_possession,Days,[integer(Days),Days>0,Days=<365]).
share_of_tenancy(Percentage):-
        ask(2,share_of_tenancy,Percentage,[numeric(Percentage),Percentage>=0,Percentage=<100]).
period_of_tenancy(Days):-
        ask(2,period_of_tenancy,Days,[integer(Days),Days>0,Days=<365]).
mountain_lands(Status):-
        ask(4,mountain_lands,Status,[]).
land_rented_for_farming(Status):-
```

```
        ask(4,land_rented_for_farming,Status,[]).
greenhouse_and_mushroom_cultivations(Status):-
        ask(4,greenhouse_and_mushroom_cultivations,Status,[]).
cultivated_area(Area):-
        ask(2,cultivated_area,Area,[numeric(Area)]).
max_cadastral_rate(Rate):-
        ask(2,max_cadastral_rate,Rate,[real(Rate)]).
income_agrarian(Amount):-
        ask(1,income_agrarian,Amount,[real(Amount)]).
tenant_for_farming(Status):-
        ask(3,tenant_for_farming,Status,[]).
labourer(Status):-
        ask(3,labourer,Status,[]).
automatic_filling(Status):-
        ask(6,automatic_filling,Status,[]).
abandon_session(Status):-
        ask(6,abandon_session,Status,[]).
```

1.2 An algorithm for causal and consistency analysis

The following code is an implementation of the program described in Chapter 5.10.5. Refer to that Section for an overview.

1.2.1 A qualitative algebra

Since the algebra described in Chapter 5.10.5 is not associative, each operation implemented below is designed to accept only two operands.

Allowable levels are stored in the variable "levels". Any number of levels can be assigned to "levels", provided they are listed in increasing order.

The functions "POSITION" and "NTH" are used in the following code for the first time:

(POSITION Element List)
(NTH Number List)

POSITION returns a number, corresponding to the position of the element "Element" in the list "List". By definition, the position of the first element of a list is 0. The position of the second element of a list is 1, of the third element is 2, etc. NTH performs the complementary task of returning a list element, given its position (argument "Number") and the list it belongs to (argument "List"). For instance, (NTH 0 List) is the same as (CAR List).

All other external functions have been defined previously; to locate their definitions, please look up the function names (in capital letters) in Appendix 2.1.

```
;;      Global variable containing the allowable levels in increasing order

(SETQ levels '(S M H))


;;      Access functions

(DEFUN sign (Label)
 (CAR Label))

(DEFUN level (Label)
 (CDR Label))

(DEFUN same-label (Label1 Label2)
 (EQUAL Label1 Label2))

(DEFUN same-sign (Label1 Label2)
 (EQUAL (sign Label1) (sign Label2)))

(DEFUN same-level (Label1 Label2)
 (EQUAL (level Label1) (level Label2)))

(DEFUN unknown-sign? (Label)
 (NULL (sign Label)))

(DEFUN make-label (sign level)
 (CONS sign level))
```

```
;;        Return label with lower level

(DEFUN inf-level (Label1 Label2)
 (IF (same-level Label1 Label2) Label1
  (IF (< (position (level Label1) levels) (position (level Label2) levels))
   Label1
   Label2)))


;;        Return label with higher level

(DEFUN sup-level (Label1 Label2)
 (IF (same-level Label1 Label2) Label1
  (IF (> (position (level Label1) levels) (position (level Label2) levels))
   Label1
   Label2)))


;;        Return level preceding the label level

(DEFUN previous-level (Label)
  (IF (EQUAL (level Label) (CAR levels)) (CAR levels)
     (nth (1- (position (level Label) levels)) levels)))


;;        Multiplication

(DEFUN label-mult (Label1 Label2)
  (make-label (sign-mult Label1 Label2)
              (level-mult Label1 Label2)))

(DEFUN sign-mult (Label1 Label2)
  (IF (unknown-sign? Label1) (sign Label2)
     (IF (unknown-sign? Label2) (sign Label1)
        (COND ((same-sign Label1 Label2) 'POS)
             (T 'NEG)))))

(DEFUN level-mult (Label1 Label2)
  (level (inf-level Label1 Label2)))


;;        Addition

(DEFUN label-add (Label1 Label2)
  (COND ((same-sign Label1 Label2) (sup-level Label1 Label2))
       ((unknown-sign? Label1)
       (make-label (sign Label2) (level (sup-level Label1 Label2))))
       ((unknown-sign? Label2)
       (make-label (sign Label1) (level (sup-level Label1 Label2))))
       ((same-level Label1 Label2)
        (LET ((result-level (previous-level Label1)))
          (LIST (make-label (sign Label1) result-level)
               (make-label (sign Label2) result-level))))
       (T (sup-level Label1 Label2))))
```

1.2.2 The propagator

The propagator is essentially a search program (see Chapter 5.8 and 5.9). The program logically consists of three separate modules, which are illustrated in Sections 1.2.2.1 to 1.2.2.3 below.

1.2.2.1 The propagation module

This module contains the propagation algorithm.

Given a model, a set of initial states with known values and a goal state, the propagation algorithm tries to assign values to the other states in the model, to be computed from the already known values and from the provided information about the strength of the causality among states (see Chapter 5.10.2 and 5.10.5). The algorithm stops as soon as it can assign definite values to the goal state.

A state can be assigned more than one value, since there might be several state properties which are of interest to the user. The propagator is not directly concerned with the structure and information content of the model states, as long as the required update functions can be specified according to the guidelines in Section 1.2.2.2. The two predicates "closed?" and "source?" (defined in Section 1.2.2.2 below) control the extent of the search:

(closed? state)

succeeds if the values of "state" can no longer be modified through further propagation. Any further causal influence on a closed state is therefore neglected. The predicate:

(source? state)

succeeds if the values of "state" can be propagated to the causally dependent states. If it fails, the propagation from "state" is temporarily suspended, waiting for some conditions to be satisfied. Such conditions are tested each time a causal impact modifies the state (see Section 1.2.2.2 below for an example of a specification).

Contexts are generated as the consequence of ambiguous results in qualitative operations; in the specific case of the algebra in Section 1.2.1 above, the addition of two labels with same levels but opposite signs returns two labels (i.e. two alternative results) rather than one. Since ambiguity is commonplace in qualitative modeling, qualitative propagators must be designed with facilities to cope with it. Two minimal specifications must be met:

- every set of alternative state values must be propagated (otherwise, potential solutions would be lost)
- propagations for each set of alternative values must be kept separate (otherwise inconsistent assignments would arise)

The above objectives can be achieved with several implementation strategies:

- the model being propagated is duplicated every time an ambiguity arises. The propagator then works on one copy at time, the propagation within one copy being non-ambiguous. This approach is however inefficient for large applications
- knowledge about which values correspond to which alternative (often called assumption) is explicitely maintained. It is easy to see that such dependency can be represented as an AND/OR graph, whose topology is determined by both the topology of the model, and the specific values/algebra used in the computations (pruning)
- the algorithm below presents a variation to the preceding option. Values in states are labeled with symbols (called *markers*). An *environment* is then defined as a collection of markers, in such a way that all values, whose labels belong to the environment, are consistent, i.e. they represent the result of the propagation under one allowable set of choices. The algorithm provides the tools to maintain the environments transparently to the user

For computational convenience, a *context* is defined as an environment together with a set of source states in that environment. Source states are upgraded each time a state satisfies the "source?" predicate in a given environment. A context is discarded when either the goal state satisfies "closed?", or no source nodes are available in the context.

Contexts are searched depth-first (see Chapter 5.8), while sources within a context are propagated breadth-first (see Chapter 5.9). This way, the causal distance between the model states can be assessed, and used as a decision criterion (see Chapter 5.10.2).

Five new built-in LISP functions are introduced in the code below.

PROGN accepts as arguments any number of expressions, evaluates all of them, and returns the value of the last expression:

```
(PROGN <expression1> <expression2> ... <expressionN>)
```

POP argument must be a list:

```
(POP List)
```

POP returns the CAR of "List" and, as a side effect, the CDR of "List" is assigned to "List". Therefore, POP is roughly equivalent to:

```
(PROG1 (CAR List) (SETQ List (CDR List)))
```

where PROG1 is a built-in predicate simlar to PROGN, except that it returns the value of the first expression.

GETHASH accepts two arguments (a key and a table), and returns the datum associated to the key in the table:

```
(GETHASH key table)
```

"table" can be roughly seen as an array, in which a datum is stored under a "key". The table is built using the built-in function MAKE-HASH-TABLE, which is explained in Section 1.2.4.

DO is a template for iteration. It is a very general iteration statement, and therefore its structure is a bit complicate:

```
(DO ((variable1 <expression1a> <expression1b>)
     (variable2 <expression2a> <expression2b>)
     :
     (variableN <expressionNa> <expressionNb>))
    (<termination predicate> <expression-result>)
       <body>
```

where:

- $variable_i$ is a variable local to the DO statement;
- the value of <$expression_{ia}$>, which is evaluated only the first time the DO is entered, is the initial value of $variable_i$
- the value of <$expression_{ib}$>, which is evaluated at each iteration, upgrades the value of $variable_i$ during the iteration
- <termination predicate> is a predicate which succeeds when termination conditions for the iteration are satisfied. If it succeeds, the function <expression-result> is evaluated, and its value is returned as the value of the DO
- <body> is a sequence of expressions, which may contain the $variable_i$ and are evaluated for side-effects only (e.g. computing the arguments of the upgrade functions)

GENTEMP is used to get fresh symbols. It returns a symbol never used before, whose first part is "string", and whose second part is a number, which is incremented each time GENTEMP is called:

```
(GENTEMP "string")
```

In the following code, GENTEMP is used to create new markers.

```
;;      Functions for creating/accessing contexts.

(DEFUN make-context (an-env a-list-of-source-nodes)
 (LIST an-env a-list-of-source-nodes))
(DEFUN get-env (a-context)
 (CAR a-context))
(DEFUN get-sources (a-context)
 (CADR a-context))


;;      Propagation algorithm

(DEFUN propagator (Goal Start-nodes model)


;;      Depth-first search over contexts

 (DEFUN recursive-propagator (Contexts)
  (IF (NULL Contexts) NIL
   (recursive-propagator
    (APPEND (process-context (get-env (CAR Contexts)) (get-sources (CAR Contexts)) '())
      (CDR Contexts)))))


;;      Breadth-first search over source nodes within a context

 (DEFUN process-context (env sources new-contexts)
  (IF (NULL sources) (return-contexts new-contexts env)
    (LET ((current (POP sources)))
     (IF (EQUAL goal current)
       (IF (closed? (GETHASH goal table)) (PROGN (answer goal env table) NIL)
         (process-context env sources new-contexts))
      (LET ((Children (state-successors (GETHASH current table))))
       (DO ((Transition (POP Children) (POP Children))
            (contexts new-contexts (merge-contexts contexts new-ctx))
           (source-nodes sources (APPEND source-nodes new-sources))
            (new-ctx NIL NIL)
            (new-sources NIL NIL))
           ((NULL Transition) (process-context env source-nodes contexts))
             (LET ((result (process-node current Transition env)))
               (SETQ new-sources (extract-sources result)
                     new-ctx (extract-new-contexts result))))))))


;;      Elementary propagation of one impact

 (DEFUN process-node (N Transition env)
  (LET ((new (CAR Transition))
        (state (GETHASH (CAR Transition) table))
        (father-state (GETHASH N table)))
   (IF (closed? state env) NIL
    (PROGN
    (update-state new state N father-state Transition env)
```

```
    (IF (source? state env) (update-context (add-result state env) (CAR env) new state)
        NIL)))))
```

```
;;      Initializations

  (SETQ first-marker (GENTEMP "marker-"))
  (SETQ table (build-model model first-marker))
  (recursive-propagator (LIST (make-context (LIST first-marker) Start-nodes))))
```

1.2.2.2 The context maintenance module

"update-context" checks if the "result" of a qualitative operation is ambiguous; if so, it returns one context for each allowable value. The context environment consists of a new marker, while the context source-list consists of the node whose value is being computed. If the result is not ambiguous, the current marker is used instead.

```
(DEFUN update-context (result marker node state)
 (IF (CDR result)
   (MAPCAR
   #'(LAMBDA (a-result)
      (LET ((new-marker (GENTEMP "marker-")))
        (update-value new-marker state a-result)
        (make-context (LIST new-marker) (LIST node))))
   result)
  (PROGN (update-value marker state (CAR result))
         (LIST (make-context (LIST marker) (LIST node))))))
```

"extract-sources" and "extract-new-contexts" are two functions for extracting information from the value of "update-context". "extract-sources" returns the source node in the case of no ambiguity (just one context returned). "extract-new-contexts" is non-NIL only in the case of ambiguity.

```
(DEFUN extract-sources (context-list)
 (IF (NULL (CDR context-list)) (get-sources (CAR context-list))))

(DEFUN extract-new-contexts (context-list)
 (IF (CDR context-list) (MAPCAR #'LIST context-list)))
```

"merge-contexts" accepts two lists of contexts in input, and returns a list of list of contexts, in which compatible contexts are combined together. Alternatively, it can be interpreted as a "cartesian" product among context lists, viewed as sets.

```
(DEFUN merge-contexts (C1 C2)
 (COND ((NULL C1) C2)
       ((NULL C2) C1)
       (T (MAPCAN #'(LAMBDA (X) (MAPCAR #'(LAMBDA (Y) (APPEND X Y))
                                                      C2))
                  C1))))
```

"return-contexts" fuses a list of compatible contexts into just one new context, by collecting together the markers and the source nodes from each context.

```
(DEFUN return-contexts (New-contexts env) ;; fusion of compatible scenarios
 (MAPCAR
     #'(LAMBDA (list-of-compatible-contexts)
        (LET ((markers (MAPCAR #'(LAMBDA (X) (CAR (get-env X))) list-of-compatible-contexts))
              (sources (MAPCAR #'(LAMBDA (X) (CAR (get-sources X))) list-of-compatible-contexts)))
          (IF (NULL (CDR markers)) (make-context (APPEND markers env) sources)
            (LET ((new-marker (GENTEMP "marker-")))
              (make-context (CONS new-marker (APPEND markers env)) sources)))))
```

New-contexts))

1.2.2.3 The state update module

The following functions show one possible implementation of state update criteria. In this implementation, "closed?" is true if "source?" is true, i.e. the sources of the propagation are at the same time the nodes with final values. Furthermore, "source?" succeeds as soon as all causal impacts to a node have been explored at least once. As a consequence of these definitions, the propagation algorithm succeeds only if all exogenous states with a causal link to the goal state (see Example 7, Chapter 5.8) are given initial values and passed as an argument (Start-nodes) to the propagator. The propagation fails if the model is underspecified, or if there are circuits. Of course, other implementations are possible for the state-upgrade functions.

In this specific example, a state is defined as follows:

```
(DEFSTRUCT state
 (successors NIL)
 (open-causes NIL)
 (causes NIL)
 (value NIL)
 (temp-impacts NIL)
 (label NIL)
 (expected-values NIL))
```

DEFSTRUCT is a built-in function for defining user-specified data types. The symbol just after DEFSTRUCT is the type name (in this case, "state"). The lists define the type fields together with the corresponding initial values (optional). The resulting data structure is similar to a record in other programming languages. As a side effect of the evaluation of DEFSTRUCT, LISP automatically defines a number of new functions:

- a type constructor, with name "make-<type name>" (in this case, "make-state") and no arguments, returning a data structure of the corresponding type
- an accessor function for each defined field, with name "<type name>-<field name>" (e.g. "state-value", "state-temp-impacts", etc.), and one argument (a data structure of the corresponding type), and returning the value stored under the specified field. The accessor functions, together with SETF, can be used to update the value of a field as well:

  ```
  (SETF (<accessor> structure) new-value)
  ```

In the current example, the field "successors" stores the successors of a state (i.e. its direct effects). This information only depends on the topology of the model (see Chapter 5.10).

The field "open-causes" contains the direct causes of a state not yet considered in a given context; each list of open causes is associated to an environment marker. "open-causes" is needed by "source?".

The field "causes" contains all direct causes of a state, as resulting from the topology of the model. Such field is obviously context-independent, and never modified by the propagation algorithm. The field "value" contains the "amplitude" of a change in a state and in a given context.

The field "temp-impacts" stores the context-dependent impacts upon which the computation of "value" is based. It is used in the computation of the "value" field, but is also a useful hook for building explanation facilities.

The field "label" is set to true if, in a given context, the state is closed.

The field "expected-values" enables the user to specify target amplitudes or set of amplitudes (i.e. constraints) for model states. By comparing the "value" and the "expected-values" fields, amplitude inconsistencies (see Chapter 5.10.2 and 5.10.5) can be easily detected, and traced back to the incompatible assumptions. Also, inconsistent contexts can be discarded early in the search process.

The following functions are constructors/accessors for single values of state fields. The structure stored under each field is a list of such elements. This is because several values may be needed, corresponding to different environments, as explained above. Some functions are not needed in the algorithm, but are nevertheless defined for the sake of completeness.

```
;;      An element of the value field of the node structure

(DEFUN make-value (a-marker a-label)
 (LIST a-marker a-label))
(DEFUN get-marker-from-value (a-value)
 (CAR a-value))
(DEFUN get-label-from-value (a-value)
 (CADR a-value))
(DEFUN no-value? (a-value)
 (NULL a-value))


;;      An element from the temp-impacts field of the node structure

(DEFUN make-impact (a-marker a-source a-label)
 (LIST a-marker a-source a-label))
(DEFUN get-marker-from-impact (an-impact)
 (CAR an-impact))
(DEFUN get-source-from-impact (an-impact)
 (CADR an-impact))
(DEFUN get-label-from-impact (an-impact)
 (CADDR an-impact))
(DEFUN empty-impact? (an-impact)
 (NULL an-impact))


;;      An element from the open-causes field of the node structure

(DEFUN make-open-causes (a-marker a-list-of-causes)
 (LIST a-marker a-list-of-causes))
(DEFUN get-marker-from-causes (an-open-cause)
 (CAR an-open-causes))
(DEFUN get-causes (an-open-cause)
 (CADR an-open-cause))
(DEFUN no-open-causes? (an-open-cause)
 (NULL (CADR an-open-cause)))


;;      An element from the closed field of the node structure

(DEFUN make-closed-flag (a-marker)
 (LIST a-marker))
```

The functions below update state fields. Field update functions are called by the top-level function "update-state".

```
(DEFUN update-state (new state N father-state Transition env)
 (update-impacts state father-state (CDR Transition) N env)
 (update-causes state N env))

(DEFUN update-value (a-marker state a-label) (PUSH (make-value a-marker a-label) (state-value state)))

(DEFUN update-impacts (state father-state strength source env)
```

```
(LET ((value (CAR (search-in-env #'state-value father-state env :one))))
 (IF (no-value? value) (break)
  (SETF (state-temp-impacts state)
   (APPEND (state-temp-impacts state)
        (LIST (make-impact (CAR env) source (label-mult (get-label-from-value value) strength))))))))

(DEFUN update-causes (state N env)
 (LET ((ctx-causes (CAR (search-in-env #'state-open-causes state env :one))))
  (PUSH (make-open-causes (CAR env) (REMOVE N (get-causes ctx-causes))) (state-open-causes state))))

(DEFUN source? (state env)
 (IF (no-open-causes? (CAR (search-in-env #'state-open-causes state env :one)))
  (PROGN (PUSH (make-closed-flag (CAR env)) (state-label state))
          (filter state env))))


;; Filter the state-temp-impacts. If just two impacts are available, they are both taken into account.
;; Otherwise, the impacts are sorted, and the two largest impacts are retained for further propagation.

 (DEFUN filter (state env)
  (LET ((impacts (search-in-env #'state-temp-impacts state env :all)))
   (IF (<= (LENGTH impacts) 2) T
    (SETF (state-temp-impacts state) (select-impacts (CAR impacts) (CADR impacts) (CDDR impacts))))))

 (DEFUN select-impacts (First Second Rest)
  (IF (NULL rest) (LIST First Second)
   (LET ((candidate (CAR Rest)))
    (COND ((NOT (EQUAL (level (sup-level (get-label-from-impact Second) (get-label-from-impact candidate)))
                        (level (get-label-from-impact Second))))
           (select-impacts First candidate (CDR Rest)))
          ((NOT (EQUAL (level (sup-level (get-label-from-impact First) (get-label-from-impact candidate)))
                        (level (get-label-from-impact First))))
           (select-impacts Second candidate (CDR Rest)))
          (T (select-impacts First Second (CDR Rest)))))))

 (DEFUN closed? (state env) (search-in-env #'state-label state env :one))


;;        Add the impact values and return the state value. May return more than one result

 (DEFUN add-result (state env)
  (LET ((impacts (search-in-env #'state-temp-impacts state env :all)))
   (IF (NULL (CDR impacts)) (LIST (get-label-from-impact (CAR impacts)))
    (LET ((result (APPLY 'label-add (MAPCAR 'get-label-from-impact impacts))))
     (IF (ATOM (CAR result)) (LIST result) result)))))


;;        Context-dependent retrieval of elements from state fields

(DEFUN search-in-env (search-function state env flag)
 (LET ((candidates (FUNCALL search-function state)))
  (FUNCALL
   (CADR (ASSOC flag '((:one SOME) (:all REMOVE-IF-NOT))))
   #'(LAMBDA (X) (AND (MEMBER (CAR X) env) (LIST X)))
   candidates)))
```

1.2.2.4 The output of the propagation

The function "answer" is called whenever a goal state is found. It may use the state fields to trace back the impacts on the goal state, as well as to detect inconsistencies.

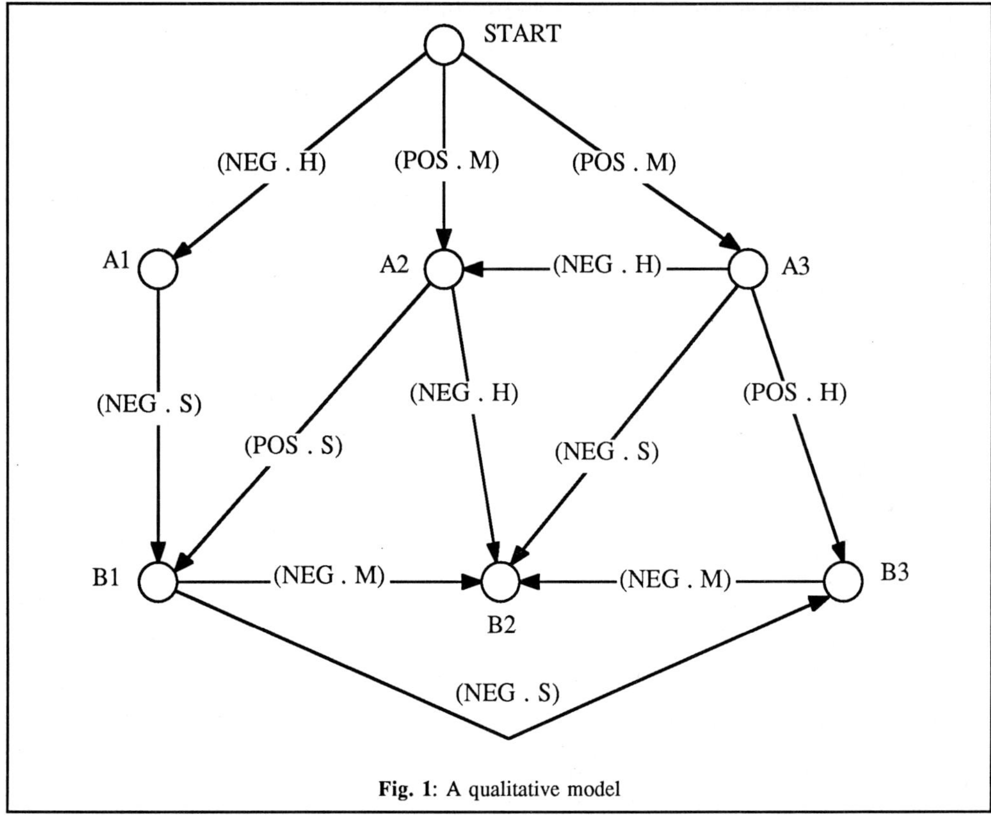

Fig. 1: A qualitative model

1.2.3 An example

Fig. 1 shows a simple model. The following code is an example of how the model is to be defined, and the propagation started. Two new built-in functions are used in the "build-model" function below:

(MAKE-HASH-TABLE :size <expression>)

returns a table data structure, with size (a keyword parameter) bound to the value of <expression>.

(DOLIST (element list <result expression>)
<body>)

is a simplification of the DO iteration. "element" is initialized to each element of "list" at each iteration. After the last iteration (corresponding to the last element of "list"), <result expression> is evaluated an its value is returned as the value of the DOLIST iteration.

```
;;      Definition of the model datatype

(DEFSTRUCT model
  (name NIL)
  (nodes NIL))
```

```
;;      The definition of the state data type is the same as in Section 1.2.2.3

(DEFSTRUCT state
 (successors NIL)
 (open-causes NIL)
 (causes NIL)
 (value NIL)
 (temp-impacts NIL)
 (label NIL)
 (expected-values NIL))


;;      The variable "my-model" stores the model in Fig. 1

(SETQ my-model (make-model :name 'TEST :nodes '(Start A1 A2 A3 B1 B2 B3)))


;;      Definition of each state

(SETQ Start (make-state
         :successors '((A1 . (NEG . H)) (A2 . (POS . M)) (A3 . (POS . M)))
         :value '(POS . H)))
(SETQ A1 (make-state :successors '((B1 . (NEG . S)))
              :causes '(Start)))
(SETQ A2 (make-state :successors '((B2 . (NEG . H)) (B1 . (POS . S)))
              :causes '(Start A3)))
(SETQ A3 (make-state :successors '((A2 . (NEG . H)) (B2 . (NEG . S)) (B3 . (POS . H)))
              :causes '(Start)))
(SETQ B1 (make-state :successors '((B2 . (NEG . M)) (B3 . (NEG . S)))
              :causes '(A1 A2)))
(SETQ B2 (make-state :successors '(())
              :causes '(B1 A2 B3 A3)))
(SETQ B3 (make-state :successors '((B2 . (NEG . M)))
              :causes '(B1 A3)))


;;      Build the hash table to be passed to the propagator. It initializes the fields used by the propagator

(DEFUN build-model (model a-marker)
 (LET ((table (MAKE-HASH-TABLE :size (LENGTH (model-nodes model)))))
  (DOLIST (node (model-nodes model) table)
   (SETF (GETHASH node table) (copy-state (EVAL node)))
   (LET ((new-state (GETHASH node table)))
    (SETF (state-open-causes new-state) (LIST (make-open-causes a-marker (state-causes new-state))))
    (AND (state-value new-state)
      (SETF (state-value new-state) (LIST (make-value a-marker (state-value new-state)))))))))


;;      Call to the propagator

(propagator 'B2 '(Start) my-model)
```

1.3 Prolog natural language parser for economic statements

Here we give the Prolog code related to the natural language (NL) understanding of economic statements as presented in Chapter 9.2. This includes:

- in Section 3.1, the vocabulary required by this application, including but also beyond the few test cases given in Chapter 9, Table 1
- in Section 3.2, the DCG grammar for NL analysis of economic statements, including but also beyond the few test cases given in Chapter 9, Table 1
- in Section 3.3, the Prolog NL parser.

1.3.1 Vocabulary for the NL parser

```
determiner(det(the))          -->  [the]
determiner(det(a))            -->  [a]
determiner(det(an))           -->  [an]
determiner(det(at))           -->  [at]
determiner(det(some))         -->  [some]
determiner(det(that))         -->  [that]
determiner(det(is))           -->  [is]
determiner(det(their))        -->  [their]
determiner(det(no))           -->  [no]

noun(noun(mass))              -->  [mass]
noun(noun(inflation))         -->  [inflation]
noun(noun(fed))               -->  [fed]
noun(noun(credit))            -->  [credit]
noun(noun(policy))            -->  [policy]
noun(noun(consumption))       -->  [consumption]
noun(noun(households))        -->  [households]
noun(noun(salaries))          -->  [salaries]
noun(noun(industry))          -->  [industry]
noun(noun(sector))            -->  [sector]
noun(noun(investment))        -->  [investment]
noun(noun(unemployment))      -->  [unemployment]
noun(noun(impotant))          -->  [important]
noun(noun(capacity))          -->  [capacity]
noun(noun(trend))             -->  [trend]
noun(noun(tendency))          -->  [tendency]
noun(noun(growth))            -->  [growth]
noun(noun(income))            -->  [income]
noun(noun(savings))           -->  [savings]

verb(verb(increase))          -->  [increase]
verb(verb(increases))         -->  [increases]
verb(verb(decrease))          -->  [decrease]
verb(verb(decreases))         -->  [decreases]
verb(verb(stabilize))         -->  [stabilize]
verb(verb(implement))         -->  [implement]
verb(verb(implements))        -->  [implements]
verb(verb(produce))           -->  [produce]
verb(verb(produces))          -->  [produces]
verb(verb(purchase))          -->  [purchase]
verb(verb(puchases))          -->  [purchases]
verb(verb(buy))               -->  [buy]
verb(verb(buys))              -->  [buys]
```

```
verb(verb(require))                      -->  [require]
verb(verb(requires))                     -->  [requires]

verb(verb(explain))                      -->  [explain]
verb(verb(explains))                     -->  [explains]
verb(verb(achieve))                      -->  [achieve]
verb(verb(achieves))                     -->  [achieves]
verb(verb(see))                          -->  [see]
verb(verb(seen))                         -->  [seen]
verb(verb(work))                         -->  [work]
verb(verb(wishes))                       -->  [wishes]
verb(verb(help))                         -->  [help]
verb(verb(helps))                        -->  [helps]
verb(verb(maximize))                     -->  [maximize]
verb(verb(maximizes))                    -->  [maximizes]
verb(verb(minimize))                     -->  [minimize]
verb(verb(minimizes))                    -->  [minimizes]
verb(verb(fix))                          -->  [fix]
verb(verb(fixes))                        -->  [fixes]
verb(verb((_))                           -->  []

adjective(adjective(monetary))           -->  [monetary]
adjective(adjective(intelligent))        -->  [intelligent]
adjective(adjective(restrictive))        -->  [restrictive]
adjective(adjective(liberal))            -->  [liberal]
adjective(adjective(tight))              -->  [tight]
adjective(adjective(expansionnary))      -->  [expansionnary]
adjective(adjective(government))         -->  [government]
adjective(adjective(private))            -->  [private]
adjective(adjective(low))                -->  [low]
adjective(adjective(lower))              -->  [lower]
adjective(adjective(lowest))             -->  [lowest]
adjective(adjective(high))               -->  [high]
adjective(adjective(higher))             -->  [higher]
adjective(adjective(highest))            -->  [highest]
adjective(adjective(small))              -->  [small]
adjective(adjective(smaller))            -->  [smaller]
adjective(adjective(smallest))           -->  [smallest]
adjective(adjective(large))              -->  [large]
adjective(adjective(larger))             -->  [larger]
adjective(adjective(largest))            -->  [largest]
adjective(adjective(stable))             -->  [stable]
adjective(adjective(increasing))         -->  [increasing]
adjective(adjective(decreasing))         -->  [decreasing]
adjective(adjective(particular))         -->  [particular]
adjective(adjective(important))          -->  [important]
adjective(adjective(percent))            -->  [percent]
adjective(adjective(million))            -->  [million]
adjective(adjective(billion))            -->  [billion]
pronoun(pronoun(they))                   -->  [they]
pronoun(pronoun(their))                  -->  [their]
pronoun(pronoun(it))                     -->  [it]
pronoun(pronoun(its))                    -->  [its]

preposition(preposition(in))             -->  [in]
preposition(preposition(many))           -->  [many]
preposition(preposition(few))            -->  [few]
preposition(preposition(all))            -->  [all]
preposition(preposition(more))           -->  [more]
preposition(preposition(most))           -->  [most]
preposition(preposition(less))           -->  [less]
preposition(preposition(least))          -->  [least]
```

```
relate(relate(with))        -->  [with]
relate(relate(of))          -->  [of]
relate(relate(and))         -->  [and]
relate(relate(for))         -->  [for]
relate(relate(or))          -->  [or]
relate(relate(but))         -->  [but]
relate(relate(to))          -->  [to]
relate(relate(after))       -->  [after]
relate(relate(before))      -->  [before]
relate(relate(from))        -->  [from]
relate(relate(up))          -->  [up]
relate(relate(down))        -->  [down]
relate(relate(as))          -->  [as]
```

1.3.2 DCG grammar for economic analysis

```
% ECONOMIC LANGUAGE PARSER
% requires first: compile(library(read_in))

sentence(sentence(NP, RP) —> noun_phrase(NP), ! , rest_phrase(RP).

rest_phrase(rest_phrase(PP,VP)) —> prep_phrase(PP) , ! , verb_phrase(VP).
rest_phrase(rest_phrase(R,NP1,VP)) —> relate(R), noun_phrase(NP1), verb_phrase(VP).
rest_phrase(rest_phrase(VP)) —> verb_phrase(VP).

noun_phrase(noun_phrase(N,R,D)) —> relate(R), determiner(D), noun(N).
noun_phrase(noun_phrase(PP)) —> prep_phrase(PP).
noun_phrase(noun_phrase(D,N))  —> determiner(D), noun(N).
noun_phrase(noun_phrase(N)) —> noun(N)
noun_phrase(noun_phrase(A,N,)) —> adjective(A), noun(N).
noun_phrase(noun_phrase(DD,N)) —> digit(DD), noun(N).
noun_phrase(noun_phrase(DD,A)) —> digit(DD), adjective(A).
noun_phrase(noun_phrase(DD,A,N)) —> digit(DD), adjective(A), noun(N).
noun_phrase(noun_phrase(D,DD,A)) —> determiner(D), digit(DD), adjective(A).
noun_phrase(noun_phrase(P,N)) —> pronoun(P), noun(N).
noun_phrase(noun_phrase(P,A,N)) —> pronoun(P), adjective(A), noun(N).
noun_phrase(noun_phrase(D,A,N)) —> determiner(D), adjective(A), noun(N).
noun_phrase(noun_phrase(D,A,A1,N)) —> determiner(D),adjective(A),adjective(A1), noun(N).
noun_phrase(noun_phrase(D,DD,N)) —> determiner(D), digit(DD), noun(N).
noun_phrase(noun_phrase(D,DD,A,N)) —> determiner(D), digit(DD), adjective(A), noun(N).
noun_phrase(noun_phrase(P)) —> pronoun(P).

prep_phrase(prep_phrase(PR,NP)) —> preposition(PR), noun_phrase(NP).
prep_phrase(prep_phrase(R,NP)) —> relate(R), noun_phrase(NP).
prep_phrase(prep_phrase(PR)) —> preposition(PR).


Verb_phrase(verb_phrase(V,PP,R,NP)) —>  verbg(V), prep_Phrase(PP), relate(R),
noun_phrase(NP).
Verb_phrase(verb_phrase(V,PP,R,NP)) —> verbg(V), relate(R), noun_phrase(NO), prep  phrase(PP).
Verb_phrase(verb_phrase(V,R,NP)) —> verbg(V), relate(R), noun_phrase(NP).
Verb_phrase(verb_phrase(V,NP)) —> verbg(V), noun_phrase(NP).
Verb_phrase(verb_phrase(V,NP,R,NP1)) —> verbg(V), noun_phrase(NP), relate(R), noun_phrase(NP1).
Verb_phrase(verb_phrase(V,NP,R,NP1,PP)) —> verbg(V), noun_phrase(NP), related(R), noun_phrase(NP1),
prep_phrase(PP).
Verb_phrase(verb_phrase(V,PP)) —> verbg(V), pre_phrase(PP).
Verb_phrase(verb_phrase(V)) —> verbg(V).
verbg(verbg(V)) —> verb(V); neg_verb(V).
neg_verb(neg_verb(V)) —> verb(V), [not].
digit(digit(DD)) —> [DD], {integer(DD)}
```

1.3.3 Parser for the Example in Sections 3.1 and 3.2

```
run:

read_in(X), n1, write(X), n1,
show(sentence( _ , _ ), X, ['.'] )).
% ..........................................................................

% Displaying of structures as they are parsed

show(Clause) :-
        Clause = .. [X] _ ],
        call(Clause),
        Clause = .. [Y,Y1| _ ],
        show 1(Y,Y1).
show(Clause) :-
        Clause = .. [X| _ ],
        !, fail.
show(sentence, S) :-
        n1,
        pp0(S).

pp0(Term) :-
        pp1(Term, 1).

pp1([],_).
pp1([H| L], X) :-
        pp1(H,X),
        pp1(L,X).
pp1(Term, X) :-
        Indent is 3 * X,
        Term = .. [Head|Args],
        tab(Indent),
        write(Head), n1,
        Next is X + 1,
        pp1(Args,Next).
```

Appendix 2 Predefined LISP and Prolog expressions

2.1 Predefined LISP functions

2.2 Predefined Prolog predicates

Bibliography

Numbers in boldface at the end of each entry refer to the pages, in which the entry is referenced.

Abelson H., G. J. Sussman with J. Sussman, (1985), Structure and Interpretation of Computer Programs, MIT Press, Cambridge, MA **133; 202**

Aho A.V., T.G. Peterson, (1972), A minimum distance error-correcting parser for context-free languages, SIAM J. Comput., Vol. 1, no 4, 1972 **249**

Aikins J.S., (1983), Prototypical knowledge for Expert Systems, Artificial Intelligence, 20, 1983, pp. 163 - 210 **100; 103**

Alexander T., (1984), Why computers cannot outthink the experts, Fortune, Aug. 20, 1984, pp.99-108

Allen J.F., (1978), Anatomy of LISP, McGraw-Hill, New York **133**

Allen J.F., (1983), Maintaining Knowledge about Temporal Intervals, Comm. of the ACM, Vol..26, no 11, Nov. 1983, pp. 832-843 **115**

Allen J.F., J.A. Koomen, (1983), Planning using a Temporal World Model, Proc. of the 8th Int. Joint Conf. on Art. Int., 1983, Morgan Kaufmann, Los Altos, CA **115**

Allen J.F., (1984), Towards a General Theory of Action and Time, Artificial Intelligence, Vol. 23, no 2, 1984, pp. 123-154 **115**

Allen J.F., P.J. Hayes, (1985), A Common-Sense Theory of Time, Proc. of the 9th Int. Joint Conf. on Art. Int., 1985, Morgan Kaufmann, Los Altos, CA **115**

Altman E.I., (1968), Financial Ratios, Discriminant Analysis and the Prediction of Corporate Bankruptcy, J. of Finance, Sept. 1968 **120**

Andren J., (1987), Future issues in implementing expert systems, Expert systems in financial institutions, Institute for International research, New York, Sept. 1987

Apte C., J. Kastner (Eds.), (1987), Special issue on financial applications, IEEE Expert, Vol. 2, no 3, Fall 1987 **285**

Arrow K.J., (1963), Social choice and individual values, J. Wiley & Sons, New York **296**

Backus J., (1978), Can Programming be liberated from the Von Neuman Style? A Functional Style and Its Algebra of Programs, Comm. of the ACM, Vol. 21, No. 8, 1978 **139**

Bahrami, A., (1988), Designing artificial intelligence based software, Sigma Press, Wilmslow, UK **198**

Bara B.G. (Ed.), (1984), Natural Language Processing, North Holland, Amsterdam **264**

Barr A., P.R. Cohen, E.A. Feigenbaum (Eds.), (1981), The Handbook of Artificial Intelligence, Vols. 1 and 2, and P.R. Cohen, E.A. Feigenbaum (Eds.), (1981), The Handbook of Artificial Intelligence, Vol. 3, William Kaufman, Los Altos, CA **10**

Behan J., (1987), Case Study: the Security Pacific Automation Company, Expert Systems in financial institutions, Institute for International Reasearch, New York, Sept. 1987

Behan J., K. Lecot, (1987), Overview of financial applications of expert systems, Security Pacific

Belkin N.J., W.B. Croft, (1987), Retrieval techniques, Annual Review of information science and technology, Vol. 22, 1987, pp. 109-145 **260**

Ben-David A., L. Sterling, (1986), A prototype expert system for credit evaluation, in [Pau, 1986]

Berber P.R., (1987), AI in action in the dealing room: the current state-of-play in the USA, System Designers, April 1987

Berge C., (1962), The theory of graphs and its applications, J. Wiley & Sons, New York **212**

Biswas G. et al., (1987), Knowledge assisted document retrieval, Parts I & II, J. of American society for information science, Vol. 38, 1987, pp. 83-96, 97-110 **260**

Blair A.R., R. Nachtmann, J.E. Olson, (1987), Forecasting foreign exchange rates: an expert system judgment approach, Socio. Econom. Planning Sciences, Vol.21, no 6, 1987, pp. 363-369

Bobrow D., A.Collins, (1975), Representation and Understanding, Academic Press, New York **264**

Bobrow D.G., (1977), A panel on knowledge representation, Proc. of the 5th Int. Joint Conf. on Art. Int., 1977, Morgan Kaufmann, Los Altos, CA, pp.983-992 **50**

Bobrow D.G., T. Winograd (1977), An overview of KRL, a Knowledge Representation Language, Cognitive Science, Vol. 1, no 1, 1977, pp. 3 - 46 **103**

Boland L.A. (1982), The foundations of economic method, George Allen and Unwin, London **295**

Bolc L. (Ed.), (1987), Natural language parsing systems, Springer-Verlag, Berlin **264; 268**

Bonarini A., (1986), Man machine interaction and artificial architecture for financial planning, in G.P.Katz (Ed), ESPRIT '85, North Holland, Amsterdam, 1986

Bond A.H., (1987), AI simplifies banker/customer relationships, Applied Artificial Intelligence reporter, Vol.4, no 4, University of Miami, April 1987

Bonissone P.P. and R.M. Tong, (1985), Reasoning with uncertainty in Expert Systems, Int. Journal of Man-Machine Studies, Vol. 22, no 3, 1985 **271**

Boyer M., R.E. Kihlstrom (Eds), (1984), Bayesian models in economic theory, North Holland, Amsterdam, ISBN 0-444-86502-0 **285**

Brachman R.J. (1983), What IS-A Is and Isn't: An Analysis of Taxonomic Links in Semantic Networks, IEEE Computer, Vol. 16, no 10, Oct. 1983, pp. 30-36 **104**

Brachman R.J., R.E. Fikes and H.J. Levesque (1983), Krypton: A Functional Approach to knowledge Representation, IEEE Computer, Vol. 16, no 10, Oct. 1983, pp. 67-73 **100**; **105**; **110**

Brachman R.J., H.J. Levesque (Eds.), (1985), Readings in knowledge representation, Morgan Kaufmann, Los Altos, CA **50**

Brams S.J. (1975), Game theory and politics, Free Press, New York **301**

Bratko, I., (1986), Prolog-programming in artificial intelligence, Addison-Wesley, Reading, MA **198**

Breiman L., (1984), Classification and regression trees, Wadsworth & Brooks, Monterey, CA **241**; **243**

Browston C., R. Farrel, E. Kant, N. Martin, (1985), Programming Expert Systems in OPS5: an introduction to rule-based programming, Addison-Wesley, Reading, MA **85**; **88**; **126**

Carré B., (1979), Graphs and networks, Claredon Press, Oxford **200**

Carter C., J. Catlett, (1987), Assessing credit card applications using machine learning, IEEE Expert, Vol. 2, no 3, Fall 1987, pp.71-79 **243**

Carter C., J. Catlett, (1987), Credit assessment using machine learning, Proceedings of the third Australian Conference on applications of expert systems, Sydney, May 1987

Case J.H., (1979), Economics and the competitive process, New York Univ. Press, New York **214**

Caudill M., (1987-1988), Neural networks Primer, AI Expert J., Vol. 2, no 12 and Vol. 3, no 2, 1987-1988 **231**

Cercone N. (Ed.), (1983), Computational linguistics, Pergamon, Oxford **264**

Charniak E., (1976), Knowledge and Inference, Part 1 in E. Charniak and Y. Wilks (Eds.), Computational Semantics, North-Holland, New York **72**; **84**

Charniak E., D. McDermott, (1985), Introduction to Artificial Intelligence, Addison-Wesley, Reading, MA **10**

Chatalic P., D. Dubois, H. Prade, (1987), An approach to approximate reasoning based on the Dempster Rule of Combination, Int. Journal of Expert Systems, Vol. 1, no 1, 1987 **277**

Clarke G., (1989), Expert Systems in the City, IBC Financial Books, London

Clocksin W.F., C.S. Mellish, Programming in Prolog, 3rd rev., Springer-Verlag, Heidelberg, 1987 **151**; **244**

Clover R. (1965), The Keynesian counterrevolution: a theoretical appraisal, in F.H. Hahn, F.F.R. Brachling (Ed), "The theory of interest rates", MacMillan, London, 1965, pp. 103-125 **296**

Cohen K.J, Maier S.F., van der Weide J.H. (1981), Recent development in management science in banking, Management Science, Vol.27, no 10, October 1981, pp. 1097 ff **285**

Cohen P.R., (1985), Heuristic reasoning about uncertainty: an artificial intelligence approach, Pitman, Boston **271**

Colmerauer A. (1984), Equations and inequations on finite and infinite trees, Proc. Conf. 5th generation computer systems, Tokio, pp. 85 ff **294**

Colmerauer A. (1987), Opening the Prolog III universe, BYTE, August 1987, pp. 177 ff **294**

Computas Expert Systems, (1988), Multiprocessing extension for Smalltalk, Computas Expert Systems, P.O.Box 410, N-1322 Høvik, Norway **251**

Cook S., (1987), Knowledge representation for financial expert systems, Presentation at banking application and artificial intelligence, SWIFT international conference, Brussels, May 1987

Cootner P.H. (Ed), (1964), The random character of the stock market, MIT Press, Cambridge, MA **245**

Davis R. (Ed), (1986), Intelligent information systems, Ellis Horwood Publ., Chichester **260**

Davis R., (1980), Meta-Rules: Reasoning about Control, Artificial Intelligence Vol. 15, 1980, pp. 179 - 222 **97**

Deo N., (1974), Graph theory with Applications to Engineering and Computer Science, Prentice-Hall, Englewood Cliffs, NJ **194**

Dhrymes P.J., (1981), Distributed lags, North Holland, Amsterdam, ISBN 0-444-86013-4 **285**

Diaper D., (Ed.), (1989), Knowledge elicitation: principles, techniques and applications, Ellis Horwood Publ., Chicester **51**

Digitalk, (1986), Smalltalk/V & Prolog/V, Digitalk, 9841 Airport Boulevard, Los Angeles, CA 90045, USA **245; 251**

Donaldson H., (1983), A critic of knowledge based systems or AI, Creativity & Innovation network, Oct.-Dec. 1983, p.172

Dowdel B., (1987), Credit evaluation for commercial loans, Expert system in the city, Banking technology conference , London, Jan.1987

Drenik R.F. (1986), A mathematical organization theory, North Holland, Amsterdam, ISBN 0-444-01080-7 **292**

Duda R.O., P.E. Hart, N.J. Nilsson, (1976), Subjective bayesian methods for rule-based inference systems, in B.W. Webber, N.J. Nilsson (Eds.), (1981), Readings in artificial intelligence, Morgan Kaufmann, Palo Alto, CA **271**

Duda R., H. Peter, R. Reboh, et al., (1987), Syntel: using a functional language for financial risk assessment, IEEE Expert, Vol.2, no 3, Fall 1987

Duffin P.H. (Ed.), (1988), Knowledge-based systems - Applications in Administrative Government, Ellis Horwood Publ., Chicester

Dulieu M., A.Fish, (1987), Artificial intelligence in the dealer/computer interface, BankAI'87, SWIFT international conference, Brussels, May 1987

Dutta S., S. Shekhar, (1989), An artificial intelligence approach to predicting bondratings, in [L.F.Pau et al., 1989], pp. 59-68 **237**

Earley J., (1970), An efficient context-free parsing algorithm, Comm.of the ACM, Vol. 14, no 7, 1970 **248**

Expert Systems J., Vol.1, no 1, July 1984, p.9 ff

Expert Systems J., Vol.1, no 2, Oct. 1984, p.102 ff

Fikes R.E., (1981), Odyssey: A Knowledge-Based Assistant, Artificial Intelligence, Vol. 16, 1981, pp. 331 - 361 **103**

Financial technology bulletin, (1976), Bath House, 56 Holborn Viaduct, London EC1A 2EX

Firlej M., (1987), Tactical dealer information system: dilemmas of using valuable knowledge, KBS'87, Online Pubblications

Fogler H.R., (1974), Pattern Recognition Model for Forecasting, Management Science, Vol. .20, no 8, April 1974, pp.1178-1189 **121**

Frankel K.A., (1985), Toward automating the software development cycle, Comm. of the ACM, Vol.28, no 6, June 1985, pp. 578-589

Fu K.S. (1975), Grammatical inference, IEEE Trans. SMC, Vol.5, Jan.1975 (Part 1) and July 1975 (Part 2) **294**

Fu K.S., (Ed), (1979), Syntactic pattern recognition applications, Springer-Verlag, New York **245**; **246**

Garvey T.D., J.D. Lowrance, M.A. Fischler, (1981), An inference technique for integrating knowledge from disparate sources, Proc.of the 7th Int. Joint Conf. on Art. Int., 1981, Morgan Kaufman, Los Altos, CA, pp. 319-325 **272**

Genesereth M.R., N.J. Nilsson (1987), Logical Foundations of Artificial Intelligence, Morgan Kaufmann, Los Altos, CA **65**

Gentry J., P. Newbold, (1985), Classifying bankrupt firms with funds flow components, J.Accounting research, Vol. 23, no 1,1985, pp.146-160 **243**

Giannesini F., H. Kanoui, R. Pasero, M. van Caneghem, (1986), Prolog, Addison-Wesley, Reading, MA **151**; **165**; **248**

Gianotti G., (1989), Estimating unobservable decisions through business surveys: Preliminary results, in [Pau et al., 1989]

Gianotti G., V. Maniezzo, (1989), A cooperative, knowledge-based approach to financial counseling, Conf. on Intell. Management Systems, Varna, Bulgaria, 1989, pp. 391-398

Gilli, M., (1978), Etude et analyse des structures causales dans les modèles économiques, Peter Lang, Berne **212**

Goldberg A., D. Robson (1983), Smalltalk-80, The language and its implementation, Addison-Wesley, Reading, MA **179**

Greenwell M., (1988), Knowledge Engineering for Expert Systems, Ellis Horwood Publ., Chichester **51**

Halim M., (1986), A computational approach to reasoning under uncertainty applied to expert systems, PhD Thesis, Dept. of Electrical and Electronics Eng., Queen Mary College, London **271**

Halloway C., (1983), Strategic management and AI, Long range planning, Vol. 16, no 5, 1983, pp.89-93

Hanssens D.M., L.J. Parsons, R.L. Schultz, (1987), Econometric and time-series research in marketing, North Holland, Amsterdam **285**

Hayes P.H., (1977), In defence of logic, Proc. of the 5th Int. Joint Conf. on Art. Int., 1977, Morgan Kaufman, Los Altos, CA **70; 71**

Hayes P.J., (1979), The Logic of Frames, in D. Metzing (Ed.), (1979), Frame Conceptions and Text Understanding, Walter de Gruiter & Co., Berlin **114**

Hendrix G.C., (1975), Expanding the utility of semantic networks through partitioning, Proc.of the 4th Int. Joint Conf. on Art. Int., 1975, Morgan Kaufman, Los Altos, CA **78**

Heuer S., U. Koch and C. Cyer (1988), Invest: An Expert System for Financial Investments, IEEE Expert, Vol. 3, no 2, Summer 1988, pp. 60 - 68 **111**

Hewitt C., G. Attardi, M. Simi (1980), Knowledge Embedding with the Description System Omega, Proc. First Annual Nat. Conf. on Art. Int., 1980, Morgan Kaufman, Los Altos, CA **100**

Hopfield J.J., D.W. Tank, (1985), Neural computation of decisions in optimization problems, Biological cybernetics, Vol. 52, 1985, pp. 141-152 **231; 234**

Hovenaars M.N., (1987), Experience at NMB bank, Presentation at banking applications and artificial intelligence, SWIFT international conference, Brussels, May 1987

Intellicorp, (1988), KEE 3.1 User's Manual **100; 126**

Israel D., (1983), The Role of Logic in Knowledge Representation, IEEE Computer, Vol. 16 no 10,1983, pp. 37 - 42 **74**

Iwasaki Y., H.A. Simon, (1986), Causality in device behavior, Artificial Intelligence, Vol. 29, 1986, pp. 3-32 **211**

Iwasaki Y., (1987), Generating behavior equations from explicit representation of mechanisms, Carnegie-Mellon University, Report CS-87-131 **211**

Iwasieczko B., J. Korczak et al., (1986), Expert systems in financial analysis, in [Pau, 1986]

Jenny C.J., (1984), Requirements on expert systems as seen by an insurance company, Zurich Insurance Co., April 1984

Journal of banking and finance, North Holland, Amsterdam

Journal of financial and quantitative analysis

Journal of money, credit and banking

Judge G.G., J.F. Yancey, (1986), Improved methods of inference in econometrics, North Holland, Amsterdam, ISBN 0-444-87936-6 **285**

Kanal L.N., J.F. Lemmer (Ed), (1986), Uncertainty in artificial intelligence, Machine intelligence and patterns recognition Series no 4, North Holland, Amsterdam, ISBN 0-444-70058-7 **286**

Kaufman P.J., (1978), Commodity trading systems and methods, J. Wiley & Sons, New York **245**

Kaufman P.J., (1978a), Technical analysis in commodities, J. Wiley & Sons, New York **245**

Kaufman P.J., (1980), Technical analysis in commodities, J. Wiley & Sons, New York **251**

Kidd A.L., (1987), Knowledge Acquisition for Expert Systems: a practical Handbook, Plenum Press **51**

Klahr P., (1987), The Authorizer's Assistant: a large financial expert system application, Proceedings of the third Australian conference on application of expert systems, Sydney, May 1987

Klein M., L. Methlie, (1990), Expert systems in finance, Addison-Wesley, Reading, MA

Klir G.J., T. Folger, (1988), Fuzzy sets, uncertainty and information, Prentice-Hall, Englewood Cliffs, NJ **271**

Kowalski R., (1979), Logic for Problem Solving, North-Holland, New York **151**; **294**

Kripke S., (1971), Semantical considerations on modal logic, in L. Linsky (Ed.), (1971), Reference and modality, Oxford Univ. Press, London **84**

Krutchen D., (1986), An expert financial portfolio management advisory system, The second international expert systems conference, Learned Information Publ., Oxford, 1986

Lee K.C., (1989), Applying machine learning to building stock market strategy, Dongnam Investment management co., Seoul, S.Korea, 1989, to appear in J.Computer science in economics and management, 1990 **243**

Leijonhufvud A. (1968), On Keinesyan economics and the economics of Keynes, Oxford University Press **296**

Les systèmes experts en France, La lettre de l'Intelligence artificielle, no 38, May 1988, pp.8-12

Les systèmes experts et la banque, Banque et informatique, 1st part, no 32, Jan-Feb. 1987, pp.71-82

Levenshtein V.I., (1966), Binary codes capable of correcting deletions, insertions and reversals, Soviet Phys. Dokl., Vol. 10, no 8, 1966 **249**

Lipmann R.P., (1987), An introduction to computing with neural nets, IEEE ASSP Magazine,Vol. 4, 1987, pp.4-22 **231**

Lowrance J.D., T.D. Garvey, (1986), A framework for evidential-reasoning systems, Proc. of the 5th Nat. Conf. on Art. Int., 1986, Morgan Kaufmann, Los Altos, CA, pp. 896-902 **277**

Lubich N., (1987), The application of artificial intelligence in the financial services industries, Proceedings of the third Australian Conference on applications of expert systems, Sidney, May 1987

Makowski P., (1987), Credit scoring branches out, Credit Management J., March 1987

Marcus M.P., (1980), A Theory of Syntactic Recognition for natural Languages (Parsifal parsing), MIT Press, Cambridge, MA **268**

Marmier E., (1987), An overview of artificial intelligence activities at Credit Suisse and Swiss brokerage convention prototype, Presentation at Banking application and artificial intelligence, SWIFT international conference, Brussels, May 1987 **23**

McCalla, W.J., (1988), Fundamentals of computer aided circuit simulation, Kluwer Academic Publishers, Boston **194**

McCarthy J., P.J. Hayes, (1969), Some philosophical problems from the standpoint of artificial intelligence, in B. Meltzer and D. Michie (Eds.), (1969), Machine Intelligence 4, Edinburgh Univ. Press **115**

McCarthy J., (1986), Applications of circumscription to formalizing common sense knowledge, Artificial Intelligence, Vol.13, 1986, pp. 89-116 **84**

McRae C.D., (1986), User control knowledge in a tax consulting system, in [Pau, 1986] **57**

Mendelson E., (1987), An introduction to mathematical logic, 3rd ed., Van Nostrand, Princeton, NJ **65**

Mesarovic M.D., D. Macko, Y. Tanaka, (1970), Theory of hierarchical, multilevel systems, Academic Press, New York **292**

Messier W., J.V. Hansen, (1989), Inducing rules for expert system development, Management science, 1989 **243**

Michalski R.S., (1983), A theory and methodology of inductive learning (AQ-Star algorithm), in R. Michalski, J. Carbonell, T. Mitchell (Eds), (1983), Machine learning, Tioga Publ. Co., Palo Alto, CA **240**

Michaelsen R.H., (1984), An expert system for federal tax planning, Expert Systems, Vol. 1, No. 2, 1984, pp.149-167 **57**

Miller R.M., (1986), Markets as logic programs, in [Pau, 1986] **294**

Miller R.M., (1990), Computer aided financial analysis, Addison-Wesley, Reading, MA **245**

Minsky M., (1975), A Framework for representing knowledge, in P.H. Winston (Ed.), (1975), The Psychology of Computer Vision, McGraw-Hill, New York, pp. 211 - 277 **84**; **100**

Mitchell T., R. Keller, (1986), Explanation based generalization: a unifying view, Machine learning J., Vol. 1, 1986, pp. 47-80 **241**

Moore R.C., (1982), The role of logic, in Knowledge representation and Commonsense Reasoning, Proc. of the 2nd Nat. Conf. on Art. Int., 1982, Morgan Kaufmann, Los Altos, CA, pp. 428-433 **83**

Naylor T.H., Thomas C. (Eds.) (1984), Optimization models for strategic planning, Studies in management science & systems no 10, North Holland, Amsterdam, ISBN 0-444-86831-3 **285**

Neely G.A., (1988), Elliott Waves motion, Elliott Wave Institute, 829 N. Fuller. Suite 7, Los Angeles, CA 90046, 1988 **254**

Nestor NDS-1000 Development system, NESTOR Inc., One Richmond Square, Providence, RI 02906, USA, 1989 **236**; **238**

Newell A., H.A. Simon, (1972), Human problem solving, Prentice-Hall, Englewood Cliffs, NJ **91**

Newell A., H.A. Simon, (1975), Computer science as empirical enquiry: symbols and search, Turing Award Lecture, 1975 **186**

Nilsson N.J., (1976), Principles of Artificial Intelligence, Tioga Publ. Co., Palo Alto, CA **10; 65; 286**

Norris G., (1986), A knowledge based system for investment appraisal, Knowledge based systems '86, Online Publ., July 1986

O'Leary D.E., P. Walkins (Eds.), Financial applications of artificial intelligence, North Holland, Amsterdam, to be published

OVUM, (1988), Expert Systems in banking and securities, OVUM Ltd **23**

Owen G. (1971), Political games, Naval Res. Logist. Quaterly, Vol.18, pp. 345-355 **301**

Pao Y.H., (1989), Adaptive pattern recognition and neural networks, Addison-Wesley, Reading, MA, 1989 **231; 234; 236; 243**

Parker R., (1983), An expert for every office, Computer design, Fall 1983, pp.37-46

Parker-Jervis G., (1987), Accountants called to Account, The Observer, 6 sept. 1987

Pau L.F., P. Valstorp, (1977), Feature extraction in the time-domain: application to the analysis of financial data and strategies over time, in K.S. Fu, A.B. Whinston (Eds), (1977), "Pattern recognition theory and application", NATO ASI Series E-22, Noordhoff, Leyden, pp. 75-90 **120; 121; 122; 229**

Pau L.F., (1979), Research on optimal control adapted to macro- and micro-economics, J. of economic dynamics and control, Vol. 1, March 1979, pp. 243-269 **285; 297**

Pau L.F., (1980), Multiple criteria decentralized control: recursive equilibrium adaptation and examples, Proc. IEEE 3rd Int. Symp. on large engineering systems, Memorial Univ. of Newfoundland, St. Johns, July 1980, pp. 9-11 **297**

Pau L.F., (1985), Inference of structure of economic reasoning from natural language analysis, Int.J.Decision support systems, Vol.1, no 4 **294**

Pau L.F. (Ed.), (1986), Artificial Intelligence in economics and management, North Holland, Amsterdam **12; 257; 285; 294**

Pau L.F., (1986a), An Expert System Kernel for the Analysis of Strategies over Time, in [Pau 1986], pp. 107-112 **119; 122**

Pau L.F., (1986b), Inference of functional economic model relations from natural language analysis, in [Pau, 1986], pp. 173-183 **26**

Pau L.F., (1986c), Survey of expert systems for fault detection, test generation and maintenance, Expert Systems, Vol. 3, no. 2, April 1986 **54**

Pau L.F., (1987), Prototyping, validation and maintenance of knowkedge-based systems software, Proc.IEEE 3rd Conf.on expert systems in government, IEEE Computer society press, Washington DC, Oct. 1987, pp. 19-23 **292**

Pau L.F., (1987a), A survey of reasoning procedures in knowledge-based systems for economics and management., Proc. 1987 Conf. on Integrated Modelling Systems, RGK Foundation, Univ. of Texas, Austin, October 1987 **12**

Pau L.F. et al, (1988), KEMEX Expert system, TUP Program report, Industry and technology agency, Copenhagen, Denmark, 1988 **245**; **246**; **251**; **255**

Pau L.F., J. Mottiwalla, Y.H. Pao (Eds), (1989), Expert systems in economics, finance and banking, North Holland, Amsterdam **257**

Pau L.F., (1989), Artificial Intelligence and Financial Services, Tutorial held at the 2nd Int.l IFIP/IFAC/IFORS Workshop on Artificial Intelligence in Economics and Management, Singapore, Jan. 9 - 13, 1989 **96**

Pau L.F., T. Gösche, (1989), An explanation facility to neural networks, T.R., EMI, Technical University of Denmark, Lyngby, Dec. 1989 **237**

Pau L.F., (1989a), Technical analysis for portfolio trading by syntactic pattern recognition, Proc. 1989 IFAC conf. on Dynamic modeling of national economics, Pergamon Press, Oxford **259**

Pau L.F., F.S. Johansen, (1990), Neural signal understanding, to appear IEEE Trans. IM, 1990, also: T.R. EMI, Technical University of Denmark, Lyngby, April 1989 **244**

Pau L.F., T. Tambo, (1990), Knowledge-based mortgage loan credit granting and risk assessment, J. of economic dynamics and control, Spring 1990 **13**

Pinson S., (1987), A multi-attribute approach to knowledge representation for loan granting, Proc. 10th Int. Joint Conf. on Art. Int., 1987, Morgan Kaufmann, Los Altos, CA, pp. 588 - 591

Popper K. (1962), Conjectures and refutations, Routlledge and Kegan Paul, London, pp. 312-335 **295**

Pring M.J., (1985), Technical analysis explained, McGraw-Hill, New York **246**

Provan G.M., (1989), An analysis of ATMS-based techniques for computing Dempster-Shafer belief functions, 11th Int. Joint Conference on Artificial Intelligence, 1989, Morgan Kaufmann, Los Altos, CA **277**

Quinlan J.R., (1979), Discovering rules from large collections of examples (ID3 algorithm), in D. Michie (Ed), (1979), Expert systems in the micro electronic age, Edinburgh University Press, Edinburgh **240**; **241**

Quinlan J.R., (1983), Inferno: a cautious approach to Uncertain Inference, The Computer J., Vol. 26, n. 3, 1983, pp. 255 - 269 **272**

Quinlan J.R., (1986), Induction of decision trees (ID3 algorithm), Machine learning J.,Vol. 1, no 1, 1986, pp. 81-106 **240**; **241**

Reiter R., (1987), FX: A foreign exchange expert advisory system, The second international expert systems conference, Learned Information Publ., Oxford, 1986, in K. Shap (Ed), (1987), Artificial Intelligence in financial trading, Intermarket, Febr.1987

Reiter R.A., (1980), A logic for default reasoning, Artificial Intelligence, Vol. 13, pp. 81- 132 **84**; **115**

Reitman W., (1987), The financial advisor and the operation advisor, 1st Int. Symp. on AI and ES, Berlin, AMK, May 1987, pp.12-22

Rendell L., (1986), A general framework for induction and a study of selective induction (PLS algorithm), Machine learning J., Vol. 1, no 2, 1986, pp. 177-26 **240**

Rich E., (1983), Artificial Intelligence, McGraw-Hill, New York **10; 65**

Rizzo T., K. Strauss, (1989), Quotron used Windows to develop new market analysis tools for real-time data, Microsoft Systems Journal, Vol. 4, no 1, Jan. 1989, p. 1-9 **257**

Robinson J.A., (1965), A Machine-Oriented Logic Based on the Resolution Principle, Journal of the ACM, Vol. 12, no 1, 1965, pp. 23-41 **76**

Rowe N.C., (1988), Artificial intelligence through Prolog, Prentice-Hall, Englewood Cliffs, NJ **198**

Roycroft A.E., (1985), ACCI, in M.A. Bramer (Ed), (1985), Research and development in expert systems, Cambridge Univ.Press, pp.127-39

Rumelhart D.E., J.L. McClelland (Ed), (1986), Parallel distributed processing, MIT Press, Cambridge, MA **231**

Sandewall E., R. Rønnqvist, (1986), A representation of action structures, Dept. of Computer and Information Science, Linkøping Univ., Linkøping, Sweden **115**

Scarf H., (1973), The computation of economic equilibria, Yale Univ. Press **296**

Sergot M.J., F. Sadri, R.A. Kowalski, F. Kriwaczek, P. Hammond, H.T. Cory, (1986), The British nationality Act as a Logic Program, Comm. of the ACM, Vol. 29, no 5, May 1986 **57**

Serre J.M., R. Voyer, (1986), Tipi: an expert system written in LISP for a French bank, The second international expert systems conference, Learned Information Publ., Oxford, 1986

Shafer G., (1976), A mathematical theory of evidence, Princeton Univ. Press **271; 272**

Shapiro S.C., (1971), A net structure for semantic information storage, deducation and retrieval, Proc. of the 2nd Int. Joint Conf. on Art. Int., 1971, Morgan Kaufmann, Los Altos, CA **80**

Shaw M.J., (1987), Applying inductive learning to enhance knowledge-based expert systems, J.Decision support systems,Vol. 3, no 4, 1987, pp.319-332 **240**

Shaw M.J., J.A. Gentry, S. Piramuthu, (1990), Inductive learning for risk classification, IEEE Expert Magazine, Vol. 5, no 1, Spring 1990, pp. 47-53 **243**

Shortliffe E.H., (1976), Computer-based medical consultation: MYCIN, American Elsevier, New York **271**

Shpilberg D., L.E. Graham, H. Schatz, (1986), ExperTAX: an expert system for corporate tax planning, Expert Systems, Vol. 3, no 3, 1986, pp. 136-151 **57**

Shubik M. (Ed.), (1983), Mathematics of conflicts, North Holland, Amsterdam ISBN 0-444-86678-7S **301**

Simon H.A., (1960), The new science of management decision, Harper and Row, New York **292**

Simon H.A., (1957), Administrative behavior, 2nd edition, MacMillian, New York **10**

Simon H.A., (1977), Models of discovery, Reidel, Dordrecht, The Netherlands **208**

Slahor L., (1987), AI in banking: intelligent workstations or mainframes, Proc.IEEE COMPEURO'87, Hamburg, May 1987, IEEE -CH-2417-4/87, pp. 851 ff

Sowa J.F., (1984), Conceptual Structures: Information Processing in Mind and Machine, Addison-Wesley, Reading, MA **72; 80**

Special issue on financial applications, IEEE Expert, Vol.2, no 3, Fall 1987

Stanfield J., (1977), COMEX: a commodity support system, Proc. of the 5th Int. Joint Conf. on Art. Int., 1977, Vol.1, Morgan Kaufmann, Los Altos, CA, pp.109 ff

Steele G.L. Jr., (1984), Common LISP, Digital Press, Billerica, MA **133**

Stefik M.J., (1979), An examination of a frame-structured representation system, Proc. of the 6th Int. Joint Conf. on Art. Int., 1979, Morgan Kaufmann, Los Altos, CA, pp. 845 - 852 **104**

Sterling L., E. Shapiro, (1986), The art of Prolog: advanced programming techniques, MIT Press, Cambridge, MA **198**

Studies in banking and finance, North Holland, Amsterdam

Swamy P.A.V.B., R.K. Conway, (1984), Peter von Zur Muehlen, The foundations of econometrics: are there any ?, Special studies paper z.11, No 182, Federal Reserve Bank, Washington DC. **295**

SWIFT, (1988), Proc. Bank AI'88, La Hulpe, Belgium,1988

Tanaka E., K.S. Fu, (1978), Error correcting parsers for formal languages, IEEE Trans., Vol. C-27, no 7, 1978 **249**

Teh T.Y., (1989), Neural logic networks, T.R., ISS, National University of Singapore **244**

Theil H., (1975), Theory and measurement of consumer demand, Vol. 1, North Holland, Amsterdam **295**

Tipi: taking the grief out of home loans, J. Expert System user, May 1987, pp.20-23

van Caneghem M., D.H.D. Warren, (1986), Logic Programming and its applications, ABLEX Publ. **151**

Van Reesema S., (1987), Expert systems on a PC in mortgages, business loans and leasing, Expert systems in the city, Banking Technology Conference, London, Jan. 1987

Walker A. (Ed.), M. McCord, J.F. Sowa, W.G. Wilson, (1987), Knowledge Systems and Prolog: A Logical Approach to Expert Systems and Natural Language Processing, Addison-Wesley, Reading, MA **72; 151**

Wallis K.F., (1980), Econometric implications of the rational expectations hypothesis, Econometrica, Vol.48, pp. 49-74 **295**

Weintraub E.R., (1977), The microfoundations of macroeconomics: a critical survey, J. of economic literature, March 1977, no 7, pp. 7-23 **296**

Welles Wilder J. Jr., (1978), New concepts in Technical Trading Systems, Trend Research, Greensboro, N.C. **186**

Wilensky R., (1983), Planning and Understanding, Addison-Wesley, Reading, MA **119**

Wilensky R., (1988), Common LISPcraft, W. W. Norton & Co., New York **133**

Williams T., (1984), A graphical interface to an economist's workstation, IEEE Computer Graphics and Applications J., Aug. 1984

Winograd T., (1975), Frame Representations and the Declarative/Procedural Controversy, in D.G. Bobrow and A.M. Collins (Eds.), (1975), Representation and Understanding: Studies in Cognitive Science, Academic Press, New York. Also published in [Brachman and Levesque, 1985] **103**

Winston P.H., (1984), Artificial Intelligence, 2nd edition, Addison-Wesley, Reading, MA **10**

Winston P.H., B.K.P. Horn, (1989), LISP, 3rd ed., Addison-Wesley, Reading, MA **133**; **198**

Woods W.A., (1983), What's Important About Knowledge Representation, IEEE Computer, Vol. 16, no 10, October 1983 **54**

Worcester R.M., J. Downham (Ed), (1986), Consumer market research handbook, North Holland, Amsterdam, ISBN 0-444-87693-6 **285**

Wyatt Software, (1989), Wy CASH+, Wyatt Software, 5335 S.W. Meadows Road, Lake Oswego, OR 97035, USA **245**; **246**; **251**

Zadeh L.A., (1978), Fuzzy sets as a basis for a theory of possibility, Fuzzy Sets and Systems, Vol. 1, pp. 3-28 **271**

Zeelenberg C., (1986), Industrial price formation, North Holland, Amsterdam, ISBN 0-444-70102-8 **285**

Subject index

A

B

C

D

E

F

G

H

I

J

K

L

M

N

O

P

Q

R

S

T

U

V

W

X

Springer-Verlag
Berlin
Heidelberg
New York
London
Paris
Tokyo
Hong Kong
Barcelona

Springer-Verlag
Berlin
Heidelberg
New York
London
Paris
Tokyo
Hong Kong
Barcelona